Braude's
Handbook of Stories
for Toastmasters
and Speakers

Braude's Handbook of Stories for Toastmasters and Speakers

Compiled and Edited by

JACOB M. BRAUDE

JUDGE OF THE CIRCUIT COURT
COOK COUNTY, ILLINOIS

Formerly *Braude's Second Encyclopedia of Stories, Quotations, and Anecdotes*

Englewood Cliffs, N. J.
PRENTICE-HALL, INC.

Reward Edition . . . . . June, 1975

Second Printing . . . . . December, 1977

Someday I hope to write a book where the royalties will pay for the copies I give away.

— CLARENCE DARROW

The trouble with the publishing business is that too many people who have half a mind to write a book do so.

He who never quotes is never quoted.

— CHARLES H. SPURGEON

Anecdotes are stories with points. They are tools—nail sinkers to drive home arguments firmly. They are the origin of all teaching.

— EDMUND FULLER

All work and no plagiarism makes a dull speech.

They say I tell a great many stories; I reckon I do, but I have found in the course of a long experience that common people, take them as they run, are more easily informed through the medium of a broad illustration than in any other way, and as to what the hypercritical few may think, I don't care.

— ABRAHAM LINCOLN

CONTENTS

PREFACE

In the interest of interest . . .

Approximately 72 per cent of the people who deliver public speeches talk too long, digress widely, include long, dreary passages of statistics, show little interest in what they're saying, are at least partially unprepared, and . . . . use far too few illustrative anecdotes. The other 28 per cent are public officials, ministers, professors, and football coaches who have been delivering the same speech for years and now know it by rote. As a result, about 96 per cent of all audiences are bored stiff—including most of those listening to public officials, ministers, professors, and football coaches.

This, of course, is a deplorable situation. There are two possible remedies: (1) eliminate public speaking altogether; (2) make the speeches interesting. Since it appears that public speaking has established itself firmly in our social structure, only the second alternative remains practical. Thus, like its immediate predecessor—*Speaker's Encyclopedia of Stories, Quotations, and Anecdotes*—this book is modestly devoted to the end of making public utterances somewhat more interesting.

I began collecting the material which makes up the contents of these two books when I took my first public-speaking course in college in 1915, and I've been building and adding to my collection ever since. The file cards on which I carefully preserve each item have now grown in number to well over 10,000. The items to follow in this book—some 2,842 stories, quips, anecdotes, poems, bits of philosophy, definitions and proverbs—are offered now as a clincher in the campaign to lighten and brighten public speeches.

This volume contains more gems of wisdom than you could use in a lifetime of speech-making. I know, because I've been making speeches for a lifetime and still haven't scratched the surface of this

1

material. Now, it's my pleasure to share these bon mots with you. I say this not only on behalf of myself, but also for the distinguished ladies and gentleman who said or wrote them in the first place.

I like to think of the cabinets which contain my carefully catalogued file cards of collected wisdom as my tool chest, from which I can draw forth, at any given time, the precise tools required to do a specific speaking or writing job well. These tools have been sharpened to a fine edge on the intellect, wit, and learning of some of the world's greatest thinkers—and a great number of lesser thinkers, too, who still had a gift for turning a phrase. I invite you to dip into my tool chest and make use of them freely, as I have. But, before you do, perhaps a few words of explanation might be in order as to how best to go about using these implements.

INTRODUCTION

Building the speech

You've been told many times how to construct a speech, and we won't belabor those instructions here. The purpose of the introduction is to show you how to use this book to mitigate audience boredom—and not to offer a course in public speaking. However, before we get into specifics, it might be well to review very briefly the steps in building a speech.

1. Have something specific and important to say. There are too many speakers who need no introductions; what they need are conclusions.

2. Determine the big idea or theme of your speech and make everything else subordinate to or pointed at the one big idea. Don't compress a lot of big words into small ideas.

3. Develop a provocative title which indicates what you are going to say—then stick to that theme. During the course of many speeches, the audience not only has trouble determining the subject but also the object.

4. Research the factual data, enlarging your own experience with facts from reference works. Every man has a right to his own opinion, but no man has a right to be wrong in his facts.

5. Build an outline:

   a. *Introduction*—Contrive an electrifying beginning to awaken your audience, then state your big idea, weaving in some local interest peculiar to the experience of your audience to win them to your side. For example, a recently naturalized U.S. citizen once shocked a fraternal organization dinner audience awake by starting his talk with: "I believe I'm the only person here who became a U.S. citizen with his clothes on."

   b. *Body of speech*—Develop the points in support of your major theme, illustrating them liberally with anecdotes, draw-

3

ing generously from your own experience, and slanting your material to your audience. Abraham Lincoln once remarked: "They say I tell a great many stories; I reckon I do, but I have found in the course of a long experience that common people are more easily informed through the medium of a broad illustration than in any other way, and as to what the hypercritical few may think, I don't care."

c. Conclusion—Build to your climax, summarize your main points, restate your big idea—then quit. Those self-righteous orators who speak for posterity often give the impression they intend to keep on talking until their chosen audience arrives. "Has he finished yet?" inquired one fugitive listener of another as the latter slipped out the auditorium door. "He finished a long time ago," was the disgusted reply, "but he just won't stop."

6. Transcribe the main points of your speech to notes, or to manuscript if you feel terribly insecure about the whole thing.

7. Familiarize yourself with your speaking material, but don't memorize it.

8. Go back and drop in a few more anecdotes where you feel the speech getting soggy.

9. Check and recheck the speaking arrangements to make sure all this effort has not been done in vain.

And in the delivery . . .

1. Speak naturally in a conversational, well-modulated tone.

2. Be animated in voice, expression, attitude, and body movements.

3. Don't worry about nervousness. The audience probably isn't expecting much, and you may turn out to be a pleasant surprise. Almost all speakers, no matter how experienced, are nervous before a speech. One well-known government official was pacing up and down a room outside a hotel auditorium, where he was soon to address an important audience, when he was accosted by a puzzled lady of his acquaintance. "Do you usually get very nervous before addressing a large audience?" she asked him. "Certainly not," he snapped. "Then," asked the lady sweetly, "why are you doing your pacing in the Ladies' Room?"

4. Use strong, simple language—and understatement. The narrower the mind, the broader the statement.

5. Look individual members of your audience straight in the eye.

6. Keep control of your audience, and deal with audience distractions promptly and effectively. During the course of a lecture he was delivering, Charles Lamb heard a loud hiss from somewhere in the audience. There was an embarrassed moment of silence, but Lamb, not turning a hair, said: "There are only three things that hiss—a goose, a snake, and a fool. Come forth and be identified."

7. Don't read your speech. Refer to a manuscript if you must, but don't read it. On this point, Bishop Fulton J. Sheen remarked: "I never resort to a prepared script. Anyone who does not have it in his head to do 30 minutes extemporaneous talking is not entitled to be heard."

8. Keep within your time limitation. James Whitcomb Riley was once asked why his talks were so successful when those of the man asking the question consistently fell flat. "Well," answered Riley, "it's like this: I talk until I get tired. Then I quit. But you talk till the audience gets tired before you quit."

The blessed index . . .

It is said that man's ability to reason is the main factor separating him from various other anthropoids. Similarly, it is the index which primarily sets apart this anthology from other collected works of first-rate interest and adaptability. This volume is designed to be useful as well as entertaining. As a tool for speaking or writing, it would be practically worthless without a detailed and efficient index. Accordingly, many hours were spent in indexing the contents of this volume in almost infinite detail—so you can track down a needed piece of philosophy or an anecdote from the very barest of clues.

Any key word, thought, idea, or broad classification can put you on the trail of what you're seeking through the General Index. Here, multiple clues are provided to every item in the book. In addition, there are two other indices to make your researching job easier. If you know the name of the author or the place where a certain piece of wisdom appeared, you can track it down through the Author and Source Index. And if you're seeking an anecdote which refers to a specific individual, you can search it out in the third index, entitled Names Referred To in the Text.

INTRODUCTION

Altogether, these three tables of index add up to more than 5,000 individual indexed references to the items contained herein. This holds to a minimum the amount of time needed to locate pertinent references.

Learning by example . . .

Now that we've reviewed the mechanics of putting together a speech and learned something about the index, let's take two hypothetical examples to show how you can use this book to meet specific speech situations.

The counterfeiter is the only person I know who gets in trouble by following a good example. The pundit who remarked, "What this country needs is less public speaking and more private thinking" must have had this book in mind when he said it. For here is collected a vast storehouse of exemplary private thinking—for your speaking and writing consumption. Now, how, specifically, shall we go about using it?

Case History No. 1—the hopeful coach

You're an assistant football coach and teacher of physical education at a small liberal arts college. You've been asked to address a meeting of the Letterman's Club of a rural high school 100 miles away to acquaint them with your college and its advantages. There are a number of boys in this group you'd like to see on your own practice field next fall, but the competition is rugged. You have little to offer in the way of scholarships or aid. You know that several universities with plenty of alumni backing have been courting some of these lads. But you're going to give it the old college try anyway to interest as many of them as possible in at least investigating your school. You have one thing on your side: the boys' parents will also attend the meeting and you plan to direct much of your talk to them since the big school glamor holds less appeal to them than to their sons.

The school is a consolidated one located in the midst of a prosperous farming area. You've just returned from an extended trip with the college track team to find that you've been committed to make this speech in place of the head coach who has taken off on a fishing trip. He left a terse note for you: "Give 'em hell, boy. We need some of these lads." You have one day to prepare your speech.

But all is not lost. You have this trusty volume and you know how to use it. So you first sit down and think of every possible topic that might relate closely to this speech, and you jot each one down as follows: ability, accomplishment, advice, athlete, college, competition, education, graduation, honesty, integrity, smallness, farmer, and farming. This is enough to start with, and you go to the General Index, seeking a theme for your speech, a framework to hang it on, and some specific stories to carry it along. After an hour's worth of digging, you come up with the following:

I. Introduction—

   A. Opening anecdote (under *Parents,* #726)
      Junior was being chided for his low grades. Robert, who lived a few doors away was held up as an example.
      "Robert doesn't get C's and D's, does he?" asked the father of Junior.
      "No," Junior admitted, "but he's different. He has very bright parents."

      The speaker then expresses gratitude that in the audience he is addressing, he sees not only bright students but bright parents as well.

   B. Local interest (under *Farmer,* #887)
      Definition of a gentleman farmer: a man with more hay in the bank than in the barn.

      The speaker then likens his position in the field of education with that of the farm people in his audience. He points out that the gentleman farmers are the big universities, but his school—like the farm parents and youngsters he is addressing—has its hay in the barn rather than the bank.

   C. Big idea or theme (under *Smallness,* #1659)
      A very small man once attended a dinner in which all of his companions seemed to be unusually large. Somebody asked him during the course of the evening, "Don't you feel rather small among all these big men?"
      "Yes, I do," the little man answered promptly, "I feel like a dime among a lot of pennies."

The speaker's small school represents a dime among the big school pennies who will be and are competing for these young athletes in his audience.

II. Body of talk (points in support of the big idea)

A. (under *Education,* #747)
"The trouble with present-day education is that it covers the ground without cultivating it."

Develop this point by illustrating the advantages of the small school in providing much closer personal attention to each student and thus "cultivating" not only his book-learning but his athletic prowess as well.

B. (under *Education,* #730)
"When an athlete is given financial inducement to attend a certain college, this is known as *hire* education."

(under *College,* #413)
"Definition of a college: Institutions which sometimes lower entrance requirements with an end in view—not to mention promising tackles and backs."

Explain that at your school the emphasis is on education and not athletics, but you can offer the athlete a well-rounded program of athletics. You have no money to buy athletes, but they are most cordially invited to compete for the scholarships available, which you list and explain.

C. (under *Enjoyment,* #2721)
"Wealth is not his who has it, but his who enjoys it."

Develop the point that an athlete—like these boys to whom you are talking—with a wealth of athletic aptitude and talent has a much greater opportunity to really enjoy sports at a smaller school where the pressures are less, the competition isn't cut-throat, and a well-rounded program turns out a well-rounded graduate.

III. Conclusion

A. Summing up and restatement of theme

B. Closing anecdote (under *Advice,* #69)

"Anyone who asks for advice nowadays just hasn't been listening."

Point out that they'll be getting lots of advice about college in the next few months and express the hope they'll remember what you said today and investigate your school before they decide.

(under *Sports,* #2424)
A baseball scout once telephoned Charley Grimm, manager of the Milwaukee Braves, in a high state of excitement. "I just watched the greatest young pitching prospect in history today," he told Grimm. "This kid just struck out 27 straight batters in a high school game. Only one man even got a foul off him. I've got him right here beside me. Should I sign him?" "First," answered Grimm, "sign the guy who got the foul off him. We need hitting."

Wind up by telling the kids that your school needs both hitting and pitching and you'll be happy for the opportunity of discussing it further with any of the boys or fathers in your audience.

Case History No. 2—the tournament chairman

Through a terrible miscarriage of justice at a meeting which you were unable to attend, you were elected chairman of your company bowling league and forced to serve in that unhappy capacity throughout the bowling season. It's all over now, and time for the annual bowling banquet. As is customary, as chairman you are also expected to serve as master-of-ceremonies at the banquet, before relinquishing your job to the newly elected chairman. Each year the president of your company—which manufactures furniture—is invited to attend the banquet, and each year he has some excuse for not making it. This year the customary invitation was proffered— and a few hours before the banquet is to take place, you have been notified the president has accepted and will be there.

Of course, he'll have to be seated at the head table and called upon to say a few words. And, of course, it will be your job to introduce him. He's a rather nice guy, although something of a stuffed shirt. You realize you'll have to be a little careful about off-color

INTRODUCTION

jokes and the usual pointed wisecracks about the company will have to be toned down a bit. Come to think of it, what *are* you going to say in introducing him? Happily, you have *Braude's Second Encyclopedia* at hand for just such emergencies, and you gratefully jot down a few categories in which to seek speech material as follows: banquet, bowling, food, drink, companionship, fellowship, employee, employer, employment, furniture, and executive.

A half-hour or so on company time with *Braude's Second Encyclopedia* and you've come up with the following:

I. Introduction

    A. Opening anecdote (under *Bowling*, #2427)

    A college football player wasn't feeling good one day and didn't want to practice. He approached the coach and said, "I'm a little stiff from bowling. Could I sit out practice today?" The coach pointed his finger at the locker room and said "Clean out your locker. You're all through. You know we don't allow any drinking on this squad."

    Point out to your audience that if they're not all too stiff from the bowling banquet, you have a special (?) treat for them tonight.

    B. Big idea or theme (under *Employer*, #784)

    Coming home on a commuting train, a suburbanite struck up a conversation with his seat mate, who turned out to be a butler for a very wealthy family in the suburbanite's home town.

    "Oh," said the suburbanite, "So you work for Mr. Jones?" The butler drew himself up haughtily. "Certainly not," he replied. "Mr. Jones works for me. He gets up at seven every morning and goes down to that dirty, stinking city to make enough money to keep this place and me going."

    Tonight's special treat is the guy who has been getting up at 7 o'clock every morning and going into the city for 35 years to keep all of us going—the president of the company.

II. Body of talk

    A. (under *Furniture*, #2269)

    When a large corporation advertised to fill a vacancy in its

10

sales force, one applicant replied: "I am at present selling furniture at the address below. You may judge my ability as a salesman if you will stop in to see me at any time, pretending that you are interested in buying furniture. When you come in, you can identify me by my red hair. And I will have no way of identifying you. Such salesmanship as I exhibit during your visit, therefore, will be no more than my usual workaday approach, and not a special effort to impress a prospective employer."

You tell your audience that you'd like to report that the young man got the job. He didn't. However, he did stay on to become president of your company.

B. Add a few boss jokes:
(under *Employer,* #2249)
You've heard of the little boy who wanted to go to a night baseball game, so he told his grandmother that his boss had died.
(under *Employment,* #779)
The only time some people work like a horse is when the boss rides them.
(under *Employer,* #2509)
One of the most tactful men I ever knew was the man who fired me from my first job. He called me in and said, "Son, I don't know how we're ever going to get along without you, but starting Monday we're sure going to try."

III. Conclusion

(Closing anecdote, under *Employer,* #782)
The boss returned in good humor from lunch one day and called the whole staff in to listen to a couple of jokes he had picked up. Everybody but one girl laughed uproariously. "What's the matter?" grumbled the boss. "Haven't you got a sense of humor?"
"I don't have to laugh," said the girl. "I'm leaving Friday, anyhow."

Wind up by telling your audience that if they aren't figuring on "leaving Friday," you suggest they laugh heartily—in

11

the right places—for their guest speaker, Mr. Company President.

Plagiarism and conclusion . . .

I should probably have pointed out in the beginning that this is no book for a hyper-developed conscience. You have just been instructed minutely in advanced techniques in the tender art of plagiarism. The further you delve into this book, the more adept you'll become at it until, finally, like me, you'll come to believe that you either said most of these things yourself or would have said them if Socrates or Irvin S. Cobb hadn't beat you to it. This, of course, is the millennium; but it takes many years of ardent digging into other people's gems to reach this plateau. In the meantime, you can content yourself with an occasional excursion into someone else's mind as you're called on to give forth with some sort of public utterance.

Just by way of showing you how valuable this gentle sort of plagiarism can be in compiling a speech or essay, 34 items from the contents of this book have been woven into the writing of this introduction, partly to prove a point and partly because I've grown so used to drawing from my files that I automatically reach for them when I start to put words together.

Don't forget, all work and no plagiarism makes a dull speech. A visiting bishop once delivered a banquet speech, then afterward requested reporters to omit from their accounts some anecdotes which he wanted to be fresh for use in another talk in the same town the next day. A rookie reporter, commenting on the speech, concluded his article with this statement: "And he told a number of stories that cannot be published."

On the pages to follow are hundreds of stories which can be published and used, over and over again. An unidentified philosopher once remarked: "The mind is a wonderful thing. It starts working the minute you're born and never stops until you get up to speak in public."

Now you no longer need to worry about this phenomenon. You have *Braude's Handbook of Stories* and the blessing of all sorts of profound people. So happy searching!

And, just in case you never make a speech (a commendable goal toward which to strive), this book makes good reading, too!

Ability

1. Genius: one who can do almost anything except make a living.

2. I add this also, that natural ability without education has oftener raised man to glory and virtue, than education without natural ability.

— CICERO, *Oratio Pro Licinio Archia*

3. Every man who can be a first-rate something—as every man can be who is a man at all—has no right to be a fifth-rate something; for a fifth-rate something is no better than a first-rate nothing.

— J. G. HOLLAND, *Plain Talks on Familiar Subjects*

4. A man was complaining about his new son-in-law: "He can't drink and he can't play cards."

"That's the kind of a son-in-law to have!" said a friend.

"Naw," said the man; "He can't play cards—and he plays. He can't drink—and he drinks."

Absence

5. The same wind snuffs candles yet kindles fires; so, where absence kills a little love, it fans a great one.

— FRANÇOIS DE LA ROCHEFOUCAULD

Absent-mindedness

6. "Alert?" repeated a Congressman when questioned concerning one of his political opponents. "Why, he's alert as a Providence bridegroom I heard of the other day. You know how bridegrooms starting off on their honeymoons sometimes forget all about their brides and buy tickets only for themselves? That is what happened to the Providence young man. And when his wife said to him, "Why Tom, you bought only one ticket," he answered without a moment's hesitation, "By Jove, you're right dear! I'd forgotten myself entirely!"

Accident

7. There is no such thing as chance or accident; the words merely signify our ignorance of some real and immediate cause.

— ADAM CLARKE

Accomplishment

8. There is no limit to what can be accomplished if it doesn't matter who gets the credit.

9. We do not count a man's years until he has nothing else to count.

— RALPH WALDO EMERSON

10. The man who has accomplished all that he thinks worth while, has begun to die.

— E. T. TRIGG

11. The worst thing about crossing a bridge before you get to it is that it leaves you on this side of the river.

12. The shortest answer is *doing* the thing.

— Old proverb

13. Large trees give more shade than fruit.

— Old proverb

14. Nothing can be made of nothing; he who has laid up no material can produce no combinations.

— SIR JOSHUA REYNOLDS

15. People forget how *fast* you did a job—but they remember how *well* you did it.

— HOWARD W. NEWTON

16. The greatest pleasure in life is doing what people say you cannot do.

— WALTER BAGEHOT

Accord

17. If men would consider not so much wherein they differ, as wherein they agree, there would be far less of uncharitableness and angry feeling in the world.

— JOSEPH ADDISON

Accumulation

18. If you add only a little to a little and do this often, soon that little will become great.

— HESIOD, *Works and Days*

Accuracy

19. Cordell Hull was an extremely cautious speaker, striving always for scientific accuracy. One day on a train a friend pointed to a fine flock of sheep grazing in a field. "Look. Those sheep have just been sheared," he remarked.

Hull studied the flock. "Sheared on this side anyway," he admitted.

20. Accuracy is the twin brother of honesty; inaccuracy is a near kin to falsehood.

— TRYON EDWARDS

21. Having completed a biography of Cordell Hull, an author submitted the manuscript to the statesman for approval. On a section telling of a time during the Spanish-American War when young Cordell won all the money in his company at poker, only one correction had been made when the manuscript was returned. In Cordell Hull's own handwriting, the word "company" had been stricken out and the word "regiment" written in.

— JONATHAN DANIELS, *Frontier on the Potomac* (The Macmillan Company)

Achievement

22. Whoever tries for great objects must suffer something.

— PLUTARCH, *Lives*

23. Nothing great was ever achieved without enthusiasm.

— RALPH WALDO EMERSON

24. The greater the difficulty the more glory in surmounting it. Skillful pilots gain their reputation from storms and tempests.

— EPICURUS

Acquiescence

25. We put up with being surpassed more easily than with being equalled.

— A. VINET

Action

26. Rome remained great as long as she had enemies who forced her to unity, vision and heroism. When she had overcome them all she flourished for a moment and then began to die.

— WILL DURANT, *Caesar and Christ*
(Simon & Schuster, Inc.)

27. Attack is the reaction; I never think I have hit hard unless it rebounds.

— DR. SAMUEL JOHNSON

28. If you have something to do that is worthwhile doing, don't talk about it, but do it. After you have done it, your friends and enemies will talk about it.

— GEORGE W. BLOUNT

Actor — actors — acting

29. The gang of robbers, out to make a killing, broke into a home for old actors by mistake. The retired, supposedly decrepit thespians put up such a battle the robbers were happy to effect their escape. Bruised and bloody, they re-formed ranks at the gang hangout.

"It ain't too bad," philosophized one. "We got twenty-two dollars between us."

The leader snarled, "I warned you lugs to steer clear of actors. We had twenty-four when we broke in!"

— BENNETT CERF, *Cerfboard*

30. Julius Tannen, after a long fame on the stage, came on hard times in Hollywood. For a number of years he was unable to get a job acting. His friends finally came to the rescue. A part was secured for him; he was to play an editor in a newspaper drama. All that remained was for the producer to see him and pass on him.

He dressed carefully and being completely bald, he wore a toupee for the occasion.

The producer listened to his "sample," shook his head and said, "I'm sorry, I don't think you will do for the part. I've always visualized a bald-headed man as the man for the part."

Julius pulled the toupee slowly off his head. "I think I can satisfy you on that score," he beamed, "I happen to be completely bald."

The producer sat studying the polished Tannen skull and then shook his head again with the pronouncement, "I'm sorry, Mr. Tannen, I simply can't visualize you as a bald-headed man."

— BEN HECHT, *A Child of the Century*
(Simon & Schuster, Inc.)

31. Fame is as much a part of an actor's equipment as elocution or gesture. An unfamous actor may please an audience but he can rarely excite it. In this fact lies one of the major secrets of the theatre —the secret of the audience's presence. People are content to live dreamily and anonymously. But they insist upon the most splendid of the dreams. Their favorite area for dreaming is the theatre and their favorite dreamselves are its actors.

— BEN HECHT, *A Child of the Century*
(Simon & Schuster, Inc.)

32. I have seldom known a greedy actor or a snobby one. The most famous of them are no more stuck up than a taxi driver. They will throw fits over their insufficient billing, but socially they wear their names in small letters.

— BEN HECHT, *A Child of the Century*
(Simon & Schuster, Inc.)

33. Some actors think they are elevating the stage when they're merely depressing the audience.

— GEORGE A. POSNER

Adjustment

34. Sailing to the Near East last summer, I often talked with the ship's 1st officer. He told me a ship riding out a storm keeps going ahead by relaxing in the waves. . . .

"The ocean is a tremendous force," he said, "and a ship is only a very small force, but we know how to make our powerful engines adapt themselves to the timing of the sea. We don't drive them relentlessly through the waves; instead, we adjust our speed to the timing of the waves, so we are practically carried along by the sea."

This technique applies to people as well as to ships. Get yourself in timing with your difficulties and look at them without tension. Then get in harmony with God and so ride out your difficulties without strain.

—Dr. Norman Vincent Peale

Adolescence

35. Adolescence is when children start bringing up their parents.

Adversity

36. Every day the world turns over on someone who has just been sitting on top of it.

37. It is good to remember that the tea kettle, although up to its neck in hot water, continues to sing.

Advertising

38. A man lost a valuable dog and advertised in a newspaper offering five hundred dollars for it, but got no replies. He called at the office.

"I want to see the advertising manager," he said.

"He's out," said the office boy.

"Well, how about his assistant?"

"He's out too, sir."

"Then I'll see the editor."

"He's out, sir."

"Goodness! Is everybody out?"

"Yes—they're all hunting your dog."

39. There was a time when Campbell Soup Co. deliberately advertised "21 kinds of soup to choose from" and listed 22. For years, from 400 to 700 alert advertisement readers annually wrote the company calling attention to the discrepancy—which pleased the company immensely; the error having been deliberately made to make people talk about it and for the added purpose of giving them an idea of how thoroughly the advertisement was read.

40. Advertising: that which makes you think you've longed all your life for something you never even heard of before.

41. The advertising man is a liaison between the products of business and the mind of the nation. He must know both before he can serve either.

— Dr. Glenn Frank

42. Advertising helps raise the standard of living by raising the standard of longing.

43. A suggestion to radio and TV advertisers: Quit talking for a minute or so and then simply say, "This silence has been brought to you through the courtesy of the So and So Company." It works!

44. "You mean to say you sold all those hats we had planned to discard?" asked the proprietor of the chapeau shoppe incredulously.

"Yes," nodded his super sales manager, "I put a little ad in the paper stating we had some hats too high-priced for the average housewife and they were all gone by noon."

45. Max Schling, New York florist, ran an advertisement in *The New York Times* entirely in shorthand. A lot of businessmen cut it out and, out of curiosity, asked their secretaries to translate it.

The ad asked secretaries to think of Schling when the boss wanted flowers for his wife.

46. Advertising begins when the first crying child advertises his wants to his mother, and ends only with the epitaph on the headstone in the village cemetery.

— Edward S. Jordan

47. Newspaper ad of an enterprising automobile dealer: "Going out of business. All Cars Guaranteed."

— Edythe Porpa, Reprinted by permission from *Coronet*, June, 1955. Copyright by Esquire, Inc., 1955

48. As we drove along a Los Angeles thoroughfare lined with spectacular advertising signs, our nine-year-old exclaimed: "Look at all the bullboards!"

— Mrs. Paul A. Cuilhe, quoted in *The Reader's Digest*

49. A storekeeper had for some time displayed in his window a card inscribed, "Fishing Tickle."

ADVERTISING

A customer drew the proprietor's attention to the spelling.

"Hasn't anyone told you of it before?" he asked.

"Hundreds," replied the dealer; "but whenever they drop in to tell me, they always spend something."

50. From the Portland Oregon Journal: "Will lady who saved $130 on automatic washer I advertised in last week's *Journal* please call me—it was the drier that my wife wanted me to sell!"

51. A codfish lays ten thousand eggs in a single day, but it is done silently. A hen lays one egg and cackles. Nobody eats codfish eggs and nearly everybody eats chicken eggs.

— George Bernard Shaw

52. Wanted: a smart young woman to act as deceptionist.

53. Advertising is wonderful. What other medium could picture children going back to school with big smiles on their faces?

54. Advertising is one of the few callings in which it is advisable to pay attention to someone else's business.

— Howard W. Newton

55. The business that considers itself immune to the necessity for advertising sooner or later finds itself immune to business.

— Derby Brown

56. "What do you use for fuel?" someone asked a South American engineer.

"Sometimes coal; sometimes wood; but more often the catalogues of your American manufacturers and mail order houses which are printed in a language we do not understand."

Advice

57. Some time ago, Edward Wilson, the son of Defense Secretary Charles E. Wilson, had a chance to invest some money in a small, promising business. In need of working capital, the firm offered him a deal on especially good terms. When Edward, with some pride, mentioned the proposed deal to his father, the Secretary, after pondering a minute, commented, "I don't think it's a good deal —it's too favorable to you."

The astonished son asked why. "Under your terms," said Wilson, "the company will still be rather hard pressed and may fail. If they succeed, by great effort, they may then feel that you pushed them a bit too hard. If these are the kind of young men you say they are, you'll want them for future friends and associates. Therefore, the terms should be made a little less favorable to you and a little better for them." Edward did this, and the father's philosophy unfolded according to plan.

— BEVERLY SMITH, quoted in "Keeping
Posted" in *Saturday Evening Post*

58. Advice: the one thing which it is "more blessed to give than to receive."

59. Two Massachusetts state senators got into an angry debate and one told the other he could "go to hell." The man thus consigned called on Governor Coolidge and asked him to do something about it.

Governor Coolidge replied: "I've looked up the law, Senator, and you don't have to go there."

60. It is surprising how many people remember the good advice that they gave you, and how few people remember the bad advice they gave you.

61. It is easy when we are well to give good advice to the sick.

— TERENCE, *Andria*

62. It is bad advice that cannot be altered.

— PUBLILIUS SYRUS

63. A woman's advice is not worth much, but he who doesn't heed it is a fool.

— PEDRO CALDERÓN,
El Médico de su Honra

64. In his own gentle, procrastinating way, Dr. George Harris did much as president of Amherst College, but the unpleasant duties of such a post he neglected or ignored. He was not really opposed to work, but I never heard him say much in favor of it. One autumn he rose in chapel to address the students at the first assembly of the year, but after three or four sentences he got tired and, breaking into a happy smile, said:

ADVICE

"I intended to give you some advice, but now I remember how much is left over from last year unused."

With that he took his hat and walked out.

— JOHN ERSKINE, *The Memory of Certain Persons.* Copyright, 1947, by John Erskine. Published by J. B. Lippincott Company.

65. A small girl whose father is a judge would often say she was Judge Brown's daughter when someone asked her name. Her mother, thinking this might sound snobbish, told her not to make that sort of reply, but simply to say that she was Dorothy Brown.

Later someone asked her if she was Judge Brown's daughter. She replied, "Well, I thought I was, but Mother says not."

66. The only thing to do with good advice is to pass it on. It is never of any use to oneself.

— OSCAR WILDE, *An Ideal Husband*

67. To the young I should offer two maxims: Don't accept superficial solutions of difficult problems. It is better to do a little good than much harm. I should not offer anything more specific; every young person should decide on his or her own credo.

— BERTRAND RUSSELL

68. Never tell a young person that something cannot be done. God may have been waiting for centuries for somebody ignorant enough of the impossible to do that very thing.

— DR. J. A. HOLMES

69. Anybody who asks for advice nowadays just hasn't been listening.

70. The people sensible enough to give good advice are usually sensible enough to give none.

— EDEN PHILLPOTTS

Affectation

71. How majestic is naturalness. I have never met a man whom I really considered a great man who was not always natural and simple. Affectation is inevitably the mark of one not sure of himself.

— CHARLES G. DAWES

Age see also *Old age*

72. Middle age: when a woman takes her high school annual out of the bookcase and hides it where the children can't find it.

73. Middle age: when you're grounded for several days after flying high for one night.
— MARJORIE JOHNSON, quoted in *The Reader's Digest*

74. Middle age: when you are sitting at home on Saturday night and the telephone rings and you hope it isn't for you.

— RING LARDNER

75. A middle-aged man is one who remembers when corn-cure ads showed only the toes.

— FRANCES RODMAN

76. An elderly lady once called her physician. After recounting the catalog of her ills, she was met by the exclamation: "What would you have me do, Madam? I have done all in my power. I cannot make you young again."

"I know that too well, doctor, but I thought you might help me to grow a little older."

— THE REVEREND P. J. THATCHER

77. Age should not have its face lifted but it should rather teach the world to admire wrinkles as the etchings of experience and the firm lines of character.

— RALPH BARTON PERRY

78. Birthdays are piling up when people call you young-looking instead of young.

— CAROLINE CLARK

79. The woman called to the stand was handsome but no longer young. The judge gallantly instructed, "Let the witness state her age, after which she may be sworn."

— JOE HARRINGTON in *Boston Post*

80. It takes a mature person to be really young.

81. We are happier in many ways when we are old than when we were young. The young sow wild oats. The old grow sage.

— SIR WINSTON CHURCHILL

82. It is not by the gray of the hair that one knows the age of the heart.

— EDWARD BULWER-LYTTON

83. He that is not handsome at 20, nor strong at 30, nor rich at 40, nor wise at 50, will never be handsome, strong, rich or wise.

— GEORGE HERBERT, *Outlandish Proverbs*

84. He lives long that lives till all are weary of him.

— HENRY GEORGE BOHN, *Handbook of Proverbs*

85. She was born in the year of our Lord only knows.

86. It's not how old you are but how you are old.

— MARIE DRESSLER

87. A woman starts lying about her age when her face begins telling the truth about it.

88. You've reached middle age when all you exercise is caution.

— FRANKLIN P. JONES in *Saturday Evening Post*

89. In a hat shop a saleslady gushed: "That's a darling hat. Really, it makes you look ten years younger."

"Then I don't want it," retorted the customer. "I can't afford to put on ten years every time I take off my hat!"

90. A dear old Quaker lady, distinguished for her youthful look, was asked what she used to preserve her appearance. She replied sweetly, "I use for the lips, truth; for the voice, prayer; for the eyes, pity; for the hand, charity; for the figure, uprightness; and for the heart, love."

— JERRY FLEISHMAN in *Ladies' Home Journal*

91. You're young when it's as easy to go upstairs as down, and you're old when it's as hard to go downstairs as up.

92. Man is like a car. Just so much mileage in him, whether he runs it out in 40 years or 80.

Agreement

93. When two men in business always agree, one of them is unnecessary.

— WILLIAM WRIGLEY, JR.

Alcohol

94. J. P. McEvoy received the following letter on gold-embossed letterhead:

Rev. Paul W. Alvin
Temperance Society
Boston, Mass.

Dear Brother J. P.:

Perhaps you have heard of me and my nationwide campaign in the cause of temperance. Each year, for the past 14 years, I have made a tour of the United States and delivered a series of lectures upon the evils of drinking.

On these tours, I have been accompanied by a young friend and associate, Herman Forsyth. He was a pathetic case; a man of good family and excellent background, whose life was ruined because of excessive indulgence in whisky, gin and rum. How much better off he would have been had he given up his evil ways!

Herman would appear with me at my lectures and sit on the platform drooling at the mouth and staring at the audience with bleary, bloodshot eyes, while I would point at him as a glaring example of what drink would do.

Unfortunately, last spring Herman died. A mutual friend has given me your name and I wonder if you would care to accompany me on my fall tour and take the place of poor Herman.

Yours in faith,
REV. PAUL W. ALVIN

— quoted in *The Reader's Digest*

95. An alcoholic is a man who has worked his way from bottoms up.

— DAN BENNETT

96. I am never called upon to explain why I don't eat oysters or calves' liver or Swiss kale; I don't have to give an account of why

25

ALCOHOL

I never go hunting or play polo. But whenever I turn down a Martini or whisky sour, the host is likely to ask sympathetically, "Ulcers?" And if I shake my head and say, "Never use the stuff," explanations are immediately and persistently demanded.

— RICHARD L. NEUBERGER, "Why I Do Not Drink" in *Christian Herald*

97. Let him who sins when drunk be punished when sober.

— Legal maxim

98. There is a story told of a somewhat tipsy man who piled into a crowded bus, and lurched into a seat beside a priest. He sat for a few minutes, blearily eyeing the priest, who was reading his Office. Then suddenly he said in a loud voice, "I ain't going to heaven, because I feel there ain't no heaven!" The priest, pretending not to hear, buried his nose in his breviary. At this the man bellowed at the top of his lungs: "I said, I ain't going to heaven, because there ain't no heaven! Now what do you say, padre?" The priest replied: "Well, go to hell then, but do be quiet about it!"

— CLARE BOOTHE LUCE

99. A man telephoned the police to report that thieves had been at work on his car.

"They've stolen the steering wheel, the brake pedal, the accelerator, the clutch pedal, and the dashboard," he complained.

A police sergeant said he would investigate. Then the telephone rang again.

"Don't bother," said the same voice—this time with a hiccup. "I got into the back seat by mistake."

100. Though a fifth will go into three with none left over, there may be one to carry.

101. A fellow we know who goes to work at 6:30 every morning told us that as he left the house one day recently he saw a neighbor fumbling drunkenly with the key to his front door. The police officer on the beat came to his aid and asked jokingly, "Where are you going at this hour?"

"To a lecture," replied the drunk.

102. Too many bourbons on the rocks can put a marriage on the skids.

103. Whisky—I like it, I always did, and that is the reason I never use it.

— GENERAL ROBERT E. LEE

Alibi

104. *Man in a flower shop:* "I want something to go with a weak alibi."

Ambition

105. Efficiency: the ability to do a job well, plus the desire to do it better.

— PAUL H. GILBERT

106. Aim at the sun, and you may not reach it; but your arrow will fly higher than if aimed at an object on a level with yourself.

— J. HAWES

107. Give me the boy who rouses when he is praised, who profits when he is encouraged and who cries when he is defeated. Such a boy will be fired by ambition; he will be stung by reproach, and animated by preference; never shall I apprehend any bad consequences from idleness in such a boy.

— MARCUS FABIUS QUINTILIAN

108. We should not, in our attempts to elevate ourselves, lose sight of safety. He who stands upon a tall man's shoulders, can look over the heads of those around him, but his footing is much less secure than theirs.

109. Ambition: the last refuge of the failure.

110. Hitch your wagon to a star. Let us not fag in paltry works which serve our pot and bag alone.

— RALPH WALDO EMERSON, *Society and Solitude*

111. I would rather be first in a little Iberian village than second in Rome.

— JULIUS CAESAR

AMBITION

112. Ah, but a man's reach should exceed his grasp. Or what's a heaven for?

— ROBERT BROWNING

113. Better to light one candle than to curse the darkness.

— Chinese proverb

114. He who sacrifices his conscience to ambition burns a picture to obtain the ashes.

— Chinese proverb

115. You should have two aims—to make a little money first, then to make it last.

America — American

116. We came to America, either ourselves or in the persons of our ancestors, to better the ideals of men, to make them see finer things than they had seen before, to get rid of the things that divide and to make sure of the things that unite. It was but an historical accident no doubt that this great country was called the "United States"; yet, I am very thankful that it has that word "United" in its title, and the man who seeks to divide man from man, group from group, interest from interest in this great Union is striking at its very heart.

— WOODROW WILSON

117. Americanism: voting to set the speed limit at 45 and demanding a car which will do 90.

118. Except the Capitol in Washington, the only place in the United States over which the American flag is allowed by law to fly each night in times of peace is the grave of Francis Scott Key in Maryland. The purpose is to make true always the line in his song, *The Star Spangled Banner:* "Gave proof through the night that our flag was still there."

119. It is infinitely easier to observe a great American's birthday than to put his principles into practice each day.

120. Every American takes pride in our tradition of hospitality to men of all races and all creeds. We must be constantly vigilant against the attacks of intolerance and injustice. We must scrupulously guard the civil rights and civil liberties of all citizens, whatever their background. We must remember that any oppression, any injustice, any hatred, is a wedge designed to attack our civilization.

— Franklin Delano Roosevelt

121. My native land! I turn to you,
  With blessing and with prayer;
Where man is brave and woman true,
  And free as mountain air.
Long may our flag in triumph wave
  Against the world combined,
And friends a welcome—foes a grave,
  Within our borders find.

— Author unknown

122. It is a noble land that God has given us; a land that can feed and clothe the world; a land whose coast lines would inclose half the countries of Europe; a land set like a sentinel between the two imperial oceans of the globe.

— Senator Albert J. Beveridge

123. *As the income tax bureau sees us:* America is the land of untold wealth.

124. Next to Washington, Lincoln stands forth as the grandest patriot in our American life. Washington was the "father of his Country"; Lincoln was her most loyal son; Washington brought the United States of America into being; Lincoln made that being immortal; Washington unfurled a new flag among the nations of the world; Lincoln made that flag a mighty power among the nations. Dead, they yet speak. The good they did will last through time and on through eternity. And so our nation has most rightly and fittingly made the birthdays of these, her illustrious sons, legal holidays, to inspire us to a purer, nobler, holier manhood.

— George H. Smythe, Jr.

125. American history: the replacement of the red Indian by red tape.

126. Americans generally spend so much time on things that are *urgent* that we have none left to spend on those that are *important*.

127. The real democratic American idea is not that every man shall be on a level with every other, but that everyone shall have liberty, without hindrance, to be what God made him.

— HENRY WARD BEECHER

128.   STARS AND STRIPES

THE FLAG of the United States of America is the fourth oldest national flag in the world. Only the flags of Denmark, Sweden and the Netherlands are older.

ONLY ONE FLAG is ever flown above the Stars and Stripes in any branch of our armed forces. This is the Chaplain's pennant on naval vessels to signal: "The crew is at divine services."

THE STAR-SPANGLED BANNER which inspired Francis Scott Key to write our National Anthem had 15 stripes and 15 stars. This flag, with 11 bullet holes, is now in the National Museum.

BOTH STRIPES AND STARS were added to the Flag when Vermont and Kentucky were admitted to the Union, in 1791 and 1792. But, in 1818, Congress reduced the number of stripes to the original 13. After that only a star was added for each new state.

— KATHLEEN MASTERSON

129. If Benjamin Franklin could have had his way, the turkey and not the eagle would have adorned the government's great seal. Proof of that fact is to be found in an article written by Franklin in 1784, which reads:

"I wish that the bald eagle had not been chosen as the representative of our country. He is a bird of bad moral character; he does not get his living honestly. You may have seen him perched on some dead tree where, too lazy to fish for himself, he watches the labor of the fishing hawk and, when that diligent bird has at length taken a fish and is bearing it to his nest for the support of his mate and young ones, the bald eagle pursues him and takes it from him. . . . Besides, he is a rank coward; the little kingbird, not bigger than a sparrow, attacks him boldly and drives him out of the district. . . . For a truth, the turkey is in comparison a much more respectable bird."

130. Some years ago, King Carol told Bruce Lockhart how he had selected 14 of the brightest young men in Rumania for training in the government service. Seven he sent to England, seven to America, to study the economic and political systems. "The seven who went to England were very smart," said Carol, "and they all now have important posts in Bucharest."

"What about the seven you sent to America?" asked Lockhart.

"They were even smarter," said the King. "They stayed there."

— LEONARD LYONS in *New York Post*

131. The typical successful American businessman was born in the country, where he worked with great energy so he could live in the city, where he worked with even greater energy so he could live in the country!

132. What is it that gives American soldiers their essential toughness? It seems to me that Americans, without really being conscious of it, are fiercely proud of being Americans. They seem to be aware instinctively that they are a mixture of all the peoples in the world—well nourished, athletic, free to think, less frustrated and so better integrated than others. . . . And with this subconscious realization comes the conviction that nothing on earth can keep an American from doing a job he knows he really has to do.

— IRA WOLFERT, *Battle for the Solomons* (Houghton Mifflin Co.)

Analysis

133. Analysis kills spontaneity. The grain once ground into flour springs and germinates no more.

— HENRI FREDERIC AMIEL

Ancestry

134. The man who has nothing to boast of but his illustrious ancestors is like a potato—the only good belonging to him is underground.

— SIR THOMAS OVERBURY

135. Ancestral pride: going forward by backing up.

136. The late Will Rogers was given to silencing persons who boasted of ancestry by making this observation on his Indian blood:

"My ancestors didn't come over on the *Mayflower* but they met the first boat."

ANCESTRY

137. The man who boasts only of his ancestors belongs to a family that is better dead than alive.

138. Every man is his own ancestor, and every man is his own heir. He devises his own future, and he inherits his own past.

— FREDERICK H. HEDGE

Anger

139. Anger: an acid that can do more harm to the vessel in which it is stored than to anything on which it is poured.

140. The greatest remedy for anger is delay.

—SENECA

141. Swallowing angry words is much easier than having to eat them.

142. As a general rule a man is about as big as the things which make him mad.

143. He is a fool who cannot be angry; but he is a wise man who will not.

— English proverb

144. Anger is a wind which blows out the lamp of the mind.

— ROBERT G. INGERSOLL

145. When a man is wrong and won't admit it, he always gets angry.

— THOMAS C. HALIBURTON

146. In a controversy the instant we feel anger we have already ceased striving for the truth, and have begun striving for ourselves.

— THOMAS CARLYLE

147. People who fly into a rage always make a bad landing.

— WILL ROGERS

Animals

148. Animals reflect their surroundings: their faces grow refined or stupid according to the people with whom they live. A domestic animal will become good or bad, frank or sly, sensitive or stupid, not only according to what its master teaches it, but according to what its master is.

— ROMAIN ROLLAND, Jean Christophe

Antagonism

149. You cannot antagonize and influence at the same time.

— J. S. KNOX

Antique — antiques

150. Henny Youngman used to tell of the time he was ejected from an antique shop. "All I did," he said, "was walk in and ask 'What's new?' "

Apology

151. When Champ Clark was Speaker of the House, Congressman Johnson of Indiana interrupted the speech of an Ohio representative, calling him a jackass. The expression was ruled to be unparliamentary and Johnson apologized.

"I withdraw the unfortunate word, Mr. Speaker, but I insist that the gentleman from Ohio is out of order."

"How am I out of order?" angrily shouted the other.

"Probably a veterinary could tell you," answered Johnson. And this was allowed to enter the record.

152. In the good old days, a king and queen were so fond of their court jester they often had him as their sole dinner guest. On one such occasion, the jester asserted: "An apology can be worse than an insult."

"Either you prove that," remarked the royal host, "or I'll have you beheaded."

After dinner, his Royal Highness happened to bend over. WHAM! The jester landed a lusty kick on the royal pants, then quickly cried: "Pardon me, Sire. I thought you were the Queen."

— ALEX F. OSBORN, quoted in The Reader's Digest

Appearances

153. Were we to take as much pains to be what we ought, as we do to disguise what we are, we might appear like ourselves without being at the trouble of any disguise at all.

— FRANÇOIS DE LA ROCHEFOUCAULD

154. The world is governed more by appearances than by realities, so that it is fully as necessary to seem to know something as it is to know it.

— DANIEL WEBSTER

Appeasement

155. An appeaser is one who feeds a crocodile—hoping it will eat him last.

— SIR WINSTON CHURCHILL

Applause

156. The silence that accepts merit as the most natural thing in the world, is the highest applause.

— RALPH WALDO EMERSON

Appreciation

157. A rabbi was once passing through a field where he saw a very old man planting an oak tree.

"Why are you planting that tree?" said he. "You surely don't expect to live long enough to see the acorn growing up into an oak tree?"

"Ah," replied the old man, "my ancestors planted trees not for themselves, but for us, in order that we might enjoy their shade and their fruit. I am doing likewise for those who will come after me."

— Talmudic story

158. A gentleman gave a friend some first-rate wine, which he tasted and drank, making no remark upon it. The owner, disgusted at his guest's want of appreciation, next offered some strong but inferior wine, which the guest had no sooner tasted than he exclaimed that it was excellent wine.

"But you said nothing of the first," remarked the host.

"Oh," replied the other, "the first required nothing being said of it, *it spoke for itself*. I thought the second needed someone to speak up for it."

159. "How can I ever show my appreciation?" gushed a woman to Clarence Darrow, after he had resolved her legal troubles.

"My dear woman," replied Darrow, "ever since the Phoenicians invented money there has been only one answer to that question."

160. People generally do not appreciate what they do not suffer for. A thing is held to be cheap if it did not cost dearly. Honor is lightly worn if it is easily attained. Inherited liberty is too often carelessly used until it is repossessed through sacrifices.

— FRED ROBERT TIFFANY, D.D.

161. Appreciation of what we have is at least one-half of the true way of life.

162. When I was a boy, my family bought a violin for me. For a year I practiced, filling the house with strange sounds. At last I was able to play something which I thought was "Home Sweet Home," but the family thought it was "The Devil's Dream" and begged me to stop, and sold the violin. But I found afterward that my practice enabled me to appreciate and enjoy violin playing far more than would have otherwise been the case.

— SAMUEL FESSENDEN CLARKE

Argument

163. Waiters, of course, are not in a position to snap back at ill-bred guests, but one English headwaiter once made the perfect retort to an uncouth customer.

"My position, sir," he said, "does not allow me to argue with you; but if it ever came to a choice of weapons, I would use grammar."

164. The way to convince another is to state your case moderately and accurately. Then scratch your head, or shake it a little and say that is the way it seems to you, but that of course you may be mistaken about it. This causes your listener to receive what you have to say, and as like as not turn about and try to convince you of it, since you are in doubt. But if you go at him in a tone of positiveness and arrogance, you only make an opponent of him.

— BENJAMIN FRANKLIN

Aristocracy

165. We no longer have an aristocracy of birth; we have rather an aristocracy of usefulness. (Compare the Duke of Windsor with General Lindbergh.)

Arrogance

166. The worst cliques are those which consist of one man.

— George Bernard Shaw

167. When men are most sure and arrogant, they are commonly most mistaken, giving views to passion without that proper deliberation which alone can secure them from the grossest absurdities.

— David Hume

Art — artist

168. Art is a veritable "fountain of youth." The ancients had a saying, "Those whom the gods love, die young." I would interpret that saying to mean not that those favored by the gods die young in years, but that by the grace of the gods they remain young to their dying day, however long that be deferred. I venture to question whether there is any tonic as stimulating, any gland-transplantation as rejuvenating, as is the quickening of the blood, the stirring of the inner, deeper self, which the powerful medicine of art can bring about. Those who love art and are truly susceptible to its spell, do die young in the sense that they remain young to their dying day.

— Otto H. Kahn

169. William Morris, the English poet, shared the feeling of many others that the Eiffel Tower of Paris was a colossal architectural monstrosity. During a long stay in Paris he very nearly cloistered himself in the restaurants of the Tower, not only taking all his meals but even doing much of his writing there.

"You must certainly be impressed by the Tower," someone once remarked to him.

"Impressed?" said Morris. "I'm not impressed. I stay here simply because it's the only place in Paris where I can avoid seeing the thing."

170. Art is the demonstration that the ordinary is extraordinary.

— AMEDEE OZENFANT

171. When a work of art appears to be in advance of its period, it is really the period that has lagged behind the work of art.

— JEAN COCTEAU

172. Art, if it is to be reckoned as one of the great values of life, must teach men humility, tolerance, wisdom and magnanimity. The value of art is not beauty, but right action.

— W. SOMERSET MAUGHAM, from *The Summing Up.*
Copyright, 1938, by W. Somerset Maugham. Reprinted by permission of Doubleday & Company, Inc.

173. The artist's sermon is more efficacious if he has no notion that he is preaching one.

— W. SOMERSET MAUGHAM, from *The Summing Up.*
Copyright, 1938, by W. Somerset Maugham. Reprinted by permission of Doubleday & Company, Inc.

174. Lorado Taft, the great Chicago sculptor, used to tell this story on himself. One blustery, rainy day as he came out of the Art Institute, he saw two nuns across the street. The wind was whipping their robes around them, and, as a sculptor, he was fascinated by the line they made. At the time he was working on a piece of sculpture of a mythological figure with robes blown by the wind, so he was delighted to have this example to study. Completely absorbed, he walked along on the opposite side of the street watching them.

Suddenly he saw that a man was deliberately following the nuns. Profoundly shocked at such an outrageous thing, the moment he could get through the traffic Mr. Taft flew across the street, caught up with the man, grabbed him by the shoulder, whirled him around and said, "How dare you?"

To his amazement, Taft found himself looking into the face of a fellow sculptor.

— DANIEL CHESTER FRENCH, quoted in *The Reader's Digest*

175. Art, like morality, consists in drawing the line somewhere.

— G. K. CHESTERTON

ATHEISM

Atheism

176. An atheist is a man who looks through a telescope and tries to explain all that he can't see.

Atomic Age

177. *Effective use of woman power:* "What's this—a program for the development of the guided Mrs.?"

— GENERAL DAVID SARNOFF

Auction — auctioneer

178. I never knew an auctioneer to lie, unless it was absolutely necessary.

— JOSH BILLINGS

179. Auction: where you get something for nodding.

Author — authorship

180. The last thing that we discover in writing a book is to know what to put at the beginning.

— BLAISE PASCAL

181. The author who speaks about his own books is almost as bad as the mother who talks about her own children.

—BENJAMIN DISRAELI

182. Nathaniel Hawthorne, having lost his government position, went home, dejected and almost desperate. His wife, after a time, learning the reason for his gloom, instead of giving way to reproaches, set pen and ink on the table, and, lighting a fire in the grate, put her arms about his shoulders and said, "Now you will be able to write your book."

He took heart and the world was enriched with *The Scarlet Letter.*

183. There is probably no hell for authors in the next world—they suffer so much from critics and publishers in this.

— CHRISTIAN BOVEE

184. Someday I hope to write a book where the royalties will pay for the copies I give away.

— CLARENCE DARROW

185. Thomas Mann always worked on each book for a very long time. Even when the manuscript was supposedly ready, he continued to work on it. When he kept changing things in *The Magic Mountain,* his publisher finally called him up and wailed, "We'll never get this book out! You've been working on it for eternity!"

"After all," was his calm reply, "I'm writing it for eternity!"

186. *Author:* "I once got ten dollars a word."
Editor: "Hmm! How was that?"
Author: "I talked back to the judge."

187. Nothing gives an author so much pleasure as to find his works respectfully quoted by other learned authors.

— BENJAMIN FRANKLIN

188. He who proposes to be an author should first be a student.

— JOHN DRYDEN

189. A young woman, interested in writing, met author Joel Sayre at a party.

"Oh, Mr. Sayre, I wonder if you'd help me out?" she asked. "Tell me, how many words are there in a novel?"

The author was taken aback, but managed a sympathetic smile. "Well, that depends. A short novel would run about 65,000 words."

"You mean 65,000 words make a novel?"

"Yes," said Sayre, hesitatingly. "More or less."

"Well, how do you like that?" shouted the girl gleefully. "My book is finished!"

190. That writer does the most who gives the reader the most knowledge and takes from him the least time.

— CHARLES C. COLTON

191. The two most engaging powers of an author are to make new things familiar, and familiar things new.

— SAMUEL JOHNSON

192. The most original authors are not so because they advance

AUTHORITY

what is new, but because they put what they have to say as if it had never been said before.

— JOHANN WOLFGANG VON GOETHE

Authority

193. Nothing more impairs authority than a too frequent or indiscreet use of it. If thunder itself were to be continual, it would excite no more terror than the noise of a mill.

— A. KINGSTON

Automobile

194. Auto driver: a person who speeds up to get in front of you so he can slow down.

195. Automobiles are like men; the less substantial they become, the more knocking they do.

Average

196. Public opinion, a vulgar, impertinent, anonymous tyrant who deliberately makes life unpleasant for anyone who is not content to be the average man.

— WILLIAM RALPH INGE, *Outspoken Essays*

197. When you're average, you're as close to the bottom as you are to the top.

198. Not doing more than the average is what keeps the average down.

— WM. M. WINANS

Averages, law of

199. Before a gathering of lawyers at a dinner some years ago, Lord Justice Matthews, the English jurist, said: When I was a young man practicing at the bar, I lost a great many cases I should have won. As I got along, I won a great many cases I ought to have lost; so on the whole justice was done.

— From *How to Win Law Suits Before Juries*
by LEWIS W. LAKE (Prentice-Hall) 1954

Aviation

200. A colored gentleman got his nerve together and took a flight in an airplane. As he climbed out after the ride, he turned to the pilot and said:

"Suh, ah has to thank you fo' both them rides."

"What are you talking about?" said the pilot. "You had only one ride."

"No suh," returned the passenger. "Ah begs yo' pardon. Ah done had two—mah fust and my last."

Bachelorhood

201. Bachelor: a chap who believes it's much better to have loved and lost than to have to get up for the 2 A.M. feeding.

202. The Department of Internal Revenue received a typed income-tax return from a bachelor who listed one dependent son. The examiner returned the blank with a penciled notation: "This must be a stenographic error."

The blank came back promptly with the notation: "You're telling me!"

203. Bachelor: the most miss-informed man in town.

204. A bachelor is a man who can be miss-led only so far.

Baldness

205. "Can you give me a prescription for my hair?" asked the balding patient of his doctor. "It worries me."

"Don't worry, old man," said the specialist, "it'll all come out all right."

206. There's one thing about baldness—it's neat.

207. When a woman makes use of false hair to improve her appearance it is referred to as a transformation, a chignon or some other fancy name. When a man does the same thing, what he is wearing is always called a toupee or a wig—both disagreeable-sounding names to a sensitive man. There's no justice in it.

—E V. DURLING, in *The Chicago American*

208. The customer in the barber shop was addressed thus: "Your hair seems to be getting thin on top, sir. Have you tried our own brand of hair tonic?"

"No, I haven't," responded the man, "so it can't be that."

— FRANCES RODMAN

209. Baldness is hereditary. If your wife's father is bald, it is probable your son will be bald when he reaches manhood.

210. I don't mind the loss of my watch, but in it I had a lock of my husband's late hair.

Bank — banks — banking

211. Bank: an institution that has a hard time getting all its vice-presidents to attend a directors meeting without giving the public the impression of a run on the bank.

212. Joint account: an account where one person does the depositing and the other the withdrawing—usually husband and wife.

213. Bank: an institution where you can borrow money if you can present sufficient evidence that you don't need it.

214. A woman in a little New England village called up the First National Bank in her community to arrange for the disposition of a $1,000 railroad bond she owned. The man at the bank to whom she talked asked:

"Is this bond for conversion or redemption?"

There was a long pause at the other end of the line. Then the woman asked:

"Am I talking to the First National Bank or the First Parish Church?"

— DAVE CASTLE, *The American Legion Magazine*

Bankruptcy

215. In the middle of the depression, the owner of a big shoe factory was summoned by the vice-president of the local bank. "About that loan of two hundred thousand," the banker started.

The manufacturer held up a hand. "Mr. James," he asked, "what do you know about the shoe business?"

"Frankly," said the banker, "nothing."

"Better learn it fast," advised the manufacturer, "you're in it."

216. When a man sits down to wait for his ship to come in, it usually turns out to be a receivership.

Bargain — bargaining

217. Late one stormy night a physician was aroused from sleep by a farmer who lived several miles out in the country. The farmer, who had the reputation of being "a little near," first inquired how much the doctor charged for country calls.

"Three dollars," snapped the doctor, impatient that the fellow would bargain under such circumstances.

Thereupon the farmer urged him to drive to his home immediately. So the doctor dressed and drove with the farmer to his house with as much speed as the muddy, slippery roads permitted. As soon as they stopped in front of the house, the farmer stepped out of the auto, took three dollars from his pocket and handed them to the doctor.

"But where is my patient?" demanded the physician.

"There ain't none," answered the country man, "but that there livery man would have charged me five dollars to bring me out here tonight."

218. A young matron, shopping, asked a butcher the price of hamburger steak.

"Seventy-nine cents a pound," he replied.

"But at the corner store it is only fifty cents," said the customer.

"Well, why didn't you buy it there?"

"Because they haven't any."

"Oh, I see," said the butcher. "When I don't have it I sell it for forty cents a pound."

Beauty

219. The master of the house rang for the maid. The girl was in the act of cleaning pots and pans, and, before she could tidy herself, her employer entered the kitchen to see what was delaying her.

BEANTY

He looked at her dirty hands and face. "My word, Mary," he said, "but you're pretty dirty, aren't you?"

Mary smiled coyly. "Yes, sir," she replied, "but I'm prettier clean."

220. At dinner one night, Chauncey M. Depew joined a small group of friends who were in the midst of an animated discussion. "Oh, Mr. Depew!" exclaimed one of the ladies, "you're just in time to settle an argument. What is the most beautiful thing in the world?"

"A beautiful woman," replied the gallant Depew, without hesitation.

But his companion seemed shocked at his levity. "I contend," she said, seriously, "that sleep is the most beautiful."

"Well," said Depew, thoughtfully, "next to a beautiful woman, sleep is!"

— ALAN GRAY M. CAMPBELL

Behavior see also *Conduct*

221. Only the young die good.

222. Poise: the act of raising the eyebrows instead of the roof.

223. Let no man be sorry he has done good because others have done evil. If a man has acted right, he has done well, though alone; if wrong, the sanction of all mankind will not justify him.

— HENRY FIELDING

224. When you are right you can afford to keep your temper; when you are wrong, you can't afford to lose it.

— R. ROY KEATON, "Avoid Hurt Feelings"

225. When adults act like children they are silly. When children act like adults they are delinquents.

226. It's easy for folks to make monkeys of themselves just by carrying tales.

— T. HARRY THOMPSON

227. *Letter to the editor of a correspondence column:*
"I am only 19 and I stayed out 'til 2 the other night. My mother objects. Did I do wrong?"

The answer: "I don't know, I wasn't there."

228. Always hold your head up but be careful to keep your nose at a friendly level.

229. Do not do unto others as you would they should do unto you. Their tastes may not be the same.
— George Bernard Shaw

230. Consider how hard it is to change yourself and you'll understand what little chance you have trying to change others.

231. We cannot always oblige, but we can always speak obligingly.
— Voltaire

Belief

232. A thing that nobody believes cannot be proved too often.
— George Bernard Shaw, *The Devil's Disciple*

Bequest

233. They tell about the Hollywood writer who left instructions that he be cremated and ten per cent of his ashes thrown in his agent's face.
— Quoted in *The Reader's Digest*

Bet — betting see also *Gambling*

234. It's bad enough to make a real wager and lose, but what is worse is to make a mental bet and lose one's mind.

235. At a golf club, a member was boasting about his strength when a puny fellow member bet him $25 that he could wheel a load in a wheelbarrow from the clubhouse to the street which the athlete couldn't wheel back. "You're on," said the boaster. A wheelbarrow was brought up to the clubhouse. "All right," said the little guy, "get in."
— "A Philadelphia Lawyer" in *Philadelphia Evening Bulletin*

Betray — betrayal

236. The best way to keep your friends is not to give them away.
— Wilson Mizner

Bible

237. The history of all the great characters of the Bible is summed up in this one sentence: They acquainted themselves with God, and acquiesced in His will in all things.

— RICHARD CECIL

238. The dog is mentioned in the Bible 18 times—the cat not even once.

— W. E. FARBSTEIN, quoted in *The Reader's Digest*

Bigness

239. A big corporation is more or less blamed for being big; it is only big because it gives service. If it doesn't give service, it gets small faster than it grew.

— WILLIAM S. KNUDSEN

Bigotry see also *Prejudice*

240. The mind of the bigot is like the pupil of the eye; the more light you pour upon it, the more it will contract.

— OLIVER WENDELL HOLMES

Birth

241. It has been said that there are three calamities which may befall one at birth, because any one of these three things will cause one to be spoiled. And these three things are: To be born comely, to be born rich, or to be the only child in the family. For if one is born comely, his comeliness will spoil him. If born rich, his money will spoil him. If the only child in the family, his parents will spoil him.

— THE REVEREND J. B. CHAPMAN

Birthday

242. "You should have seen my birthday cake," a young woman told a friend. "Seventeen candles—one for each year."

There was a skeptical silence, then: "Seventeen candles! Did you burn some of them at both ends?"

243. Ethel Barrymore once invited friends to a birthday party. "There'll be a birthday cake, I suppose?" someone asked.

"Yes, there'll be a birthday cake, never fear," Miss Barrymore replied.

"And candles, of course?"

"My friend," said Miss Barrymore, "it's to be a birthday party, not a torchlight procession."

Blame

244. "It seems to me," said the judge, "that you've been coming up before me for the last 20 years."

"Can I help it if you don't get promoted?"

Blessings

245. The world's greatest blessings are the fruit of the world's greatest sorrows.

Blind — blindness

246. None so blind as those that will not see.

— MATTHEW HENRY, *Commentaries*

247.   LOUIS BRAILLE

When the blind lead the blind, they do not always fall into the ditch. Take the life of Louis Braille, a blind French farm boy who, by the time he was 18, had perfected the raised alphabet which bears his name.

Little is known of Louis' life except that it was plagued by ill health and ill fortune. Biographies are hard to find and often contradictory. But it is known that in 1812, at the age of 3, he was blinded while playing with an awl in his father's saddlemaking shop near Paris. France was in turmoil and nobody gave a hoot about the blind anyway; to most people, they were beggars and thieves. What chance was there for little Louis?

But when he was 10, at a friend's urging, his father put him in an obscure school for blind children in Paris, where they used the regular alphabet, embossed so that it could be read by the blind but not written. Louis studied music, but several times became discouraged and ran away, only to return because there was nothing in Paris for a blind child but ridicule and rough treatment.

When he was 14, death took his father, his mother, his best school friend and the devoted school director. But he plodded on, became an accomplished organist, and was made a teacher at the school.

Meanwhile he heard of a system of nightwriting used by the French army and based on punching holes in cardboard. He spent three years developing this into his system. He demonstrated it before the Royal Academy and was ignored. The new school director forbade him to teach it because the books were in the old system. For 20 more years he lived on, playing the organ, teaching, trying to find support for his system, and gradually succumbing to tuberculosis, which took his life at the age of 43, in 1852.

It was years before his system was accepted, and that due to many of his pupils who had learned it surreptitiously.

* * *

And there is a local sequel to the Braille story. In 1915, at the age of 55, the late William Hadley, a Latin teacher at Lake View High school, lost his sight; but, like Braille, he refused to surrender. He studied Braille, and founded the Hadley Correspondence School for the Blind—which has probably given more blind people an education than any other organization in the world. Now, directed by Dorrance Nygaard, this Winnetka school has students in every state and 36 foreign countries; and Mr. Nygaard tells us that even Chinese and Japanese are being translated into Braille.

Here is proof, certainly, that the blind can, and do, lead the blind.

—J. T. McCutcheon, Jr., "A Line
O'Type or Two," *Chicago Tribune*

Books see also *Reading*

248. I would rather be a poor man in a garret with plenty of books than a king who did not love reading.

—Thomas B. Macaulay

249. There is no such thing as a moral or an immoral book. Books are well written, or badly written.

—Oscar Wilde

250. I have somewhere seen it observed that we should make the same use of a book that the bee does of a flower; she steals sweets from it, but does not injure it.
— CHARLES C. COLTON

251. It is with books as with men; a very small number play a great part, the rest are lost in the multitude.
— VOLTAIRE

252. A man is himself—plus the books he reads.

253. We are as liable to be corrupted by books as by companions.
— HENRY FIELDING

254. If time is precious, no book that will not improve by repeated readings deserves to be read at all.
— THOMAS CARLYLE

255. The true university of these days is a collection of books.
— THOMAS CARLYLE, *Heroes and Hero Worship*

256. Laws die. Books never.
— EDWARD BULWER-LYTTON, *Richelieu*

257. God deliver me from a man of one book.
— Old proverb

258. A good book is the purest essence of the human soul.
—THOMAS CARLYLE

Bore — boredom

259. I spent a year in that town, one Sunday.
— WARWICK DEEPING

260. Bore: one who insists upon talking about himself when you want to talk about yourself.

261. Big gun: frequently an individual of small caliber and immense bore.

262. Often the happiest moment of the evening comes when a tiresome guest announces he must leave.

263.   The minister was just about to begin his sermon. Directly in front of him, in the first row, sat a rather elderly lady of stern mien. Rather slowly and deliberately she opened up a little kit, assembled the various parts of an elaborate hearing mechanism and affixed it to her ears. For ten minutes she listened to the discourse, then suddenly took off the earpieces, unscrewed the mechanism and packed it neatly away in its neat little container, and thereafter sat with her hands folded in her lap through the rest of the sermon.

264.   Bore: a man who deprives you of solitude without providing you with company.

— GIAN VINCENZO GRAVINA

Borrow — borrowing

265.   Acquaintance: a person whom we know well enough to borrow from, but not well enough to lend to.

266.   Borrowing is not much better than begging.

— GOTTHOLD LESSING, *Nathan der Weise*

Bragging

267.   An American visitor was rather perturbed because his stories of the wonders of his country made little impression on his English friends. He could not seem to bring home to them the gigantic size of his state or, for that matter, the superior speed of American transport. "You know," he said at last, "you can get into a train in the State of Texas at dawn and twenty-four hours later you'll still be in Texas."

"Ah, yes," politely murmured one of his friends. "We've got some pretty slow trains in this country, too."

Brains

268.   There was once a girl who didn't have much upstairs—but, Oh! what a stairway!

Brevity

269.   George Bernard Shaw once received an invitation from a celebrity hunter: "Lady X will be at home Thursday between four and six."

The author returned the card; underneath, he had written: "Mr. Bernard Shaw likewise."

270. Blessed are the brief for they will be invited again.

271. "There are four requisites to a good short story," explained the English teacher to the class. "Brevity, a reference to religion, some association with royalty and an illustration of modesty. Now, with these four things in mind, I will give you thirty minutes to write a story."

Ten minutes later the hand of Sandy went up:

"That is fine, Sandy," she complimented, "and now read your story to the class."

Sandy read: "My Gawd, said the Countess, take your hand off my knee."

272. As it is the mark of great minds to say many things in a few words, so it is that of little minds to use many words to say nothing.

— François de La Rochefoucauld

Brotherhood

273. There is a destiny that makes us brothers,
    No one goes his way alone;
All that we send into the lives of others,
    Comes back into our own.

— Edwin Markham

Budget

274. Budget: an orderly system of living beyond your means.

Business see also Industry

275. Business is like a man rowing a boat upstream. He has no choice; he must go ahead or he will go back.

— Lewis E. Pierson

276. Big business can't prosper without small business to supply its needs and buy its products. Labor can't prosper so long as capital lies idle. Capital can't prosper while labor is unemployed.

— De Witt M. Emery

277. Business is never so healthy as when, like a chicken, it must do a certain amount of scratching for what it gets.

—Henry Ford

278. Among at least three quarters of the people of the world, goods bought and sold seldom have a fixed value. The price paid is determined only after negotiations between buyer and seller. Prices for rugs in Persia and rubies in Burma are settled by the two men squeezing each other's hands beneath a table or a piece of cloth. When the parties wish to keep the price a secret, the negotiations are carried on in a finger code under cover.

— *Collier's,* by permission of Crowell-Collier Publishing Co.

279. The most successful business man is the man who holds on to the old just as long as it is good and grabs the new just as soon as it is better.

— Robert P. Vanderpoel

280. Bankruptcy: a legal proceeding in which you put your money in your pants pocket and give your coat to your creditors.

281. A large company had the following legend printed on its salary receipt forms:

"Your salary is your personal business, and should not be disclosed to anyone else."

The new employee, in signing the receipt, added after his signature: "I won't mention it to a soul. I'm just as much ashamed of it as you are."

282. *Patron:* "Sir, I have not yet received a statement of my account."

Merchant: "Oh, we never ask a gentleman for money."

Patron: "Indeed! How, then, do you manage if he doesn't pay?"

Merchant: "Well, after a certain time we conclude he is no gentleman; and then we ask him."

283. Formerly when great fortunes were only made in war, war was business; but now when great fortunes are only made by business, business is war.

— Christian Bovee

284. The old proverb about having too many irons in the fire is an abominable old lie. Have all in, shovel, tongs and poker.

— Adam Clarke

285. During the depression days business was so quiet you could even hear the passing of the dividends.

286. It is never safe to entrust your business to the man who neglects his own.

287. Business is like a wheelbarrow—it stands still unless someone pushes it.

288. The biggest corporation, like the humblest private citizen, must be held to strict compliance with the will of the people.

— Theodore Roosevelt, speech in
Cincinnati, 1902

289. You generally hear that what a man doesn't know doesn't hurt him, but in business what a man doesn't know does hurt him.

— E. S. Lewis

290. I often tell my people that I don't want any fellow who has a job working for me; what I want is a fellow whom a job has. I want the job to get the fellow and not the fellow to get the job. And I want that job to get hold of this young man so hard that no matter where he is the job has got him for keeps. I want that job to have him in its clutches when he goes to bed at night, and in the morning, I want that same job to be sitting on the foot of his bed telling him it's time to get up and go to work. And when a job gets a fellow that way, he'll amount to something.

— Charles F. Kettering, when vice-president
of General Motors Corporation

291. Don't learn the tricks of the trade—learn the trade.

292. These days, the prices of most items in the stores are counter-irritants.

BUSINESS

293. Every young man would do well to remember that all successful business stands on the foundation of morality.

— HENRY WARD BEECHER

294. The proprietor of a highly successful optical shop was instructing his son as to how to charge a customer.

"Son," he said, "after you have fitted the glasses, and he asks what the charge will be, you say, 'The charge is $10.' Then pause and wait to see if he flinches."

"If the customer doesn't flinch, you then say, 'For the frames. The lenses will be another $10.' Then you pause again, this time only slightly, and watch for the flinch. If the customer doesn't flinch this time, you say firmly, 'Each'."

295. The cloak and suit manufacturer received a wire from a customer reading: "Cancel our order at once." To which he replied: "Regret your order cannot be cancelled at once, you will have to wait for your turn."

Candor

296. If people would dare to speak to one another unreservedly there would be a good deal less sorrow in the world a hundred years hence.

— SAMUEL BUTLER, *The Way of All Flesh*

Capacity

297. Attempt only what you are able to perform.

— CATO, *Distichia*

Capital — capitalism see also *Labor-Communism*

298. If you divorce capital from labor, capital is hoarded, and labor starves.

— DANIEL WEBSTER

299. The number of useful and productive laborers is everywhere in proportion to the quantity of capital stock which is employed in setting them to work and to the particular way in which it is so employed.

— ADAM SMITH, *The Wealth of Nations*

300. When commercial capital occupies a position of unquestioned ascendancy, it everywhere constitutes a system of plunder.

— KARL MARX, *Das Kapital*

301. It is assumed that labor is available only in connection with capital; that nobody labors unless somebody else, owning capital, somehow by the use of it, induces him to labor. This assumed, it is next considered whether it is best that capital shall hire laborers, and thus induce them to work by their consent. Having proceeded so far, it is naturally concluded that all laborers are either hired laborers or what we call slaves.

Now, there is no such relation between capital and labor as here assumed . . . Labor is prior to and independent of capital. Capital is only the fruit of labor and could never have existed if labor had not first existed. Labor is the superior of capital, and deserves much the higher consideration.

— ABRAHAM LINCOLN

302. Capitalism and communism stand at opposite poles. Their essential difference is this: The communist, seeing the rich man and his fine home, says: "No man should have so much." The capitalist, seeing the same thing, says: "All men should have as much."

— PHELPS ADAMS

Card-playing

303. The old quarrel between North and South has spread out to include East and West and is now called contract bridge.

Career

304. He didn't carve his career—he chiseled it.

— WALTER WINCHELL

Catharsis

305. Many a man's profanity has saved him from a nervous breakdown.

CAUSE

Cause

306.
They never fail who die
In a great cause.

— LORD BYRON, *Marino Faliero*

Cause and effect

307. Nothing prompts the payment of an old dental bill like a new toothache.

308. Because of the law of gravitation the apple falls to the ground. Because of the law of growth the acorn becomes a mighty oak. Because of the law of causation, a man is "as he thinketh in his heart." Nothing can happen without its adequate cause.

— DON CARLOS MUSSER

Caution

309. Look before you leap, for snakes among sweet flowers do creep.

— Old proverb

310. Wait till it is night before saying it has been a fine day.

— French proverb

311. Better put a strong fence 'round the top of the cliff,
Than an ambulance down in the valley.

— JOSEPH MALINES, *A Fence or an Ambulance*

312. A Georgia cracker sitting, ragged and barefoot, on the steps of his tumbledown shack, was accosted by a stranger who stopped for a drink of water. Wishing to be agreeable, the stranger said, "How is your cotton coming on?"

"Ain't got none," replied the cracker.

"Didn't you plant any?" asked the stranger.

"Nope," said the cracker. " 'Fraid of boll weevils."

"Well," said the stranger, "how is your corn?"

"Didn't plant none. 'Fraid there wa'n't going to be no rain."

The stranger, confused but persevering, added: "Well, how are your potatoes?"

56

"Ain't got none. Scairt o' potato bugs."
"Really, what did you plant?" asked the astonished visitor.
"Nothin' " answered the cracker. "I jes' played safe."

313. It's well for the girl with a future to avoid the man with a past.

Censorship

314. A judge who was asked to ban a book ruled that it was not obscene—and the author took an appeal.

315. Don't think that you are going to conceal faults by concealing evidence that they ever existed. Don't be afraid to go in your library and read every book, as long as that document does not offend your own ideas of decency. That should be the only censorship.

— DWIGHT D. EISENHOWER at Dartmouth
College Commencement Exercises, 1953

316. Every burned book enlightens the world.

— RALPH WALDO EMERSON, *Compensation*

317. Unfortunately it has been our experience that there is a distinct affinity between fools and censorship. It seems to be one of those treading grounds where they rush in.

— HEYWOOD BROUN, *Censoring the Censor*

Censure

318. He who would acquire fame must not show himself afraid of censure. The dread of censure is the death of genius.

— WILLIAM G. SIMMS

319. As high mountains attract clouds and vapors, so do eminent men attract censure. They act like the conductors placed on lofty buildings to draw the lightning from less elevated objects.

— LADY MARGUERITE BLESSINGTON

320. You cannot raise a man up by calling him down.

— WILLIAM J. H. BOETCKER

Change

321. They must often change who would be constant in happiness or wisdom.

— OLIVER GOLDSMITH, *Citizen of the World*

322. All progress stems from change but all change is not necessarily progress.

323. When you're through changing, you're through.

— BRUCE BARTON

324. Change is an easy panacea. It takes character to stay in one place and be happy there.

— ELIZABETH DUNN, quoted in *The Reader's Digest*

325. Every custom was once an eccentricity; every idea was once an absurdity.

— HOLBROOK JACKSON

Character

326. I would rather be adorned by beauty of character than by jewels. Jewels are the gift of fortune, while character comes from within.

— PLAUTUS, *Poenulus*

327. By nothing do men show their character more than by the things they laugh at.

— JOHANN WOLFGANG VON GOETHE

328. Personality has the power to open many doors, but character must keep them open.

329. The test of our religion is whether it fits us to meet emergencies. A man has no more character than he can command in a time of crisis.

— RALPH W. SOCKMAN, D.D.

330. As diamond cuts diamond, and one hone smooths a second, all the parts of intellect are whetstones to each other; and genius, which is but the result of mutual sharpening, is character too.

— ADOLFO BARTOLI

331. A man is what he is, not what men say he is. His ~
no man can touch. His character is what he is before God. His repu~
tation is what men say he is. That can be damaged. For reputation
is for time. Character is for eternity.

— JOHN B. GOUGH

332. A man's treatment of money is the most decisive test of
his character—how he makes it and how he spends it.

— JAMES MOFFATT

333. You can prevent a man from robbing you, but you can't
stop him from being a thief.

— NAPOLEON BONAPARTE

334. Character is not made in a crisis—it is only exhibited.

— ROBERT FREEMAN

335. A pat on the back develops character, if administered
young enough, often enough, and low enough.

Charity — philanthropy

336. A man there was and they called him mad; the more he
gave the more he had.

— JOHN BUNYAN

337. One must be poor to know the luxury of giving.

— GEORGE ELIOT

338. No man ever stood so straight as when he stooped to help
a crippled child.

— Motto inscribed over the doorway of each
Shrine Hospital for Crippled Children

339. THE EIGHT DEGREES OF CHARITY
As Set Down by
MAIMONIDES
Theologian, Philosopher, and Physician, 1135-1204

The first and lowest degree is to give, but with reluctance or regret. This is the gift of the hand, but not of the heart.

The second is, to give cheerfully, but not proportionately to the
distress of the sufferer.

The third is, to give cheerfully, and proportionately, but not until solicited.

The fourth is, to give cheerfully, proportionately, and even unsolicited, but to put it in the poor man's hand, thereby exciting in him the painful emotion of shame.

The fifth is, to give to charity in such a way that the distressed may receive the bounty, and know their benefactor, without their being known to him. Such was the conduct of some of our ancestors, who used to tie up money in the corners of their cloaks, so that the poor might take it unperceived.

The sixth, which rises still higher, is to know the objects of our bounty, but remain unknown to them. Such was the conduct of those of our ancestors who used to convey their charitable gifts into poor people's dwellings, taking care that their own persons and names should remain unknown.

The seventh is still more meritorious, namely, to bestow charity in such a way that the benefactor may not know the relieved persons, nor they the names of their benefactors, as was done by our charitable forefathers during the existence of the temple. For there was in that holy building a place called the Chamber of the Silent, wherein the good deposited secretly whatever their generous hearts suggested, and from which the poor were maintained with equal secrecy.

Lastly, the eighth, and the most meritorious of all, is to anticipate charity by preventing poverty: namely, to assist the reduced fellow man, either by a considerable gift, or a sum of money, or by teaching him a trade, or by putting him in the way of business, so that he may earn an honest livelihood, and not be forced to the dreadful alternative of holding out his hand for charity—this is the highest step and the summit of charity's golden ladder.

340. As the youngster was setting out for Sunday School one morning, he was given two nickels—one for the collection plate and one for himself. As he was rambling down the street he played with the coins. One of them slipped out of his hand, rolled away from him and disappeared irretrievably into a sewer. Gazing ruefully down through the grate he observed rather sadly, "Well, there goes the Lord's nickel."

341. Beware of the saint with an open mouth and a closed pocketbook.

342. Our credit in heaven is not determined by what we give but by what we have left.

343. They who give have all things; they who withhold have nothing.

— Hindu proverb

344. The child had just received a bright new dime and was starting out to invest it in an ice cream soda.

"Why don't you give your money to the missionaries?" asked the minister, who was calling at the house.

"I thought about that," said the child, "but I think I will buy the ice cream soda, and let the druggist give the money to the missionaries."

345. "Look what the good Lord has done for all of you," exhorted the preacher. "Each of you ought to give a tenth of all you get."

"Amen," shouted one of the brethren catching the spirit of the occasion, "but a tenth ain't enough. I say, let's raise it to a twentieth."

346. The gift without the giver is bare;
Who gives himself with his alms feeds three,—
Himself, his hungering neighbor, and me.

— JAMES RUSSELL LOWELL, *The Vision of Sir Launfal*

347. To pity distress is but human: to relieve it is Godlike.

— HORACE MANN, *Lectures on Education*

348. I expect to pass through this world but once. Any good therefore that I can do, or any kindness that I can show to any fellow creature, let me do it now. Let me not defer or neglect it for I shall not pass this way again.

— STEPHEN GRELLET

349. In nothing do men more nearly approach the gods than in doing good to their fellow men.

— CICERO, *Pro Ligario*

350. He who bestows his goods upon the poor,
Shall have as much again, and ten times more.

— JOHN BUNYAN, *Pilgrim's Progress*

351. You must be fit to give before you can be fit to receive.

— JAMES STEPHENS, *The Crock of Gold*

352. Behold, I do not give lectures or a bit of charity,
when I give of myself.

— WALT WHITMAN, *Song of Myself*

353. *Notice in a Scot church:* "Those in the habit of putting buttons instead of coins in the collection plate will please put in their own buttons and not buttons from the cushions on the pews."

354. He who defers his charities till his death is liberal with another man's rather than with his own.

355. A cup that is already full cannot have more added to it. In order to receive the further good to which we are entitled, we must give of that which we have.

— MARGARET BECKER, "There Is But One
Source," *Weekly Unity*

356. Talmudic writers encourage charity and denounce covetousness, telling of the fox who wanted to steal grapes but could not get through the small hole in the stone wall. He fasted for three days, became thin, forced his way through, ate all he could and found he could not get out. He had to fast three more days, which may remind some of their stock gambling experiences.

357. You must give some time to your fellow man. Even if it's a little thing, do something for those who have need of help, something for which you get no pay but the privilege of doing it.

— DR. ALBERT SCHWEITZER

358. Philanthropist: one who gives away when he should be giving it back.

359. No great spiritual blessing ever comes to one who gives selfishly and grudgingly. Some years ago a man was complaining to his pastor about the church asking for money. He fumed, "This business of Christianity is just one continuous give, give, give." The preacher thought for a moment, and then replied, "I want to thank you for one of the best definitions of Christianity I have ever heard."

360. The poor man's charity is to wish the rich man well.

361. Generosity during lifetime is a very different thing from generosity in the hour of death; one proceeds from genuine liberality and benevolence, the other from pride or fear.

— HORACE MANN

362. The only thing which is of lasting benefit to a man is that which he does for himself. Money which comes to him without effort on his part is seldom a benefit and often a curse. . . . And so with regard to money or other things which are given by one person to another. It is only in the exceptional case that the receiver is really benefited. But if we can help people to help themselves, then there is a permanent blessing conferred.

— JOHN D. ROCKEFELLER, SR., *Random Reminiscences of Men and Events*

363. Old timer: one who remembers when charity was a virtue and not an organization.

Charm

364. There is no personal charm so great as the charm of a cheerful temperament. It is a great error to suppose this comes entirely by nature—it comes quite as much by culture.

— HENRY VAN DYKE

365. If you have charm, you don't need to have anything else; and if you don't have it, it doesn't matter what else you have.

Child – children

366. Children are natural mimics—they act like their parents in spite of every attempt to teach them good manners.

367. Give me a newborn child, and in ten years I can have him so scared he'll never dare lift his voice above a whisper, or so brave he'll fear nothing.

— Dr. George A. Dorsey, quoted in
The Reader's Digest

368. Joy of motherhood: What a woman experiences when all the kids are in bed.

369. Children do not grow all in a straight line. Day by day they do not get better and better. Like it or not, humans grow and develop in a zigzag fashion. The whole trend is toward better behavior but all of us have ups and downs.

— Dr. James L. Hymes, Jr.

370. "Mother," asked a little girl out of a sudden silence, "when will I be old enough to wear the kind of shoes that kill you?"

371. A friend of mine with three children in college was badly upset when her physician told her she was going to have another child. "I simply can't go through it again, Doctor!" she wailed.

"Did you have complications with your other pregnancies?" he asked sympathetically.

"Heavens, no! Having babies never bothered me a bit, physically. It's the PTA that gets me down."

— Marie Hamel

372. He who pleases children will be remembered with pleasure by men.

— James Boswell

373. After you have children, the economic law reverses to Demand and Supply.

— Marcelene Cox in *Ladies' Home Journal*

374. Instead of telling the modern child he should be seen, not heard, parents could phrase it more understandably by suggesting he may continue the video portion of his program if he interrupts the audio.

375. The only things that children wear out faster than shoes are parents and teachers.

376. Children need love, especially when they don't deserve it.

— Harold S. Hulbert

377. Children are small people who are not permitted to act as parents did at that age.

— JOSEPHUS HENRY

378. One should no more be affectionate in front of a child without including him than eat in front of him while he remains hungry.

— ERIC BERNE, M.D., *The Mind in Action*
(Simon & Schuster, Inc.)

379. The whole business about bringing up children is to know when to lose one's patience.

— ELIZABETH TAYLOR

380. All children are born good.

— LORD PALMERSTON

Childbirth

381. "If a mother is disquieted," wrote Robert Burton in *The Anatomy of Melancholy,* in 1621, "or if by any casualty she be affrighted by some fearful object, she endangers her child."

In his book *Ourselves Unborn,* the embryologist, George Washington Corner, laughed off Burton's catalogue of prenatal horrors with one of his own: "As an honest man of science, I have to admit that I myself know of a remarkable case. A woman of my acquaintance had a craving to read *David Copperfield* while she was expecting and, upon my word, her child was full of the Dickens."

Choice

382. Young men, life is before you. Two voices are calling you —one coming out from the swamps of selfishness and force, where success means death and the other from the hilltops of justice and progress, where even failure brings glory. Two lights are seen in your horizon—one, the fast fading marsh light of power, and the other the slowly rising sun of human brotherhood. Two ways lie open for you—one leading to an even lower and lower plain, where are heard the cries of despair and the curses of the poor, where manhood shrivels and possession rots down the possessor; and the other leading to the highlands of the morning, where are heard the glad

CHOICE

shouts of humanity and where honest effort is rewarded with immortality.

— JOHN P. ALTGELD

383. He who chooses the beginning of a road, also chooses its destination.

384. Groucho Marx saw a friend standing in the rain in front of a swank Hollywood night club. "What are you going to do?" he asked. "Stay outside and get wet or go in and get soaked?"

Christmas

385. I am thinking of you today because it is Christmas and I wish you happiness, and tomorrow because it will be the day after Christmas, I shall still wish you happiness and so on through the year. I may not be able to tell you about it every day, because I may be far away; or because both of us may be very busy; or because I cannot even afford to pay the postage on so many letters, or find the time to write them, but that makes no difference, the thought and the wish will be here just the same. Whatever joy or success comes to you will make me glad without pretense, and in plain words, goodwill to you is what I mean, in the spirit of Christmas.

— HENRY VAN DYKE

Church see also *Religion*

386. One reason we have so many pennies in the church collection is because we have no smaller coins.

387. It is generally agreed that the Founder of the Church, Jesus Christ, wished the spiritual power to be distinct from the civil, and each to be free and unhampered in doing its own work, not forgetting however, that it is expedient for both, and in the interest of everybody, that there be a harmonious relationship.

— POPE LEO XIII, *Arcanum Divinae Sapientaie* (1880)

388. Overheard some children inside our church admiring the stained-glass window depicting Christ at prayer. "It's beautiful here," one boy said, with greater wisdom than he realized, "but it ain't no good if you are outside."

— Burton Hillis, courtesy of *Better Homes and Gardens* magazine

389. The difference between listening to a radio sermon and going to church is like the difference between calling your girl on the phone and spending the evening with her.

— The Reverend L. Gene Stewart, *Christian Advocate*

390. One day the telephone rang in the Rector's office of the Washington church which President Franklin Roosevelt attended. An eager voice inquired, "Tell me, do you expect the President to be in church this Sunday?"

"That," the Rector explained patiently, "I cannot promise. But we expect God to be there, and we fancy that will be incentive enough for a reasonably large attendance."

— John T. Watson, quoted in *The Reader's Digest*

Citizen – citizenship

391. A man who neglects his duty as a citizen is not entitled to his rights as a citizen.

— Tiorio

392. In medieval times, the police force of the town was selected by rotation from among the burghers: the duty of watch and ward. In modern times we have such service only for war or some sudden disaster, and it is a serious question whether the leaving of such functions to a professional police has not weakened the sense of civic responsibility and done away with an effective means of education.

To patrol one's city at night; to know its dark alleys under the moon, or with no light at all except one's lantern; to enjoy the companionship of the watch—was this not an early practical example of William James' *Moral Equivalent of War,* more useful, more humane than any national scheme of military training?

The American school child, in assuming the policeman's duty of regulating traffic at school crossings, is perhaps recovering some of that sense of responsibility which disappeared in the 18th century with the final collapse of the medieval municipality.

— Adapted from *The Culture of Cities*
by LEWIS MUMFORD. Copyright, 1938,
by Harcourt, Brace and Company, Inc.

393. A good citizen is one who behaves as if there were no laws.

394. At a fraternal organization dinner when the guests got up to introduce themselves, one of them, a naturalized citizen, had this to say: "I believe I am the only person here who became a United States citizen with my clothes on."

City — cities

395. Frank Lloyd Wright, among others, thinks the modern big city is doomed. But it's hard to envision major leagues made up of teams representing decentralized shopping centers.

Civilization

396. Civilization: a system under which a man pays a quarter to park his car so he won't be fined a dollar while spending a dime for a cup of coffee.

397. Civilization is a limitless multiplication of unnecessary necessaries.

— MARK TWAIN

Civil liberty

398. Civil liberties lie in the habits and customs which tolerate dissent.

— JUDGE LEARNED HAND

399. There is no truth to be gathered from all history more certain, or more momentous, than this:

That civil liberty cannot long be separated from religious liberty without danger and, ultimately, without destruction of both.

Whenever religious liberty exists, it will, first or last, bring in and establish civil liberty.

Wherever the State establishes one Church, suppressing all others, the State Church will, first or last, become the engine of despotism and overthrow, unless it be itself overthrown, every vestige of political right.

— JOSEPH STORY

Clarity

400.   To be able to ask a question clearly is two-thirds of the way to getting it answered.

— JOHN RUSKIN

Cleanliness

401.   "Cleanliness is next to Godliness"—Carefulness leads to cleanliness; cleanliness to purity; purity to humility; humility to saintliness; saintliness to fear of sin; fear of sin to holiness; and holiness to immortality.

— The *Talmud*

Cleverness

402.
If all good people were clever,
And all clever people were good,
The world would be nicer than ever
We thought that it possibly could.
But somehow, 'tis seldom or never
The two hit it off as they should;
The good are so harsh to the clever,
The clever so rude to the good.

— DAME ELIZABETH WORDSWORTH,
St. Christopher and Other Poems

403.   There was once a village half-wit who was the butt of much ridicule. Whenever people offered him the choice between a nickel and a dime he invariably chose the nickel. After this had gone on for years someone took pity on him and told him a dime was worth more than a nickel. To which he replied: "But if I took the dime, people would stop offering me the money and I wouldn't even get the nickel."

404.   Cleverness is serviceable for everything, sufficient for nothing.

— HENRI-FRÉDÉRIC AMIEL

CLOTHES — DRESS — FASHION

Clothes — dress — fashion

405. Heavy women command more attention than thin ones, and usually have more friends. They're not so apt to be preoccupied with clothes. Women who think of nothing but clothes bore men because they haven't time to be nice to them.
— ELSA MAXWELL

406. A girdle is a device to keep an unfortunate situation from spreading.

407. Girdle: the difference between fact and figure.

408. In these days of low cut gowns, it takes a lot of will power to look a woman in the eye.
— Quoted by BRUCE PATTERSON, King Features Syndicate, Inc.

409. You are never fully dressed until you wear a smile.

410. "Now," said the saleslady in a millinery shop, assuring a prospective customer, "here's a number that will never go out of style. It will look just as ridiculous year after year."

411. If women really dressed to please their husbands, they'd be wearing last year's clothes.

College — university

412. College graduate: a person who had a chance to get an education.

413. Colleges: institutions which sometimes lower entrance requirements with an end in view—not to mention promising tackles and backs.

414. In our anxiety to give everyone a college degree, we are giving no one an education.
— RUSSELL KIRK, *Academic Freedom* (Henry Regnery Co.)

415. College is just like a laundry—you get out of it what you put into it—only you never recognize it.

416. People sometimes refer to higher education as the higher learning, but colleges and universities are much more than knowledge factories; they are testaments to man's perennial struggle to make a better world for himself, his children, and his children's children. This, indeed, is their sovereign purpose. They are great fortifications against ignorance and irrationality; but they are more than places of higher learning—they are centers and symbols of man's higher yearning.

— Professor W. H. Cowley,
Stanford University

417. A student government officer at the University of San Francisco wrote to the University of California concerning the use of the honor system during exams and received this reply: "The University of California abandoned the honor system several years ago when it became evident that the professors had the honor and the students had the system."

— Dick Friendlich, *San Francisco Chronicle* columnist

418. The remarkable thing about college reunions is that your classmates have gotten so stout and bald they hardly recognize you.

419. College professors are not made overnight. They reach the height of their profession by degrees.

420. It seems a shame that college education should be wasted on high school graduates, who already know everything.

— Oren Arnold, *Kiwanis Magazine*

421. The farmer sent his son to college, and the lad came home at the end of the first year jubilantly announcing that he stood second in his class.

"Second?" said his father. "Second? Why weren't you first? What do you think I'm sending you to school for, anyway?"

Filled with determination, the boy plowed into his books, and returned home from his sophomore year with top honors in studies. His father looked at him silently for a few minutes, then shrugged his shoulders and grumbled, "At the head of the class, eh? Well, it can't be much of a college!"

— *The Rotarian* magazine

422. You can lead a boy to college but you can't make him think.

— George Ade

71

423. A college education is not a quantitative body of memorized knowledge salted away in a card file. It is a taste for knowledge, a taste for philosophy, if you will; a capacity to explore, to question, to perceive relationships, between fields of knowledge and experience.

— A. WHITNEY GRISWOLD

424. A college education is one of the few things a person is willing to pay for and not get.

— WILLIAM LOWE BRYAN, president emeritus of Indiana University

Committee

425. Committee: a group which succeeds in getting something done only when it consists of three members, one of whom happens to be sick and another absent.

— HENDRIK VAN LOON

426. Committee: a group of the unfit, appointed by the unwilling to do the unnecessary.

— VICTOR RIESEL, Hall Syndicate

427. At meeting of clubs, by an effort of will,
I always contrive to keep perfectly still,
For it takes but a word of annoyance or pity
And wham! there I am on another committee.

— ALICE F. STURGIS, *Learning Parliamentary Procedure*, by permission of RICHARD ARMOUR (McGraw Hill Book Company)

Common interest

428. We didn't all come over on the same ship, but we're all in the same boat.

— BERNARD M. BARUCH

429. In a boat at sea one of the men began to bore a hole in the bottom of the boat. On being remonstrated with, he answered: "I am only boring under my own seat." "Yes," said his comrades, "but when the sea rushes in we shall all be drowned with you."

— The *Talmud*

Common sense

430. One pound of learning requires ten pounds of common sense to apply it.

— Persian proverb

431. Common sense in an uncommon degree is what the world calls wisdom.

— SAMUEL T. COLERIDGE

432. Dr. Karl Compton of M.I.T. used to tell that his sister who lived in India was having some wiring done by a native electrician. He came to her over and over again for instructions. Finally in exasperation she said, "You know what I want. Why don't you just use your common sense and go ahead?"

He made a grave, courtly bow and said, "Madam, common sense is a rare gift of God, I have only a technical education."

— PAUL GARRETT, vice-president, General Motors Corporation

433. Common sense is the knack of seeing things as they are, and doing things as they ought to be done.

— C. E. STOWE

Communism

434. *Free enterprise:* You furnish your own ladder and the government merely stands by to steady it as you climb.

Socialism: The government furnishes the ladder for free, but with no rungs.

Communism: The Comrades, finding you already well up the ladder, jerk it out from under you, bust it up and beat you to death with the pieces.

435. What is a Communist? One who has yearnings for equal division of unequal earnings.

436. *Nationalist Chinese Radio, answering propaganda broadcast from Chinese Reds:* "We have American advisers, just as you have Russian advisers. We are friendly with Americans, but we speak out frankly. . . . To prove it, we will shout three times, 'The Americans are S.O.B.'s' and we dare you to say just once, 'The Russians are S.O.B.'s.' " (From the Reds, no response.)

Companionship

437. I hold that companionship is a matter of mutual weaknesses. We like that man or woman best who has the same faults we have.

— George Jean Nathan

Competition

438. Don't knock your competitors. By boosting others you will boost yourself. A little competition is a good thing and severe competition is a blessing. Thank God for competition.

— Jacob Kindleberger

Compliment — complimentary

439. Perhaps the wittiest and most graceful tribute ever spoken by a man of his wife was said by Joseph H. Choate.

Someone asked him: "Mr. Choate, if you could not be yourself, who would you rather be?"

Instantly came the reply: "Mrs. Choate's second husband."

440. At a dinner given in honor of Chauncey Depew the speakers had paid him generous compliments. At last came his turn to reply. He began as follows: "It's nice to get these words while I'm still alive. I'd rather have the taffy than the epitaphy."

441. Dubious compliment: She is as pretty as she can be.

442. It is a great mistake for men to give up paying compliments, for when they give up saying what is charming, they give up thinking what is charming.

— Oscar Wilde

443. Though compliments should arise naturally out of the occasion, they should not appear to be prompted by the spur of it, for then they seem hardly spontaneous. Applaud a man's speech at the moment when he sits down and he will take your compliment as exacted by the demands of common civility; but let some space intervene, and then show him that the merits of his speech have dwelt with you, and he will remember your compliment for a much longer time than you have remembered his speech.

— Sir Henry Taylor

444. The surest way to knock the chip off a fellow's shoulder is by patting him on the back.

445. If you wish to compliment someone, compliment him on a detail. In praising a man's home, avoid a vague generality like "Nice place you've got here." Select something specific, such as the view from a window or the shrewd arrangement of a room. Don't tell a woman her hat is merely "becoming." Mention its angle or its color.

— DOROTHY WALWORTH, quoted in
The Reader's Digest

Compromise

446. Compromise: a deal in which two people get what neither of them wanted.

447. We learned once and for all that compromise makes a good umbrella but a poor roof; that it is a temporary expedient, often wise in party politics, almost sure to be unwise in statesmanship.

— JAMES RUSSELL LOWELL, *Democracy*

Compulsion

448. One fact stands out in bold relief in the history of man's attempts for betterment. That is that when compulsion is used, only resentment is aroused, and the end is not gained. Only through moral suasion and appeal to man's reason can a movement succeed.

— SAMUEL GOMPERS

Conceit

449. Conceit, God's gift to little men.
— BRUCE BARTON

450. Is he conceited? Well, I'd just like to buy him at my price, and sell him at his!

451. A man wrapped up in himself makes a very small package.

452. Here's to the man who is wisest and best,
Here's to the man who with judgment is blest.

CONCEIT

Here's to the man who's as smart as can be—
I mean the man who agrees with me.

453. Conceit may puff a man up but it never props him up.

— JOHN RUSKIN

454. "Do you like conceited men better than the other kind?"
"What other kind?"

455. Gen. Alfred M. Gruenther, former supreme commander of the Atlantic alliance in Europe, used to tell this story about the Soviet delegation to Belgrade:

Nikita S. Khrushchev went to his tailor with a bolt of expensive cloth specially woven for him. He asked the tailor to make up a three-piece suit. After measuring the portly, vodka-guzzling Red czar, the tailor said he would not have enough cloth for a vest. Khrushchev grumpily decided against ordering the suit and took the cloth with him on his visit to Belgrade. There he tried a Yugoslav tailor who measured him and found he could make a stylish suit including the vest. Khrushchev, puzzled, asked how come the Russian tailor couldn't cut the cloth to make the vest. "In Moscow you are a bigger man than you are here," the Belgrade tailor replied.

— *Chicago Tribune*

456. Have you heard the new beatitude for school administrators? "Blessed are they who run around in circles, for they shall be known as big wheels."

457. Men who "know all about it" can never learn anything; while those who are most *learned* are always students.

— RICHARD HARRIS, *Illustrations in Advocacy* (Stevens and Haynes)

458. The ass who thinks himself a stag discovers his mistake when he comes to the hurdle.

459. Whenever nature leaves a hole in a person's mind, she generally plasters it over with self-conceit.

— HENRY WADSWORTH LONGFELLOW

460. Every man has a right to be conceited until he is successful.

— BENJAMIN DISRAELI

461. A modest man often seems conceited because he is delighted with what he has done, thinking it better than anything of which he believed himself capable, whereas the conceited man is inclined to express dissatisfaction with his performances, thinking them unworthy of his genius.

    — HESKETH PEARSON, *The Man Whistler*
    (Harper and Brothers)

Condescension

462. 'Tis looking downward makes one dizzy.

    — ROBERT BROWNING

Conduct see also *Behavior*

463. If evil be said of thee and if it be true, correct thyself; if it be a lie, laugh at it.

    — EPICTETUS

Conference

464. Conference: a place where conversation is substituted for the dreariness of labor and the loneliness of thought.

Confession

465. Confession of our faults is the next thing to innocence.

    — PUBLILIUS SYRUS

466. "Did I understand you to say that this boy voluntarily confessed his share in the mischief done to the schoolhouse?" asked the judge, addressing the determined-looking female parent of a small and dirty boy who was charged with having been concerned in a recent raid upon an unpopular schoolmaster. "Yes sir, he did," the woman responded. "I just had to persuade him a little, and then he told the whole thing, voluntarily." "How did you persuade him?" queried the judge. "Well, first I gave him a good licking," said the firm parent, "and then I put him right to bed without any supper and I took all his clothes away and told him he'd stay in bed till he told me what he'd done, if 'twas the rest of his days, and I should lick him again in the morning. And in less than half an hour, sir, he told me the whole story voluntarily."

Confidence

467. Nature has written a letter of credit upon some men's faces that is honored wherever presented. You cannot help trusting such men. Their very presence gives confidence. There is "promise to pay" in their faces which gives confidence and you prefer it to another man's endorsement. Character is credit.

468. Confidence: the cocky feeling you have just before you know better.

Conformity

469. In all men there must arise a spark of the dissenter if civilization is to survive. Society has less to lose from these subversive individuals who are willing to pervert the right of free inquiry than it has by denying freedom to the host of honest men and women who are genuinely concerned to learn what is not now known, to create knowledge now sorely needed.

> — RICHARD B. BALLOU, *The Individual and the State: The Modern Challenge to Education* (The Beacon Press)

470. The intellectuals, the educated men, must come out from behind their books long enough to reassert themselves.

The conformists did not make America what it is today. Thos. Jefferson was not a conformist; he was a bristling intellectual. And what about Abraham Lincoln . . . Theodore Roosevelt, Woodrow Wilson, or FDR? The conformists in American history have been forgotten—because they did so little to make the United States the great nation it is today. It was the innovators, the men who thought, the men, if you please, who read books, who did it.

> — Editorial, *Decatur* (Illinois) *Herald*

471. A lecturer of some renown was asked to speak at a nudist camp. He was greeted by ladies and gentlemen with no more on than nature saw fit to bestow upon them. They suggested that he would probably like to get ready for dinner. He went upstairs realizing that he must disrobe like the rest of them. He paced the floor in an agonized panic of indecision. The dinner bell rang. With the courage of utter desperation he stripped, and in Adamite splendor descended the staircase—only to find that all the guests had put on evening clothes to do him honor.

— DONALD CULROSS PEATTIE, quoted in
The Reader's Digest

Confusion

472. It seems to me that we're all in the same boat with Christopher Columbus. He didn't know where he was going when he started. When he got there he didn't know where he was, and when he got back he didn't know where he had been.

473. If you can't convince 'em—confuse 'em.

Conscience

474. Conscience: the still small voice that makes you feel still smaller.

475. A man's own conscience is his sole tribunal, and he should care no more for that phantom "opinion" than he should fear meeting a ghost if he crossed the churchyard at dark.

— EDWARD G. BULWER-LYTTON

476. A good conscience is to the soul what health is to the body; it preserves a constant ease and serenity within us, and more than countervails all the calamities and afflictions that can possibly befall us.

— JOSEPH ADDISON

477. Conscience gets a lot of credit that belongs to cold feet.

478. When you have a fight with your conscience and get licked, you win.

Conservative

479. A conservative is a person with sense enough to know that change isn't necessarily progress.

Constancy

480. It is often constancy to change the mind.

— JOHN HOOLE

Contempt

481. One day when Thaddeus Stevens, the famous American statesman and abolitionist, was practicing in the courts, he did not like the ruling of the presiding judge. A second time when the judge ruled, "Old Thad," turned scarlet and his lips quivered. He began, tremblingly, tying up his papers as if to quit the courtroom.

"Do I understand, Mr. Stevens," asked the judge, eyeing "Old Thad" indignantly, "that you wish to show your contempt for this court?"

"No sir," returned "Old Thad,"—"no sir, I don't want to show my contempt, sir—I'm trying my best to conceal it."

Contentment

482. A man who is contented with what he has done will never become famous for what he will do.

483. Who lives content with little possesses everything.

— NICOLAS BOILEAU

484. There are two kinds of discontent in this world: the discontent that works, and the discontent that wrings its hands. The first gets what it wants, and the second loses what it had. There is no cure for the first but success, and there is no cure at all for the second.

— ELBERT HUBBARD, *Scrapbook*

485. A strong determination to get the best out of life, a keen desire to enjoy what one has, and no regrets if one fails: this is the secret of the Chinese genius for contentment.

— LIN YUTANG, *My Country and My People*

486. My motto is, "contented with little, yet wishing for more."

— CHARLES LAMB

487. It is right to be contented with what we have, never with what we are.

488. Just think how happy you'd be if you lost everything you have right now—and then got it back again.

— LEONARD M. LEONARD in *Journal of Living*

489. Being "contented" ought to mean in English, as it does in French, being pleased. Being content with an attic ought not to mean being unable to move from it and resigned to living in it: it ought to mean appreciating all there is in such a position. For true contentment is a real, even an active virtue—not only affirmative but creative. It is the power of getting out of any situation all there is in it.

> —Reprinted by permission of Dodd, Mead & Company from *A Miscellany of Men* by G. K. CHESTERTON

Continuity

490. Even as the generations of leaves, so are also those of men. As for the leaves, the wind scatters some upon the earth, but the forest as it buds brings forth new leaves when the spring is come; even so one generation of men arises and another passes away.

> — HOMER

Contradictions

491. *Apparent contradictions:*

Look before you leap.
—He who hesitates is lost.
A man gets no more than he pays for.
—The best things in life are free.
Leave well enough alone.
Progress never stands still.

Convention — conventional

492. Convention: an excuse for doing the unconventional.

Conversation

493. No matter how flat your conversation, most people would like to have it flatter.

494. When you talk you only say something that you already know—when you listen you learn what someone else knows.

495. A conversation is like a good meal. You should leave it just before you have had enough.

496. The great gift of conversation lies less in displaying it ourselves than in drawing it out of others. He who leaves your company pleased with himself and his own cleverness is perfectly well pleased with you.

— JEAN DE LA BRUYÈRE

497. The secret of polite conversation is never to open your mouth unless you have nothing to say.

498. The real art of conversation is not only to say the right thing in the right place but to leave unsaid the wrong thing at the tempting moment.

— DOROTHY NEVILL, *Under Five Reigns* (Methuen)

Convincing

499. Before you try to convince anyone else be sure you are convinced, and if you cannot convince yourself, drop the subject.

— JOHN H. PATTERSON

500. In theory it is easy to convince an ignorant person; in actual life, men not only object to offering themselves to be convinced, but hate the man who has convinced them.

— EPICTETUS

Cooperation

501. "How long was your last cook with you?"
"She was never with us. She was against us from the start."

— HENRY SWICEGOOD in *Young America*

502. Coming together is a beginning; keeping together is progress; working together is success.

503. Remember the banana; when it left the bunch it got skinned.

504. One hand cannot applaud.

— Arabian proverb

505. When bad men combine, the good must associate; else they will fall, one by one, in unpitied sacrifice, in a contemptible struggle.

— EDMUND BURKE

506. You may be on top of the heap—but remember you're still part of it.

— FRANCES RODMAN

Corruption

507. Because men are everywhere corruptible and always corrupted, no man or group of men can be trusted with too much power and indeed with no power at all which is not balanced or checked by the power of other men.

— From *The Bent World* by J. V. LANGMEAD CASSERLEY. Copyright, 1955, by Oxford University Press, Inc.

Courage

508. Keep your face to the sun and the shadows will fall behind

509. Let him not imagine who aims at greatness that all is lost by a single adverse case of fortune; for if fortune has at one time the better of courage, courage may afterwards recover the advantage. He who is prepossessed with the assurance of overcoming at least overcomes the fear of failure; whereas he who is apprehensive of losing loses, in reality, all hopes of subduing. Boldness and power are such inseparable companions that they appear to be born together; and when once divided, they both decay and die at the same time.

— ARCHBISHOP VENN

510. It is better to die on your feet than to live on your knees.

— *La Pasionaria*

511. To see what is right and not to do it is want of courage.

— CONFUCIUS, *Analects*

512. Cowards die many times before their deaths;
The valiant never taste of death but once.

— WILLIAM SHAKESPEARE, *Julius Caesar*

COURAGE

513. Success is never final and failure never fatal. It's courage that counts.

514. Courage is resistance to fear, mastery of fear—not absence of fear. Except a creature be part coward it is not a compliment to say it is brave; it is merely a loose misapplication of the word. Consider the flea!—incomparably the bravest of all the creatures of God, if ignorance of fear were courage. Whether you are asleep or awake he will attack you, caring nothing for the fact that in bulk and strength you are to him as are the massed armies of the earth to a suckling child; he lives both day and night and all days and nights in the very lap of peril and the immediate presence of death, and yet is no more afraid than is the man who walks the streets of a city that was threatened by an earthquake ten centuries before. When we speak of Clive, Nelson and Putnam as men who "didn't know what fear was," we ought always to add the flea—and put him at the head of the procession.

— Source unknown

515. A great deal of talent is lost to the world for want of a little courage. Every day sends to their graves obscure men whom timidity prevented from making a first effort.

— Sydney Smith

516. Courage is the first of human qualities because it is the quality which guarantees all others.

— Sir Winston Churchill

Courtesy see also Politeness

517. Courtesy is really nothing more than a form of friendliness. It is amazing what a warming influence it can have on an otherwise dreary world. It has been said that a rise of one degree Fahrenheit in the mean annual temperature of the globe would free both polar regions from their ice. It is thrilling to contemplate what frigidity might be dispelled in the world of human relations if people made just a little better effort to be friendly.

— M. Bartos

518. Nothing is ever lost by courtesy. It is the cheapest of the pleasures; costs nothing and conveys much. It pleases him who gives and him who receives, and thus, like mercy, is twice blessed.

— Erastus Wiman

519. We cannot always oblige, but we can always speak obligingly.

— VOLTAIRE

Courtship

520. Behind every successful man there is always a woman—and usually she catches him.

Creativity

521. Most men have died without creating; not one has died without destroying.

— ALEXANDRE DUMAS

522. If you would create something you must *be* something.

— JOHANN WOLFGANG VON GOETHE

Credit — creditor

523. Creditor: a man who has a better memory than a debtor.

524. Bill collector: a man who doesn't believe in putting off until tomorrow what can be dunned today.

Credo

525. *My Creed*

My creed is: Give the best you have to the highest you know and do it now. If we do the duty next to us and then the duty next to that, light begins to break on life's ultimate issues. And when we persevere to the apparent limit of our own strength, a Higher Power comes to our help, provided our purpose is to serve with honor and not for honor.

— DR. RALPH W. SOCKMAN

526. I believe, with all my heart, that the Spirit of God is within every man, however mean, ugly, or diseased; and that when we visit indignities upon other men, we are affronting our Creator, and we are also harming ourselves.

— BARTLEY C. CRUM

Credulity

527. I prefer credulity to skepticism and cynicism, for there is more promise in almost anything than in nothing at all.

— RALPH BARTON PERRY

Crime see also *Delinquency—Juvenile delinquency*

528. Whoever profits by the crime is guilty of it.

— French proverb

529. The first prison I ever saw had inscribed on it—"Cease to Do Evil; Learn to Do Well"; but as the inscription was on the outside, the prisoners could not read it.

— GEORGE BERNARD SHAW

530. Of equal if not greater importance than deterrence and retributive justice (in the treatment or punishment of the offender) are the rehabilitative goals to be achieved through different types of penalties and by bringing to bear correctional processes. More and more reliance is being placed on this factor as we come to realize that men's attitudes and habits and way of life can be changed by bringing to bear the teachings of the psychiatrists, the sociologists, and religious leaders.

— JAMES V. BENNETT, "Operation: Assize," *Journal of the American Judicature Society*

531. The man who starts out with the notion that the world owes him a living generally finds that the world pays its debt in the penitentiary or the poorhouse.

— WILLIAM GRAHAM SUMNER, *The Forgotten Man and Other Essays*

532. Attending a charity dinner at a Park Avenue address, foreign correspondent Frank Sparks was seated next to a criminologist who was dull and annoying. After listening to 20 minutes of tiresome chatter, Sparks managed to slip away to another room.

"He's a bit dull, isn't he?" the host said. Fred nodded. "But he's got a remarkable mind," the host continued. "They tell me he's found a way to commit the perfect crime."

"I know," hissed Sparks, "he almost bored me to death, too."

— From *Champagne Before Breakfast*, by HY
GARDNER. Copyright, 1954, by HY GARD-
NER. Used by permission of Henry Holt and
Company

533. Let no one be naive enough to assume crime will decrease
in proportion to the increase in police power. You may as well try
to stop a leaky water faucet by placing a pan under it to catch the
overflow, as try to stop crime merely by catching criminals. In either
instance it is the plumbing that needs attention. Put the emphasis
on character-building, and crime will vanish as darkness vanishes
with the lighting of an incandescent bulb.

534. Probation represents a distinct break with the classical
theory of criminal law, for it attempts to deal with offenders as
individuals rather than as classes or concepts, to select certain offenders who can be assisted while at liberty to form correct habits
and attitudes without a penalty, and to use a great variety of methods
for this purpose. It represents, also, a distinct break with the retributive theory of punishment. It does not attempt to make the offender suffer; it attempts to prevent him from suffering. Some suffering results from the status, to be sure, but it is not intentional and is
avoided as far as possible. Consequently there is no good reason for
insisting that probation is punishment, as some authors have in the
effort to win approval for the system.

— EDWIN H. SUTHERLAND

535. It can reasonably be estimated that $20 billion annually
is the cost of crime in this country. This represents a cost of $495
for each family in the U.S.; for every $1 spent on education, $1.82
goes to crime; for every $1 donated to churches, $10 goes to crime.

— JUDGE IRVING BEN COOPER, "The Courts and
Juvenile Delinquency," *American Scholar*

536. Great Britain has one answer to the problem which in one
year resulted in a drop of 14 per cent in juvenile delinquency, of
which only 5 per cent was violent. Britain's attitude is that children
are not naturally good citizens until society has made them so, therefore their methods include strong disciplinary powers for teachers,
including whipping; establishment of youth clubs; strict control of

child consumption of movies, television, and comic books; frequent courtroom fines for the parent instead of punishment for the child.

537. He who spares the guilty threatens the innocent.

—Legal maxim

538. Eighty per cent of our criminals come from unsympathetic homes.

—HANS CHRISTIAN ANDERSEN

539. Criminals become so—not from hardening of the arteries but from hardening of the heart.

—DOROTHY THOMPSON, "Educating Emotions Prevents Juvenile Delinquency," *Ladies Home Journal*

540. Arson: fire caused by friction between the insurance policy and the mortgage.

541. For more than many decades, about three-quarters of the criminals sent to our state and federal prisons "for life" have completed their sentences and have been discharged in less than ten years.

Critic — criticism

542. Critics are sentinels in the grand army of letters, stationed at the corners of newspapers and reviews, to challenge every new author.

—HENRY WADSWORTH LONGFELLOW

543. Producer Alfred de Liagre took his small son and daughter to a Broadway musical. Just before the curtain went up, he cautioned: "Remember, now: no talk, no coughing, no fidgeting."

"But, Papa," persisted five-year-old Christine, "if I get sick, may I vomit?"

De Liagre leaned over to the man in front of him, predicted ruefully: "She'll grow up to be a critic!"

—JOHN MASON BROWN, quoted by BENNETT CERF in *Saturday Review*

544. Mrs. Cholmondely Jones entertained at a musical afternoon in her home. The feature was a great and well known violinist. When it was all over, everybody crowded around the musician.

"I've got to be very frank with you," one of the guests said. "I think your performance was terrible."

Whereupon the hostess interposed: "Pay no attention to him. He doesn't know what he's talking about. He only repeats what he hears everyone else say."

545. When New York newspaper reviews hooted at Liberace's Madison Square Garden performance—packed to the rafters with palpitating females—he wired each detractor, "Your cruel remarks made me so unhappy I cried all the way to the bank."

— BENNETT CERF in *Saturday Review*

546. Music critic's comment on a woman singer: "All her high notes are promissory."

— LYDEL SIMS in Memphis *Commercial Appeal*

547. She ran the gamut of emotions from *A* to *B*.

548. Criticism of our contemporaries is not criticism; it is conversation.

— BRANDER MATTHEWS

549. The value of compassion cannot be overemphasized. Anyone can criticize. It takes a true believer to be compassionate. No greater burden can be borne than to know no one cares or understands.

— ARTHUR H. STAINBACK, D.D.

550. George Bernard Shaw was once asked how he enjoyed the playing of a new young violinist. "He reminds me of Paderewski," he replied. "Oh, but Mr. Shaw, Paderewski is not a violinist," said the prodigy's sponsor.

"Just so, just so," was the response.

551. Aversion from reproof is not wise. It is mark of a little mind. A great man can afford to lose; a little insignificant fellow is afraid of being snuffed out.

— ROBERT CECIL

552. If it's very painful for you to criticize your friends, you're safe in doing it. But if you take the slightest pleasure in it, that's the time to hold your tongue.

553. It is a thing of no great difficulty to raise objections against another man's oration—nay, it is a very easy matter; but to produce a better in its place is a work extremely troublesome.

— PLUTARCH

554. Criticism should be as constructive as possible. But we can't expect it always to be so, nor can we feel always obliged to make it so. As Ralph Ingersoll once put it: "When a man points out that you've got a counterfeit bill, he's not obliged to replace it with a good one."

— LEONARD M. LEONARD in *Journal of Living*

555. Of a poor play, Heywood Broun once wrote: "It opened at 8:40 sharp and closed at 10:40 dull."

556. If you stop every time a dog barks, your road will never end.

— Arabian proverb

Culture

557. Culture is what is left after everything we have learned has been forgotten. It consists of a deepened understanding, a breadth of outlook, an unbiased approach and a heart that has deep sympathy and strength of courage.

— BISHOP G. BROMLEY OXNAM

Curiosity

558. *Doctor:* "Now you see what comes of eating green apples when your mother told you not to."
Boy: "I didn't eat them because I liked them. I ate them to find out why she told me not to."

Customs

559. The floors of a building are called "stories" because early European builders used to paint picture stories on the sides of their houses. Each floor of the house had a different story.

560. The Chinese believe that when there are too many policemen, there can be no individual liberty; when there are too many lawyers, there can be no justice; and when there are too many soldiers, there can be no peace.

— LIN YUTANG, *Faith and Freedom*

561. Kisses and embraces are unknown in Japan as tokens of affection except between mothers and little children. After babyhood, kissing is held to be highly immodest. Parents and children do not kiss; husbands and wives may meet after years of absence, yet they will only kneel down and salute one another, smile and perhaps cry a little for joy. They never rush into each other's arms or utter phrases of affection, but show their love through acts of exquisite courtesy and kindness.

> —LAFCADIO HEARN, *Out of the East*
> (Houghton Mifflin Company)

562. For centuries the position of Arab women was lowly. When traveling, the man always rode the family donkey, while the woman, carrying the household goods, walked behind. But with the coming of war and the British and American troops, many customs changed. The man still rode the donkey but the woman was emancipated. She walked in front. There might be land mines!

> —Quoted in *The Reader's Digest*

Cynic — cynicism

563. The cynic makes fun of all earnestness; he makes fun of everything and everyone who feels that something can be done. . . . But in his heart of hearts he knows that he is a defeated man and that his cynicism is merely an expression of the fact that he has lost courage and is beaten.

> —GEORGE E. VINCENT

564. Cynics build no bridges; they make no discoveries; no gaps are spanned by them. Cynics may pride themselves in being realistic in their approach, but progress and the onward march of Christian civilization demand an inspiration and motivation that cynicism never affords. If we want progress we must take the forward look.

> —PAUL L. McKAY, D.D.

565. Cynicism is nothing but idealism gone sour in the face of frustration.

> —BUELL G. GALLAGHER

Danger

566. Better face a danger once than be always in fear.

Dating

567. Few things are more expensive than a girl who is free for the evening.

— EARL WILSON, Hall Syndicate

Death

568. A certain man had three friends, two of whom he loved dearly but the other he lightly esteemed. It happened one day that the king commanded his presence at court at which he was greatly alarmed, and wished to procure an advocate. Accordingly, he went to the two friends whom he loved; one flatly refused to accompany him; the other offered to go with him as far as the king's gate, but no farther. In his extremity he called upon his third friend, whom he least esteemed, and he not only went willingly with him, but so ably defended him before the king that he was acquitted.

In like manner, every man has three friends when Death summons him to appear before his Creator. His first friend, whom he loves most, namely, his money, cannot go with him a single step; his second, relations and neighbors, can only accompany him to the grave, but cannot defend him before the Judge; while his third friend, whom he does not esteem—his good works—goes with him before the King, and obtains his acquittal.

— A Talmudic tale

569. To live in hearts we leave behind is not to die.

— THOMAS CAMPBELL

570. Some people are so afraid to die that they never begin to live.

— HENRY VAN DYKE

571. We are too stupid about death.
We will not learn
How it is wages paid to those who earn;
How it is the gift for which on earth we yearn,
To be set free from bondage to the flesh;
How it is turning seed corn into grain,
How it is winning Heaven's eternal gain,
How it means freedom evermore from pain,
How it untangles every mortal mesh.

We are too selfish about death.
We count our grief
Far more than we consider their relief,
When the Great Reaper gathers in the sheaf,
No more to know the season's constant change;
And we forget that it means only life,
Life with all rest, peace, joy and glory rife,
The victory won and ended all the strife,
And Heaven no longer far away or strange.

—W. C. DOANE

Debate

572. It is better to debate a question without settling it than to settle a question without debating it.

—JOSEPH JOUBERT

Debt

573. Running into debt doesn't bother me; it's running into my creditors that's so upsetting.

—GUS EDSON in New York *Daily News*

574. Two men were discussing their status in life. "I started out on the theory that the world had an opening for me," said one.

"And you found it?" asked the other.

"Well, rather," replied the first, "I'm in the hole now."

Deception

575. "So, you deceived your husband," said the judge gravely.

"On the contrary, your honor, he deceived me. He said he was going out of town and he didn't go."

576. I do not care to "fool" any man. When he discovers I have fooled him, he will do me more harm than my cunning did me good.

—EDGAR W. HOWE

Decisions

577. Three baseball umpires were exchanging experiences. Said the first: "I call some strikes and I call some balls. But I calls 'em as

93

DECISIONS

I sees 'em." The second chimed in: "I call some strikes and I call
some balls. You see, I call 'em as they are." Spoke up the third: "I,
too, call some strikes and I, too, call some balls; but until I calls 'em
they ain't nuthin'."

578. In making our decisions, we must use the brains that God
has given us. But we must also use our hearts which He also gave us.

— FULTON OURSLER

579. Decide promptly, but never give any reasons. Your decisions may be right, but your reasons are sure to be wrong.

— LORD MANSFIELD

Defeatism

580. Beaten paths are for beaten men.

— ERIC JOHNSTON

581.
If you think you are beaten, you are,
If you think that you dare not, you don't,
If you'd like to win, but you think you can't,
It's almost certain you won't.

If you think you'll lose, you've lost,
For out in the world you'll find
Success begins with a fellow's will—
It's all in the state of mind.

If you think you are out-classed, you are;
You've got to think high to rise;
You've got to be sure of yourself before
You can ever win a prize.

Life's battles don't always go
To the stronger or faster man;
But soon or late the man who wins
Is the man who thinks he can.

— Author unknown

Deflation

582. Behind every famous man stands a woman telling him he's
not so good.

Delay   see also *Procrastination*

583.   If you want to make an easy job seem mighty hard, just keep putting off doing it.

> — OLIN MILLER, Chicago Sun Times Syndicate

584.   *Housewife to plumber:* "It must have been the family living here before that sent for you, but they moved out over a year ago."

585.   One of the most tragic things I know about human nature is that all of us tend to put off living. We are all dreaming of some magical rose garden over the horizon—instead of enjoying the roses that are blooming outside our windows today.

> — DALE CARNEGIE, *How to Stop Worrying and Start Living* (Simon & Schuster, Inc.)

Delegation of Authority

586.   No matter how much work a man can do, no matter how engaging his personality may be, he will not advance far in business if he cannot work through others.

> — JOHN CRAIG

Delinquency   see also *Crime—Juvenile Delinquency*

587.   Youth is an age of imagination; its choice may be made on imitation; and nothing is so strong an incentive to do right or wrong as imitation of someone who captures the imagination of youth. Many a youth has been branded a delinquent whose career started in imitation of someone "accepted" in the community.

> — CHAS. A. TONSOR, *Youth and the Awful Power of Choice*

588.   Half of juvenile delinquency starts in boredom. Boys and girls of 12-18 have terrific energy and too little to do with it; they also have the most lively and eager imaginations, for which almost nothing is provided. If they show any imagination in dress, for instance, they are promptly marked down as rebels and nuisances, and respond very naturally by rebellion. If they show any interest in reading, it is odds on that the books will be labelled obscene and thrown on the fire. And then it is highly likely that they will stop reading altogether, and simply get on with gangsterism.

— JOYCE CARY

589. The United States has some 19 million youngsters between the ages of 10 and 18 and more than a million of them, or about 5 per cent, are in some sort of trouble with the police each year.

590. Happy laughter and friendly voices in the home will keep more kids off the streets at night than the loudest curfew.

— BURTON HILLIS, courtesy of *Better Homes and Gardens* magazine

591. The children now love luxury. They have bad manners, contempt for authority, they show disrespect to their elders and love to chatter in places of exercise. They no longer rise when elders enter the room. They contradict their parents, chatter before company, gobble up dainties at the table, cross their legs and are tyrants over their teachers.

— Attributed to SOCRATES

Democracy

592. Democracy is something we must always be working at. It is a process never finished, never ending. And each new height gained opens broader vistas for the future. Thus it has been as one looks back over the sweep of history; thus it must continue to be if democracy is to continue as a working tool in the hands of free men.

— EDMUND DE S. BRUNNER

593. Democracy as I understand it, requires me to sacrifice myself *for* the masses, not *to* them. Who knows not that if you would save the people, you must often oppose them?

— JOHN C. CALHOUN

594. We aren't educated until we come truly to find democracy not just in the machinery of government but in the hearts of men.

— JAMES M. SPINNING

595. Democracy is based upon the conviction that there are extraordinary possibilities in ordinary people.

— HARRY EMERSON FOSDICK

596. When everybody is somebody, then nobody is anybody.

597. Ultimately there can be no freedom for self unless it is vouchsafed for others; there can be no security where there is fear, and a democratic society presupposes confidence and ardor in the relations of men with one another and eager collaboration for the larger ends of life instead of the pursuit of petty, selfish or vainglorious aims.

— JUSTICE FELIX FRANKFURTER

598. Democracy means not "I am equal to you" but "you are equal to me."

— JAMES RUSSELL LOWELL

599. Democracy is the theory that the common people know what they want, and deserve to get it good and hard.

— H. L. MENCKEN

600. The essential ingredient of democracy is not doctrine but intelligence, not authority but reason, not cynicism but faith in man, faith in God. Our strength lies in the fearless pursuit of truth by the minds of men who are free.

— DAVID LILIENTHAL, *This I Do Believe*
(Harper and Brothers)

601. Democracy is a way of life. Democracy is sincerity, friendliness, courage and tolerance. If your life and mine do not exemplify these characteristics, we do not have the right to call ourselves fullfledged citizens of the world's greatest democracy.

— MELVIN J. EVANS

602. There can be no democracy unless there is a basic respect for opposing ideas and a willingness on both sides "to live and let live."

— GEORGE R. HAVENS, *The Age of Ideas*
(Henry Holt and Company)

Dentist — dentistry

603. "I am sorry," said the dentist, "but you cannot have an

appointment with me this afternoon. I have eighteen cavities to fill."
And he picked up his golf bag and went out.

604. Dentist: a prestidigitator who, putting metal into your
mouth, pulls coin out of your pocket.

— AMBROSE BIERCE

605. They call them dental parlors because they are drawing
rooms.

Dependence

606. Without the help of thousands of others, any one of us
would die, naked and starved. Consider the bread upon our table,
the clothes upon our backs, the luxuries that make life pleasant; how
many men worked in sunlit fields, in dark mines, in the fierce heat
of molten metal, and among the looms and wheels of countless factories, in order to create them for our use and enjoyment.

— ALFRED E. SMITH

Depletion

607. Taking out without putting in soon comes to the bottom.

— Old proverb

Depression

608. Depression: a period during which we have to get along
without the things our grandparents never dreamed about.

Destiny

609. Choice, not chance, will determine our eternal destiny.

Destructive

610. No man is self-made who unmakes others.

— STEPHEN VORIS

Determination see also *Will—Persistence*

611. *Walk* fast till you get upon the right ground. Then *stand*
fast.

612. Poverty is uncomfortable; but nine times out of ten the best thing that can happen to a young man is to be tossed overboard and compelled to sink or swim.

— JAMES A. GARFIELD

613. Everyone has his superstitions. One of mine has always been when I started to go anywhere, or to do anything, never to turn back or to stop until the thing intended was accomplished.

— ULYSSES S. GRANT

Development

614. Great occasions do not make heroes or cowards; they simply unveil them to the eyes of men. Silently and imperceptibly, as we wake or sleep, we grow strong or we grow weak, and at last some crisis shows us what we have become.

— BROOKE FOSS WESTCOTT

Dictator — dictatorship

615. The purse strings of the world are better manipulated by the many hands of the homemakers of the world than by the powerful fists of a few dictators.

— R. G. BRESSLER, JR., "Purse Strings of the World," *Journal of Home Economics,* September, 1954

616. Adolf Hitler was once described as suffering from deep melancholia, arising from a pronounced inferiority complex. After getting unsatisfactory results from many Aryan psychiatrists, he was finally persuaded to consult a distinguished Jewish psychiatrist. After a complete diagnosis, he advised Hitler to repeat constantly to himself: "I am important; I am significant; I am indispensable." Whereupon, Hitler shouted: "That is bad advice." When the psychiatrist inquired why, Hitler replied: "I never believe a word I say."

617. Dictator: one who thinks he can take it—no matter to whom it belongs.

618. Adolf Hitler was known to frequent astrologers, soothsayers and others of that ilk. A certain astrologer was asked by him, "On what day will I die?"

After peering over his charts, the astrologer announced, "You will die on a Jewish holiday."

"But, which one?" demanded Hitler, much perturbed.

"I do not know," replied the astrologer.

With this, Hitler became very angry. "You must know," he shouted, "I insist upon the truth."

"I tell you I do not know," persisted the astrologer, "because any day you die will be a Jewish holiday."

619. Totalitarian state: a place where the people in jail are better than the people who put them there.

620. At the total level the Communists will beat us every time, because they can totalize ruthlessly and process men to the pattern they desire. But at the person-to-person level we have something to give that they cannot match. We have the fundamental proposition of our Revolution to give: that man is the child of Nature's God; that he carries within him a spark that links him with the universe and differentiates him from the animals . . . By practical person-to-person democracy we can teach the world to see in every individual that individual spark which gives to the principles of freedom a godlike validity.

— RUSSELL DAVENPORT, *The Dignity of Man*
(Harper and Brothers)

621. There must be no majority decisions . . . Every man shall have councillors at his side, but the decision shall be made by one Man.

— ADOLF HITLER, *Mein Kampf*

622. It is a paradox that every dictator has climbed to power on the ladder of free speech. Immediately on attaining power each dictator has suppressed all free speech except his own.

— HERBERT HOOVER

623. Totalitarianism has an insidious, a sinister appeal. It appeals to those who prefer leadership to initiative, blueprints to enterprise. It appeals to those who find it difficult to bend democracy to serve their economic or political self-interest.

— WENDELL WILLKIE

Diet see also *Food*

624. All the things I really like to do are either imm⟨ ⟩ ⟨ ⟩ or fattening.

— ALEXANDER WOOLLCOTT

625. Diet: something to take the starch out of you.

626. Reducing experts live on the fat of the land.

Differences

627. There's a difference between good sound reasons and reasons that sound good.

628. Honest differences of views and honest debate are not disunity. They are the vital process of policy-making among free men.

— HERBERT HOOVER

Difficult — difficulty

629. Difficulty is the excuse history never accepts.

— SAMUEL GRAFTON in *New York Post*

630. I believe in getting into hot water; it keeps you clean.

— G. K. CHESTERTON

631. All things are difficult before they are easy.

— THOMAS FULLER

632. Undertake something that is difficult; it will do you good. Unless you try to do something beyond what you have already mastered, you will never grow.

— RONALD E. OSBORN

633. What is difficulty? Only a word indicating the degree of strength requisite for accomplishing particular objects; a mere notice of the necessity for exertion; a bugbear to children and fools; only a mere stimulus to men.

— SAMUEL WARREN

634. There are two ways of meeting difficulties: you alter the difficulties, or you alter yourself to meet them.

— PHYLLIS BOTTOME

IFFICULTY

635. Life affords no higher pleasure than that of surmounting difficulties, passing from one step of success to another, forming new wishes and seeing them gratified. He that labors in any great or laudable undertaking has his fatigues first supported by hope and afterwards rewarded by joy.

— Dr. Samuel Johnson

Dignity

636. Dignity consists not in possessing honors, but in the consciousness that we deserve them.

— Aristotle

637. It is only people of small moral stature who have to stand on their dignity.

— Arnold Bennett

Dilemma

638. G. K. Chesterton is credited with the story of the wily bandit who was finally captured by the king's troopers. The king, a man fond of games and riddles, posed this one to the bandit: "You may make one statement. If you tell the truth in it, you will be shot. If you lie, you will be hanged." The bandit put everything in a fine mess with this reply:

"I am going to be hanged."

639. "When I look at this congregation," said the preacher, "I ask myself, 'Where are the poor?' But when I look at the collection, I say to myself 'Where are the rich?' "

640. Among the guests at a dinner party given by my parents were a rabbi and a Catholic priest. When the party sat down to dinner, they were confronted with one of those seemingly insurmountable moments—who was going to say grace? Everyone looked meekly down at his plate; my mother and father gulped for words. At the crest of the terrible moment, the priest looked around at the table and said: "If you don't mind, I'd like to say an old Jewish prayer."

They all bowed their heads, and the priest said grace—in Hebrew.

— Paul Marcus in *The Reader's Digest*

Diplomacy

641. Diplomacy is to do and say
The nastiest thing in the nicest way.

— Isaac Goldberg

642. Diplomacy: a peaceful substitute for shooting.

643. A diplomat is one who can bring home the bacon without spilling the beans.

644. Georges Clemenceau, "the Tiger of France," was riding to the Versailles peace conference, and his young secretary was complaining about all the diplomatic baloney.

"It's nothing but a lot of hot air," grumbled the assistant as their car rolled along the Paris streets.

"All etiquette is hot air," answered the premier, "but that's what's in our automobile tires and see how it eases the bumps."

— John Taylor in *Catholic Digest*, February, 1955

645. Diplomat: one who can keep a civil tongue in his cheek.

646. When Joseph Choate was American ambassador to Great Britain, many amusing incidents arose. For one, he had gained quite a lot of weight while in England. When he returned to this country, some of his friends, remembering his slight build, remarked about his corpulence. "Why, Mr. Choate," said one, "you have been getting stout since you went abroad." "Oh, yes," replied he, "I found it necessary to meet the Englishman half way."

Disagreement

647. The people to fear are not those who disagree with you, but those who disagree with you and are too cowardly to let you know.

Disappointment

648. It may be proper for all to remember that they ought not to raise expectations which it is not in their power to satisfy; and

103

that it is more pleasing to see smoke brightening into flame than flame sinking into smoke.

— Dr. Samuel Johnson

649. *Indignant woman to luscious-looking librarian:* "Funny you haven't that book. My husband said you have everything."

Discipline

650. There is a mistaken notion prevailing among some parents that discipline is the same thing as punishment. It is not. Discipline comes from a Latin word meaning "to teach." The best discipline is that which teaches, not the kind that hurts.

— From *How Christian Parents Face Family Problems* by J. C. Wynn. Copyright, 1955, by W. L. Jenkins, The Westminster Press. Used by permission.

651. Discipline is not as simple nor as easy as it might appear. A little girl said to her father, "I don't think mama knows much about bringing up children." The father asked, "Why?" The little girl replied, "Well, she makes me go to bed when I'm not sleepy and makes me get up when I am sleepy."

— Perry F. Webb

Discouragement

652. A dentist at work in his vocation always looks down in the mouth.

— George D. Prentice

653. People seldom want to walk over you until you lie down.

— Elmer Wheeler

Discretion

654. Mention not a rope in the house of one whose father was hanged.

— Old proverb

655. Sir Lewis Morris was complaining to Oscar Wilde about the neglect of his poems by the press. "It is a complete conspiracy of silence. What ought I do, Oscar?"

"Join it," replied Wilde.

656. Experience teaches that whenever anything is on the tip of one's tongue it is probably best that it be kept there.

657. *Teacher:* "If your mother gave you a large apple and a small one and told you to divide with your brother, which would you give him?"

Johnnie: "Do you mean my little brother, or my big one?"

658. Better shun the bait than struggle in the snare.

— JOHN DRYDEN

Discrimination see also *Intolerance*

659. A small Negro boy stood watching the balloon man at the county fair. Suddenly, a red balloon broke loose and soared upward until it could scarcely be seen. So many people were attracted by the incident that the vendor thought it might be good business to let another go. So he snipped the string of a bright yellow balloon and, later, a white one.

The little boy stood there, as if waiting for something. Finally, he asked, "Mister, if you sent the black one up, would it go as high as the others?"

The balloon man, with an understanding smile, released the black balloon as he said, "Sonny, it isn't the color—it's the stuff inside that makes it rise."

— LYLE D. FLYNN in *Quote*

Discussion

660. He is more apt to contribute heat than light to a discussion

— WOODROW WILSON

Display

661. The girl with cotton stockings never sees a mouse.

Doctor — doctors see also *Medicine*

662. Many persons call a doctor when all they want is an audience.

DOCTOR — DOCTORS

663. Doctors think a lot of patients are cured who have simply quit in disgust.

—Don Herold

664. Double jeopardy: when your doctor calls in a consulting physician.

665. Doctor: a man who suffers from good health.

666. Doctor: a guy who tells you if you don't cut out something he'll cut something out of you.

667. "You've been a pretty sick man," said the doctor. "In fact, I may say that it was only your strong constitution that pulled you through."

"Good," replied the convalescent, "I hope you'll remember that when you come to make out your bill."

668. "But, doctor," said the worried patient, "are you sure I'll pull through? I've heard of cases where the doctor has made a wrong diagnosis, and treated someone for pneumonia who has afterwards died of typhoid fever."

"Nonsense," spluttered the affronted physician. "When I treat a patient for pneumonia, he dies of pneumonia."

669. A man was found sprawled in a gutter and rushed to a hospital. In the emergency operating room, a young interne unbuttoned his coat to prepare him for surgery, only to find the following note pinned to the lining:

"To the members of the Medical Profession: I am merely stinking drunk. Just let me sleep it off. Do not attempt to remove my appendix. You already took it out *twice.*"

670. No physician, in so far as he is a physician, considers his own good in what he prescribes, but the good of his patient; for the true physician is also a ruler having the human body as his subject, and is not a mere money-maker.

—Plato, *The Republic*

671. Who shall decide when doctors disagree?

—Alexander Pope, *Moral Essays*

672. That patient is not likely to recover who makes the doctor his heir.

673. Illegibility: a doctor's prescription written with a post-office pen in the rumble seat of a second-hand car.

674. And when the physician said, "Sir, you are an old man," "That happens," replied Pausania, "because you never were my doctor."

— PLUTARCH

675. Doctors and lawyers are alike in one respect; some defend the constitution while others destroy it.

676. No doctor is a good doctor who has never been ill himself.

— CONFUCIUS

677. A surgeon was taking a walk with his wife when a young and vivid blonde greeted him gaily. The doctor's wife eyed him narrowly. "Where," she asked, "did you meet that person, my dear?"

"Just a young woman I met professionally," he explained.

"I see," murmured his wife. "Yours, or hers?"

678. "I reckon you get paid right handsome for looking after the rich Johnson boy," observed the cleaning woman to the doctor.

"Why, yes. I get pretty good fees," he replied, somewhat perplexed. "Why do you ask?"

"I just hope you won't forget that it was my boy what threw the brick that hit him."

679. He was the kind of doctor who diagnosed your ailment by feeling your purse.

680. *Sign in a hospital in the West:* "During this intense weather, and owing to the scarcity of coal, no unnecessary operations will be performed."

681. Consultant: a colleague who is called in at the last moment to share the blame.

682. *Nurse, comforting a patient:* "Don't let the doctors frighten you. Doctors are like politicians—they view with alarm so they can point with pride!"

683. There are more old drunkards than old doctors.

— BENJAMIN FRANKLIN, *Poor Richard's Almanac*

DOCTOR

684. Mrs. Brown was complaining to her doctor that his bill was unreasonably high. "Don't forget," he reminded her, "that I made eleven visits to your home while your son had the measles."

"And don't you forget," she countered, "that he infected the whole school."

Doom

685. Who, like the hindmost chariot wheels are curst,
Still to be near, but ne'er to reach the first.

— PERSIUS, *Satires*

Double-meaning

686. Dr. Emil G. Hirsch, one of the outstanding rabbis of his day and known for his sharp tongue and wit, once rather terrified an early teenager whose mother and father he had united in marriage, by saying to her: "I married your mother but I am not your father."

Doubt

687. To believe with certainty we must begin with doubting.

— STANISLAUS LESCYNSKI, *Maxims and Moral Sentences*

688. Who knows most, doubts most.

— ROBERT BROWNING

689. I respect faith, but doubt is what gets you an education.

— WILSON MIZNER

Drama

690. Like the telegram, drama is constricted to a few cautiously chosen words of information. Delivered to the right address it may arouse violent emotion. At the wrong address it will be stared at blankly.

— BEN HECHT, *A Child of the Century*
(Simon & Schuster, Inc.)

Dreams

691. We grow great by dreams. All big men are dreamers. They see things in the soft haze of a spring day or in the red fire of a long winter's evening. Some of us let these great dreams die, but others nourish and protect them; nurse them through bad days till they bring them to the sunshine and light which comes always to those who sincerely hope that their dreams will come true.

— WOODROW WILSON

Drudgery

692. The everyday cares and duties, which men call drudgery, are the weights and counterpoises of the clock of time, giving its pendulum a true vibration, and its hands a regular motion; and when they cease to hang upon the wheels, the pendulum no longer swings, the hands no longer move, and the clock stands still.

— HENRY WADSWORTH LONGFELLOW

Drug store

693. Restaurant: an eating place that does not sell drugs.

Durability

694. An American soldier who hailed from Texas and was stationed in England sauntered into the West London Synagogue for the New Year Holyday services, and asked:

"What kind of show do you have here? Is it good?"

"It should be," replied the rabbi who had overheard the question. "It's been running for nearly six thousand years."

— ISRAEL H. WEISFELD, *The Pulpit Treasury of Wit & Humor* (Prentice-Hall, Inc.)

Duty

695. Duty: what the normal man looks forward to with distaste, does with reluctance, and boasts about forever after.

696. He who eats the fruit should at least plant the seed.

— HENRY DAVID THOREAU

DUTY

697. Let men laugh when you sacrifice desire to duty, if they will. You have time and eternity to rejoice in.

— THEODORE PARKER

698. Be content with doing calmly the little which depends upon yourself, and let all else be to you as if it were not.

— FRANÇOIS FÉNELON

699. When any duty is to be done, it is fortunate for you if you feel like doing it; but, if you do not feel like it, that is no reason for not doing it.

— W. GLADDEN

700. Never mind your happiness; do your duty.

— WILL DURANT

Eating see also Food

701. We may live without books,—
What is knowledge but grieving.
We may live without hope,—what is hope but deceiving.
We may live without love,—what is passion but pining;
But where is the man who can live without dining?
   (Let's eat!)

— OWEN MEREDITH

Eccentricity

702. That so few now dare to be eccentric marks the chief danger of the time.

— JOHN STUART MILL, On Liberty

Economy — economist see also Thrift

703. An economist is a man who knows more about money than people who have it know.

704. It is cheaper to buy milk than keep the cow.

— GEORGE BERNARD SHAW, Pen Portraits
and Reviews: Samuel Butler

705. He who is taught to live upon little owes more to his father's wisdom than he who has a great deal left him does to his father's care.

— WILLIAM PENN

706. If all the economists were laid end to end, they'd still point in all directions.

Education see also *Teaching*

707. Education is the cheap defense of nations.

— EDMUND BURKE

708. You should have education enough so that you won't have to look up to people; and then more education so that you will be wise enough not to look down on people.

— M. L. BOREN

709. The aim of education should be to convert the mind into a living fountain, and not a reservoir. That which is filled by merely pumping in, will be emptied by pumping out.

— JOHN M. MASON

710. The whole art of teaching is only the art of awakening the natural curiosity of young minds for the purpose of satisfying it afterwards.

— ANATOLE FRANCE

711. All education does today is develop the memory at the expense of imagination.

— OWEN JOHNSON quoted in *The Reader's Digest*

712. Education makes a people easy to lead, but difficult to drive; easy to govern, but impossible to enslave.

— LORD BROUGHAM

713. A good teacher has been defined as one who makes himself progressively unnecessary.

— THOMAS J. CARRUTHERS

714. Education: that mysterious process whereby information passes from the lecture notes of the professor through the fountain pen and onto the notebooks of the students.

715. Education is what a man gets when he sits in his living room with a group of teen-agers.

716. Let us be honest with youth and tell them that there is no one magic formula of education for war or peace, no fruit of the tree of knowledge which, swiftly eaten, can make us wise as gods, nothing good and evil. Even in these critical days, when educated persons are so desperately needed, the process of education requires time and work and striving.

> — VIRGINIA C. GILDERSLEEVE, *Many a Good Crusade* (The Macmillan Company)

717. I am like a teacher who enjoys hearing your ideas, who enjoys telling you his own, but has no plan to make you think as he does. If you think as he does that may please him; but if you do not, the honesty of your thought will please him just as much. That is just the difference between education and indoctrination.

> — Reprinted by permission of the publishers, J. B. Lippincott Company, from *The Land and People of South Africa* by ALAN PATON. Copyright 1955 by ALAN PATON.

718. True education makes for inequality; the inequality of individuality; the inequality of success; the glorious inequality of talent, of genius; for inequality, not mediocrity, individual superiority, not standardization, is the measure of the progress of the world.

> — FELIX E. SCHELLING in the *Chicago Tribune*

719. Every person has two educations—one which he receives from others, and one more important, which he gives himself.

720. One is never too old to learn something one really wants to learn, never too old to take up a new interest. Interest is the operative word. If you are interested you will concentrate and if you concentrate you can learn something new at any age.

721. "And how do you like going to school, Roger?" a kindly lady inquired of a very small lad.

"Oh, I like the going all right," the boy replied, "and I like coming back, too. It's having to stay after I get there that bothers me."

722. Education will broaden a narrow mind, but there is no known cure for a big head.

> — J. GRAHAM

723. Learning is not wisdom.

724. If we do not prepare children to become good citizens— if we do not develop their capacities, if we do not enrich their minds with knowledge, imbue their hearts with the love of truth and duty and a reverence for all things sacred and holy, then our republic must go down to destruction, as others have gone before it; and mankind must sweep through another vast cycle of sin and suffering before the dawn of a better era can arise upon the world. It is for our government, and for that public opinion which in a republic governs the government, to choose between these alternatives of weal or woe.

— HORACE MANN

725. No school can offset the evil influence not merely of a bad home, but of a home with low moral, disciplinary and intellectual standards. If fathers and mothers offer their children no more intellectual fare than comic books, a television set, and picture magazines; if they make of the home merely a place to sleep, drink and eat—and not the center of life—they have no right to complain of the schools.

— GRAYSON KIRK, in address before the National Education Association

726. Junior was being chided for his low grades. Little Robert, who lived a few doors away, was held up as an example.

"Robert doesn't get C's and D's, does he?" asked his father.

"No," Junior admitted, "but he's different. He has very bright parents."

727. The best board of education—is sometimes a shingle.

728. Life is but one continual course of instruction. The hand of the parent writes on the heart of the child the first faint characters which time deepens into strength so that nothing can efface them.

— R. HILL

729. Education is not to teach men facts, theories or laws, not to reform or amuse them or make them expert technicians. It is to unsettle their minds, widen their horizons, inflame their intellect, teach them to think straight, if possible, but to think nevertheless.

— ROBERT MAYNARD HUTCHINS

730. Hire education: when an athlete is given financial inducements to attend a certain college.

EDUCATION

731. A teacher in Hillside, N.J., supplements his salary by operating a bull-dozer during vacations. Not long ago he made an application for credit to purchase a home, stating that he was a teacher.

It was turned down.

The teacher resubmitted the application, this time putting down his occupation as a bull-dozer operator.

The application was promptly approved.

> — From the *Hillside* (N.J.) *Times* quoted in
> *The Reader's Digest*

732. A teacher affects eternity; he can never tell where his influence stops.

> — HENRY ADAMS, *The Education of Henry Adams*

733. Education which is simply intellectual taxidermy—the scooping out of the mind and the stuffing in of facts—is worthless. The human mind is not a deep-freeze for storage but a forge for production; it must be supplied with fuel, fired, and properly shaped.

> — WILLIAM A. DONAGHY, S.J., president, Holy Cross University

734. What is done in our classrooms today will be reflected in the successes or failures of civilization tomorrow.

> — LINDLY C. BAXTER in the *New Jersey Educational Review*

735. Mere accumulation of information without a sound philosophy is not education.

> — BELLA V. DODD, *School of Darkness* (P. J. Kenedy & Sons)

736. Education does not mean teaching people what they do not know. It means teaching them to behave as they do not behave. It is not teaching the youth the shapes of letters and the tricks of numbers, and then leaving them to turn their arithmetic to roguery, and their literature to lust. It means, on the contrary, training them into the perfect exercise and kingly continence of their bodies and souls. It is a painful, continual and difficult work, to be done by kindness,

by watching, by warning, by precept and by praise, but above all—
by example.

— JOHN RUSKIN

737. Education means developing the mind, not stuffing the
memory.

738. Our responsibility as educators is to teach youth to have
respect for those who differ from the customary ways as well as for
those who conform. In simpler words, we have a profound obligation both to education and to society itself to support and strengthen
the right to be different, and to create a sound respect for intellectual
superiority.

— ROBERT C. POOLEY, *Wisconsin*
Journal of Education

739.   A little learning is a dangerous thing;
Drink deep or taste not the Pierian spring;
There shallow draughts intoxicate the brain,
And drinking largely sobers us again.

— ALEXANDER POPE

740. I want my son to have a college education, but I cannot
give it to him unless he asks for it and wants it. If I make available
for him the money he needs, he must cooperate by opening his mind
through study in order to receive the education. The reason we do
not receive the answers to our prayers may be in us—in our failure
to cooperate.

— From *When the Heart Is Hungry* by
CHARLES L. ALLEN. Fleming H. Revell
Company

741. "I can't get my report card back," said the boy to his
teacher. "You gave me an A in something and they're still mailing
it to relatives."

742. They who educate children well, are more to be honored
than they who produce them; for these only gave them life, those the
art of living well.

— ARISTOTLE

743. Our schools must encourage brains, for our world needs
brains. We can no longer be content with mediocrity, with the second rate. There is nothing undemocratic about this. To develop an

EDUCATION

intellectual elite is no more undemocratic than to develop an athletic elite or journalistic elite. We must learn to take brains in our stride, as we do expertness on the football field, the basketball floor, the state, or the newsroom.

> — HENRY STEELE COMMAGER, "Our Schools and the Climate of Freedom," *National Parent-Teacher*

744. Arriving in Calcutta, the U.S. educator opened his suitcase and presented his passport. Quickly, the customs official closed the suitcase without the slightest examination and returned the passport. "We are accustomed," he said, "to respect teachers."

745. If these distracted times prove anything, they prove that the greatest illusion is reliance upon the security and permanence of material possessions. We must search for some other coin. And we will discover that the treasurehouse of education has stood intact and unshaken in the storm. The man of cultivated life has founded his house upon a rock. You can never take away the magnificent mansion of his mind.

> — JOHN CUDAHY

746. Fortunately or otherwise, we live at a time when the average individual has to know several times as much in order to keep informed as he did only thirty or forty years ago. Being "educated" today, requires not only more than a superficial knowledge of the arts and sciences, but a sense of interrelationship such as is taught in few schools. Finally, being "educated" today, in terms of the larger needs, means preparation for world citizenship; in short, education for survival.

> — NORMAN COUSINS

747. The trouble with present-day education is that it covers the ground without cultivating anything in it.

> — DR. E. N. FERRIS

748. Training is everything. The peach was once a bitter almond; cauliflower is nothing but cabbage with a college education.

> — MARK TWAIN

749. Formal education is but an incident in the lifetime of an individual. Most of us who have given the subject any study have come to realize that education is a continuous process ending only when ambition comes to a halt.

— R. I. REES

750. Perhaps the most valuable result of all education is the ability to make yourself do the thing you have to do, when it ought to be done, whether you like it or not; it is the first lesson that ought to be learned; and however early a man's training begins, it is probably the last lesson that he learns thoroughly.

— THOMAS HENRY HUXLEY

751. *Small boy on telephone:* "Now, then, page four, problem six. What answer does *your* dad get for that one?"

752. A man cannot leave a better legacy to the world than a well educated family.

— THOMAS SCOTT

753. *Teacher to teacher:* "TV programs are ruining this school —every time a pupil answers a question he wants to get paid!"

754. It is impossible to educate anyone. All that can be done is to put him in a position where he can find an education. Motivation is the first necessity for this. He must wish to learn and he must wish to develop. He must be curious, he must be eager, and he must be serious.

— BARNABY C. KEENEY, president,
Brown University

755. The secret of education lies in respecting the pupil.

— RALPH WALDO EMERSON

756. Instruction ends in the schoolroom, but education ends only with life.

— F. W. ROBERTSON

757. Education is the knowledge of how to use the whole of oneself. Many men use but one or two faculties out of the score with which they are endowed. A man is educated who knows how to make a tool of every faculty—how to open it, how to keep it sharp, and how to apply it to all practical purposes.

— HENRY WARD BEECHER

758. Education commences at the mother's knee, and every word spoken in the hearing of the little children tends toward the formation of character. Let parents always bear this in mind.

— HOSEA BALLOU

759. Education is the gradual adjustment to the spiritual possessions of the race, with a view to realizing one's own potentialities and assisting in carrying forward that complex of ideas, acts and institutions which we call civilization.

— NICHOLAS MURRAY BUTLER

Efficiency

760. Efficiency expert: a man who is smart enough to tell you how to run your business, and too smart to start one of his own.

761. There can be no economy where there is no efficiency.

— BENJAMIN DISRAELI

Effort

762. "I can't do it" never yet accomplished anything; "I will try" has performed wonders.

— GEORGE P. BURNHAM

763. If you want to kill time, why not try working it to death.

764. It's one thing to be trying; it's altogether another to be very trying.

765. Nothing will make a man put his best foot forward like getting the other one in hot water.

— O. A. BATTISTA

766. Nothing worthwhile comes easily. Half effort does not produce half results. It produces no results. Work, continuous work and hard work, is the only way to accomplish results that last.

— HAMILTON HOLT

767. For every action there is an equal and opposite reaction. If you want to receive a great deal, you first have to give a great deal. If each individual will give of himself to whomever he can, wherever he can, in any way that he can, in the long run he will be compensated in the exact proportion that he gives.

— R. A. HAYWARD

768. Triumph is just "umph" added to "try."

769. God gives every bird its food, but He does not throw it into the nest.

— J. G. HOLLAND

Egotism

770. Egotism is the anesthetic which nature gives us to deaden the pain of being a fool.

— HERBERT SHOFIELD

771. A few seasons ago Notre Dame's star center, Frankie Szymanski, appeared in a South Bend court as a witness in a civil suit. "Are you on the Notre Dame football team this year?" queried the judge.

"Yes, Your Honor."

"What position?"

"Center, Your Honor."

"How good a center?"

Szymanski squirmed in his chair, but in confident tones admitted, "Sir, I'm the best center Notre Dame ever had."

Coach Frank Leahy, who was in the courtroom, was surprised because the lad had always been modest and unassuming. When proceedings were adjourned, the coach asked him why he had made such a statement. Szymanski blushed. "I hated to do it, coach," he explained, "but after all, I was under oath."

772. One of the hardest secrets for a man to keep is his opinion of himself.

Eloquence

773. The truest eloquence is that which holds us too mute for applause.

— EDWARD G. BULWER-LYTTON

Embarrassment

774. My husband likes to tell of a baptism he attended many years ago in Sioux Falls, S.D. One couple was having some difficulty quieting their infant son. In an effort to put the parents at ease, the

119

pastor beamed at the congregation as he happily remarked, "and the baptism of this little baby gives me great pleasure—it was such a very short time ago I married this couple."

— Mrs. Carroll M. Dewey

775. An embarrassing situation marked the passing of a well-known fire chief. And none of the members of his family have spoken since the funeral to any members of his engine company. For these firemen, while well-intentioned, committed the unpardonable sin of sending to the wake a high floral tribute inscribed in gold letters—GONE TO HIS LAST FIRE.

— *Journal of the American Medical Association*

776. The most embarrassing moment in the life of Jane Wyman happened when she was entertaining very special guests. After looking over all the appointments carefully, she put a note on the guest towels, "If you use these I will murder you." It was meant for her husband. In the excitement she forgot to remove the note. After the guests had departed, the towels were discovered still in perfect order, as well as the note itself.

— Kay Mulvey in *Woman's Home Companion.*
Copyright 1942, The Crowell-Collier Publishing Co.

Emotion

777. Sixty years of contact with the public mind through books, journalism and teaching, a period divided about equally between France, the United States and Britain, have convinced me that our worst dangers arise, *not* from evil intention (the intentions of most men are good), but from the distortion of judgment by mass emotions like those which mark nationalism, partisanship, doctrinaire fanaticism. This phenomenon was illustrated by the Germans under Hitler and is revealed at present by the passing of a third of the world's population to Communism.

The problem is not new. The passions displayed in the Wars of Religion were such that had the antagonists possessed the H Bomb they would have destroyed Western civilization. Today we do possess the H Bomb, giving old passions a new danger.

To discipline these emotional forces we must recognize them, not deny their danger by such slogans as "The Voice of the People is the Voice of God." (Which we did not believe of Germans and Japanese.) Only by facing the fact that the voice of a mass (say a lynching party) may be the voice of Satan, can we hope to develop that sense of moral obligation to discipline emotion by reason which will enable us to meet the twin dangers of Communism and the H Bomb.

— SIR NORMAN ANGELL

Employment

778. *Employer:* I'd like to compliment you on your work— when do you start?

779. The only time some people work like a horse is when the boss rides them.

780. You shouldn't blame the boss for being a crank if the employees aren't self-starters.

781. When you hire people who are smarter than you are, you prove you are smarter than they are.

— R. H. GRANT

782. The boss returned in a good humor from lunch and called the whole staff in to listen to a couple of jokes he had picked up. Everybody but one girl laughed uproariously. "What's the matter?" grumbled the boss. "Haven't you got a sense of humor?"

"I don't have to laugh," said the girl. "I'm leaving Friday anyhow."

— BENNETT CERF, *Laughing Stock*
(Grosset & Dunlap)

783. I once had a friend who worked as a waiter in an insane asylum; his job was carrying soup to nuts.

784. A chap we know shared a commuter's seat the other day with a brisk, informative little man who said he was a butler at a Libertyville estate. "Oh," said our friend, "you work for Mr. Jones?"

The brisk little man drew himself up haughtily. "Certainly not. Mr. Jones is working for me. He gets up at seven every morning and goes down to that dirty, stinking city to make enough money to keep this place and me going."

— MARCIA WINN in the *Chicago Tribune*

121

Emulation

785. Emulation lives so near to envy that it is sometimes difficult to establish the boundary lines.

— HENRY GILES

Encouragement

786. She was not pretty, but she might have been handsome if somebody had kept telling her that she was pretty.

— J. B. PRIESTLEY

787. Don't discourage the other man's plans unless you have better ones to offer.

788. Correction does much, but encouragement does more. Encouragement after censure is as the sun after a shower.

— JOHANN WOLFGANG VON GOETHE

789.   ENCOURAGEMENT

It takes so little to make us sad,
Just a slighting word or a doubting sneer,
Just a scornful smile on some lips held dear;
And our footsteps lag, though the goal seemed near,
And we lose the courage and hope we had—
So little it takes to make us sad.

It takes so little to make us glad,
Just a cheering clasp of a friendly hand,
Just a word from one who can understand;
And we finish the task we long had planned,
And we lose the doubt and the fear we had—
So little it takes to make us glad.

— IDA GOLDSMITH MORRIS

England

790. Oats: a grain, which in England is generally given to horses but in Scotland supports the people.

— DR. SAMUEL JOHNSON

Enthusiasm

791. Fires can't be made with dead embers, nor can enthusiasm be stirred by spiritless men. Enthusiasm in our daily work lightens effort and turns even labor into pleasant tasks.

— JAMES MARK BALDWIN

792. If you can give your own son only one gift; let it be enthusiasm.

— BRUCE BARTON

793. The fellow who is fired with enthusiasm for his boss is seldom fired by the boss.

794. No prudent man will embark on an undertaking until his first enthusiasm has passed away.

795. The worst bankrupt in the world is the man who has lost his enthusiasm. Let a man lose everything else in the world but his enthusiasm and he will come through again to success.

— H. W. ARNOLD

796. If you can't get enthusiastic about your work, it's time to get alarmed—something is wrong. Compete with yourself; set your teeth and dive into the job of breaking your own record. No one keeps up his enthusiasm automatically. Enthusiasm must be nourished with new actions, new aspirations, new efforts, new vision. It is one's own fault if his enthusiasm is gone; he has failed to feed it. If you want to turn hours into minutes, renew your enthusiasm.

Envy

797. For the first time in my life I envied my feet. They were asleep!

— MONTY WOOLLEY

798. To be born without envy is the surest sign that one possesses great qualities.

— FRANÇOIS DE LA ROCHEFOUCAULD

799. If there is any sin more deadly than envy, it is being pleased at being envied.

Epitaph

800.   SOME SELF-COMPOSED EPITAPHS

Pardon me for not rising.

        — CLIVE BROOK

Excuse my dust.

        — DOROTHY PARKER

The tomb monument of a certain genial host bears his name and the following inscription: This Is on Me.

This is too deep for me.

        — DON HEROLD

Well, I've played everything but a harp.

        — LIONEL BARRYMORE

Here lies an author—as usual.

        — OWEN DAVIS

On the whole, I'd rather be in Philadelphia.

        — W. C. FIELDS

I had a hunch something like this would happen.

        — FONTAINE FOX

Here's something I want to get off my chest.

        —WILLIAM HAINES

This is the first time I've ever taken anything lying down.

        — CARL BRISSON quoted in *The Reader's Digest*

Over my dead body.

        — GEORGE KAUFMAN quoted in *The Reader's Digest*

This is all over my head.

        — ROBERT BENCHLEY quoted in *The Reader's Digest*

This one's on me.

        — MILTON BERLE quoted in *The Reader's Digest*

I've finally gotten to the bottom of things.

        — ILKA CHASE quoted in *The Reader's Digest*

801.   Epitaph for a waiter: God finally caught his eye.

802. After reading the epitaphs in a cemetery, you wonder where they bury the sinners.

— *Coronet*

Equality

803. The doctrine of human equality reposes on this: that there is no man really clever who has not found that he is stupid. There is no big man who has not felt small. Some men never feel small; but these are the few men who are.

— G. K. CHESTERTON

804. They who say all men are equal speak an undoubted truth; if they mean that all men have an equal right to liberty, to their property and to their protection of the laws. But they are mistaken if they think men are equal in their station and employments, since they are not so by their talents.

— VOLTAIRE

Error see also *Mistake*

805. An error is more menacing than a crime, for an error begets crime.

— G. K. CHESTERTON

806. The longer a man is wrong, the surer he is he's right.

Etiquette

807. Good breeding consists in concealing how much we think of ourselves and how little we think of the other person.

— MARK TWAIN

808. "I've had a wonderful evening," said Groucho Marx to his hostess as he was leaving a dull Hollywood party, "but this wasn't it."

809. President Coolidge once invited some Vermont friends to dine at the White House. They were worried about their table manners, so decided to do everything Coolidge did. The meal passed smoothly until coffee was served and Coolidge poured his into a saucer. The guests followed suit. Then he added sugar and cream.

125

ETIQUETTE

The visitors did likewise. Then Coolidge leaned over and gave his to the cat.

— HENRY CHARLES SUTER

810. On a day when the fire of hell seemed to be heating New York, a man entered an elegant restaurant and took off his suit coat. The waiter rushed over and reminded, "Sir, please. That's not allowed here."

"The queen of England gave me permission to do so!"

The waiter, astonished, hurried to get the headwaiter, who in turn rushed over and admonished the newcomer.

"The queen of England . . ."

"Nonsense!"

"She most certainly did. I recently started to remove my coat at her court, and then she said, 'Sir, you can do that in America, but not here.'"

811. When Stuyvesant Fish was president of the Illinois Central Railroad, there walked into his office one morning an Irishman, hat on and pipe in mouth, who said: "I want a pass to St. Louis."

"Who are you?" asked President Fish, somewhat startled.

"I'm Pat Casey, one of your switchmen."

Mr. Fish, thinking it was a good chance to impart a lesson in etiquette, said, "Now, Pat, I'm not going to say that I will refuse your request, but there are certain forms a man should observe in asking a favor. You should knock at the door, and when I say 'Come in' you should enter and, taking off your hat and removing your pipe from your mouth, you should say, 'Are you President Fish?' I would say, 'I am. Who are you?' Then you should say, 'I am Pat Casey, one of your switchmen.' Then I would say, 'What can I do for you?' Then you would tell me, and the matter would be settled. Now you go out and come in again and see if you can't do better."

So the switchman went out. About two hours later there was a knock on the door and President Fish said, "Come in." In came Pat Casey with his hat off and pipe out of his mouth.

"Good morning," he said, "are you President Fish of the Illinois Central Railroad?"

"I am. Who are you?"

"I am Pat Casey, one of your switchmen."

"Well, Mr. Casey, what can I do for you?"

126

"You can go to hell. I got a job and a pass on the Wabash."

> — B. A. BOTKIN & ALVIN F. HARLOW, "A
> Treasury of Railroad Folklore," in the
> *Merrill* (Iowa) *Record*

Eulogy

812. This minister was attempting to eulogize the deceased in a funeral sermon: "We have here only the shell; the nut is gone."

813. Called upon for a few words of condolence at the death of one he cordially detested, Voltaire at first refused. He was finally persuaded and penned this brief but reluctant statement: "I have just been informed that Monsieur ———— is dead. He was a sturdy patriot, a gifted writer, a loyal friend and an affectionate husband and father—provided he is really dead."

Evasion

814. A businessman called his stenographer and told her to write a letter to John White of Buffalo, making an appointment to meet him in Schenectady.

"How do you spell *Schenectady,* Mr. Smith?"

"Why the idea! Don't you know how to spell *Schenectady?*"

"No sir, I'm sorry I don't."

"Why, er— Oh, well, never mind. Just tell him I'll meet him in Albany."

Evil

815. There can be no such thing as a necessary evil. For, if a thing is really necessary, it cannot be an evil and if it is an evil, it is not necessary.

> — TIORIO

816. The sorrow of knowing that there is evil in the best is far out-balanced by the joy of discovering that there is good in the worst.

> — DR. AUSTEN FOX RIGGS

817. All that is necessary for the triumph of evil is that good men do nothing.

> — EDMUND BURKE

Evolution

818. Very few of us are impelled by clearly reasoned doctrine. What actually motivates us is not so much a philosophy as a mood or an emotional opinion. This mood or personal "philosophy" changes as we move on through the years. The best way to judge what motivates us at any stage is to notice what sort of people we prefer.

Years ago I preferred clever people. There was a joy in beholding the phenomenon of a mind joyously creative, inhering thoughts quickly translated into words, or ideas expressed in a new way. I find now, that my taste has changed. Verbal fireworks often bore me. They seem motivated by self-assertion and self-display. I now prefer another type of person:—one who is considerate, understanding of others, careful not to break down another person's self-respect, and willing to arrive at a consensus of opinion. My preferred person today is one who is always aware of the personality needs of others, or their pain and fear and unhappiness, and their search for self-respect.

Perhaps my change in taste has come about from a change in the world. People once felt that ignorance was the only bar to social happiness. Now, having seen mass murder in the age of culture, we know that human happiness is barred by active evil in human character, callousness and active cruelty. There is so much man-made misery in the world that one begins to hunger for a little considerateness and a little patience. Whether or not this change of taste reveals a basic change in my personal motivation, I know that I have come to prefer a different type of person. I once liked clever people. Now I like good people.

— RABBI SOLOMON B. FREEHOF, D.D.

Exaggeration

819. A Texan was trying to impress upon a Bostonian the valor of the heroes of the Alamo. "I bet you never had anybody so brave around Boston," he said.

"Did you ever hear of Paul Revere?" asked the Bostonian.

"Paul Revere?" said the Texan. "Isn't that the guy who ran for help?"

Example

820. The first great gift we can bestow on others is a good example.

— THOMAS MORELL

821. A counterfeiter is a guy who gets into trouble by following a good example.

822. We may well ask ourselves how successful will the school be in teaching honesty when in the home father boasts gleefully at the dinner table about a sharp business deal or how lucky he was when the filling station attendant forgot to charge him for that extra quart of oil.

— GEORGE E. ROTTER

823. You can preach a better sermon with your life than with your lips.

— OLIVER GOLDSMITH

824. He that gives good advice builds with one hand; he that gives good counsel and example builds with both; but he that gives good admonition and bad example builds with one hand and pulls down with the other.

— FRANCIS BACON

Excess

825. ... He saw his duty and overdid it!

Exchange

826. If I visit your house and we exchange ten-dollar bills, we part no richer; but if I visit your house and we exchange ideas, both of us come away from the meeting enriched.

827. You have a shilling. I have a shilling. We swap. You have my shilling and I have yours. We are no better off. But suppose you have an idea and I have an idea. We swap. Now you have two ideas and I have two ideas. We have increased our stock of ideas 100 per cent.

— A. S. GREGG

Excuse

828. On hearing the excuses given by the Russians for not favoring certain Balkan measures in the United Nations, Warren Austin was reminded of the story about the Vermont farmer whose neighbor wanted to borrow an axe. "Sorry, Jim," said the farmer, "I've got to shave tonight."

His wife later took him to task, saying, "Why did you give Jim such a silly excuse?"

"If you don't want to do a thing," the farmer replied, "one excuse is as good as another."

Executive

829. Executive ability is deciding quickly and getting somebody else to do the work.

—J. G. POLLARD

Expectation

830. Blessed is he who expects nothing, for he shall never be disappointed.

—JONATHAN SWIFT

Experience

831. Experiment is folly where experience shows the way.

—ROGER W. BABSON

832. The only complete catastrophe is the catastrophe from which we learn nothing.

—WILLIAM ERNEST HOCKING, *Experiment in Education* (Henry Regnery Co.)

833. Experience is a school where a man learns what a big fool he has been.

—JOSH BILLINGS

834. Experience enables us to defend in age the prejudices of our youth, and belatedly to realize ambitions forsaken in earlier youth. This would seem to be true not only of individuals but of institutions also.

—C. A. MACE, *Sibylla* (Routledge & Kegan Paul Ltd., London)

835. We cannot advance without experiments in living, but no wise man tries every day what he has proved wrong the day before.

— JAMES TRUSLOW ADAMS

836. Experience without learning is better than learning without experience.

— American proverb

837. An employer, interviewing an applicant, remarked: "You ask high wages for a man with no experience."

"Well," the prospect replied, "it's so much harder work when you don't know anything about it."

838. Only part of us learn by other people's experience—the rest of us have to be the other people.

Experiment

839. During his campaign for governor of New Jersey in 1940, Charles Edison, son of the inventor, introduced himself by explaining, "People will inevitably associate me with my father, but I would not have anyone believe that I am trading on the name Edison. I would rather have you know me merely as the result of one of my father's earlier experiments."

— CARL JOHN BOSTLEMANN quoted in
The Reader's Digest

Expert

840. Make ten consecutive correct guesses and you've established a reputation as an expert—which lasts until you've made one little mistake.

841. Economist: a man who tells you what to do with your money after you have done something else with it.

Explanation

842. One of the curiosities some time ago shown at public exhibition, professed to be a skull of Oliver Cromwell. A gentleman present observed that it could not be Cromwell's, as he had a very large head, and this was a small skull. "Oh, I know all about that," said the exhibitor, undisturbed, "but, you see, this was his skull when *he was a boy.*"

Extraordinary

843. God does not want us to do extraordinary things; He wants us to do ordinary things extraordinarily well.

— BISHOP CHARLES GORE

Extravagance

844. A man in anticipation of death bought the finest casket available, for delivery at the appropriate time. He told a friend what he had done, describing the gold fittings, teakwood carvings and other features, and mentioned the cost of the casket. His friend expressed horror and urged him to cancel the deal.

"Don't you realize that for only a few hundred dollars more you could be buried in a Cadillac?"

— SAMUEL PACE quoted in *The Reader's Digest*

845. A miser grows rich by seeming poor; an extravagant man grows poor by seeming rich.

— WILLIAM SHAKESPEARE

Facts

846. President Coolidge was once asked by a visitor whether the people where he came from said, "A hen lays or a hen lies." "The people where I come from," he replied, "lift her up to see."

847. Facts mean nothing unless they are rightly understood, rightly related and rightly interpreted.

— R. L. LONG

848. Get the facts, or the facts will get you. And when you get 'em, get 'em right, or they will get you wrong.

849. Facts that are not frankly faced have a habit of stabbing us in the back.

— SIR HAROLD BOWDEN

850. Let us keep our mouths shut and our pens dry until we know the facts.

— DR. ANTON J. CARLSON

851. Every man has a right to his opinion, but no man has a right to be wrong in his facts.

— BERNARD M. BARUCH

852. True opinions can prevail only if the facts to which they refer are known; if they are not known, false ideas are just as effective as true ones, if not a little more effective.

— WALTER LIPPMANN

853. I do believe one ought to face facts. If you don't they get behind you and may become terrors, nightmares, giants, horrors. As long as one faces them one is top dog. The trouble is not to steel oneself but to face them calmly, easily—to have the habit of facing them.

— *Letters to John Middleton Murry*
(Alfred A. Knopf, Inc.)

Failure See also *Success*

854. Many a good man has failed because he had his wishbone where his backbone ought to have been.

855. One of the saddest experiences which can ever come to a human being is to awaken, grey-haired and wrinkled near the close of an unproductive career, to the fact that all thru the years he has been using only a small part of himself!

— V. M. BURROWS, *The Wages of a Fellow Craft*

856. Many a man never fails because he never tries.

— NORMAN MACEWAN

857. Sometimes a noble failure serves the world as faithfully as a distinguished success.

858. There are two kinds of failures: the man who will do nothing he is told, and the man who will do nothing else.

— PERLE THOMPSON

859. I don't like to lose, and that isn't so much because it is just a football game, but because defeat means the failure to reach your objective. I don't want a football player who doesn't take defeat to heart, who laughs it off with the thought, "Oh, well, there's another

Saturday." The trouble in American life today, in business as well as in sports, is that too many people are afraid of competition. The result is that in some circles people have come to sneer at success if it costs hard work and training and sacrifice.

— Knute Rockne

860. Because a fellow has failed once or twice, or a dozen times, you don't want to set him down as a failure till he's dead or loses his courage—and that's the same thing.

— George Horace Lorimer

861. We have forty million reasons for failure, but not a single excuse.

— Rudyard Kipling

862. You and I must not complain if our plans break down if we have done our part. That probably means that the plans of One who knows more than we do have succeeded.

— Edward Everett Hale

863. He who stops being better stops being good.

— Oliver Cromwell

864. Failures are divided into two classes—those who thought and never did, and those who did and never thought.

— John Charles Salak

865. When a man blames others for his failures, it's a good idea to credit others with his successes.

— Howard W. Newton

866. Failure is the line of least persistence.

Fair play

867. The man who will use his skill and constructive imagination to see how much he can give for a dollar, instead of how little he can give for a dollar, is bound to succeed.

— Henry Ford

Faith

868. Faith is to believe what we do not see; and the reward of this faith is to see what we believe.

— St. Augustine

869. Faith is not trying to believe something regardless of the evidence. Faith is daring to do something regardless of the consequences.

— SHERWOOD EDDY

870. All I have seen teaches me to trust the Creator for all I have not seen.

— RALPH WALDO EMERSON

871. Despotism may govern without faith, but Liberty cannot.

— ALEXIS CHARLES HENRI DE TOCQUEVILLE

Fame

872. Fame: the advantage of being known to those who do not know us.

873. It is the penalty of fame that a man must ever keep rising. "Get a reputation, and then go to bed," is the absurdest of all maxims. "Keep up a reputation or go to bed," would be nearer the truth.

— E. H. CHAPIN

874. One afternoon John Barrymore strolled into a haberdashery on Hollywood Boulevard and asked to be shown some hats. After looking over several, he selected one. "I'll take that," he said. "Just charge it."

"Yes, sir," the clerk said eagerly, "and to whom shall I charge it?"

One famous eyebrow went up. "Barrymore," the Great Profile said icily.

"Yes, sir," said the clerk, "and what's the first name, please?"

That was too much for the actor. "Ethel!" he barked, and stormed out of the store.

— AMASA B. WINDHAM in *The Birmingham News*

Family — family life

875. No family should have fewer than three children, because if there is one genius among them, there should be two to support him.

876. Of all my wife's relations I like myself the best.

877. Take the word "family." Strike out the "m" for mother and the "y" for youth—and all you have left is "fail."

— OMAR BURLESON, M.C.

878. Otto Kahn, the well-known financier, was one day driving through the lower East Side of New York when he saw a large sign reading: "Samuel Kahn, cousin of Otto Kahn." He immediately called up his lawyer, instructing him to have the sign changed, sparing no expense. A few days later, Kahn drove by the place again. The offending sign had been changed. "Samuel Kahn, formerly cousin of Otto Kahn."

879. There are better things than curfews to bring kids home and off the streets at night: a mother singing in the kitchen and a dad whistling around the house.

— BURTON HILLIS, courtesy of *Better Homes & Gardens* magazine

880. Speaking of trade relations, almost everyone would like to.

— *Wall Street Journal*

881. If we want better people to make a better world, then we will have to begin where people are made—in the family.

Fanaticism

882. The prosecuting witness in a rape case, asked if she were a virtuous woman, replied that she was but that she was no fanatic on the subject.

883. Fanaticism consists in redoubling your effort when you have forgotten your aim.

— GEORGE SANTAYANA

Farm — farming

884. A man, interested in buying a farm that was for sale, stopped in to see how a nearby farmer was faring.

Man: "Do you think I would prosper if I bought that farm?"

Farmer: "Nope, I wouldn't say that, but on the other hand, if yer luck holds like mine, there ain't nothin' to lose. There weren't nothin' here when I came, and there ain't nothin' here now. A feller can't ask for more than an even break."

885. Of all occupations from which gain is secured, there is none better than agriculture, nothing more productive, nothing sweeter, nothing more worthy of a free man.

— CICERO, *De Officiis*

886. No race can prosper till it learns that there is as much dignity in tilling a field as in writing a poem.

— BOOKER T. WASHINGTON, *Up from Slavery*

887. Gentleman farmer: a man with more hay in the bank than in the barn.

Fate

888. I do not believe in that word Fate. It is the refuge of every self-confessed failure.

— ANDREW SOUTAR

Father

889. Charles Coburn, the actor, tells this story:

As a boy, I fell in love with the theater and started seeing plays whenever possible. "One thing, son, you must never do," my father warned me. "Don't go to burlesque houses."

I, of course, asked why.

"Because you would see things you shouldn't," Father replied.

That settled it. The next time I managed to get the price of admission, I went straight to a burlesque house.

Father was right. I saw something I shouldn't have seen—my father.

— LOUIS AZRAEL in *Baltimore News-Post*

Father's Day

890. When, every day, throughout the year we've gone the same old way,

It's difficult to make a change for one specific day.

Often he sang us funny songs when we were very small,
And later taught us how to walk, and then to catch a ball,
And helped us with our lessons too, and pulled us through our ills,
And gave us talks on life and love, and always paid the bills.
All year we've tossed no praise at him—this creature known as father,
Why build the old man up today?
You'll find it's worth the bother!

— Sunshine Magazine

Fault

891. A fault confessed is more than half amended.

— Sir John Harrington, Epigrams

892. Almost all our faults are more pardonable than the methods we think up to hide them.

— François de La Rochefoucauld

893. The faults of others are like headlights on an automobile. They only seem more glaring than our own.

Fault-finding

894. Two things are bad for the heart—running up stairs and running down people.

— Bernard M. Baruch

Faux pas

895. At a dinner party, a shy young man had been trying to think of something nice to say to his hostess. At last he saw his chance when she turned to him and remarked, "What a small appetite you have, Mr. Jones."

"To sit next to you," he replied gallantly, "would cause any man to lose his appetite."

Fear

896. Wise fear beats care.

897. The man who has ceased to fear has ceased to care.

— FRANCIS BRADLEY

Finance

898. Some men wrest a living from nature; this is called work. Some men wrest a living from those who wrest a living from nature; this is called trade. Some men wrest a living from those who wrest a living from those who wrest a living from nature; this is called finance.

— VINCENT McNABB

Fish — fishing

899. The fastest growing thing in nature is a fish—from the time a guy catches it until he tells about it.

900. Fishing is just a jerk at one end of the line waiting for a jerk at the other end.

— ERNIE FORD

901. Accordion: an instrument invented by the man who couldn't decide how big the one was that got away.

902. Spike Jones tells about the irate wife of a movie star who had gone off fishing and left her alone. Asked where her husband might be, she replied, "Just go down to the bridge and look around until you find a pole with a worm on each end!"

— JIMMY STARR in *Los Angeles Evening Herald and Express*

Flattery

903. Baloney is flattery laid on so thick it cannot be true, and blarney is flattery laid on so thin we like it.

— BISHOP FULTON J. SHEEN

904. Nothing is so great an instance of ill-manners as flattery. If you flatter all the company, you please none; if you flatter only one or two, you affront all the rest.

— JONATHAN SWIFT

FLATTERY

905. As far as the United States is concerned, immigration is still the sincerest form of flattery.

906. No flattery is so irresistible as second-hand flattery.

907. If you can't think of any other way to flatter a man, tell him he's the kind of man who can't be flattered.

908. A man is never so weak as when some woman is telling him how strong he is.

909. I hate careless flattery, the kind that exhausts you in your effort to believe it.

— WILLIAM MIZNER

910. The mischief of flattery is, not that it persuades any man that he is what he is not, but that it suppresses the influence of honest ambition by raising an opinion that honor may be gained without the toil of merit.

— DR. SAMUEL JOHNSON

911. Just praise is only a debt but flattery is a poisoned gift.

912. The best way to turn a woman's head is to tell her she has a nice profile.

— MARTIN BLOCK

Flirtation

913. Flirting is the gentle art of making a man feel pleased with himself.

— HELEN ROWLAND, *Reflections of a Bachelor Girl*. All rights reserved by the McBride Company, 1955.

Flowers

914. Sign in front of the flower garden on the grounds of a western town's city hall: "Love 'em and leave 'em."

— *Wall Street Journal*

915. How faithful flowers are! With the first call of the sun in early spring the leaders of the gay procession never fail to appear, followed by all the others of the happy company, each of them seeming to know when it is time for it to arrive.

— SAMUEL FESSENDEN CLARKE

Food see also *Diet—Eating*

916. Chef: a man with a big enough vocabulary to give the soup a different name every day.

917. Snack: the pause that refleshes.

Fool – folly

918. Tommy's uncle was wont to give out bits of hardheaded advice to his young nephew.

"Yes, Tommy," he said one day, "fools are certain; wise men hesitate."

"Are you sure, Uncle John?" asked Tommy.

"Yes, my boy; certain of it."

919. The best way to convince a fool that he is wrong is to let him have his own way.

920. A learned fool is one who has read everything, and simply remembered it.

— Josh Billings

921. Any fool can criticize, condemn, and complain—and most fools do.

— Dale Carnegie, *How to Win Friends and Influence People* (Simon & Schuster, Inc.)

922. Most everyone seems to be willing to be a fool himself, but he can't bear to have anyone else be one.

— Josh Billings

923. He that makes himself an ass must not take it ill if men ride him.

— Old proverb

924. Hope is the fool's income.

925. A fool always finds a greater fool to admire him.

— Nicolas Boileau-Despréaux

926. There are two kinds of fools. One says, "This is old, therefore it is good." The other says, "This is new, therefore it is better."

— Dean William Ralph Inge

927. A very affected young man who had been holding forth at great length remarked, "I simply *can't* bear fools!"

"How odd," chimed in Dorothy Parker. "Apparently your mother could."

— Olga Swanson quoted in
The Reader's Digest

928. Nobody can make a fool out of a person if he isn't the right kind of material for the job.

929. A fool and his money are soon spotted.

Football see also *Sports*

930. Football season: time of the year when girls whistle at men in sweaters.

Forewarning

931.
There was a young lady from Kent
Who said that she knew what it meant
When men asked her to dine
Gave her cocktails and wine
She knew *what it meant*—but she went.

Forget – forgetfulness

932. We may with advantage at times forget what we know.

— Publilius Syrus

933. A young lady calling on Agnes Repplier, got ready to go, put on her hat and coat, put her hands in her muff, took them out, picked up a parcel, laid it down, shifted from one foot to another and then said, "There was something I meant to say, but I've forgotten."

"Perhaps, my dear," Miss Repplier replied, "it was *good-bye*."

— From *Conversation, Please* by Loren Carroll,
copyright © 1939, used by special permission of
the publishers, The Bobbs-Merrill Company, Inc.

Forgiveness

934. In the sphere of forgiveness, too many hatchets are buried alive.

— Lem Hubbard in the *Chicago Tribune*

935. The best thing to give to your enemy is forgiveness; to an opponent, tolerance; to a friend, your heart; to your child, a good example; to a father, deference; to your mother, conduct that will make her proud of you; to yourself, respect; to all men, charity.

— Lord Arthur J. Balfour

936. The tennis courts of an Iowa high school adjoined the grounds of a church rectory. Occasionally, exuberant youngsters whammed a tennis ball over the fence onto the trim lawns. One day a player, chasing a stray ball, came face to face with a large sign which read: NO TRESPASSING. The sign came down overnight, however, when the tennis club erected its own sign directly opposite. This one read: FORGIVE US OUR TRESPASSES.

— *Texas Outlook*

937. "I can forgive, but I cannot forget," is only another way of saying, "I cannot forgive."

— Henry Ward Beecher, *Life Thoughts*

938. They who forgive most, shall be most forgiven.

— Josiah W. Bailey

939. He that cannot forgive others, breaks the bridge over which he must pass himself; for every man has need to be forgiven.

— Lord Herbert

940. To be wronged is nothing unless you continue to remember it.

— Confucius

941. Beware of the man who does not return your blow; he neither forgives you nor allows you to forgive yourself.

— George Bernard Shaw

942. He who cannot forgive himself with regard to you will never forgive you.

— Francis Bradley

Fraud

943. The first and worst of all frauds is to cheat one's self.

— Philip James Bailey

FREEDOM

Freedom

944. Freedom is the coin of the realm in the kingdom of human worth and dignity, and the coin has two sides. On one side are inscribed the rights and privileges of free men. On the other side are the responsibilities. Unless both sides are genuine and deeply cut, the coin is counterfeit.

— P. E. KAY, *The Other Side of Freedom, New Outlook*

945. Freedom: being able to do what you please without considering anyone except the wife, police, boss, life insurance company, state, federal and city authorities, and the neighbors.

946. Many politicians lay it down as a self-evident proposition that no people ought to be free till they are fit to use their freedom. The maxim is worthy of the fool in the old story, who resolved not to go into the water till he had learned to swim.

— THOMAS B. MACAULAY

947. If a nation values anything more than freedom, it will lose its freedom; and the irony of it is that, if it is comfort or money that it values more, it will lose that too.

— From *Strictly Personal*, by W. SOMERSET MAUGHAM. Copyright 1940, 1941 by W. SOMERSET MAUGHAM, reprinted by permission of Doubleday & Company, Inc.

948. The fight for freedom is an endless battle. Its victories are never final, its defeats are never permanent. Each generation must defend its heritage, for each seeming conquest gives rise to new forces that will attempt to substitute fresh means of oppression for the old. There can be no peace in a world of life and growth—every battle the fathers thought finished will have to be fought anew by their children if they wish to preserve and extend their freedom.

— PHILIP VAN DOREN STERN

949. To its own people and to the world the United States has from its inception embodied the idea of freedom. Like all ideals, this one has never been fully realized in practice, and at times it has suffered serious abridgments. But because it has always remained a vital and dynamic force, living not only in phrases and institutions

144

but in the spirit of a people, it has triumphed over temporary set-backs and gone on to achieve new meaning and new dimensions.

— From *American Security and Freedom* by
MAURICE J. GOLDBLOOM, copyright, 1954,
by The American Jewish Committee

Freedom of Speech

950. It is by the goodness of God that in our country we have those three unspeakably precious things: freedom of speech, freedom of conscience, and the prudence never to practice either of them.

— MARK TWAIN

951. I may disapprove of what you say, but will defend to the death your right to say it.

— VOLTAIRE

952. What this country needs is more free speech worth listening to.

— HANSELL B. DUCKETT

953. If there be any among us who would wish to dissolve this Union, or to change its Republican form, let them stand undisturbed as monuments of the safety with which error of opinion may be tolerated where reason is left free to combat it.

— THOMAS JEFFERSON

954. Lincoln defended his interference with freedom of speech and press by asking: "Must I shoot a simple-minded soldier boy who deserts, while I must not touch a hair of the wily agitator who induces him to desert?"

Friend — friendship

955. False friends are like our shadow, keeping close to us while we walk in the sunshine but leaving us when we cross into the shade.

— CHRISTIAN BOVEE

956. It's smart to pick your friends—but not to pieces.

957. What is a friend? A single soul dwelling in two bodies.

— ARISTOTLE

958. Unless you bear with the faults of a friend, you betray your own.

— Publilius Syrus, *Maxims*

959. Cocktail party: where they cut sandwiches and friends into little pieces.

960. Money lent to a friend must be recovered from an enemy.

— German proverb

961. Speak well of your enemies; remember, you made them.

962. To keep your friends, treat them kindly; to kill them, treat them often.

963. Rejected courtesy becomes enmity. If the extended hand is refused, the mere closing of the fingers changes it into a *fist*.

964. One enemy is too much for a man in a great post, and a hundred friends are too few.

— Old proverb

965. A friend is one to whom we may pour out the contents of our hearts, chaff and grain together, knowing that the gentlest of hands will sift it, keep what is worth keeping, and with a breath of kindness, blow the rest away.

966. Friends: persons who stick together until debt do them part.

967. Real friends are those who, when you've made a fool of yourself, don't feel that you've done a permanent job.

— Erwin T. Randall quoted in *The Reader's Digest*

968. Every man should keep a fair-sized cemetery in which to bury the faults of his friends.

— Henry Ward Beecher

969. It is great to have friends when one is young, but indeed it is still more so when you are getting old. When we are young, friends are, like everything else, a matter of course. In the old days we know what it means to have them.

— Edvard Grieg

970. One does not make friends; one recognizes them.

> — ISABEL PATERSON, *If It Prove Fair Weather*
> (G. P. Putnam's Sons)

971. Recipe for having friends: be one.

> — ELBERT HUBBARD

972. A friend is a present you give yourself.

> — ROBERT LOUIS STEVENSON

Future

973. Every tomorrow has two handles. We can take hold of it with the handle of anxiety or the handle of faith. We should live for the future, and yet should find our life in the fidelities of the present; the last is only the method of the first.

> — HENRY WARD BEECHER

974. My interest is in the future because I'm going to spend the rest of my life there.

> — CHARLES F. KETTERING

975. Live only for today, and you ruin tomorrow.

> — C. SIMMONS

976. It will be a shock to men when they realize that thoughts that were fast enough for today are not fast enough for tomorrow. But thinking tomorrow's thoughts today is one kind of future life.

> — CHRISTOPHER MORLEY

977. The men who built this country, and those who have made it prosper in good times and bad, have always been men whose faith in its future was unshakable. Men of courage, they dared to go forward despite all hazards; men of vision, they always looked forward, never backward. Always their thoughts were of the future, like those of the late Elihu Root, who, at the age of 91, declared: "Keep looking out in front; the future looks better out there than it has ever looked in the history of the world."

978. There is no squabbling so violent as that between people who accepted an idea yesterday and those who will accept the same idea tomorrow.

> — CHRISTOPHER MORLEY, *Religio
> Journalistici*

FUTURE

979. He that will not look forward must look behind.

— Gaelic proverb

980. I have no economic radar to penetrate the future, but we can make it what we will it to be. Of that I am sure.

— BERNARD M. BARUCH

981. SUPERMAN OF THE FUTURE

In Half Million Years Human Beings Will Be Taller and Have Less Hair and Fewer Toes

Man 500,000 years from now will probably be taller with a larger head. He will have a smaller face and jaw, and fewer teeth.

Our taller man will probably have either lost his little toe entirely or it will only be a nubbin. It isn't of much use to us anyway and we would not miss it if it were gone. In many people today it is very small and often has no nail at all or only a vestige of one. The line of leverage of our foot in walking has passed from the middle of the foot as in the early primates over to the big toe. Thus that has grown to be bigger and more important with a progressive decrease in size and function as one moves to the little toe. Nature likes to get rid of useless organs eventually even though it takes a long time. Therefore I think our little toe is doomed.

Most unhappy of all, man of the future is likely to have little if any hair on his body and become bald very early in life. In the course of human evolution the pelt has constantly diminished. We don't need hair to keep us warm when clothes do the job—therefore, why have body hair? Some races, like the Mongoloids, have advanced further in this respect than have white men and their body hair has almost entirely disappeared. It is true also that baldness is much more frequent among highly civilized races of mankind than among the primitive people of nature. If we continue to remain civilized in the way we are today, physical anthropologists draw a picture of the man of thirty, 500,000 years from now, as having a head resembling the surface of a billiard ball.

We can remember, however, that our judgment of what is or is not beautiful will have changed with our bodily characters. The man of the future may well look back upon us with our big faces and small heads, with five toes instead of four, with all our teeth and hair on

148

the top of our heads, with the same amusement that women find in the hats which their mothers wore in the gay nineties.

—Roy Chapman Andrews, *This Amazing Planet* (G. P. Putnam's Sons)

982. It's like the cab driver told the tourist riding past the government archives building. The tourist looked at the carved words, "What Is Past Is Prologue," and wanted to know what it meant.

"It means," said the driver, "that you ain't seen nothing yet."

983. We can pay our debt to the past by putting the future in debt to ourselves.

—John Buchan

984. The best thing about the future is that it only comes one day at a time.

—Dean Acheson

985. Hats off to the past; coats off to the future.

986. The future that we study and plan for begins today.

—Chester O. Fischer

Gambling see also *Betting*

987. A dining car patron on an Eastern railroad received his luncheon check, which amounted to $1.45, and gave the waiter two one-dollar bills. In due time, the waiter brought his change—a fifty-cent piece and a nickel. After a moment's hesitation, the annoyed patron picked up the half-dollar, leaving the nickel on the plate. To his surprise, the waiter grinned broadly.

"That's all right, sir," he said. "I just gambled and lost."

988. A drunk, armed with nickels, entered an Automat, stopped in front of the slot marked "Ham Sandwich." He dropped in two nickels and got a sandwich. He dropped two more nickels and out came another sandwich. After he'd collected 20 ham sandwiches, someone suggested: "Hey, don't you think you've had enough?"

"I should quit now?" replied the drunk. "Now—when I'm on a winning streak?"

989. A bookie is just a pickpocket who lets you use your own hands.

—Henry Morgan

GAMBLING

990. Do you frequently toss a coin to decide something? If so, let the other fellow do the calling. Those who call say "heads" seven times out of ten. Checking indicates a coin comes up heads only on an average of five times out of ten. So the percentage is against the caller. Don't gamble! However, if you cannot resist the temptation to gamble, you should as a matter of self-protection make a study of that thing called "percentage."

> —E. V. Durling in *The Chicago American*

991. Race track: a place where windows clean people.

992. There is little bona fide gambling in the U.S. Most of what is called gambling is really the donation of suckers to swindlers.

> —E. M. Duvall & Reuben Hill, *When You Marry* (D.C. Heath and Company)

993. When it comes to trading on the Stock Exchange, the bears win sometimes and the bulls win sometimes but the hogs always lose.

994. Gambling: a way of getting nothing for something.

> —Wilson Mizner

995. A teacher, making a trip with a group of children, stopped for lunch at a restaurant where one youngster noticed a slot machine and asked what it was. The teacher launched into a lecture on the evils of gambling. To emphasize the futility of getting something for nothing, she said she'd show them what she meant. She marched up to the machine, put in a nickel, pulled the handle—and hit the jackpot.

> —Herman M. Patton quoted in *The Reader's Digest*

996. The longest odds in the world are those against getting even.

997. Play not for gain but for sport; who plays for more than he can lose with pleasure stakes his heart.

> —George Herbert

998. The urge to gamble is so universal and its practice so pleasurable that I assume it must be evil.

> —Heywood Broun

Garden

999. Gardener: someone who thinks that what goes down must come up.

— I. B. GIBSON

1000. To cultivate a garden is to walk with God.

— CHRISTIAN BOVEE

Garrulity

1001. Speaking much is a sign of vanity; for he that is lavish in words is a niggard in deed.

— SIR WALTER RALEIGH

Genealogy

1002. Genealogy: tracing yourself back to people better than you.

— JOHN GARLAND POLLARD

Generosity

1003. He who is not liberal with what he has, does but deceive himself when he thinks he would be more liberal if he had more.

— W. S. PLUMER

Genius

1004. Genius is entitled to respect only when it promotes the peace and improves the happiness of mankind.

— LORD ESSEX

1005. What makes genius is the combination of natural gifts for creation with an idiosyncrasy that enables its possessor to see the world personally in the highest degree and yet with such catholicity that his appeal is not to this type of man or to that type, but to all men.

— From *The Summing Up*, by W. SOMERSET
MAUGHAM. Copyright 1938 by W. SOMERSET MAUGHAM, reprinted by permission of Doubleday & Company, Inc.

GENIUS

1006. Genius is only the power of making continuous efforts. The line between failure and success is so fine that we scarcely know when we pass it; so fine that we are often on the line and do not know it. How many a man has thrown up his hands at a time when a little more effort, a little more patience would have achieved success. As the tide goes clear out, so it comes clear in. In business, sometimes, prospects may seem darkest when really they are on the turn. A little more persistence, a little more effort, and what seemed a hopeless failure may turn into a glorious success. There is no failure except in no longer trying. There is no defeat except from within, no really insurmountable barrier save your own inherent weakness of purpose.

— Author unknown

1007. Genius is one per cent inspiration and ninety-nine per cent perspiration.

— Thomas A. Edison

1008. Men of genius are often dull and inert in society, as a blazing meteor when it descends to earth, is only a stone.

— Henry Wadsworth Longfellow

1009. If you have genius, industry will prove it; if you have none, industry will supply its place.

— Sir Joshua Reynolds

1010. Genius is the infinite capacity not only for taking pains but for giving them.

Gentleman

1011. Essential characteristics of a gentleman: The will to put himself in the place of others; the horror of forcing others into positions from which he would himself recoil; the power to do what seems to him to be right, without considering what others may say or think.

— John Galsworthy

1012. A gentleman is one who is too brave to lie, too generous to cheat, and who takes his share of the world and lets other people have theirs.

1013. A gentleman is a gardener who can call a spade a spade without adding any qualifying adjectives.

— ALBERT D. LASSETER in
Saturday Evening Post

1014. The gentleman is a man of culture, a man of refinement, above all an honest man; possessing that good taste which is the conscience of the mind, that conscience which is the good taste of the soul.

— JAMES RUSSELL LOWELL

Ghosts

1015. World's shortest ghost story: The last man on earth sat in his room. There was a knock on the door!

Gift

1016. Take gifts with a sigh; most men give to be repaid.

— JOHN BOYLE O'REILLY, *Rules of the Road*

1017. The manner of giving shows the character of the giver more than the gift itself.

— JOHANN KASPAR LAVATER

1018. What is bought is cheaper than a gift.

— MIGUEL DE CERVANTES

1019. "Darling," sighed the enraptured young man, "when I think that tomorrow is your birthday, and when I think that a year ago I didn't even know you . . ."

"Sweetheart," murmured his darling, "don't let's talk about our past. Let's talk about my present."

— LOUIS UNTERMEYER, *A Treasury of Laughter* (Simon & Schuster, Inc.)

Girl

1020. Boys will be boys, but these days girls are running them a close second.

— HAL COCHRAN quoted in
The Reader's Digest

GIVING

Giving see also *Charity*

1021.   Not what we give, but what we share—
For the gift without the giver is bare.

> — JAMES RUSSELL LOWELL, *The
> Vision of Sir Launfal*

1022.   All we can hold in our cold dead hands is what we have given away.

> — Old Sanscrit proverb

1023.   In giving, a man receives more than he gives, and the more is in proportion to the worth of the thing given.

> — GEORGE MACDONALD, *Mary Marston*

1024.   A benefit consists not in what is done or given, but in the intention of the giver or doer.

> — SENECA, *De Beneficiis*, I. 6

1025.   He gives twice who gives quickly.

> — Credited to many, including: PUBLIUS
> MIMUS, ERASMUS, EURIPEDES, AUSONIUS

1026.   Getters generally don't get happiness; givers get it. You simply give to others a bit of yourself—a thoughtful act, a helpful idea, a word of appreciation, a lift over a rough spot, a sense of understanding, a timely suggestion. You take something out of your mind, garnished in kindness out of your heart, and put it into the other fellow's mind and heart.

> — CHARLES H. BURR

1027.   Happiness is not so much in having or sharing. We make a living by what we get, but we make a life by what we give.

> — NORMAN MACEWAN

1028.   While touring in Spain, an American musician was entertained at a grandee's house, where there was much of the grandeur of the past though less of the wealth of the present. The musician happened to admire some old battle flags of embroidered silk, trophies of the past glories of the grandee's ancestors. Soon after his visit, the Spaniard sent him one of the flags, asking him to receive it as a gift, an appreciation of the joy which his music had given the sender. The musician deprecated receiving such a gift, priceless to the giver, an article of curiosity only to him. So he returned it. But the flag was again sent after him with this explanation: "Your art, sir, gave me unusual pleasure. I want to mark my appreciation in an unusual manner. I know that you admire this banner of silk, for it be no more than that to you. To me, as the symbol of a brave deed of one of our family, it means much more; and I wish to give you something the giving of which I shall feel."

—FELIX E. SCHELLING, *Summer Ghosts and Winter Topics* (J. B. Lippincott Company)

1029. The best gifts are always tied with heartstrings.

1030. Blessed are those who can give without remembering, and take without forgetting.

—ELIZABETH BIBESCO

1031. Dwight L. Moody, the great evangelist, was calling with a certain minister, on a wealthy lady, to ask her help in a building operation. On the way over, Moody asked the minister what sum he had in mind. "Oh," said the pastor, "perhaps $250."

"Better let me handle the matter," suggested the evangelist.

"Madam," said Moody, after the usual introductions, "we have come to ask you for $2000 toward the building of the new Mission."

The lady threw up her hands in horror. "Oh, Mr. Moody!" she exclaimed, "I couldn't possibly give more than $1000."

And the pair walked away with a check for just that sum.

1032. He that gives all, though but little, gives much; because God looks not to the quantity of the gift, but to the quality of the giver.

—FRANCIS QUARLES

1033. What I gave, I have; what I spent, I had; what I kept, I lost.

—Old proverb

1034. You can't take your money with you but you can send it on ahead.

God see also *Religion*

1035. I believe we are all part of a universe that has certain forms, patterns, interrelations and compensations, even for the worst of personal tragedies. And, if things go wrong, the concept of God

GOD

not only can give us hope and succor, it also relieves us of some responsibility. Of course I believe in God.

— JOHN GUNTHER

1036. What we are is God's gift to us. What we become is our gift to God.

— LOUIS NIZER in *Brooklyn Law Review*

Gold-digger

1037. Gold-digger: a girl who knows a good thing when she sues it.

1038.
Here's to the maid who is thrifty,
And knows it is folly to yearn,
And picks out a lover of fifty,
Because he has money to burn.

1039. Gold-digger: a woman after all.

Golf see also *Sports*

1040. Man blames fate for other accidents but feels personally responsible when he makes a hole-in-one.

1041. Golf is a lot like taxes—you drive hard to get to the green and then wind up in the hole.

1042. Suburbanite: a man who hires someone to mow his lawn so he can play golf for exercise.

1043. Golf is like a love affair; if you don't take it seriously, it's no fun; if you do take it seriously, it's apt to break your heart.

— ARNOLD DALY

1044. A golf professional, hired by a big department store to give golf lessons, was approached by two women. "Do you wish to learn to play golf, madam?" he asked one.

"Oh, no," she replied, "it's my friend who wants to learn. I learned yesterday."

1045. "My wife says that if I don't give up golf she'll leave me."
"Say, that's really tough, old man."
"Yes, it is. You know, I'm going to miss her."

1046. Caddie: a boy who stands behind a golfer and who didn't see where it went either.

1047. My golf is finally improving. Today I hit a ball-in-one.

— ROBERT Q. LEWIS, CBS-TV

1048. Golfer: a guy who can walk several miles toting 25 pounds of equipment but who has Junior bring him an ash tray.

1049. A couple of duffers were beating each other's brains out on the golf course one day. Things were pretty even for the first few holes. After the fourth hole, one of the duffers turned to his friend who was marking the card.

"How many did you take on that one?" he asked.

"Nine," replied his friend.

"That was my hole then," said the first one. "I only took eight."

After the next hole had been played, the first duffer asked his friend the same question.

"Oh, no," said the other bitterly, "it's my turn to ask first this time!"

1050. A murderer, condemned to be hanged, was visited by the warden the night before the execution.

"Is there anything you'd like to do before we—er—spring the trap?" asked the warden.

"Yes, I would," replied the murderer, who happened to be a golf nut. "I'd like to try a practice swing."

1051. "Now," said the golf pro, "suppose you just go through the motions without driving the ball."

"But that's precisely the difficulty I'm trying to overcome," said his pupil.

Good — goodness

1052. The fundamental idea of good is that it consists in preserving life, in favoring it, in wanting to bring it to its highest value, and evil consists in destroying life, doing it injury, hindering its development.

— DR. ALBERT SCHWEITZER, *Personnel and Guidance Journal*

1053. The heart of a good man is the sanctuary of God.

— MADAME ANNE DE STAËL

1054. By doing good with his money, a man, as it were, stamps the image of God upon it, and makes it pass current for the merchandise of heaven.

— J. RUTLEDGE

1055. The smallest good deed is better than the grandest good intention.

— GASPARD DUCHET

1056. When you are good to others you are best to yourself.

— American proverb

1057. You may depend upon it that he is a good man whose intimate friends are good.

— JOHANN KASPAR LAVATER

Good-will

1058. Good-will, like a good name, is got by many actions, and lost by one.

— LORD FRANCIS JEFFREY

1059. I have found it helpful to keep constantly in mind that there are really two entries to be made for every transaction—one in terms of immediate dollars and cents, the other in terms of good-will.

— RALPH HITZ

Gossip

1060. More people are run down by gossip than by automobiles.

1061. You can't believe everything you hear—but you can repeat it.

1062. This is the advice which a father cannibal gave to his son: "Don't talk if you have people in your mouth."

1063. Women seldom repeat gossip—the way they heard it.

1064. You can never tell about a girl, and if you can you shouldn't.

1065. Secret: something a woman can keep with a telling effect.

— PAUL H. GILBERT

1066. Gossip: a person who will never tell a lie if the truth will do as much damage.

1067. Gossip: someone who will chin and bear it.

1068. Some people just shift their brains into neutral and let their tongues idle on.

1069. There is so much good in the worst of us, and so much bad in the best of us, that it behooves all of us not to talk about the rest of us.

— ROBERT LOUIS STEVENSON

1070. Animals when they have once gained our affection never lose it; they cannot talk.

— IVAN NIKOLAYEVICH PANIN

1071. The only thing worse than being talked about is not being talked about.

— OSCAR WILDE

1072. Of course I wouldn't say anything about her unless I could say something good. And, oh boy, is this good . . .

— BILL KING in *Collier's*

1073. Gossip has been well defined as putting two and two together, and making five.

Government

1074. Most of us don't understand that we will get just as bad government as we are willing to stand for and just as good government as we are willing to fight for.

— JUDGE LUTHER YOUNGDAHL, U.S. District Court, "Make a House a Home"

1075. Overheard in government building coffee bar: "Gee, I'd better get back to the office or I'll be late for quitting time."

GOVERNMENT

1076. No man is good enough to govern another man without that other's consent.

— ABRAHAM LINCOLN

1077. Experience should teach us to be more on our guard to protect our liberties when the government's purposes are beneficent . . . The greatest dangers to liberty lurk in insidious encroachment by men of zeal, well meaning but without understanding.

— JUSTICE LOUIS D. BRANDEIS

1078. The power to tax is the power to destroy.

— CHIEF JUSTICE JOHN MARSHALL

1079. This government is ours whether it be local, county, State or Federal. It doesn't belong to anybody but to the people of America. Don't treat it as an impersonal thing; don't treat it as something to sneer at; treat it as something that belongs to you.

— HARRY HOPKINS, Speech, 1939

1080. I place economy among the first and important virtues, and public debt as the greatest of dangers. . . . We must make our choice between economy and liberty, or profusion and servitude. If we can prevent the government from wasting the labors of the people under the pretense of caring for them, they will be happy.

— THOMAS JEFFERSON

1081. Government originated in the attempt to find a form of association that defends and protects the person and property of each with the common force of all.

— JEAN JACQUES ROUSSEAU

1082. No man has a right to rule who is not better than the people over whom he rules.

— CYRUS THE ELDER in PLUTARCH'S
Moralia: Sayings of Kings

1083. The office of government is not to confer happiness, but to give men opportunity to work out happiness for themselves.

— WILLIAM ELLERY CHANNING

1084. A society of sheep must in time beget a government of wolves.

— BERTRAND DE JOUVENEL

1085. If Patrick Henry thought taxation without representation was bad, he should see it *with* representation.

1086. I believe in as little government as possible, in complete freedom of thought and speech; and in all of the things which support the dignity of the individual man as against an all-powerful State.

— BARTLEY C. CRUM

1087. Bad officials are elected by good citizens who do not vote.

Graciousness

1088. After a Town Hall meeting in a midwestern city, a woman saw Alexander Woollcott standing alone in the lobby. Impulsively she went up to tell him of the pleasures his lecture had given her. "And," said this lady who had grown grandchildren and admitted having passed 70, "I was encouraged to speak to you because you said you loved old ladies."

"Yes," replied Woollcott, "I do. But I also like them your age."

— FANNIE CAMPBELL quoted in
The Reader's Digest

Grandchildren

1089. One of the great mysteries of life is how the boy who wasn't good enough to marry the daughter can be the father of the smartest grandchild in the world.

Gratitude

1090. Too great haste to repay an obligation is a kind of ingratitude.

— FRANÇOIS DE LA ROCHEFOUCAULD

1091. Gratitude is an idiotic word; it is put in the dictionary, but it does not exist in the human heart.

1092. Men who are grateful are usually good.

Greatness see also *Simplicity*

1093. Once there was a man whose neighbors held him to be a great man. . . . "We know he is a great man," they said, "because when we are with him we ourselves feel bigger."

— JAMES M. SPINNING, "Democracy Obliges," *Nation's Schools*

1094. If a man was great while living, he becomes tenfold greater when dead.

— THOMAS CARLYLE, *Heroes and Hero Worship*

1095. Formerly we used to canonize our heroes. The modern method is to vulgarize them. Cheap editions of great books may be delightful, but cheap editions of great men are absolutely detestable.

— OSCAR WILDE

1096. The wisest man could ask no more of Fate
Than to be simple, modest, manly, true,
Safe from the Many, honored by the Few;
To count as naught in the World, or Church or State,
But inwardly in secret to be great.

— JAMES RUSSELL LOWELL

1097. The superiority of some men is merely local. They are great because their associates are little.

— DR. SAMUEL JOHNSON

1098. The nearer we come to great men the more clearly we see that they are only men. They rarely seem great to their valets.

— JEAN DE LA BRUYÈRE, *Caractères*

1099. One reason why the big apples are at the top of the basket is because a lot of little apples are keeping them up there.

1100. Great men suffer hours of depression through introspection and self-doubt. That is why they are great. That is why you will find modesty and humility the characteristics of such men.

— BRUCE BARTON

1101. If any man seeks for greatness, let him forget greatness and ask for truth, and he will find both.

— HORACE MANN

1102. Greatness is a two-faced coin—and its reverse is humility.

— MARGUERITE STEEN

1103. Great men are very apt to have great faults; and the faults appear the greater by their contrast with their excellencies.

— G. SIMMONS

1104. A man's true greatness lies in the consciousness of an honest purpose in life, founded on a just estimate of himself and everything else, on frequent self-examinations, and a steady obedience to the rule which he knows to be right, without troubling himself about what others may think or say, or whether they do or do not that which he thinks and says and does.

— MARCUS AURELIUS

Guilt

1105. He that relates another man's wicked jest with delight adopts it to be his own.

— THOMAS FULLER

Gullibility

1106. If we don't stand for something, we will fall for anything.

Habit

1107. A Florida woman was so incensed when her favorite cure-all could no longer be purchased without a doctor's prescription that she went to Washington to lodge a protest with Senator George A. Smathers. He checked with the Food and Drug Administration, found that the remedy had been banned because it is habit-forming.

"It is not habit-forming!" she cried indignantly. "I know it's not, because I've been taking it every day for 25 years!"

— GEORGE DIXON quoted in
The Reader's Digest

1108. An old story tells of a father who, in guiding his son, told him to drive a nail into a post every time he did an evil thing, and to withdraw one nail each time he did a good act. The son did so, but regretted he could not pull out the nail holes. So with the record of every life. We may amend, change our program, turn over a new leaf —but some flaws remain. Habits long continued become hard to break. The nail holes stay, and they remind us of bad decisions.

1109.   Habits are at first cobwebs—then cables.

1110.   Habits are either bobs and sinkers, cork or lead. They hold you up or they hold you down.

Handicap

1111.   Most people know that Thomas A. Edison was deaf but only a few of his close friends knew that his deafness was more psychological than physical. Once an ear specialist called on Edison and unfolded a plan of treatment which he was sure would restore his hearing. To the proposition that he submit to treatment, Edison gave an emphatic "no."

"What I am afraid of," he said, "is that you will be successful. Just think what a lot of stuff I'd have to listen to that I don't want to hear! To be a little deaf and be the only one who knows how deaf you are has its advantages. I prefer to leave well enough alone."

Handwriting

1112.   The physician had been sent an invitation to dinner. In reply, the hostess had received an absolutely illegible note. "I've got to know if he accepts or refuses," she told a friend, "but I simply can't read this note."

"Take it to a druggist," the friend advised. "No matter how badly written, a druggist can always read a doctor's handwriting."

The druggist looked at the slip of paper, disappeared into a back room and returned in a few minutes with a small bottle. "Here you are," he said, "that will be one seventy-five."

Happiness

1113.   Happiness lies in the absorption in some vocation which satisfies the soul.

— Sir William Osler

1114.   Not what we have, but what we use;
Not what we see, but what we choose;
These are the things that mar or bless the sum of human happiness.

— Joseph Fort Newton

1115. We have no more right to consume happiness without producing it than to consume wealth without producing it.

— George Bernard Shaw

1116. After you have sought over the wide world, you learn that happiness is to be found only in your own home.

— Voltaire

1117. I remember how on summer nights when I was a little girl, I used to catch "lightning bugs," put them in a bottle, and seal them up tight so the tiny bright lights would glow there in the dark. Next morning all the "glow" was gone. The lightning bugs had died.

It is the same way with a human being. If we try too hard to find happiness, we don't find it. But when we share ourselves with God's world and His other children, happiness is right there "glowing" and waiting for us.

1118. Happiness is the only thing we can give without having.

1119. Happiness is not given but exchanged.

1120. Happiness? That's nothing more than good health and a poor memory.

— Dr. Albert Schweitzer, reprinted from
Forbes Magazine of Business

1121. Some of our foremost successful men, Edison, Ford, Belasco, Roosevelt and Carnegie, have told how happy they were in their work, and how their success was the result of the love they put into it. Neither money, fame, nor luxury was the goal of these men; these are merely the things which are added to those who succeed in doing their work well. The richest men and the greatest artists all testify that it is the work itself which constitutes happiness.

— Richard Lynch, *Work and Supply*

1122. Temptation: something which when resisted gives happiness and which when yielded to gives even greater happiness.

1123. Be happy if you can, but do not despise those who are otherwise, for you know not their troubles.

1124. In the cornerstone for its new office building in Minneapolis, the Prudential Life Insurance Company placed predictions by

HAPPINESS

20 leading citizens as to what life in the United States will be like in the year 1975.

Among the forecasts was one from Harry Bullis, chairman of General Mills. First he gave some eye-opening estimates of increased population, wealth, income and living standards. These he topped off with this wise and wonderful reminder:

"In 1975, men and women will still struggle for happiness—*which will continue to lie within themselves.*"

1125. Make one person happy each day and in forty years you have made 14,600 human beings happy for a little time at least.

1126. Happiness is a rebound from hard work. One of the follies of man is to assume that he can enjoy mere emotion. As well try to eat beauty! Happiness must be tricked. She loves to see men work. She loves sweat, weariness, self-sacrifice. She will not be found in palaces, but lurking in cornfields and factories, and hovering over littered desks. She crowns the unconscious head of the busy child.

— DAVID GRAYSON, *Adventures in Contentment*

1127. All the Constitution guarantees is the pursuit of happiness; you have to catch up with it yourself.

1128. It isn't your position that makes you happy or unhappy. It's your disposition.

1129. If one only wished to be happy, this could be easily accomplished; but we wish to be happier than other people, and this is always difficult, for we believe others to be happier than they are.

— BARON DE LA MONTESQUIEU

1130. Happiness is not a station you arrive at, but a manner of traveling.

1131. The belief that youth is the happiest time of life is founded on a fallacy. The happiest person is the person who thinks the most interesting thoughts, and we grow happier as we grow older.

— WILLIAM LYON PHELPS

1132. The foolish man seeks happiness in the distance;
The wise grows it under his feet.

— JAMES OPPENHEIM

1133. The world would be both happier and brighter, if we would dwell on the duty of happiness as well as on the happiness of duty.

— Sir John Lubbock

1134. Much happiness is overlooked because it doesn't cost anything.

1135. Happiness? It is an illusion to think that more comfort means more happiness. Happiness comes of the capacity to feel deeply, to enjoy simply, to think freely, to risk life, to be needed.

— Storm Jameson

1136. Happiness does not come from possessions, but from our appreciation of them. It does not come from our work, but from our attitude toward that work. It does not come from success, but from the spiritual growth we attain in achieving that success.

Haste

1137. No man who is in a hurry is quite civilized.

— Will Durant

1138. The man who saves time by galloping loses it by missing his way; the shepherd who hurries his flock to get them home spends the night on the mountain looking for the lost; economy does not consist in haste, but in certainty.

— J. Ramsay MacDonald

Hate — hatred

1139. A rattlesnake, if cornered, will become so angry it will bite itself. That is exactly what the harboring of hate and resentment against others is—a biting of oneself. We think we are harming others in holding these spites and hates, but the deeper harm is to ourselves.

— E. Stanley Jones

1140. Hate is only power to love misused.

1141. Charles Lamb once said: "Don't introduce me to that man! I want to go on hating him, and I can't hate a man whom I know."

1142. The man who is consumed by hate is not only a misery to himself, but a source of misery to all around him, not because of the menace he offers to our interests but because he defiles the atmosphere we breathe and debases the currency of our kind.

— A. G. GARDINER

1143. Whenever I hear a man or woman express hatred for any race, I wonder just what it is in themselves they hate so much. You can always be sure of this: You cannot express hatred for anything or anybody unless you make use of the supply of hatred within yourself. The only hatred you can express is your own personal possession. To hate is to be enslaved by evil.

— THOMAS DREIER

1144. When we hate our enemies, we give them power over us—power over our sleep, our appetites, our blood pressure, our health, and our happiness. Our enemies would dance with joy if they surmised that they worry and lacerate us. Our hatred is not hurting them at all; it only turns our own days and nights into a hellish turmoil.

— Author unknown

Hazard

1145. A fallen lighthouse is more dangerous than a reef.

Health

1146. Be true to your teeth and they won't be false to you.

1147. Convalescent: a patient who is still alive.

1148. Gastric ulcer: something you get mountain climbing over molehills.

1149. Hypochondriac: a man who can't leave being well enough alone.

1150. A nice old gentleman of 75 or so went to a physician and requested a general checking-up as to the state of his health.

After looking him over thoroughly, the doctor smilingly reported that everything was fine and shipshape. "Tell me," he asked as the old chap paid his fee, "have you followed any regular regimen which would account for your excellent physical condition?"

"Well, it's this way," his patient replied. "When I was married some 50 years ago, I entered into an agreement with my wife to the effect that whenever I lost my temper and began to blow off steam, she was to remain silent. When she, on the other hand, lost her temper I agreed to leave the house. Well, for over 50 years I have enjoyed a fine outdoor life, which no doubt accounts for my present condition."

Helpfulness

1151. A mother had been lecturing her small son, stressing that we are in this world to help others. He considered this for some time, then asked somberly: "What are the others here for?"

1152. A helping hand to one in trouble is often like a switch on a railroad track—an inch between wreck and smooth-rolling prosperity.

— HENRY WARD BEECHER

1153. There is a loftier ambition than merely to stand high in the world. It is to stoop down and lift mankind a little higher.

— HENRY VAN DYKE

Heredity

1154. Heredity is an omnibus in which all our ancestors ride, and every now and then one of them puts his head out and embarrasses us.

— OLIVER WENDELL HOLMES

Hidden talent

1155. Although men are accused of not knowing their own weakness, yet perhaps few know their own strength. It is in men as in soils, where sometimes there is a vein of gold which the owner knows not of.

— JONATHAN SWIFT

History — historical

1156. After you have heard two eye-witness accounts of an auto accident, you begin to wonder about history.

1157. Historic continuity with the past is not a duty, it is only a necessity.

— Justice Oliver Wendell Holmes

1158. Anybody who thinks the past can't be altered is rather naive about historians.

1159. History after all is the story of people: a statement that might seem too obvious to be worth making if it were not for the fact that history so often is presented in terms of vast incomprehensible forces moving far under the surface, carrying human beings along, helpless, and making them conform to a pattern whose true shape they never see. The pattern does exist, often enough, and it is important to trace it. Yet it is good to remember that it is the people who make the pattern, not the other way around.

— Bruce Catton, *American Heritage,*
Vol. VI, Number One

1160. All the historical books which contain no lies are extremely tedious.

— Anatole France

1161. History repeats itself. That's one of the things wrong with history.

— Clarence Darrow

Hobby

1162. A man who has no hobby does not know all the good that is to be drawn out of life. A hobby is a happy medium between a passion and a monomania.

Hollywood

1163. Hollywood pal: someone who is always around when he needs you.

Home

1164. A lot of homes have been spoiled by inferior desecrators.

— Frank Lloyd Wright quoted in *Time*

1165. When Charles (Hell-and-Maria) Dawes was Ambassador to Great Britain the story was told of his buying a newspaper from a London newsboy who charged him the usual price of a penny.

"I'd have to pay double the price for this paper in America," Dawes remarked.

"Well, guv'nor," said the newsboy, "you can pay me double if it'll make you feel at 'ome."

1166. I do not care so much where, as with whom, I live. If the right folks are with me I can manage to get a good deal of happiness in the city or in the country. After all, a palace without affection is a poor hovel, and the meanest hut with love in it is a palace for the soul.

— ROBERT G. INGERSOLL

Honesty see also Integrity

1167. The more honesty a man has, the less he affects the air of a saint.

— JOHANN KASPAR LAVATER

Honor

1168. You can be deprived of your money, your job and your home by someone else, but remember that no one can ever take away your honor.

— WILLIAM LYON PHELPS

1169. An old Springfield neighbor of Lincoln, after an evening at the White House, asked, "How does it feel to be President of the United States?"

"You have heard," said Lincoln, "about the man tarred and feathered and ridden out of town on a rail? A man in the crowd asked him how he liked it, and his reply was that, if it wasn't for the honor of the thing, he would rather walk."

— From *Abraham Lincoln: The War Years* by CARL SANDBURG. Copyright, 1939, by Harcourt, Brace and Company, Inc.

Hope

1170. There is nothing so well known as that we should not expect something for nothing, but we all do, and call it Hope.

— EDGAR W. HOWE

HORSE SENSE

Horse sense

1171. Horse sense is when a fellow knows enough to stay away from a nag.

Hospital

1172. After two days in the hospital I took a turn for the nurse.

— W. C. FIELDS

Hotel

1173. Joe E. Lewis once spent a night at Saratoga's old Grand Union Hotel. The railroad was directly below, and a switching engine kept shunting cars back and forth incessantly. Finally Joe summoned the night clerk. "Maybe you can tell me," he suggested, "what time this hotel reaches Chicago!"

— BENNETT CERF in *Saturday Review*

Human nature

1174. *A sad commentary on human nature:* When a person says, "I'm only human," he's apologizing rather than boasting.

1175. A great feast was to be held in a medieval village. To insure its success a huge cask was built into which each participant agreed to pour a bottle of wine.

"If I fill my bottle with water," soliloquized one, "and empty the water into the barrel with others, surely it won't be noticed."

The big day arrived. All the villagers assembled. The great cask was tapped. Lo, only water flowed forth.

Each of the villagers had also reasoned, "My bit won't be missed."

— From *Anecdotes for All Occasions* (Droke House)

Humility see also Pride

1176. The proud man counts his newspaper clippings—the humble man his blessings.

— BISHOP FULTON J. SHEEN

1177. It is no great thing to be humble when you are brought low; but to be humble when you are praised is a great and rare attainment.

— St. Bernard

1178. Humility is not self-contempt but the truth about ourselves coupled with a reverence for others . . . A man who is 6 ft., 4 in's., is not humble when he says: "Oh, no, really I am only 4 ft., 4 in's."—because that is not the truth; neither is an opera singer humble when she says, "Oh, I really am nothing in the singing profession"; neither is a beautiful person humble when she says: "I am really ugly."

Such protestations against the truth are marks of pride, rather than humility. Humility in such cases consists of the acknowledgment of the truth that we have received the gifts for which we are praised.

— Bishop Fulton J. Sheen

1179. Humility, like darkness, reveals the heavenly lights.

— Henry David Thoreau

Husband and wife see also Marriage

1180. A good husband is merely a good son grown up.

— Mary Antin

1181. The wife of a careless man is almost a widow.

— Hungarian proverb

Hypochondria

1182. Dr. Oliver Wendell Holmes once warned a hypochondriac patient found reading up on his disease: "Look out! or you'll die of a misprint some day."

Hypocrisy

1183. The only vice which cannot be forgiven is hypocrisy. The repentance of a hypocrite is itself hypocrisy.

— William Hazlitt

1184. If the world despises hypocrites, what must be the estimate of them in heaven?

— Madame Marie Jeanne Roland

HYPOCRISY

1185. Hypocrite: a man who sets good examples when he has an audience.

1186. Hypocrite: one who talks on principles and acts on interest.

1187. The worst sort of hypocrite and liar is the man who lies to himself in order to feel at ease.

— HILAIRE BELLOC

1188. A man who hides behind the hypocrite is smaller than the hypocrite.

— W. E. BIEDERWOLF

Idea — ideas

1189. A good idea that is not shared with others will gradually fade away and bear no fruit, but when it is shared it lives forever because it is passed on from one person to another and grows as it goes.

— LOWELL FILLMORE, *Things to Be Remembered*

1190. If you have on hand (in your store), on July 1st, a pair of socks, you will have them still on hand on August 1st, or else cash in your till to correspond, assuming honest and successful management. But, in spite of unlimited honesty and efficiency, you have no guarantee that an idea on hand on July 1st may not have been simply removed by August 1st without any equivalent remaining on hand.

— From *The Standardization of Error,* by
V. STEFANSSON (Kegan Paul, Trench,
Trubner & Co., Ltd., London)

1191. A fresh mind keeps the body fresh. Take in the ideas of the day, drain off those of yesterday. As to the morrow, time enough to consider it when it becomes today.

— EDWARD G. BULWER-LYTTON

1192. Talking about a famous Hollywood Producer who hasn't had a hit film in years, Ben Hecht commented: "He can compress the most words into the smallest ideas of any man I ever met."

1193. Ideas are like children; your own are very wonderful.

Ideal – ideals

1194. If some people lived up to their ideals they would be forever stooping.

1195. Show me the man you honor, and I will show you the kind of a man you are, for it shows me what your ideal of manhood is, and what kind of a man you long to be.
— THOMAS CARLYLE

1196. A man's ideal, like his horizon, is constantly receding from him as he advances towards it.
— W. G. T. SHEDD

Identification

1197. *Boss:* "Why did you engage that man as cashier? Didn't you notice he squints, has a crooked nose and protruding ears?"
Personnel manager: "Of course I did. But that will make him so easy to identify if anything ever goes wrong."

Idleness

1198. To rest is to rust.

1199. Idleness is emptiness; the tree in which the sap is stagnant, remains fruitless.
— HOSEA BALLOU, *Sermons*

Imagination

1200. A panic is a sudden desertion of us, and a going over to the enemy of our imagination.
— CHRISTIAN BOVEE

1201. Man consists of body, mind and imagination. His body is faulty, his mind is untrustworthy, but his imagination has made his life on this planet an intense practice of all the lovelier energies.
— JOHN MASEFIELD

Immaturity

1202. You are only young once, but you can stay immature indefinitely.

175

Immortality

1203.   Death cannot be and is not the end of life.

Man transcends death in many altogether naturalistic fashions. He may be immortal biologically, through his children; in thought, through the survival of his memory; in influence, by virtue of the continuance of his personality as a force among those who come after him; and ideally, through his identification with the timeless things of the spirit.

When Judaism speaks of immortality it has in mind all these. But its primary meaning is that man contains something independent of the flesh and surviving it; his consciousness and moral capacities, his essential personality; a soul.

— MILTON STEINBERG, *Basic Judaism*

Impatience

1204.   Impatient people are like the bees; they kill themselves in stinging others.

— FRANCIS BACON

Importance

1205.   It isn't the common man at all who is important; it's the uncommon man.

— LADY NANCY ASTOR

Impossible

1206.   The one thing you can't saw is sawdust.

— Editorial in *Chicago Tribune*

1207.   Impossible is a word to be found only in the dictionary of fools.

— NAPOLEON BONAPARTE

Impractical

1208.   One who has both feet firmly planted in the air.

Improvement

1209.   Where we cannot invent, we may at least improve; we may give somewhat of novelty to that which was old, condensation to that which was diffuse, perspicuity to that which was obscure, and currency to that which was recondite.

— CHARLES C. COLTON

Impulsiveness

1210. He who loses his head is usually the last one to miss it.

Inaccuracy

1211. I do not mind lying, but I hate inaccuracy.

— SAMUEL BUTLER

Inattention

1212. A wandering mind gathers nothing, and inattention often leads to a false move which may ruin the cause.

— RICHARD HARRIS, *Illustrations in Advocacy*
(Stevens and Haynes, London)

1213. The English tell the story of the Irish counsellor who had developed an inexhaustible argument upon an exhaustible case. After he had gone on for four hours the presiding judge of the court said to him, "Mr. Murphy, is it any good for you to continue? Everything you say goes in at one ear and comes out of the other."

"Why not," said the counsel, "there is little enough to stop it."

1214. One morning Mose came to work with a black eye, a swollen lip, and other troubles. "Mose," asked his boss, "what in the world happened to you?"

"Well, boss, I was a-talkin' when I shoulda been a-listenin'."

— EDISON MARSHALL

1215. At a wedding reception in Charlotte, N.C., a friend of the groom decided to find out whether anyone in the receiving line knew what the hundreds of people filing past were saying. As he moved along, he purred, "My grandmother just died today."

"How nice!" "Thank you so much!" "How sweet of you to say so!"—were the responses to his announcement. No one had the

INATTENTION

slightest idea what he said, least of all the groom, who exclaimed
jovially, "It's about time you took the same step, old man!"

— UNA TAYLOR

1216. To demonstrate how little attention people pay to actual
words, a hostess said smilingly as she passed the cakes at a tea:
"These green ones are colored with Paris green, the pink have strych-
nine in them." Every guest unconcernedly took a cake and thanked
her.

— GLADYS BORCHERS, *Living Speech*
(Harcourt, Brace and Company)

Incentive

1217. A multi-millionaire, being interviewed about his self-
made fortune, commented: "I never hesitate to give full credit to
my wife for her assistance."

"In what way did she help?" the reporter asked.

"Well, if you want the whole truth," replied the wealthy man, "I
was curious to find out if there was any income she couldn't live
beyond."

— JOE HARRINGTON

Inconsistency

1218. Millionaire: a man who travels between his air-conditioned home and air-conditioned office in an air-conditioned car,
then pays $50 to go over to the steam room at the club and sweat.

Indecision

1219. Of all the small annoyances that weight our mental buoy-
ances,
No chaff or cold derision is so sad as indecision.

— SIR WILLIAM S. GILBERT, *The Bab Ballads*

1220. You seldom get what you go after unless you know in
advance what you want. Indecision has often given an advantage to
the other fellow because he did his thinking beforehand.

— MAURICE SWITZER

Indifference

1221. Too many people don't care what happens so long as it doesn't happen to them.

— WILLIAM HOWARD TAFT

1222. The worst sin toward our fellow creatures is not to hate them but to be indifferent to them; that's the essence of inhumanity.

— GEORGE BERNARD SHAW

Indispensability

1223. You cannot afford to make the mistake of thinking you cannot be replaced. And your employer cannot afford to have a man around that he cannot afford to do without.

— FRANK IRVING FLETCHER

1224. History records only one indispensable man—Adam.

1225. Whenever I get to feeling indispensable, I take another look at the old saddle hanging in the garage.

— J. J. CLAYTON, *Corydon* (Iowa) *Times Republican*

Individual

1226. This sovereign faith of ours in the freedom and dignity of the individual is infinitely more than a dry and lifeless philosophic doctrine. It is the nerve and the fiber of our very laws. The supreme ideal—not merely the votes of so many Senators or Congressmen—is what sends aid to drought-stricken areas, guarantees an income to farmers, banishes needless restrictions on individual enterprise, guards the free union of workers, extends the protection of social insurance to the aged and to the needy. This sovereign ideal we believe to be the very source of the greatness and the genius of America.

— DWIGHT D. EISENHOWER, address at Boston Gardens, 1953

Industry — industrious see also *Business*

1227. A man who gives his children habits of industry provides for them better than by giving them a fortune.

— RICHARD WHATELY

INDUSTRY — INDUSTRIOUSNESS

1228. Every industrious man, in every lawful calling, is a useful man.—And one principal reason why men are so often useless is that they neglect their own profession or calling, and divide and shift their attention among a multitude of objects and pursuits.

— NATHANIEL EMMONS

1229. The more we do, the more we can do; the busier we are, the more leisure we have.

— WILLIAM HAZLITT

1230.
Sitting still and wishing
Makes no person great.
The good Lord sends the fishing
But you must dig the bait.

Influence

1231. You can only make others better by being good yourself.

— HUGH R. HAWEIS

1232. The work an unknown good man has done is like a vein of water flowing hidden underground, secretly making the ground green.

— THOMAS CARLYLE, *Essays*

1233. It would be difficult to exaggerate the degree to which we are influenced by those we influence.

Information

1234. "Mummy," asked the ten-year-old daughter of an English friend, "how did Princess Elizabeth know she was going to have a baby?"

Before the mother could reply, the younger daughter, aged five, piped up scornfully, "Well, she can read, can't she? It was in all the papers."

1235. I attribute the little I know to my not having been ashamed to ask for information, and to my rule of conversation with all descriptions of man on those topics that form their own peculiar professions and pursuits.

— JOHN LOCKE

Ingenuity see also *Resourcefulness*

1236. On dull Mondays a certain grocer in Slinger, Wisconsin, had a novel way of boosting business. An alarm clock, its face covered, was set for an unknown hour. Whenever the alarm went off, the merchant made no charge for groceries being purchased at the moment. Curious and hopeful housewives were thus encouraged to come early and prolong their shopping.

1237. In the lobby of a large New York office building are two identical candy booths, selling the same candies and managed by two equally pleasant girls. Yet one always has twice as many customers as the other. I asked the more successful girl what her magic formula was.

"It's all in the scooping," she said. "An indifferent scoop usually puts too much candy on the scales. That means you have to take some of it away, and the customer feels cheated. I'm always careful to scoop too little the first time and then add a little more. The customer thinks he's getting a bonus. It's amazing how business has increased."

1238. A Hollywood photographer puts vanity to work in collecting overdue bills from famed female patrons. With his past-due notice he encloses an unretouched proof of the customer and requests permission to exhibit it in his studio window as a sample of his work. The patron usually shows up next day, cash in hand.

— IRVING HOFFMAN in *Coronet*

1239. Cornelia Otis Skinner declares that as a child she was so ugly that her mother used to weep. "But I did have a genius for something even then," she says. "I was good at trade and I made money from Dad. He thought I was a good correspondent. I was; for every letter I wrote him, I received an answer. I cut the 'Cornelia' from the address on the envelope containing his reply, and sold the 'Otis Skinner' as my father's autograph. Sometimes it brought a dime, sometimes a quarter."

1240. A young lady applying for a position in a large establishment was given a very lengthy application blank to fill out. On the last page of the blank was a boxed space reserved for the employing

INGENUITY

official to fill in the amount of salary to be paid. Above it were the words: "Do Not Write in This Space."

The applicant, endowed with a sense of humor, wrote in: "Do Right in This Space."

She got the job.

1241. Because popcorn boxes littered his movie theater after Saturday matinees, the manager decided to take steps. Numbering each box, he announced one Saturday afternoon that there would be a prize for the holder of the lucky number, drawn after the show. As the youngsters left the theater, they showed their boxes, dumped them into a well-marked receptacle, and the winner collected his prize. The scheme has been working well every week since.

—HELEN H. BOILEAU quoted in
The Reader's Digest

1242. A manufacturing plant in the Panama Canal Zone employed 20 local women. After a few months they all quit their jobs. Offers of shorter hours and more pay failed to entice them back— they had earned enough money to satisfy their wants.

The problem was solved when the manager wired a mail-order house to send each woman a catalog showing its products. All 20 women returned to their jobs.

1243. Alexander, the world conqueror, came across a simple people in Africa who knew not war. He lingered to learn their ways. Two citizens appeared before their chief with this point of dispute: One had bought a piece of land and discovered a treasure in it; he claimed that this belonged to the seller, and wished to return it. The seller, on the other hand, declared he sold the land with all it might contain. So he refused to accept the treasure. The chief, turning to the buyer, said: "Thou hast a son?" "Yes." And addressing the seller, "Thou hast a daughter?" "Yes." "Then marry one to the other and make the treasure their portion."

— A Talmudic story

1244. There's a brilliant future ahead for the boy who found a purse containing a ten-dollar bill. He returned the money to the owner—but first changed the bill to ten ones.

1245. Two London "barrow boys," trying to sell their fruit on the same street at the same prices, were doing very little business—

182

until tney began to trade on everyone's desire for a "bargain." One boy raised his prices a few pennies. Fruits in the less expensive barrow began to sell rapidly—and its owner restocked in a side street from the other barrow. This way both boys sold nearly everything they had in a morning.

1246. Around the Pentagon they tell the story of the air force pilot who was assigned to fly a hazardous mission over the jungle. He was given an escape and invasion kit to help him in case he crashed.

He pointed to two vials in the kit, one filled with a colorless liquid and the other with an amber liquid. "What are those for?" he asked the intelligence officer.

"Why, they will help you get out of the jungle," replied the G-2 officer. "One is filled with gin and the other with vermouth. All you have to do when you are lost in the jungle is to start mixing a martini. No sooner do you start that, when someone is sure to appear and start telling you that you don't know how to mix a martini. Then you ask him the direction to the nearest town."

— Chicago Tribune

1247. A trumpet player we know never hesitates to hock his watch or clock. He explains, "I live in an apartment house, and when I want to know what time it is during the night, all I have to do is start running the scales on my trumpet, and it ain't long before somebody will holler: 'What the h--l is the idea of playing the cornet at 3:30 in the morning?"

— Ollie James in the Cincinnati Enquirer

1248. A New Orleans woman planning a cocktail party thought the invitations ought to read "from six to eight," but her husband objected that this would appear to be telling the guests when to go home. So the invitations merely stated "cocktails at six," with the inevitable result. Long after midnight the party was still going strong.

Shortly after one, the cops arrived. Somebody in the neighborhood had complained, and the racket would have to stop. The host was outraged, said he couldn't imagine one of his neighbors making a complaint. But the sergeant was adamant. A complaint had been received.

That broke up the party. As the last guest filed out, the hostess turned to her husband and murmured: "I wonder who called the police?"

Replied her weary husband: "I did."

— THOMAS GRIFFIN in *The New Orleans Item*

1249. Mr. Holt, the proprietor of a cigar store, was worried. His competitor was attracting crowds to his window by employing a vivacious Spanish girl to sit in it and roll cigars, meanwhile "giving the eye" to the boys outside. Mr. Holt hit upon an idea. Next morning a blonde was rolling cigars in his window—but with her back to the street. There soon was a crowd—*inside* the store.

1250. A customs inspector at San Ysidro, Calif., once told of stopping a young Mexican bicycling across the border with two large sacks draped across the handle bars. "What you got in those sacks, Miguel?" asked the inspector.

"Sand."

"How about dumping the sand on the ground, Miguel?"

"O. K."

After the sixth trip, customs sternly asked the youth, "Come, now, what are you taking across the border, young man?" And got this confession:

"New bicycles."

— *Chicago Tribune*

1251. *Husband:* "Why is that big transfer truck backed up to the door?"

Wife: "The furniture people are here to repossess the piano."

Husband: "But I gave you the money for the next installment."

Wife: "Yes, I know, dear, but don't say anything to the men yet. I decided I'd rather have the piano in the downstairs sitting room than upstairs, but I didn't want to pay all that money for getting it moved. I'll pay the installment as soon as they get the piano downstairs."

Ingratitude

1252. My chief memory of life is the ingratitude of those to whom I have given myself. It is only toward what they cannot have or own that people feel grateful. Give them something, and contempt for the gift grows in them.

— BEN HECHT in *A Child of the Century*
(Simon & Schuster, INC.)

1253. Not to return one good office for another is inhuman; but to return evil for good is diabolical.

— SENECA

Initiative

1254. A famous admiral always encouraged his officers to act on their own initiative.

One day he received a message from one of the captains in his fleet: "Am lost in fog. Shall I proceed to destination or return to base?"

The admiral replied: "Yes."

Soon after, another message arrived: "Do you mean yes, I should proceed to destination or, yes, I should return to base?"

This time the reply was: "No."

1255. Men who will do things without being told draw the most wages.

— EDWIN H. STUART

Innocence

1256. Innocence needs no eloquence.

1257. It is better that ten guilty persons escape than that one innocent suffer.

— SIR WILLIAM BLACKSTONE, *Commentaries*

Insincerity

1258. Philanderer: a man who considers himself too good to be true.

Installment purchase see also *Credit*

1259. Car sickness: that feeling you get every month when the payment falls due.

1260. Many people who buy on time forget to pay that way.

Institution

1261. An institution is the lengthened shadow of one man.

— RALPH WALDO EMERSON, *Essay, Self Reliance*

INSULT

Insult

1262. He who allows himself to be insulted deserves to be so; and insolence, if unpunished, increases!

— PIERRE CORNEILLE, *Heraclius*

Insurance

1263. A 97-year-old man presented himself at the insurance office and said he wished to take out a policy on his life. He filled out an application blank but was very much annoyed when he was turned down.

"You folks are making a big mistake," he said, "if you look over your statistics you'll discover that mighty few men die after they're 97."

1264. The insistent salesman had his prospect backed up against the wall. "Take our accident insurance policy," he insisted.

The prospect still had some fight left. "Why should I?" he asked defensively.

"Listen!" boasted the salesman. "One month ago a man took out a policy with us. The other day he broke his neck and we paid him $5,000. Now think: Tomorrow you may be the lucky one!"

1265. Dave Randall, of Scribner's Rare Book Department, tells the story of the owner of one of the 13 copies of the American Declaration of Independence, who stubbornly refused all Randall's blandishments until one Friday he telephoned out of the blue and said he had changed his mind. The next day Mrs. Randall drove her triumphant husband out to Greenwich, Conn. In his library the old gentleman handed them a beautiful morocco slipcase, and Mr. Randall presented him with a check.

"That check's not certified," the old gentleman said brusquely. "That's no way to do business, Mr. Randall."

"But it's not mine; it's Mr. Scribner's personal check."

"Can't help that. And what were you intending to do with my property until Monday?"

"I was going to take it back to my house."

"Might easily burn down."

"Well, it hasn't for 150 years," said Mr. Randall, getting rather impatient.

186

"Young man, that won't stop it burning down tomorrow. I will bring the document in by train on Monday—insured all the way—and bring it to your office and you will then hand me a certified check."

"Pernickety old fool," said Mr. Randall to his wife as they drove away.

On Monday the happiest old man in America handed over the document and took the check. He had just been told that on Sunday Mr. Randall's house burned to the ground.

— "Atticus" in *The Sunday Times* (London)

1266. Some weeks after receiving £400 compensation for the loss of her jewelry an elderly woman informed an Auckland insurance company that she had found the missing property in a cupboard. "I didn't think it would be fair to keep both the jewels and the money, so I thought you would be pleased to know that I have sent the £400 to the Red Cross," she wrote.

— Christchurch, New Zealand, *Star-Sun*

Integrity see also *Honesty*

1267. Nothing more completely baffles one who is full of tricks and duplicity than straightforward and simple integrity in another.

— CHARLES C. COLTON

1268. A country is not made by the number of square miles it contains, but by the number of square people it contains.

Intelligence

1269. Human intelligence is millions of years old, but it doesn't seem to act its age.

1270. The man of intelligence understands the value of sound knowledge and provides himself with it. The ignorant despise knowledge and are punished with "poor luck."

— W. D. HOARD

Interference

1271. A man who lives in a Nob Hill hotel noticed that the

contents of a bottle of fine bourbon were dropping at a fast rate.
So he made a tiny pencil mark on the label opposite the current level.
Returning home that night, he found a note from the chambermaid:
"Please don't put a pencil mark on the bottle, because I don't want
to have to put water in such good whisky."

— HERB CAEN in *The San Francisco Chronicle*

1272. When you find a man who knows his job and is willing
to take responsibility, keep out of his way and don't bother him with
unnecessary supervision. What you may think is co-operation is
nothing but interference.

— THOMAS DREIER

Interruption

1273. When your work speaks for itself, don't interrupt.

Intolerance see also *Discrimination*

1274. It is not a merit to tolerate, but rather a crime to be
intolerant.

— PERCY BYSSHE SHELLEY

1275. "What did the puritans come to this country for?" asked
a teacher in a class in American history.

"To worship in their own way, and make other people do the
same," was the reply.

1276. The most ominous sign of our time is the indication of
the growth of an intolerant spirit. It is the more dangerous when
armed, as it usually is, with sincere conviction. . . . Our institutions
were not devised to bring about uniformity of opinion; if they had
been, we might well abandon hope. It is important to remember that
the essential characteristic of true liberty is that under its shelter,
many different types of life and character and opinion and belief
can develop unmolested and unobstructed.

— CHARLES EVANS HUGHES

Introduction of Speaker see also *Public Speaking*

1277. "I had expected to find Mr. Lloyd George a big man in
every sense," playfully remarked the chairman when introducing the

statesman to a meeting, "but you can see for yourselves he is quite small in stature."

Lloyd George was not a bit abashed. "In North Wales from where I come," he remarked, "we measure a man from his chin up. You evidently measure him from his chin down."

1278. Dr. Abraham Cronbach, retired Professor of Social Studies at the Hebrew Union College, often tells about the way he was once introduced to a Negro audience. Meaning to praise the speaker for his understanding of Negro problems, the introducer said, "Dr. Cronbach may be white, but, my friends, his heart is black."

1279. "It affords me great pleasure," began Chauncey M. Depew in introducing Dr. Vincent to a New York audience, "to present the president of the University of Minnesota, popularly acclaimed as the 'Cyclone of the Northwest.'"

"I appreciate the designation," said Dr. Vincent in arising, "by the most eminent wind authority of the East."

Intuition

1280. Intuition: that which enables a woman to put two and two together and get your number.

1281. Intuition: the ability women have to read between the lines on a blank page.

Invention

1282. A lady shopping in the garden department of a local department store noticed an object strange to her and asked the clerk what it was.

"It's a sundial," he told her, and patiently explained how the sun's shadow moving across the dial would indicate the time of day.

"My," said the lady, "what will they think of next!"

— FRANK ROSSITER in *The Savannah Morning News*

1283. People think of the inventor as a screwball, but no one ever asks the inventor what he thinks of other people.

— CHARLES F. KETTERING

Isms

1284. *Socialism:* If you have two cows, you give one to your neighbor.

Communism: If you have two cows, you give them to the government and the government gives you some milk.

Fascism: If you have two cows, you keep the cows and give the milk to the government; then the government sells you some milk.

New Dealism: If you have two cows, you shoot one and milk the other, then you pour the milk down the drain.

Nazism: If you have two cows, the government shoots you and keeps the cows.

Capitalism: If you have two cows, you sell one and buy a bull.

Janitor

1285. I am reminded of the story of the two janitors in a large city office building: They were broommates; they even swept together; in fact they were dust inseparable.

Jealousy

1286. One often wonders why a man who hasn't kissed his wife in five years will take a poke at a man who does it for him.

1287. The grass may look greener next door, but it's just as hard to cut.

Joint effort

1288. A flea and an elephant walked side by side over a little bridge. Said the flea to the elephant, after they had crossed it: "Boy, we sure did shake that thing."

Journalism see *Newspaper*

Joy

1289. Real joy comes not from ease or riches or from the praise of men, but from doing something worth while.

— SIR WILFRED GRENFELL

Judge — judges see also *Law*

1290. Judge Jeffreys, of notorious memory, pointing with his cane to a man who was about to be tried, remarked: "There is a rogue at the end of my cane," and the man to whom he pointed, looking at him, said: "At which end, my Lord."

1291. The "posies" English judges carry even to this day as they proceed to the bench are inspiring bits of pageantry symbolic of the majesty of the law. Unfortunately, also, they are reminders of a time when the courts tried to ward off disease by smelling nosegays of sweet flowers and measured justice on hunch, superstition or the need to replenish the king's coffers.

— JAMES V. BENNETT, "Operation Assize,"
Journal of the American Judicature Society

1292. The upright judge condemns the crime but does not hate the criminal.

— SENECA

Judgment

1293. A businessman's judgment is no better than his information.

— R. P. LAMONT

1294. Do not condemn the judgment of another because it differs from your own. You may both be wrong.

— DANDEMIS

Justice see also *Law*

1295. He who decides a case without hearing the other side, though he decide justly, cannot be considered just.

— SENECA, *Medea CXCIX*

1296. A miscarriage of mercy is as much to be guarded against as a miscarriage of justice.

— ROBERT LYND in the *New Statesman*

1297. He who allows himself to be a worm must not complain if he is trodden upon.

1298. Justice: what we get when the decision is in our favor.

—JOHN W. RAPER, *What This World Needs*

Juvenile Delinquency see also *Delinquency—Crime*

1299. Juvenile delinquency can be prevented. It is not a scourge which rules with an inevitable necessity. One of the best weapons with which to attack this malady is religious training. The young boy and girl trained in the teachings of the Bible have a moral reliance which serves as a compass for everyday living. They know the difference between right and wrong, good and evil. They are able to conquer the temptations of life.

—J. EDGAR HOOVER

1300. We wouldn't have so many delinquents if their mothers hugged them and kissed them, and when necessary spanked them . . . A child who knows that he is loved can accept discipline, even the woodshed type.

—BENJAMIN FINE, *1,000,000 Delinquents* (The World Publishing Company)

1301. I'm convinced that every boy, in his heart, would rather steal second base than an automobile.

—JUSTICE TOM C. CLARK

1302. Reform schools are not reform schools, but crucibles wherein boil the worst instincts of humanity and where innocence vanishes and insolence takes its place.

1303. One way to curb delinquency is to take parents off the street at night.

—MORRIE GALLANT quoted in *The Reader's Digest*

1304. Juvenile delinquency: modern term for what adults did as kids.

Kindness

1305. When you have anything to communicate that will distress the heart of the person whom it concerns, be silent, in order that he may hear it from someone else.

—SAADI, *The Gulistan*

1306. True kindness only exists between those who care nothing for each other: it is love that leads us to act well towards our friends and, with regard to our enemies, self-respect that bids us wish them well.

— COMTESSE DIANE

1307. As "unkindness has no remedy at law," let its avoidance be with you a point of honor.

— HOSEA BALLOU

1308. Kindness consists in loving people more than they deserve.

1309. Kindness is the oil that takes the friction out of life.

Kiss — kissing

1310. The difference between kissing your sister and somebody else: about 45 seconds.

1311. Kiss: a contraction of the mouth due to an enlargement of the heart.

1312. Kiss: a noun, though often used as a conjunction; it is never declined; it is more common than proper and is used in the plural and agrees with all genders.

1313. Kiss: the anatomical juxtaposition of two orbicularis oris muscles in a state of contraction.

1314. A man may sometimes be forgiven the kiss to which he is not entitled, but never the kiss he has not the initiative to claim.

1315. Men who kiss and tell are not half as bad as those who kiss and exaggerate.

1316. Merle Oberon, the actress, visiting the wounded in London, asked one soldier, "Did you kill a Nazi?" The soldier said he had. "With which hand?" Miss Oberon asked. She decorated his right hand with a kiss.

Then she asked the next patient, "Did *you* kill a Nazi?"

"I sure did!" came the ready answer. "I bit 'im to death!"

1317. A kiss is a pleasant reminder that two heads are better than one.

1318. Kissing a girl is like opening a bottle of olives—if you get one the rest come easy.

1319. All girls act the same when they want a kiss. The difference consists in their actions when they want another one.

Know-how

1320. A New York socialite came into the salon of Walter Florell, mad milliner to movie stars and socialites, and announced that she needed a hat at once for a cocktail party. Walter took a couple of yards of ribbon, twisted it around, put it on her head and said, "There is your hat, madam." The lady looked in the mirror and exclaimed, "It's wonderful."

"Twenty-five dollars," said Walter.

"But that's too much for a couple of yards of ribbon!" she gasped.

Florell unwound the ribbon and handed it to her saying, "The ribbon, madam, is free."

— ERSKINE JOHNSON

Knowledge see also Wisdom

1321. Most men believe that it would benefit them if they could get a little from those who *have* more. How much more would it benefit them if they would learn a little from those who *know* more.

— WILLIAM J. H. BOETCKER

1322. Knowledge comes by taking things apart, analysis. But wisdom comes by putting things together.

— JOHN A. MORRISON, president, Anderson College, *The Role of Religion in Education*

1323. He who knows not, and knows not that he
knows not, is a fool. Shun him.
He who knows not, and knows that he knows not
is simple. Teach him.
He who knows, and knows not that he knows,
is asleep. Waken him.
He who knows, and knows that he knows is
wise. Follow him.

— Arabian proverb

1324. Strange how much you've got to know before you know how little you know.

1325. Knowledge is of two kinds. We know a subject ourselves or we know where we can find information upon it.

— DR. SAMUEL JOHNSON

1326. It is the province of knowledge to speak, and it is the privilege of wisdom to listen.

— OLIVER WENDELL HOLMES, *The Poet at the Breakfast Table*

1327. Knowledge that sleeps doth die.

— BEN JONSON

1328. Knowledge is power—if you know it about the right person.

1329. It's what you learn after you know it all that counts.

1330. There can be no knowledge and no truth without accurate facts. But all the facts in the world do not add up to knowledge.

— DOROTHY THOMPSON, *Matrix*

1331. Knowledge always desires increase: it is like fire, which must first be kindled by some external agent, but which will afterwards propagate itself.

— DR. SAMUEL JOHNSON

1332. It is a platitude to say you can't give what you don't have, but the platitude is true. You can't. Nevertheless, we often make the mistake of trying to give what we don't have. There are those, for example, who think they know everything about everything and if they do not know they pretend. They can give advice on any subject. Now and then, of course, they reveal the fact they are speaking with authority from a vacuum of knowledge.

Abraham Lincoln was vastly disturbed during the Civil War because he was so often denounced and criticized by people who pretended to be wise on a minimum diet of facts and information. They offered wisdom they did not possess. So, whimsically he told the story of a backwoods traveler lost in a terrific thunderstorm. The rider floundered thru the mud until his horse gave out. Then he stood alone in the middle of the road while lightning streaked and thunder

LABOR

roared around him. One crash seemed to shake the earth underneath, and it brought the traveler to his knees. He was not a praying man but he made a petition short and to the point: "O Lord, if it is all the same to you, give us a little more light and a little less noise."

The points is, we cannot give light or wisdom we do not have, and we do more damage than good when we speak with authority from a vacuum of knowledge and information.

— HAROLD BLAKE WALKER, *Magazine Section,*
Chicago Sunday Tribune

Labor see also *Capital—Work—Effort*

1333. A champion of the working man has never yet been known to die of overwork.

— FROST

1334. Capital is a result of labor, and is used by labor to assist it in further production. Labor is the active and initial force, and labor is therefore the employer of capital.

— HENRY GEORGE, *Progress and Poverty*

1335. Labor is the capital of our workingmen.

— GROVER CLEVELAND, *Message to the*
Congress, December, 1885

Language

1336. Professor Ernest Brennecke of Columbia is credited with inventing a sentence that can be made to have eight different meanings by placing the word "only" in all possible positions in the sentence: "I hit him in the eye yesterday."

Laughter

1337. Laugh, and the world laughs with you; weep, and they give you the laugh.

— O. HENRY, *The Count and the*
Wedding Guest

1338. The vulgar often laugh, but seldom smile; whereas well-bred people often smile, but seldom laugh.

— LORD CHESTERFIELD

1339. I laugh because I must not cry.

— ABRAHAM LINCOLN

1340. Laugh, and the world laughs with you;
Weep, and you weep alone.
For the sad old earth must borrow its mirth,
But has troubles enough of its own.

— ELLA WHEELER WILCOX

1341. He who laughs—lasts.

— Norwegian proverb

1342. Like all explosives, laughter is a powerful and dangerous thing. Laughter detects the impostors. It preserves the sane and the normal.

— MARTIN ARMSTRONG

1343. With the fearful strain that is on me night and day, if I did not laugh I should die.

— ABRAHAM LINCOLN

1344. Laughter is a weapon more terrible than a bullet and travels further. Long after one forgets what was said, one will be unable to forget that laughter was set loose in the air.

— Paraphrased from a short story by
L. G. BARNARD

1345. The human race has only one really effective weapon and that is laughter.

— MARK TWAIN

1346. Max Eastman once asked Charlie Chaplin what it was in his pictures that made people laugh, and he said, "It's telling them the truth of things. For instance, when I walk up and slap a *grande dame* who gave me a contemptuous look, it's the right way to behave. They can't admit it, but they laugh because they know it's true!"

Law — lawyer see also *Legal—Courts—Legislation*

1347. A lawyer had his portrait taken in his favorite attitude—standing with his hands in his pockets. An old farmer remarked that the portrait would have been more like the lawyer if it had represented him with his hands in another man's pockets, instead of his own.

1348. *Why is a Lawyer Called an Attorney?*

No word has been more persistently persecuted by the pseudoety-mologists than attorney. For nearly two centuries law dictionaries have told us that an attorney was so called because he acts in the turn of somebody else. This is a poor guess that ought not be repeated seriously. Certain other writers, who prefer fiction to fact when dealing with the history of words and who insist in ascribing every word to a romantic source, tell us that attorney originally signified one who appeared in a medieval tourney or tournament and fought in the place of another. That too is sheer nonsense. As a matter of fact there is nothing very romantic in the history of the word. It is derived from Old French àtorné, the past participle of àtourner, being composed of *à, to,* and *tourner,* to turn, and literally meaning to turn to. From this the sense of attorn, assign, attribute or delegate was an easy step. Thus an attorney was originally one appointed or delegated to act for another. The word has been used in this sense in English since the fourteenth century. In Great Britain most of its legal significance has been absorbed by solicitor. Attorney was so often associated with pettifoggers and treated contemptuously that in 1873 it was abolished as a title for British lawyers, being retained only in the title of the attorney-general.

— GEORGE W. STIMPSON

1349. In Ohio a Negro was arrested on a charge of horse theft and was duly indicted and brought to trial. When his day in court came he was taken before the judge and the prosecuting attorney solemnly read the charge in the indictment to him.

The prosecuting attorney put the question: "Are you guilty or not guilty?"

The Negro rolled uneasily in his chair. "Well, boss," he finally said, "ain't dat the very thing we're about to try to find out?"

1350. The judge is condemned when the guilty are acquitted.

— PUBLILIUS SYRUS

1351. It was the boast of Augustus . . . that he found Rome of brick and left it of marble. . . . But how much nobler will be the sovereign's boast when he shall have it to say that he found law dear and left it cheap; found it a sealed book, left it a living letter; found it the patrimony of the rich, left it the inheritance of the poor; found it the two-edged sword of craft and oppression, left it the staff of honesty and the shield of innocence.

— HENRY BROUGHAM

1352. Just laws are no restraint upon the freedom of the good, for the good man desires nothing which a just law will interfere with.

— JAMES A. FROUDE, *Short Stories on Great Subjects*

1353. As civilization progresses, we should improve our laws basically, not superficially. Many things that are lawful are highly immoral and some things which are moral are unlawful.

— HENRY L. DOHERTY

1354. The strictest law sometimes becomes the severest injustice.

— TERENCE, *Heauton Timorumenos*

1355. All clients knew that, with old Abe as their lawyer, they would win their case—if it was fair; if not, that it was a waste of time to take it to him. After listening one day to a would-be client's statement, with his eyes on the ceiling, he swung around in his chair and exclaimed:

"Well, you have a pretty good case in technical law, but a pretty bad one in equity and justice. You'll have to get some other fellow to win this case for you. I couldn't do it. All the time while standing talking to that jury I'd be thinking, 'Lincoln, you're a liar,' and I believe I should forget myself and say it out loud."

1356. The law cannot make all men equal, but they are equal before the law and equally the subject of protection and their duties of enforcement.

— SIR FREDERICK POLLOCK

1357. As a man is known by his associates, so we think may the character of the creditor be known by his attorney: the sharp employ the sharp.

— DOUGLAS JERROLD

1358. A case in which Smith, the eminent counsel, was employed, came up for a hearing late in the afternoon, and Mr. Smith asked the judge to allow it to go over until the following day.

"I have been speaking all day in another court," he said, "and I am rather exhausted." His request was granted.

The clerk called the next case, and immediately a young attorney rose who, for some reason of his own, did not want the case to be tried at that time. He also requested that his case might be postponed.

"Why?" asked the judge coldly.

"May it please Your Honor," the young attorney said, "I, too, am in a state of exhaustion, for I have been listening all day to Mr. Smith."

1359. Ignorance of the law excuses no man: not that all can know the law, but because it is an excuse everyone will plead, and no man can tell how to refute him.

—JOHN SELDEN, *Table Talk*

1360. A businessman who had consulted his attorney for some legal advice ran into an acquaintance to whom he recounted his experience.

"But why spend money for a lawyer?" the friend asked. "Didn't you see all those law books while you sat in his office? Well, the answers were all there. What he told you, you could easily have read for yourself in those very books and you would have saved having to pay a big fee."

"Yes," said the businessman, "that's all very true. The only difference is that the lawyer knows what page it's on."

1361. No man is above the law and no man is below it; nor do we ask any man's permission when we require him to obey it.

—THEODORE ROOSEVELT, *Message to the Congress*, January, 1904

1362. I know no method to secure the repeal of bad or obnoxious laws so effective as their stringent enforcement.

—ULYSSES S. GRANT, *Inaugural Address,* March 4, 1869

1363. I will not say with Lord Hale, that "the law will admit of no rival," . . . but I will say that it is a jealous mistress, and requires a long and constant courtship. It is not to be won by trifling favors, but by lavish homage.

— JUDGE JOSEPH STORY, *The Value and Importance of Legal Studies*

1364. If there were no bad people there could be no good lawyers.

— CHARLES DICKENS, *The Old Curiosity Shop*

1365. Lawyer: a fellow who is willing to go out and spend your last cent to prove he's right.

1366. Lawyer: he who is summoned when a felon needs a friend.

1367. Lawsuit: a machine which you go into as a pig and come out of as a sausage.

— AMBROSE BIERCE, *The Devil's Dictionary*

1368. 'Tis easier to make certain things legal than to make them legitimate.

— NICHOLAS CHAMFORT

1369. Once a lawyer interrupted Rufus Choate, the famous "wizard of the bar" in the midst of a patent case to say: "Look here; there's nothing original in your patent; your client did not come by it naturally."

Choate, surprised, looked up at his opponent. "What does my brother mean by naturally?" he inquired suavely. "We don't do anything naturally. Why, naturally, a man would walk down the street with his pantaloons off!"

The laughter that followed obscured the point of the other lawyer's remarks which was precisely what Choate intended it to do.

— W. ORTON TEWSON in *An Attic Saltshaker*

1370. The man was facing trial and possible imprisonment. "I know the evidence is against me," he told his lawyer, "but I've got $50,000 in cash to fight this case."

"You'll never go to prison with that amount of money," the lawyer assured him.

He didn't. He went there broke.

1371. If we could make a great bonfire of the thousands of laws we have in this country, and start all over again with only the Golden

Rule and the Ten Commandments, I am sure we would get along much better.

— COLEMAN COX

1372. It is to law alone that men owe justice and liberty. It is this salutary organ of the will of all which establishes in civil rights the natural equality between men. It is this celestial voice which dictates to each citizen the precepts of public reason, and teaches him to act according to the rules of his own judgment and not to behave inconsistently with himself. It is with this voice alone that political leaders should speak when they command.

— JEAN JACQUES ROUSSEAU

1373. Discourage litigation. Persuade your neighbor to compromise whenever you can. As a peacemaker the lawyer has a superior opportunity of being a good man. There will still be business enough.

— ABRAHAM LINCOLN

1374. "Judge," said the prisoner, "I don't know what to do."
"Why, what is the matter?" asked the judge.
"I swore to tell the truth, but every time I try some lawyer objects."

1375. A young attorney had been talking for about four hours to a jury, who, when he had finished, felt like lynching him.
His opponent, a grizzled old professional, then arose and, looking sweetly at the judge, said, "Your Honor, I will follow the example of my friend who has just finished and submit the case without argument."

1376. *Lawyer to all male jury:* "Gentlemen, shall this charming young lady be cast into a lonely cell, or shall she return to her beautiful little apartment at 34 Wilson Avenue, telephone 8-7765?"

1377. A well-known lawyer had just finished an important case which he had lost. He was upset and worried and, unable to sleep, he went wandering through the train on which he was a passenger.
By mistake he got into a car that had been reserved for mental patients just as the man in white was checking up on his charges.
"One, two, three, four, five," the man counted, and then he spotted the unfamiliar face of the lawyer. "Who are you?" the attendant asked.

"I'm a lawyer," he answered with sheepish pride.

The male nurse nodded his head with understanding and continued counting ". . . six, seven, eight, nine . . ."

1378. A young lawyer, who had only recently passed his state bar exams and hung out his shingle, got his first client last week and had to appear on his behalf at City Court, before Judge Parella. A fledgling attorney's first court appearance is as big an occasion for him as a young surgeon's first incision, and this fellow waited with bride-like excitement for his case to be called. When the word finally came, he laid his hat and coat on a bench and stepped up before the judge. "Young man, I assume that this is your first experience in this court," the judge said, sternly. With that awful what-have-I-done-wrong feeling, the lawyer said, "Yes, sir." "I thought so," Judge Parella said, fretfully. "Before we proceed, get your hat and coat and put them where you can watch them."

> — Reprinted by permission. © 1940 The New Yorker Magazine, Inc.

1379. It is difficult to make our material condition better by the best laws, but it is easy enough to ruin it by bad laws.

> — THEODORE ROOSEVELT

1380. Lawyers on opposite sides of a case are like the two parts of shears; they cut what comes between them but not each other.

1381. The law itself is on trial in every case as well as the cause before it.

> — JUSTICE HARLAN F. STONE

Laziness

1382. The origin of civilization is man's determination to do nothing for himself which he can get done for him.

> — H. C. BAILEY

1383. Hard work: an accumulation of easy things you didn't do when you should have.

1384. Men are as lazy as they can afford to be, but not as lazy as they want to be.

1385. Don't be misled into believing that somehow the world owes you a living. The boy who believes that his parents, or the government, or anyone else owes him a livelihood and that he can collect it without labor will wake up one day and find himself working for another boy who did not have that belief and, therefore, earned the right to have others work for him.

— GENERAL DAVID SARNOFF

1386. Truth as old as the hills is bound up in the Latin proverb, "Necessity is the mother of invention." It is surprising what a man can do when he has to, and how little most men will do when they don't have to.

— WALTER LINN

1387. The reason a dollar won't do as much as it once did is because people won't do as much for a dollar as they once did.

1388. I was spending the night with a Kentucky mountaineer and his 19-year-old son. They sat silently in front of the fire, smoking their pipes, crossing and uncrossing their legs. Finally after a long period of silence, the father remarked, "Son, step outside and see if it's raining."

Without looking up, the son answered, "Aw, Pop, why don't ye jest call in the dog and see if he's wet?"

— W. K. WELCH quoted in
The Reader's Digest

1389. Some think they are following their natural bent when they are just too lazy to straighten up.

— EARL RINEY

Leadership

1390. Executive ability: deciding quickly and getting somebody else to do the work.

— JOHN GARLAND POLLARD

1391. "Safety first" has been the motto of the human race for half a million years; but it has never been the motto of leaders. A leader must face danger. He must take the risk and the blame, and the brunt of the storm.

— Quoted from the writings of
HERBERT N. CASSON

1392. The right of commanding is no longer an advantage transmitted by nature; like an inheritance, it is the fruit of labors, the price of courage.

— VOLTAIRE

1393. The best executive is the one who has sense enough to pick good men to do what he wants done, and self-restraint enough to keep from meddling with them while they do it.

— THEODORE ROOSEVELT

1394. No man will ever be a big executive who feels that he must, either openly or under cover, follow up every order he gives and see that it is done—nor will he ever develop a capable assistant.

— JOHN LEE MAHIN

1395. The ability to keep a cool head in an emergency, maintain poise in the midst of excitement, and refuse to be stampeded are the true marks of leadership.

— R. SHANNON

1396. You will never be a leader unless you first learn to follow and be led.

— TIORIO

1397. A great leader never sets himself above his followers except in carrying responsibilities.

— JULES ORMONT

1398. The character and qualifications of the leader are reflected in the men he selects, develops and gathers around him. Show me the leader and I will know his men. Show me the men and I will know their leader. Therefore, to have loyal, efficient employees—be a loyal and efficient employer.

— ARTHUR W. NEWCOMB

1399. The best leaders are those most interested in surrounding themselves with assistants and associates smarter than they are— being frank in admitting this—and willing to pay for such talents.

— AMOS PARRISH

1400. Who hath not served cannot command.

— JOHN FLORIO, *First Fruits*

LEADERSHIP

1401. A ship, to run a straight course, can have but one pilot and one steering wheel. The same applies to the successful operation of a business. There cannot be a steering wheel at every seat in an organization.

— JULES ORMONT

1402. I light my candle from their torches.

— ROBERT BURTON, *The Anatomy of Melancholy*

1403. The trouble with being a leader today is that you can't be sure whether the people are following you or chasing you.

1404. When a girl applies for admission to Vassar, a questionnaire is sent to her parents. A father in a Boston suburb, filling out one of these forms, came to the question, "Is she a leader?" He hesitated, then wrote, "I am not sure about this, but I know she is an excellent follower."

A few days later he received this letter from the president of the college: "As our freshman group next Fall is to contain several hundred leaders, we congratulate ourselves that your daughter will also be a member of the class. We shall thus be assured of one good follower."

— *Journal of Education*

1405. When two men ride a horse, one must ride behind.

— WILLIAM SHAKESPEARE

1406. He who governs should possess energy without fanaticism, principles without demagogy, severity without cruelty; he must neither be weak, nor vacillating, nor, so to express it, must he be ashamed of his duty.

— NAPOLEON BONAPARTE

1407. The great leader is one who never permits his followers to discover that he is as dumb as they are.

Lecture see also *Public Speaking*

1408. Lecture: a process by which the notes of the professor become the notes of the student, without passing through the minds of either.

Legal see also *Law*

1409. Protocol required Supreme Court Justice Hugo Black to attend the funeral of a man he had cordially detested for years. A colleague who was late for the services whispered in Justice Black's ear, "How far has the service gone?" Justice Black whispered back, "They just opened the defense."

— BENNETT CERF

1410. Bursting into the lawyer's office, the butcher demanded, "If a dog steals a piece of meat from my shop, is the owner liable?"

"Of course," said the lawyer.

"Well, your dog took a piece of steak worth half a dollar about five minutes ago."

"All right," said the lawyer without blinking. "Give me the other half dollar and that will cover my fee."

Legislation see also *Law*

1411. With the tourist season moving into full volume in Washington, Capitol restaurants stepped up the amount of bean soup prepared daily. It was always a major attraction for out-of-towners, many of whom probably didn't know the reason a law was passed requiring it to be served daily in the U. S. House restaurant. The late House Speaker Joe Cannon, who loved bean soup, walked into the restaurant one day in 1904 and found it wasn't on the menu. "Thunderation!" he shouted and went upstairs to the House chamber. Within a very short time, he had railroaded a resolution through forcing the soup to be served daily without fail.

1412. In one of his books, Curtis Bok recounted the historical fact that in one section of ancient Greece it long was the custom that when a man proposed a law in the popular assembly, he did so on a platform with a rope around his neck. "If his law passed, they removed the rope; if it failed, they removed the platform.

— GERALD HORTON BATH,
Whatsoever Things

Leisure

1413. Leisure without books is death, and burial of a man alive.

— SENECA

LENDING

1414. Leisure: the two minutes rest a man gets while his wife thinks up something for him to do.

1415. The real problem of one's leisure is to keep other people from using it.

1416. Leisure for men of business, and business for men of leisure, would cure many complaints.

1417. Nothing adds to a man's leisure time like doing things when they're supposed to be done.

— O. A. BATTISTA

Lending

1418. If you lend a friend five dollars and you never see him again, it's worth it.

Liberty see also *Freedom*

1419. The love of liberty is the love of others; the love of power is the love of ourselves.

— WILLIAM HAZLITT, *Political Essays*

1420. Liberty is the right to do everything that the law permits.

— CHARLES DE SECONDAT DE MONTESQUIEU, *L'Esprit des Lois*

1421. He that would make his own liberty secure must guard even his enemy from oppression.

— THOMAS PAINE, *Dissertation on First Principles of Government*

1422. Those who would give up essential liberty to purchase a little temporary safety, deserve neither liberty nor safety.

— BENJAMIN FRANKLIN

1423. The condition upon which God has given liberty to man is eternal vigilance.

— JOHN PHILPOT CURRAN

1424. What this country needs is not more liberty, but fewer people who take liberties with liberty.

— EARL RINEY, *Church Management*

1425. It is the privilege and duty of the present generation to pass on to its successors, unimpaired, the heritage of liberty bequeathed to it by the founders of the Republic.

— GEORGE B. CORTELYOU

1426. Liberty is always dangerous, but it is the safest thing we have.

— DR. HARRY EMERSON FOSDICK

1427. There is no liberty worth anything which is not a liberty under law.

— NATHANIEL J. BURTON

1428. Some of the most menacing encroachments upon liberty invoke the democratic principle and assert the right of the majority to rule. The interests of liberty are peculiarly those of individuals and hence of minorities, and freedom is in danger of being slain at her own altars if the passion for uniformity and control of opinion gathers head.

— CHIEF JUSTICE CHARLES EVANS HUGHES

Library see also *Books—Reading*

1429. The founding of a library is one of the greatest things we can do . . . It is one of the quietest things; but there is nothing that I know of at bottom more important. Everyone able to read a good book becomes a wiser man. He becomes a similar center of light and order, and just insight into the things around him. A collection of good books contains all of the nobleness and wisdom of the world before us. A collection of books is the best of all universities.

— THOMAS CARLYLE

1430. To add a library to a house is to give that house a soul.

— CICERO

Life see also *Death*

1431. Where life is more terrible than death, it is then the truest valor to want to live.

— THOMAS BROWNE

1432. One man gets nothing but discord out of a piano; another gets harmony. No one claims the piano is at fault. Life is about the same. The discord is there, and the harmony is there. Study to play it correctly, and it will give forth the beauty; play it falsely, and it will give forth the ugliness. Life is not at fault.

1433. When death consents to let us live a long time, it takes successively as hostages all those we have loved.

— NINON DE LENCLOS

1434. Income these days is something you cannot live without or within.

1435. Life without mirth is a lamp without oil.

— SIR WALTER SCOTT, *The Pirate*

1436. Only those are fit to live who are not afraid to die.

— GENERAL DOUGLAS MACARTHUR to Filipino
Air Force, 1941

1437. When Michelangelo, already well along in years, was discussing life with an old friend, the latter commented, "Yes, after such a good life it's hard to look death in the eye."

"Not at all!" contradicted Michelangelo. "Since life was such a pleasure, death coming from the same great Source cannot displease us."

— *Temmler Werke* publication, Hamburg.
Quote translation

1438. Life is like a bank account. You only get back what you put in. Experience is the interest.

1439. The life given us by nature is short; but the memory of a well spent life is eternal.

— CICERO, *Philippicae*

1440. Life has a value only when it has something valuable as its object.

— GEORGE WILHELM FRIEDRICH HEGEL

1441. You can only live once—but if you live right, once is enough!

— JOE E. LEWIS

1442. It's all right to live it up, if you can live it down.

1443. This life is a round-and-round affair. People eat animals,

animals eat smaller animals, smaller animals eat vegetables, vegetables eat animalculae, animalculae eat bacilli, bacilli eat microbes, and microbes eat us. The cannibal takes the short cut.

— *Wall Street Journal*

1444. We live our best so intermittently that when we need it most we find only the mediocre at our service.

1445. Life: living expensively to impress people who live expensively to impress us.

1446. To live in hearts we leave behind, is not to die.

— THOMAS CAMPBELL

1447. It is a funny thing about life: If you refuse to accept anything but the best you very often get it.

— W. SOMERSET MAUGHAM

1448. I want to be thoroughly used up when I die for the harder I work, the more I live.

— GEORGE BERNARD SHAW

1449. Though we seem grieved at the shortness of life in general, we are wishing every period of it at an end. The minor longs to be at age, then to be a man of business, then to make up an estate, then to arrive at honors, then to retire.

— JOSEPH ADDISON

1450. Life is no brief candle to me. It is a sort of splendid torch which I have got hold of for the moment, and I want to make it burn as brightly as possible before handing it on to future generations.

— GEORGE BERNARD SHAW

1451. A good man doubles the length of his existence; to have lived so as to look back with pleasure on our past life is to live twice.

— MARTIAL

1452. Most of life is routine—dull and grubby, but routine is the momentum that keeps a man going. If you wait for inspiration you'll be standing on the corner after the parade is a mile down the street.

— BEN NICHOLAS

1453. There is more to life than increasing its speed.

— MOHANDAS K. GANDHI

1454. Life is a garment; when it is dirty, we must brush it; when it is ragged, it must be patched; but we keep it as long as we can.

— HONORÉ DE BALZAC

1455. To be able to live, at ease but without complacency, with one's prejudices is good. To be able to live, with regret but without shame or agony, with one's limitations is still better.

— CLIFTON FADIMAN, "On Being Fifty," *Holiday*

1456. Thus we never live, but we hope to live; and always disposing ourselves to be happy, it is inevitable that we never become so.

— BLAISE PASCAL, *Thoughts*

1457. Life is made up, not of great sacrifices or duties, but of little things, in which smiles and kindnesses, and small obligations, given habitually, are what win and preserve the heart and secure comfort.

— SIR HUMPHREY DAVY

1458. The whole secret of life is to be interested in one thing profoundly and in a thousand things well.

— HUGH WALPOLE

1459. About the time one learns to make the most out of life, most of it is gone.

1460. "Have you lived here all your life?" asked the traveler in the Blue Ridge Mountains of the old man sitting at a cabin door. "Not yit," replied the old gent patiently.

— JOHN KIERAN

1461. Life is a one-way street. No matter how many detours you take, none of them leads back. And once you know and accept that, life becomes much simpler. Because then you know you must do the best you can with what you have and what you are and what you have become.

— ISABEL MOORE, *I'll Never Let You Go* (Farrar & Rinehart)

1462. The game of life requires all one's energy to play it at one's best. The present gives us the only chance we have for doing. To use it in futile grief or regret is to leave something worth while undone, indulge in something that does no one any good and interferes with maintaining a cheerful spirit that brings happiness to self and to others.

— SAMUEL FESSENDEN CLARKE

1463. Live one day at a time. You can plan for tomorrow and hope for the future, but don't live in it. Live this day well, and tomorrow's strength will come tomorrow.

— CHARLES W. SHEDD

1464. Live your life each day as you would climb a mountain. An occasional glance toward the summit keeps the goal in mind, but many beautiful scenes are to be observed from each new vantage point. Climb slowly, steadily, enjoying each passing moment; and the view from the summit will serve as a fitting climax for the journey.

— HAROLD V. MELCHERT

Literature

1465. The difference between literature and journalism is that journalism is unreadable, and literature is not read.

— OSCAR WILDE, *The Critic as Artist*

Living see *Life*

Logic

1466. Logic: an organized procedure for going wrong with confidence and certainty.

Lonesomeness

1467. People are lonely because they build walls instead of bridges.

— JOSEPH FORT NEWTON

Loquacity

1468. Just before leaving for a hunting trip in Africa, Theodore

LOQUACITY

Roosevelt invited a famous English big-game hunter to give him some pointers for his trip. After a two-hour conversation at the White House, during which the two were not disturbed, the Englishman came out.

"And what did you tell the President?" asked a reporter.

"I told him my name," said the wearied visitor.

— EMILY BAX, *Miss Bax of the Embassy*
(Houghton Mifflin Company)

Love

1469. In lovers' quarrels, the party that loves most is always most willing to acknowledge the greater fault.

— SIR WALTER SCOTT

1470. As a neglected garden is soon invaded by weeds, so a love carelessly guarded is quickly submerged by unkind feelings. Everything threatens it: ennui, monotony, illness, the spitefulness of third parties. Against these I know of only two remedies. The first is that which makes the very essence of marriage—the vow: "I will not give up; I will defend our union and happiness; I will tie up again every broken thread; I will reconstruct, untiringly, faithfully, each part of the fallen wall." The second is sincerity without reserve. Mystery may be compatible with light and transient loves. Marriage must live in confidence and certitude. Treachery has no power against two beings who confide all. Thus only is it possible to form an admirable affection, incomprehensible to those who do not know by experience this strange mixture of love and friendship, of sensuality and respect, of indulgence and admiration, an amazing blending of the human and divine, which constitutes the true marriage.

— ANDRE MAUROIS

1471. There is at least enough in love to keep everybody hopeful about it.

— EDGAR W. HOWE

1472. The quarrels of lovers are the renewal of love.

— TERENCE, *Andria*

1473. Of all heavy bodies, the heaviest is the woman we have ceased to love.

— LEMONTEY

1474. It is as absurd to pretend that one cannot love the same always as to pretend that a good artist needs several violins to execute a piece of music.

— HONORÉ DE BALZAC

1475. No lover should have any insolence to think of being accepted at once, nor should any girl have the cruelty to refuse at once, without seven reasons.

— JOHN RUSKIN

1476. Love is real only for the young. The mature must look at it with wiser eyes, and see it for the many other things it is—selfishness, robbery and the hiatus between deceits.

— BEN HECHT, *A Child of the Century*
(Simon & Schuster, Inc.)

1477. A Chinese woman sat in the graveyard fanning the earth beneath which her husband lay buried.

"What a tender heart that still hopes to comfort him with her loving fan," sighed an onlooker.

The Chinese woman had promised her husband not to marry again until the earth on his grave was dry.

— BEN HECHT, *A Child of the Century*
(Simon & Schuster, Inc.)

1478. Those who love deeply never grow old; they may die of old age, but they die young.

— ARTHUR WING PINERO

1479. The way to love anything is to realize that it might be lost.

— G. K. CHESTERTON

1480. We like someone *because*. We love someone *although*

— Reprinted from *Pity for Women* by HENRI
DE MONTHERLANT, by permission of Alfred
A. Knopf, Inc.

1481. Love is the feeling that brings a woman to the point where she brings a man to the point.

— *Quote*

Loyalty

1482. When put to the test, an ounce of Loyalty is worth a pound of Cleverness.

— ELBERT HUBBARD

Luck

1483. Fortune is like glass—the brighter the glitter, the more easily broken.

— PUBLILIUS SYRUS

1484. Every man who holds a big job gets there through luck. All he has to do is cultivate a pleasing personality, make himself well-liked by others, sow seeds of kindness and good cheer wherever he goes, perform his work better than the "unlucky" man does, render the most and best service possible regardless of the salary he is getting. Luck does the rest.

1485. Sometimes it may be bad luck to have good luck too soon.

— M. K. SARGENT, quoted in *Toastmaster*

1486. It never occurs to fools that merit and good fortune are closely united.

— JOHANN WOLFGANG VON GOETHE

1487. Luck is the sense to recognize an opportunity and the ability to take advantage of it. Everyone has bad breaks, but everyone also has opportunities. The man who can smile at his breaks and grab his chances gets on.

1488. Whether or not it's bad luck to meet a black cat depends upon whether you are a man or a mouse.

1489. Luck means the hardships and privations which you have not hesitated to endure; the long nights you have devoted to work. Luck means the appointments you have never failed to keep; the trains you have never failed to catch.

— MAX O'RELL

1490. The important thing is to be on the spot at the moment most favorable for gaining the desired advantage; and it will be found that of men who get what they want in this world, both those who seem to hasten and those who seem to lounge are always at the right place at the right time.

— DAVID GRAHAM PHILLIPS

1491. Good and bad luck is a synonym in the great majority of instances, for good and bad judgment.

— JOHN CHATFIELD

1492. No accidents are so unlucky but that the wise may draw some advantage from them; nor are there any so lucky but that the foolish may turn them to their own prejudice.

— FRANÇOIS DE LA ROCHEFOUCAULD

1493. What helps luck is a habit of watching for opportunities, of having a patient, but restless mind, of sacrificing one's ease or vanity, of uniting a love of detail to foresight, and of passing through hard times bravely and cheerfully.

— VICTOR CHERBULIEZ

1494. I am a great believer in luck. The harder I work the more of it I seem to have.

— COLEMAN COX

1495. A peddler of lottery tickets tried to sell a chance to Baron Rothschild, head of the famous European banking family.

"What would I want with a lottery ticket?" protested the annoyed Baron.

"Oh, come on," pleaded the peddler. "They're only fifty cents each. Go on, take a chance."

In order to get rid of the nuisance, Baron Rothschild bought the lottery ticket. The next day, bright and early, the peddler was on the Baron's doorstep. "You won first prize!" he cried, "$300,000!"

"Well!" exclaimed the pleased Baron. "I suppose I ought to reward you." He thought a moment. "Which would you rather have?" he asked at last. "$12,000 in cash or $3,600 a year for the rest of your life?"

"Give me the $12,000," said the peddler. "With the kind of luck you Rothschilds have, I wouldn't live another six months."

1496. A stout heart breaks bad luck.

— MIGUEL DE CERVANTES

Luxury

1497. Economy: denying ourselves a necessity today in order to buy a luxury tomorrow.

Machinery

1498. One machine may do the work of fifty ordinary men. No machine can do the work of one extraordinary man.

— ELBERT HUBBARD, *The Philistine*

Madness

1499. There is a pleasure sure
In being mad which none but madmen know.

— JOHN DRYDEN, *The Spanish Friar*

Majority

1500. The oppression of a majority is detestable and odious; the oppression of a minority is only by one degree less detestable and odious.

— WILLIAM E. GLADSTONE, speech, House of Commons, 1870

Man see also Men

1501. Man's worst enemy is man, I say!
— PRATHER MOXEY

1502. Men are like fish; neither would get into trouble if they kept their mouths shut.

1503. A man needs a woman to take care of him so she can make him strong enough for her to lean on.

1504. Every child comes with the message that God is not yet discouraged of man.

— RABINDRANATH TAGORE

1505. Man: a creature who buys football tickets three months in advance and waits until Christmas Eve to do his gift shopping.

1506. Man: a large irrational creature who is always looking for home atmosphere in a hotel and hotel service around a home.

1507. Taste is the mark of an educated man, imagination the sign of a productive man, and emotional balance the token of a mature man.

— PHILIP N. YOUTZ, *The Forum*

1508. Cruel men are the greatest lovers of mercy, avaricious men of generosity, and proud men of humility; that is to say in others, not in themselves.

— CHARLES C. COLTON

Manicurist

1509. Manicurist: a girl who makes money hand over fist.

Mankind

1510. A brick is made of clay. So is a man.
A brick is square and plumb and true. So a man ought to be.
A brick is useless until it has been through the fire. So is a man.
A brick is not as showy as marble, but it is more useful. Man is not for show, but for service.
When a man fulfills this description, he has a right to be called a brick.

Manners see also *Etiquette*

1511. Fundamentally, good manners are the embodiment of one's moral respect and consideration for others.

— HAROLD W. DODD

1512. If company manners are very proper, they are proper in the home—when no company is present.

— DR. LOUIS L. MANN

Married Life — marriage see also *Husband* and *Wife*

1513. The most popular record chosen from the selection in a juke-box installed in one American bar and grill is a "novelty" number playing only the sound of typewriters working. The reason for its popularity is that it is played every time one of the regulars phones home to say he is working late at the office.

1514. A distinguished gentleman came to Abercrombie and Fitch's in New York and asked to see shotguns. The clerk, sizing him up as a man of means, showed him a fine English model priced at $450. "That is a splendid gun," the gentleman said, "but a little expensive."

The clerk brought out a Belgian model priced at $275. "Still a little too expensive," observed the gentleman.

A bit discouraged, the clerk said: "Well, here is a Winchester mass production stock model at $17.50."

With that the gentleman brightened. "That will do nicely. After all, it's only a small wedding."

— JENNIE JUSTIN

1515. She had begged her husband for months to have his picture taken. At last he gave in, but when the proofs arrived, she exclaimed, "There's only one button on your coat."

"Thank heaven!" he exclaimed, "you've noticed it at last."

1516. A bachelor is a fellow who doesn't think the bonds of matrimony are a good investment.

— MAURICE SEITTER

1517. When a man and woman marry, they become one. Of course, they must decide which one, and that is often where the storm starts.

— *Spiritual Revolution* by PIERCE HARRIS. Copyright 1952 by PIERCE HARRIS, reprinted by permission of Doubleday & Company, Inc.

1518. The honeymoon is over when the bushels of kisses are reduced to little pecks.

— TAD ROBINSON in *Country Gentleman and Better Farming*

1519. A hotel manager received this letter: "Have you suitable accommodations where I can put up with my wife?"

1520. With so many showers for June brides, nearly everyone gets soaked.

— VESTA N. KELLY, *Quote*

1521. *He:* "How come you aren't married?"
She: "I'm looking for the perfect man."
He: "Haven't you found him?"
She: "Yes, but he was looking for the perfect woman!"

1522. There are two kinds of people at every party: those who want to leave early and those who don't, and the trouble is, they're married to each other.

1523. Don't ever question your wife's judgment. After all, she married you.

1524. When air lines were young and people were wary of flying, a promotion man suggested to one of the lines that they permit wives of businessmen to accompany their husbands free, just to prove that flying was safe. The idea was quickly adopted, and a record kept of the names of those who accepted the proposition. In due time the air line sent a letter to those wives, asking how they enjoyed the trip. From a large percentage of them came back a baffled reply, "What airplane trip?"

> — From *And So to Bedlam* by MARGUERITE LYON, copyright 1943, used by special permission of the publishers, The Bobbs-Merrill Company

1525. Many a man finds that burning a candle at both ends makes it twice as hard to keep his wife in the dark.
> — RALPH PAUL

1526. Never forget to make your wife believe you really love her or she may succumb to the natural temptation to try out her feminine powers on some other man. A woman needs confirmation of her power.
> — LEON BLUM

1527. *News item:* Police can find no reason for the suicide. The man was unmarried.

1528. The chief cause of divorce is matrimony.

1529. A working girl is one who quit her job to get married.

1530. ICE CREAM EVERY MEAL

Does Dr. Popenoe ("Are You a Good Husband?") actually think

a husband should say "I love you" at least once a day? Wouldn't that be like having ice cream with chocolate sauce for every meal? "I love you" can be said with a glance or a touch. A husband expresses his love for his wife in every word if it is spoken with genuine kindliness and reverence . . . He says it when he refuses to go out unless she consents to go too, and when he buys her a bottle of perfume out of his own spending money, and when he makes his own coffee and toast if she oversleeps. In fact, he is saying "I love you" by making a living for her and the children. Every good wife knows this and does not ask for a ritual of words every twenty-four hours.

— Mrs. J. H. Beebe, Zion, Ill.

1531. "I'm the head of my house," remarked one recently-wed husband to another. "After all, I should be; I'm the one who earns the money."

"Well," said the other, "my wife and I have a different arrangement. We've agreed that I should decide all the major problems and she the minor ones."

"And how is that working out," asked the first.

"Well, all I can report is that so far, no problems of major importance have come up."

1532. Jack was unusually late getting home one night and his apprehensive wife sent the following telegram to five of his closest friends. "Jack not home. Is he spending the night with you?" Shortly thereafter, Jack arrived home and was followed by five telegrams all bearing the same one word, "Yes."

1533. One good husband is worth two good wives; for the scarcer things are the more they are valued.

— Benjamin Franklin

1534. I once asked my father why a man is not allowed to have more than one wife, and he said: "Son, when you're older you'll realize that the law protects those who are incapable of protecting themselves."

— Ernie Ford

1535. A conscientious father was advising his son, who was about to be married: "Cooperation is the foundation of a successful marriage. You must do things together. For instance, if your wife wants to go for a walk, go for a walk with her. If she wants to go to the movies, go to the movies with her. If she wants to do the dishes, do the dishes with her."

The son listened dutifully and then asked, "Suppose she wants to mop the floor?"

1536. *Bank teller to man at window:* "Sorry, sir. Your wife beat you to the draw."

1537. Some women work so hard to make good husbands that they never quite manage to make good wives.

1538. Hollywood marriage: much "I do" about nothing.

1539. Every famous man's wife must have an uneasy feeling that something will happen to open the world's eyes.

1540. Marriages may be made in heaven, but man is responsible for the maintenance work.

1541. Keep your eyes open before marriage; half shut afterwards.

— BENJAMIN FRANKLIN

1542. It is well to remember that a misplaced "I" can transform the marital relation into a martial one.

1543. Reno: the land of the free and the grave of the home.

1544. Perfect man: my wife's first husband.

1545. A truly happy marriage is one in which a woman gives the best years of her life to the man who made them the best.

— Quoted by CYNTHIA GREY in the
San Francisco News

1546. Wedding: a ceremony at which a man loses complete control of himself.

1547. Wedding ring: smallest handcuff in the world.

1548. "While he never actually struck me," explained Mrs Jones, who was suing Mr. Jones for divorce, "he would go arounc slamming his fist against the doors and saying: 'I wish it was you.'"

1549. It is not marriage that fails; it is people that fail. All that marriage does is show people up.

— HARRY EMERSON FOSDICK, *Marriage*

1550. Marriage is popular because it combines the maximum of temptation with the maximum of opportunity.

— GEORGE BERNARD SHAW

1551. Alimony: a splitting headache.

1552. If you do housework at $20 a week, that's domestic service; if you do it for nothing, that's matrimony.

1553. When a man takes his wife to a convention, he has twice the expense—and half as much fun.

1554. It takes two to make a marriage—a girl and an anxious mother.

1555. Bigamist: a man who makes the same mistake twice.

1556. An optimist is a single man contemplating marriage; a pessimist is a married person contemplating it.

1557. Someone has compared marriage to a dollar bill. You cannot spend half of it when you tear it in two. The value of one half depends upon the other. And so it is with regard to husband and wife.

— S. C. MICHELFELDER, *Houston Times*

1558. "Papa, how much does it cost to get married?"
"That, my son, depends on two things: how much you've got, and how long you live."

1559. To the Man whose Wife Is Out of Town

Of all the insidious
Temptations invidious,
Devised by the Devil,
For pulling men down,
There's none more delusive,
Seductive, abusive,
Than the snare to a man
When his wife's out of town.

He feels such delightfulness
Such stay-out-all-nightfulness,
And sure to get tightfulness
I own it with pain,

224

A sort of back-rakishness,
What-will-you-takishness,
It's hard to explain.

His wife may be beautiful,
Tender and dutiful,
It is not her absence
That causes delight,
But the curs'd opportunity,
The baleful immunity,
That scatters his scruples
As day scatters night.

— LAWRENCE J. WOLFRAM

1560. Man may be the head of the family, but far better than that, woman is the heart of it.

1561. A woman who has made fun of her husband can love him no more.

— HONORE DE BALZAC

1562. "My wife tells me that I talk in my sleep, Doctor. What should I do?"
"Nothing that you shouldn't."

1563. *A:* "I'm a man of few words."
B: "I'm married, too."

1564. Nowadays it is easy to tell whether a man is married. All you have to do is watch when he opens his wallet. If he turns his back while doing it, he's married.

1565. *Sign on the house of a Justice of the Peace:*
"Are You Fit to Be Tied?"

1566. Cupid: one who when he hits the mark usually Mrs. it.

1567. Best people: the ones your wife knew before she married you.

1568. Bigamy: when a man marries a beautiful girl and a good housewife.

1569. Extravagance: buying whatever is of no earthly value to your wife.

1570. A good husband is one who feels in his pockets every time he passes a mail box.

1571. Desertion: the poor man's method of divorce.

1572. Debutante: a young girl with bride ideas.

1573. If a husband's words are sharp, maybe it's from trying to get them in edgewise.

1574. Martyrdom: telling your wife the exact truth and then having her refuse to believe a word of it.

1575. The trouble with marriage is that a fellow can't support a wife and the government on one income.

1576. Marriage is a great thing—no family should be without it.

1577. The girl who marries a man with money to burn usually makes a good match.

1578. Maxim for wives: you never know what you can do till you cry.

1579. Every man who is high up loves to think that he has done it all himself; and the wife smiles, and lets it go at that.

— JAMES MATTHEW BARRIE

1580. Many a man today is living by the sweat of his *frau.*

— O. O. McINTYRE

1581. Many a husband, knowing nothing about music, learns he can produce real harmony in the home by playing second fiddle.

1582. Wedding license: a certificate that gives a woman the legal right to drive a man.

1583. Marriage: the only life sentence that is suspended by bad behavior.

1584. Many a wife has made her own marital grave with a series of little digs.

1585. When a man brings his wife flowers for no reason— there's a reason.

1586. Plutarch tells of a Roman, divorced from his wife, who was blamed by friends for the separation.

"Was she not beautiful?" they chorused. "Was she not chaste?"

The Roman, holding out his shoe for them to see, asked if it were not good-looking and well made. "Yet," he added, "none of you can tell where it pinches me."

1587. The great secret of successful marriage is to treat all disasters as incidents and none of the incidents as disasters.

— HAROLD NICOLSON

1588. The plural of spouse is spice.

— CHRISTOPHER MORLEY

1589. Often the difference between a successful marriage and a mediocre one consists of leaving about three or four things a day unsaid.

— HARLAN MILLER, courtesy of
Better Homes & Gardens

1590. Don't marry for money; you can borrow it cheaper.

— Scotch proverb

1591. A disciple once asked Socrates whether it was better to marry or not to marry.

"Whichever you do," replied Socrates, "you will regret it."

Matter-of-fact

1592. As William Dean Howells and Mark Twain were coming out of church one morning, it commenced to rain heavily.

"Do you think it will stop?" asked Howells.

"It always has," answered Twain.

Maturity

1593. You grow up the day you have your first real laugh— at yourself.

— ETHEL BARRYMORE

Maxims

1594. A maxim consists of a minimum of sound and a maximum of sense.

— MARK TWAIN

Medicine see also *Doctors*

1595. The best cure for the body is to quiet the mind.

— Napoleon Bonaparte

1596. Medicine is a science. Making a practice of it is an art.

1597. After sending a parcel to European relatives, we received a very grateful letter with this paragraph:

"If you can, please send us more pills. We didn't know what they were until Cousin Lempi came—she has studied English, you know—and read the name for us. Then we gave them all to Uncle Paul who has been suffering from rheumatism and he feels much better now. He says it is the best medicine he ever took. The pills are called Life Savers."

— Alice Murdock in *Pageant*

Mediocrity

1598. Mediocrity requires aloofness to preserve its dignity.

— Charles G. Dawes

1599. Mediocrity is excellence to the mediocre.

— Joseph Joubert

1600. Nothing in the world is more haughty than a man of moderate capacity when once raised to power.

Meekness

1601. Meekness is not weakness.

— Sir William Gurney Benham, *Proverbs*

Membership

1602. A hobo, wandering around the golf course of a fashionable country club, dropped off to sleep in a sand trap. A little later, he was rudely awakened by a none too gentle kick in the ribs. He opened his weary eyes and looked up.

"What's the idea?" he demanded. "Who do you think you are?"

"I'm the chairman of the membership committee," replied the man sternly.

The tramp rose to his feet. "All right," he grumbled as he staggered away, "all I can say is, this is a heck of a way to get new members."

1603. Groucho Marx once explained that he resigned from the Friars Club with the simple, chilly explanation: "I don't want to belong to any club that would accept me as one of its members."

— JOHN CROSBY in the *New York Herald Tribune*

Memory

1604. A man's real possession is his memory. In nothing else is he rich, in nothing else is he poor.

— ALEXANDER SMITH

1605. Historian W. E. Woodward, writing about the Judd Gray and Ruth Snyder murder case, pointed up a small thing that played an important role in sending Gray to the electric chair. Among the witnesses was a taxi driver who remembered him on the night of the murder. Why? Because on a $3.50 fare, Gray had given him only a five-cent tip.

"Five cents!" the taxi driver said. "I took a good look at his face, and I'll never forget him. There he sits, right over there." And he pointed to Judd Gray.

1606. A retentive memory is a good thing, but the ability to forget is the true token of greatness.

— ELBERT HUBBARD

1607. Each man's memory is his private literature, and every recollection affects us with something of the penetrative force that belongs to the work of art.

— ALDOUS HUXLEY, *Texts and Pretexts*
(Harper and Brothers)

1608. Of all the conventional methods of greeting an important person, "Do you remember me?" is probably the most inconsiderate.

Charles U. Bay, the former Ambassador to Norway, answered the sometimes-impossible-to-answer question without giving offense, by replying: "Sure I remember you. Say, how'd you ever get out of that trouble you were in?"

Charles Michelson, the late publicity director for the Democratic

National Committee, had a reputation for never forgetting a name, though he once confessed he didn't deserve the reputation because he rarely mentioned names. Whenever a man asked, "Do you remember me?"—and he couldn't remember him—he said, "Yes—and it turned out you were right, didn't it?"

Winston Churchill has the perfect squelch for those indiscreet enough to ask, "Do you remember me?" Sir Winston replies, "Why should I?"

Men see also *Man*

1609. Most men need two women in their lives—a secretary to take everything down and a wife to pick everything up.

1610. To believe in men is the first step in helping them.

Military

1611. The army doctor was examining a prospective serviceman. "Sit down in that chair," ordered the doctor sternly.

The reluctant prospect obeyed.

"A-1," cried the doctor. "Next."

"What!" exclaimed the recruit. "Why, you haven't even looked at me."

"Well," said the doctor, "you heard me tell you to sit down, you saw the chair, and you had enough intelligence to carry out the order. Move on, soldier!"

1612. Unaware that the War of 1812 was already over, General Andrew Jackson's troops fought and won the Battle of New Orleans 140 years ago. (1815)

1613. Guests in a Cairo hotel, hearing a scream in the corridor, discovered a damsel in negligee being pursued by a gentleman who was, to put it bluntly, nude. Later it developed that the impetuous Romeo was an English major, who was promptly court-martialed. His lawyer won him an acquittal, however, by virtue of the following paragraph in the army manual: "It is not compulsory for an officer to wear a uniform at all times, as long as he is suitably garbed for the sport in which he is engaged."

— MABEL DANA LYON, quoted by BENNETT
CERF in *Saturday Review*

1614. A good general not only sees the way to victory; he also knows when victory is impossible.

— POLYBIUS, *Histories*

1615. "Comrades, you have lost a good captain to make a bad general."

— SATURNIUS

1616. One of the very young Air Force colonels, who were a dime a dozen in the Pentagon, lost his way in the maze of corridors. Seeing a sailor standing confidently ahead of him, the colonel called, "Sergeant." The call went unheeded. Again he called, and still the sailor made no reply. The colonel quickened his pace, tapped the sailor on the shoulder and said, "Sergeant, don't you speak when you're spoken to?"

"I'm sorry, sir," answered the sailor, "I'm a second class petty officer, not a sergeant."

"What difference does that make?" snapped the colonel. "If you were in the Air Force you would be a sergeant."

"No, sir," came the proud reply, "if I were in the Air Force, I'd be a colonel!"

1617. Military science: that remarkable art in which the lessons learned in winning one war, if strictly followed, lose the next.

1618. A colonel was transferring to a new command. On reaching his depot, he found stacks of old documents accumulated in the archives of his predecessors, so he wired headquarters for permission to burn them. The answer came back: "Yes, but make copies first."

1619. It was out on the rifle range, and the green recruits were curdling the blood of the tough old Army rifle instructor. He stomped over to the prone form of one rookie whose misses were nothing short of spectacular.

"Son, where the blazes are your shots going?" the sergeant bellowed in his finest tones.

The rookie looked up innocently. "I dunno, sir," he replied. "They're leaving this end all right."

1620. Rank.
A girl turned up at work the other day wearing two officer's silver

231

bars pinned to her sweater. One of her office mates asked, "Is your boy friend a captain?"

"Goodness, no," she said. "Two lieutenants."

— Reprinted by permission. Copyright 1943, The New Yorker Magazine, Inc.

1621. Two draftees were discussing the war. "Are you ready to go?" one asked.

"No," said the other, "I ain't ready, but I'm willing to go, unready."

1622. *Private:* I feel like telling that sergeant where to get off again.

Second Private: What do you mean "again?"

Private: I felt like it yesterday, too.

1623. A noncommissioned officer wrote this in an essay: "It is commonly supposed that the first duty of a good soldier is to die for his country. This is a mistake. The first duty of a soldier is to make his enemies die for theirs."

— DAVID GOLDBERG in *The Chicago Sun*

1624. The cute little thing entered the Doc's office with a worried look.

"Doctor," she said, "I need an operation."

"Major?" asked the Doctor.

"No," she said, "sergeant."

Mind

1625. Professor Louis Agassiz of Harvard was one of the greatest naturalists of his day and among other of his accomplishments was the first to formulate the "glacial theory." To give recognition to his genius, the city of San Francisco erected a monument to his memory. During the earthquake and fire of 1906, the statue of Professor Agassiz toppled from its pedestal and landed head foremost in the cement sidewalk immediately in front, its feet and lower extremities projecting high into space.

Professor William H. Hobbs of the University of Michigan, in referring to this occurrence in his freshman classes in geology, invariably commented that it had always been known that Professor

Agassiz had a penetrating mind but that this was a concrete example of that fact.

1626. A dose of poison can do its work but once, but a bad book can go on poisoning minds for generations.

— W. JOHN MURRAY

1627. The human mind should be like a good hotel: open the year round.

— WILLIAM LYON PHELPS

1628. Only fools and dead men don't change their minds. Fools won't. Dead men can't.

— JOHN H. PATTERSON

1629. A weak mind is like a microscope, which magnifies trifling things, but cannot receive great ones.

— LORD CHESTERFIELD

1630. The mind is like the stomach. It is not how much you put into it that counts, but how much it digests.

— A. J. NOCK

1631. Man's mind stretched by a new idea never goes back to its original dimensions.

— OLIVER WENDELL HOLMES

Minority

1632. President Eisenhower (surrounded by sixteen Democrats and four Republicans at a luncheon meeting): "I'm bipartisan when I'm in the minority."

1633. A perfect example of minority rule is a baby in the house.

Miracle

1634. An old woman of the Ulster frontier was asked if she had anything to declare. No, nothing at all. But what was in the bottle? Oh, only holy water; holy water from Lourdes. The custom officer pulled the cork. "Whisky it is," said he.
"Glory be to God!" cried the offender. "A miracle."

1635. Miracle: an event described by those to whom it was told by men who did not see it.

— ELBERT HUBBARD, *Epigrams*

Misfortune

1636. If all our misfortunes were laid in one common heap, whence everyone must take an equal portion, most people would be content to take their own and depart.

— SOCRATES

Mistake see also Error

1637. If you make a mistake, make a new one each time.

1638. A kindergarten teacher smiled pleasantly at the gentleman opposite on the trolley car. He did not respond. Realizing her error, she said aloud, "Oh, please excuse me. I mistook you for the father of two of my children."

She got out at the next corner.

— Wall Street Journal

1639. Humility leads to strength and not to weakness. It is the highest form of self-respect to admit mistakes and to make amends for them.

1640. Alibi: slip cover.

1641. Sign across the window of an automobile agency in a newly constructed building:

OPENED BY MISTAKE

1642. The man in the barber's chair was comfortably emulsified under a pack of steaming towels when suddenly a boy rushed into the shop shouting, "Mr. Balsam, Mr. Balsam, your store is on fire."

Horrified, the customer leaped from his chair, ripped off the apron and sped wildly up the street. After two or three blocks, he stopped suddenly, scratched his head and cried out in great perplexity: "What in the heck am I doing? My name isn't Balsam."

1643. Half our mistakes in life arise from feeling where we ought to think, and thinking where we ought to feel.

— JOHN C. COLLINS

1644. The Duke of Wellington, at the height of his fame, was walking down Piccadilly when a gentleman came up, took off his hat, and said: "Mr. Brown, I believe?" The Duke's answer was simple and direct. It was: "Sir, if you believe that, you'll believe anything."

— *Time*

1645. A mistake at least proves somebody stopped talking long enough to do something.

1646. The greatest mistake you can make is to be continually fearing that you'll make one.

— ELBERT HUBBARD

1647. There is nothing final about a mistake, except its being taken as final.

— PHYLLIS BOTTOME, *Strange Fruit*
(Curtis Brown, Ltd.)

1648. A hundred mistakes is a liberal education—if you learn something from each one.

1649. If a man makes a stupid mistake, the other men say: "What a fool that man is." If a woman makes a stupid mistake, the men say: "What fools women are!"

— H. C. L. JACKSON in *The Detroit News*

1650. A British captain in Cairo ripped open a cablegram from England, goggled in mute horror at the message: "Son born." Frantic inquiries at the cable office disclosed that form 185 had been substituted for No. 85 "Receiving letters occasionally." The error made a difference to the captain: he had not seen his wife in two years.

Misunderstanding

1651. At Arthur Murray's dancing studio, an overanxious pupil frequently danced the steps without waiting for her tutor's lead. Finally, he said, "Pardon me, but aren't you anticipating?"

"Why, Mr. Fowler," she said blushing furiously, "I'm not even married."

1652. A middle-aged woman wandered into the Senate Interstate and Foreign Commerce Committee one day and asked if a Mr. Sexauer worked there. A helpful employe thought she might be looking for the Banking and Currency Committee, offered to check by telephone. When a feminine voice answered his ring, he inquired politely: "Do you have a Sexauer over there?"

"Listen," she snapped, "we don't even have a ten-minute coffee break any more."

> — RUTH MONTGOMERY, reprinted by permission Chicago Tribune-New York News Syndicate, Inc.

1653. Mr. Ginsburg, returning from Europe, was assigned by the head steward to a table for two. Presently he was joined by a polite Frenchman who, before sitting down, bowed, smiled, and said, *"Bon appetit."* Not to be outdone, Mr. Ginsburg rose, bowed, and said, "Ginsburg."

This little ceremony was repeated at each meal for three days. The Frenchman always came late, always said, *"Bon appetit,"* and his bewildered table companion always rose and replied, "Ginsburg."

On the fourth day, Mr. Ginsburg confided his perplexity to a man in the smoking lounge:

"It was like this, you see. This Frenchman tells me his name—Bon Appetit—and then I tell him mine. So we are introduced. That's fine. But why keep it up day after day, meal after meal?"

"Oh, but you don't understand, Mr. Ginsburg," replied the other. "Bon appetit is not his name. He is merely wishing you a good appetite; he is hoping that you have a pleasant meal."

"Ah, now I understand," exclaimed Ginsburg. "Thanks for helping me out. Now I'll have to show him that I know what he means."

That evening it was Ginsburg who arrived late for dinner. Before sitting down he bowed ceremoniously, and said, "Bon appetit."

Whereupon the Frenchman rose, smiled, and murmured, "Ginsburg."

Mob

1654. The Mob has many heads, but no Brains.

> — THOMAS FULLER, *Gnomologia*

Moderation

1655. Be not the first by whom the new are tried.
Nor yet the last to lay the old aside.

> — ALEXANDER POPE, *An Essay on Criticism*

1656. Even moderation ought not to be practiced to excess.

Modern

1657. Men have always lived in "modern" times but they have not always been as much impressed with the fact.

— CRANE BRINTON, *The Shaping of the Modern Mind*

Modesty

1658. As former Postmaster General James A. Farley was leaving after a friendly call on Postmaster General Arthur Summerfield, Farley's eyes lit on the line of oil paintings of other men who have held the cabinet office. "There have been only three great postmasters general," Farley observed. "Who was the other one?" Summerfield chuckled. "Benjamin Franklin," laughed Farley.

1659. Comic Sam Levenson is a short man but does not brood about this fact. At a dinner he once attended he found himself surrounded by an unusual number of tall actors. "Don't you feel rather small among all these big men?" somebody asked him.
"Yes, I do," Levenson answered promptly. "I feel like a dime among a lot of pennies."

1660. Modesty is the art of imperfectly concealing your talents.

1661. Real merit of any kind cannot long be concealed; it will be discovered, and nothing can depreciate it but a man exhibiting it himself. It may not always be rewarded as it ought; but it will always be known.

— LORD CHESTERFIELD

Momentum

1662. Our maid asked for an advance on her week's salary. "Our preacher is leaving the church this Sunday," she told us, "and the congregation wants to give him a little momentum."

— FRED G. MCKNIGHT in *Coronet*

Money

1663. "Your friend Rogers is a good fellow," someone said to Mark Twain of H. H. Rogers of Standard Oil fame. "It's a pity his money is tainted."

"It's twice tainted," drawled Mark. " 'Tain't yours and 'tain't mine."

— FRANCIS WILSON's *Life of Himself*

1664. Paper Money

Man learns slowly; sometimes it seems that he does not learn at all. Six centuries ago the famous traveler, Marco Polo, among other proofs of the wisdom and the experience of the Chinese, brought back to Europe this quotation from an ancient Chinese sage: "In olden times the emperors of China began to issue paper money. One of the great ministers got a great revenue by this scheme. But it soon came about that for ten thousand bills you could scarcely buy a bowl of rice. The people were in misery, and the government was ruined." How many rulers of the nations—not to speak of the less instructed peoples themselves—have not yet learned the lesson that this old Chinaman knew several hundreds of years ago?

1665. No amount of pay ever made a good soldier, a good teacher, a good artist, or a good workman.

— JOHN RUSKIN

1666. The love of money is the root of all evil.

— New Testament, Timothy VI

1667. You must spend money, if you wish to make money.

— PLAUTUS, *Asinaria*

1668. Money is not the measure of man, but it is often the means of finding out how small he is.

1669. The bit in "two bits" used to refer to a small coin in England. It came to America through English colonists in the West Indies, who called the Spanish real (one-eighth of a dollar) by that name.

— JOSEPH DIGIOVANNI in the *Catholic Digest*

1670. The Indian on the Indian Head penny is no Indian, so the story goes. "He" was modeled after Sarah Longacre, daughter of a chief engraver of the Philadelphia mint.

1671. Before Dixie came to mean the South, it was a New Orleans $10 bill, with one side printed in English and the other in French. Dix is the French word for ten, and Dixie is the land where dixies were circulated.

1672. Money may be the husk of many things, but not the kernel. It brings you food, but not appetite; medicine but not health; acquaintances, but not friends; servants, but not faithfulness; days of joy, but not peace or happiness.

— Henrik Ibsen

1673. The chief value of money lies in the fact that one lives in a world in which it is overestimated.

— H. L. Mencken

1674. If a man runs after money, he's money-mad; if he keeps it, he's a capitalist; if he spends it, he's a playboy; if he doesn't get it, he's a ne'er-do-well; if he doesn't try to get it, he lacks ambition. If he gets it without working for it, he's a parasite; and if he accumulates it after a lifetime of hard work, people call him a fool who never got anything out of life.

— Vic Oliver

Monument

1675. The erection of a monument is superfluous; our memory will endure if our lives have deserved it.

— Pliny the Younger, *Epistulae*

Morale

1676. Morale is faith in the man at the top.

— Albert S. Johnstone

Morality

1677. Physical deformity calls forth our charity. But the infinite misfortune of moral deformity calls forth nothing but hatred and vengeance.

— CLARENCE DARROW

1678. When Rome's youth became debased and enervated, when regard was lost for men's honor and women's purity, when the sanctity of the home was violated, when her literature became cynical and debased, her dominion ended. The moral life of any people rises or falls with the vitality or decay of its religious life.

— JOHN S. BONNELL, D.D.

1679. Morality is religion in practice; religion is morality in principle.

— RALPH WARDLAW

Moral support

1680. There's no better exercise for strengthening the heart than reaching down and lifting people up.

— *Woman's Home Companion,* December 1951 issue. Copyright 1951, The Crowell-Collier Publishing Co.

Mother — motherhood

1681.   Courage

The courage that my mother had
    Went with her, and is with her still;
Rock from New England quarried;
    Now granite in a granite hill.

The golden brooch my mother wore
    She left behind for me to wear;
I have no thing I treasure more;
    Yet, it is something I could spare.

Oh, if instead she'd left to me
    The thing she took into the grave!—

That courage like a rock, which she
Has no more need of, and I have.

> —EDNA ST. VINCENT MILLAY, *Mine the
> Harvest: A Collection of New Poems*
> (Harper and Brothers)

1682. Simply having children doesn't make mothers.

> —JOHN A. SHEDD, *Salt from My Attic*

1683. God could not be everywhere and therefore He made mothers.

> —Jewish proverb

1684. Men are what their mothers made them.

> —RALPH WALDO EMERSON

1685.   What Is a Mother?

If there is something one cannot do without, it is Mother. Father loves her, daughter imitates her, son ignores her, salesmen thrive on her, motorists hurry around her, teacher phones her, and the woman next door confides in her.

She can be sweeter than sugar, more sour than a lemon, all smiles, and crying her heart out all within any given two-minute period.

She likes sewing, detective stories, having her birthday remembered, church, a new dress, the cleaning woman, Father's praise, a little lipstick, flowers and plants, canasta, dinner out on Sunday, policemen, one whole day in bed, crossword puzzles, sunny days, tea, and the newspaper boy.

She dislikes doing the dishes, Father's boss, having her birthday forgotten, the motorist behind her, spring cleaning, Junior's report card, rainy days, the neighbors' dog, stairs, and the man who was supposed to cut the grass.

She can be found standing by, bending over, reaching for, kneeling under, and stretching around, but rarely sitting on.

She has the beauty of a spring day, the patience of a saint, the appetite of a small bird, and the memory of a large elephant.

She knows the lowest prices, everybody's birthday, what you should be doing, and all your secret thoughts.

She is always straightening up after, reminding you to, and taking care of, but never asking for.

MOTHER

Yes, a Mother is one thing that nobody can do without. And when you have harassed her, buffeted her about, tried her patience, and worn her out, and it seems that the end of the world is about to descend upon you, then you can win her back with four little words, "Mom, I love you!"

— WILLIAM A. GREENEBAUM II

1686. The commonest fallacy among women is that simply having children makes one a mother—which is as absurd as believing that having a piano makes one a musician.

— SYDNEY J. HARRIS, *The Chicago Daily News*

1687. Extravagant girl: one who usually makes a poor mother and a bankrupt father.

1688. A modern mother is one who worries if her daughter gets in too early.

Mother-in-law

1689. "My mother-in-law has been living with us for years and is driving me crazy."
"Why don't you ask her to move?"
"I'd love to but I can't. It's her house."

1690. A mother, asked if she had yet made the long trip across the country to visit her son and his new wife, replied: "No, I've been waiting until they have their first baby."
"You don't want to spend the money for the trip until then?"
"No," the wise lady explained. "It's just that I have a theory that grandmas are more welcome than mothers-in-law."

— *Wall Street Journal*

1691. Mother-in-law: a woman who is never outspoken.

Motive

1692. The noblest motive is the public good.

— SIR RICHARD STEELE

Music

1693. Give me the making of the songs of a nation and I care not who makes its laws.

—THOMAS D'URFEY

1694. Psychologists have found that music does things to you whether you like it or not. Fast tempos invariably raise the pulse, respiration, and blood pressure; slow music lowers them.

—DORON K. ANTRIM

Narrow-mindedness

1695. Some people get so narrow-minded they have to stack their ideas vertically.

1696. The narrower the mind the broader the statement.

—TED COOK

Nation

1697. There is no such thing as a little country. The greatness of a people is no more determined by their number than the greatness of a man is determined by his height.

—VICTOR HUGO, speech, 1862

1698. The Jews are among the aristocracy of every land; if a literature is called rich in the possession of a few classic tragedies, what shall we say to a national tragedy lasting for fifteen hundred years, in which the poets and the actors were also the heroes.

—GEORGE ELIOT, *Daniel Deronda*

Native talent

1699. Whatever you are by nature, keep to it; never desert your own line of talent. Be what nature intended you for, and you will succeed; be anything else and you will be ten thousand times worse than nothing.

—SYDNEY SMITH

Nautical

1700. Battleships are named for states and cruisers for large cities. Destroyers bear the names of persons distinguished in naval or marine history, the christening being done when possible by relatives of those persons. Carriers are named for historic naval vessels or for famous battles; submarines for fish; minesweepers for birds; seagoing gunboats for small cities, and river gunboats for islands. Submarine tenders preserve the memory of pioneers in submarine development. Repair ships draw their names from mythology. Oilers have names of rivers, cargo ships of stars, destroyer tenders of natural areas of the United States.

1701. At a party not long ago, I raised the question of why everyone invariably refers to a boat as a "she." Here are some of the reasons the group came up with:

"A boat is called a she because there's always a great deal of bustle around her . . . because there's usually a gang of men around . . . because she has a waist and stays . . . because she takes a lot of paint to keep her looking good . . . because it's not the initial expense that breaks you, it's the upkeep . . . because she's all decked out . . . because it takes a good man to handle her right . . . because she shows her topsides, hides her bottom and, when coming into port, always heads for the buoys."

—GEORGE L. MOSES, in the Falmouth, Mass., *Enterprise*

Necessity

1702. Necessity may render a doubtful act innocent, but it cannot make it praiseworthy.

—JOSEPH JOUBERT

Neglect

1703. No man ever sank under the burden of the day. It is when tomorrow's burden is added to the burden of today that the weight is more than a man can bear.

—GEORGE MACDONALD

244

Neighbor

1704. Good fences make good neighbors.

— ROBERT LEE FROST, *Mending Wall*

1705. A woman in the suburbs was chatting over the back fence with her next-door neighbor. "We're going to be living in a better neighborhood soon," she said.

"So are we," her neighbor volunteered.

"What? Are you moving, too?"

"No, we're staying here."

1706. Most people repent of their sins by thanking God they ain't so wicked as their neighbors.

— JOSH BILLINGS

1707. No one is rich enough to do without a neighbor.

— Danish proverb

Neutrality

1708. The hottest places in Hell are reserved for those who, in a period of moral crisis, maintain their neutrality.

— DANTE

1709. Neutrality, as a lasting principle, is an evidence of weakness.

— LOUIS KOSSUTH

1710. When during World War I, a U-boat wrecked a ship and landed the survivors in South Ireland, two Civic Guards discussed the problem. "We ought to intern them."

"And why, I'm asking?"

"Why? Because we're neutral."

"Sure we are. But who are we neutral against?"

— "Critic" in *The New Statesman and Nation*

Newspaper

1711. Mark Twain, in his reporting days, was instructed by an editor never to state anything as a fact that he could not verify from personal knowledge. Sent out to cover an important social event soon afterward, he turned in the following story: "A woman giving the name of Mrs. James Jones, who is reported to be one of the society leaders of the city, is said to have given what purported to be a party yesterday to a number of alleged ladies. The hostess claims to be the wife of a reputed attorney."

1712. One answer to the problem of how to treat reporters is: "Treat them frequently."

— F. H. BRENNAN in *Vanity Fair*

1713. Walter Winchell's favorite story, which may be apocryphal, is about an editorial feud between the old *New York Sun* and the *New York Post,* when both were conservative papers. One day the very proper and staid *Post* lost its temper and editorially called the *Sun* a yellow dog. The *Sun* replied in its starchiest manner: "The *Post* calls the *Sun* a yellow dog. The attitude of the *Sun,* however, will continue to be that of any dog toward any post."

— *Variety*

1714. The newspaper is an institution developed by modern civilization to present the news of the day, to foster commerce and industry, to inform and lead public opinion, and to furnish that check upon government which no constitution has ever been able to provide.

— ROBERT R. MCCORMICK

1715. If words were invented to conceal thought, I think that newspapers are a great improvement on a bad invention.

— HENRY DAVID THOREAU

1716. Curious ideas about anatomy prevail in the press. Recently a newspaper item proclaimed that a certain colonel was "shot in the ticket office." Another paper stated that a man was shot in the "suburbs" as "he kissed her passionately upon her reappearance." She is then alleged to "have whipped him upon his return," whereupon he "kissed her back." Another periodical relates a story in which "Mr. Jones walked in upon her invitation" and that she "seated herself upon his entering" whereas it was thought that she sat down "upon her being asked." To climax it all, it was reported that she "fainted upon his departure."

1717. Gen. Alfred M. Gruenther's favorite newspaperman's

story is of a world traveling newspaperman who was shipwrecked some years ago when cannibalism was still the vogue in some South Sea islands. The natives prepared to drag the journalist to the boiling cauldron when he protested that his newspaper would bring official wrath upon their heads. He demanded to see the chief. The chief asked the newspaperman what his job was on the newspaper. "I'm an assistant editor," the reporter said boasting a bit. "Well, you will soon be promoted to editor-in-chief," said the cannibal chief, smacking his lips.

— *Chicago Tribune*

1718. The following correction appeared in a small town paper: "Our paper carried the notice last week that Mr. John Jones is a defective in the police force. This was a typographical error. Mr. Jones is really a detective in the police farce."

1719. Newspaper: a publication that condemns gambling on the editorial page and prints racing tips on the sports page.

Objective

1720. Lots of times you have to pretend to join a parade in which you're not really interested, in order to get where you are going.

— From *Kitty Foyle* by CHRISTOPHER MORLEY.
Copyright 1939 by CHRISTOPHER MORLEY.
Published by J. B. Lippincott Company

Observation

1721. I have a friend who's a weather forecaster. He bases his forecasts on reports cabled him by experts in all parts of the world. And he's a rotten forecaster—because he never looks out the window.

— DR. HARVEY CUSHING

1722. If I were to prescribe one process in the training of men which is fundamental to success in any direction, it would be thoroughgoing training in the habit of accurate observation. It is a habit which every one of us should be seeking evermore to perfect.

— EUGENE G. GRACE

Obstacle

1723. The greater the obstacle the more glory in overcoming it.

Obstinacy

1724. Obstinacy and heat in argument are surest proofs of folly. Is there anything so stubborn, obstinate, disdainful, contemplative, grave, serious, as an ass?

— MICHEL DE MONTAIGNE

Obstructionist

1725. The worst obstructionist in any community is not the man who is opposed to doing anything, but the man who will not do what he can because he cannot do what he would like to do.

— J. L. LONG

Old age

1726. Those who enjoy the large pleasures of advanced age are those who have sacrificed the small pleasures of youth.

— CHARLES E. CARPENTER

1727. Nobody grows old by merely living a number of years. People grow old only by deserting their ideals. Years wrinkle the face, but to give up enthusiasm wrinkles the soul. Worry, doubt, self-interest, fear, despair—these are the long, long years that bow the head and turn the growing spirit back to dust.

1728. Advice in old age is foolish; for what can be more absurd than to increase our provisions for the road the nearer we approach to our journey's end?

— CICERO

1729. A comfortable old age is the reward of a well-spent youth. Instead of its bringing sad and melancholy prospects of decay, it should give us hopes of eternal youth in a better world.

1730. Old-timer: one who remembers when a man did his own withholding on his take-home pay.

1731. An eighty-year-old man with young ideas had married a girl of twenty-two, and more than anything else in the world he wanted a son. He went to his doctor and explained the situation.

"I'm sorry," said the doctor. "You may be heir-minded, but you're not heir-conditioned."

1732. Old age is when you find yourself using one bend-over to pick up two things.

1733. Old men are fond of giving good advice to console themselves for their inability to give bad examples.

— François de La Rochefoucauld

1734. Forty is the old age of youth, fifty is the youth of old age.

— Victor Hugo

1735. The hell for women who are only handsome is old age.

— Charles de Saint Denis Evremond

1736.   Resignation

> Better to ride
> The rising tide
> Of time's incessant call
> Than to tussle in rage
> With advancing age—
> And get nowhere at all.

1737. The best thing about getting old is that all those things you couldn't have when you were young you no longer want.

— Earl Wilson, Hall Syndicate

1738. There is a uselessness of men above sixty years of age, and an incalculable benefit would result in commercial, political, and in professional life if, as a matter of course, men stopped work at this age.

— Sir William Osler, address at Johns Hopkins University, 1905

1739. Whenever a man's friends begin to compliment him about looking young, he may be sure they think he is growing old.

— Washington Irving

OLD AGE

1740. If life were lived backwards, from old age to youth, there'd be a lot more juvenile delinquents.

1741. I am an old man and have known a great many troubles, but most of them have never happened.

— MARK TWAIN

1742. Growing old is no more than a bad habit which a busy man has no time to form.

— ANDRÉ MAUROIS, *The Art of Living*
(Harper and Brothers)

Old-fashioned

1743. It is better to be old-fashioned and right than to be up-to-date and wrong.

— TIORIO

1744. If a thing is old, it is a sign that it was fit to live. Old families, old customs, old styles survive because they are fit to survive. The guarantee of continuity is quality. Submerge the good in a flood of the new, and the good will come back to join the good which the new brings with it. Old-fashioned hospitality, old-fashioned politeness, old-fashioned honor in business had qualities of survival. These will come back.

1745. Too many of us keep looking forward to the good old days.

Old maid

1746. The girl who lays all her cards on the table is usually left playing solitaire.

Omission

1747. Admiral Sir Andrew Cunningham was aboard his flagship in a Mediterranean port when a cruiser made a sloppy job of tying up to her berth.

The cruiser's captain, dreading the message he knew would come from his commander-in-chief, was relieved, if puzzled, when it was delivered. It consisted of the one word, "Good."

Fifteen minutes later, the captain was interrupted in his bath with a supplement reading, "To previous message please add the word 'God.' "

— The Boston Globe

Opinion

1748. The foolish and dead alone never change their opinion.

—James Russell Lowell,
My Study Windows

1749. Opinions cannot survive if one has no chance to fight for them.

—Thomas Mann

1750. Opinions that are well rooted should grow and change like a healthy tree.

—Irving Batcheller

1751. Your opinion of others is apt to be their opinion of you.

—B. C. Forbes

1752. No one agrees with other people's opinions; he merely agrees with his own opinions expressed by somebody else.

—Sydney Tremayne

Opportunity

1753. Mrs. Smythe was making final arrangements for an elaborate reception. "Nora," she said to her veteran servant, "for the first half-hour I want you to stand at the drawing-room door and call the guests' names as they arrive."

Nora's face lit up. "Thank you, ma'am," she replied. "I've been wanting to do that to some of your friends for the last twenty years."

—Neal O'Hara, McNaught Syndicate

1754. The doors of Opportunity are marked "Push" and "Pull."

1755. I have always thought that the opportunity to do something worth while is the substance, and trying to get something is the shadow.

—Elihu Root

OPPORTUNITY

1756. Small opportunities are often the beginning of great enterprises.

— DEMOSTHENES

1757. Too many people are thinking of security instead of opportunity. They seem more afraid of life than death.

— JAMES F. BYRNES

1758. Opportunities multiply as they are seized; they die when neglected.

1759. Many do with opportunities as children do at the sea shore; they fill their little hands with sand, and then let the grains fall through, one by one, till all are gone.

1760. There exist limitless opportunities in every industry. Where there is an open mind, there will always be a frontier.

— CHARLES F. KETTERING

1761. A customer in a Copenhagen department store complained to the management about the attendant in the ladies' rest room, who had given her a frosty stare when she failed to leave a generous tip.

"Why, we have no attendant in the ladies' room," said the manager.

A check revealed that the "attendant" was a woman who had wandered in for a rest a year ago. While relaxing with her knitting the woman had received coins from patrons who thought she was the attendant. Recognizing opportunity when it knocked, the woman had come in regularly ever since, netting while she knitted.

— WALTER KIERNAN

1762. Times of change are times of fearfulness and times of opportunity. Which they may be for you, depends upon your attitude toward them. Remember that life is not fighting you. No natural powers work against you. They work for everything and everyone that works with them.

Men used to fear the lightning; but one man faced that age-old fear, and found out how to make the lightning serve him and others.

Men feared the uncharted spaces of the seas, until one brave soul set out to face that fear, and found a new world. The oceans that kept continents apart have become lanes of intercourse.

Men feared the skies. They pictured witches on broomsticks, hobgoblins, demons in the air. Intrepid fliers faced the fear, and banished the fearful fancies.

Wise men of today face the future unafraid.

— ERNEST C. WILSON

Opposition

1763. Never ascribe to an opponent motives meaner than your own.

— JAMES MATTHEW BARRIE

1764. I am the inferior of any man whose rights I trample underfoot.

— HORACE GREELEY

Oppression

1765. I am a man of peace. God knows I love peace. But I hope I shall never be such a coward as to mistake oppression for peace.

— LOUIS KOSSUTH

Optimism see also Pessimism

1766. Optimism: waiting for a ship to come in when you haven't sent one out.

1767. Optimist: a woman who leaves the dinner dishes because she will feel more like washing them in the morning.

1768. An optimist is a person who already has his bad breaks relined.

1769. An optimist is one who makes the best of conditions, after making the conditions the best possible.

— DR. LOUIS L. MANN

Oratory see also Public speaking

1770. Orators are most vehement when they have the weakest cause, as men get on horseback when they cannot walk.

— CICERO

ORATORY

1771. An orator or author is never successful till he has learned to make his words smaller than his ideas.

— RALPH WALDO EMERSON

Originality

1772. The more intellectual people are, the more originality they see in other men. To commonplace people all men are much alike.

— BLAISE PASCAL

Origins

1773. What is the origin of "Auld Lang Syne?" Is it a version of an old Irish song? Was it sung to the accompaniment of a harp by itinerant poets 300 years before Robert Burns was born? There are indications such was the case. In any event, wandering entertainers in the Wicklow Mountains in the early 15th century featured a song, the title of which, translated from the Gaelic, was "The Days of Old Long Since." And the theme of the song was that old acquaintances should not be forgotten.

— E. V. DURLING

1774. The term "cow college" got its start 65 years ago (1890) as the first collegiate dairying course began at the University of Wisconsin.

1775. The Horseshoe

According to legend, the ancient Greeks originated the horseshoe to protect the feet of their horses. The first form of shoe was a slipper made of a kind of fiber called Spanish broom (sparta), used as a binding for the diseased feet of both horses and cattle. The Romans called this safeguard for tender feet the "solea spartea" or broom sandal.

The Greeks and Romans later extended the idea to a more permanent shoe for horses and mules and hammered it out of metal, such as iron. It was bound on the hoof and not fastened with nails like the modern horseshoe. Later on the "solea ferrea" (iron shoe) had seven holes for nails. Since the shoe resembled the crescent moon, it became a good luck symbol.

1776. The term *southpaw* is particularly associated with baseball and refers to a left-handed pitcher. It is believed to have had its origin among newspaper sports writers during the earlier days of baseball.

In general, a baseball diamond is laid out with the first base line to the south, so that the sun is kept out of the eyes of the batters as much as possible. Thus a pitcher throwing with his left hand or "paw" (his left to the south), became known as a "southpaw."

1777. Do you know the origin of the word mossback?

Its meaning as a "reactionary" (and later as "outdated") was first applied politically to the Democratic party's conservatives in 1885. It is said to have been derived from an old moss-covered turtle that had stayed put in the same pond.

1778. Fiasco is the Italian word for bottle or flask. It is said that when the Italian glassblowers, in making their beautiful glassware, discovered a flaw in the bulb, they would convert it into an ordinary flask or fiasco. Hence, "fiasco" came to be synonymous with "failure."

Others

1779. The eyes of other people are the eyes that ruin us. If all but myself were blind, I should want neither fine clothes, fine houses, nor fine furniture.

— BENJAMIN FRANKLIN

Paradox

1780. The truest sayings are paradoxical.

— LAO-TSE

Parenthood

1781. The father who does not teach his son his duties is equally guilty with the son who neglects them.

1782. Out of the mouths of babes come words we shouldn't have said in the first place.

1783. Infant prodigies: young people with highly imaginative parents.

PARENTHOOD

1784. Parents wonder why the streams are bitter when they themselves have poisoned the fountain.

— JOHN LOCKE

1785. Too many parents are not on spanking terms with their children.

1786. Most parents allow their children to make a certain number of mistakes. The really wise ones avoid saying "I told you so" afterward. I remember once a parent saying to his 14-year-old boy, "You wouldn't have made that foolish mistake if you had used good judgment." The boy said, "Well, how do you get good judgment?" and the parent rather slowly answered, "By making mistakes, of course." . . . Wise children ought to suspect their too-wise parents of having been rather too-foolish children.

— JOHN F. SCHERESCHEWSKY, *You and Your Child*

1787. To parental misconduct is traceable a great part of the domestic disorder commonly accredited to the perversity of children, and the defects of children mirror the defects of their parents.

1788. Being a parent used to be one of the most simple, natural, inevitable developments in the world. But, nowadays, one has no business to be married unless, waking and sleeping, one is conscious of the responsibility.

— DR. ABRAHAM FLEXNER

1789. Children begin by loving their parents. As they grow older, they judge them. Sometimes they forgive them.

1790. Parents: persons who spend half their time worrying how a child will turn out, and the rest of the time wondering when a child will turn in.

— TED COOK

Past, The

1791. An old-timer is one who remembers when he could buy a pound of steak for a dime, but forgets he had to work an hour to earn the dime.

Patience

1792. The anvil lasts longer than the hammer.

— Old proverb

1793. A teacher told Johnny to give a sentence using the word "I."

"I is—," began Johnny.

"No, no. Not 'I is' " interrupted the teacher. "Always say 'I am'."

"All right," Johnny agreed. "I am the ninth letter of the alphabet."

1794. A handful of patience is worth more than a bushel of brains.

— Dutch proverb

1795. Patience: being able to wait for the first coat of paint to dry before adding the second.

1796. There is no road too long for the man who advances deliberately and without undue haste; no honors too distant to the man who prepares himself for them with patience.

— JEAN DE LA BRUYÈRE

1797. John Wesley, the founder of Methodism, used to recall that as a youth his behavior often displeased his father. His mother was more forbearing. "How can you have the patience," exploded the elder Wesley, "to tell that blockhead John the same thing 20 times over?"

"Why," replied Mrs. Wesley, "if I had told him but 19 times I had wasted my breath!"

Patriotism

1798. The proper means of increasing the love we bear to our native country is to reside some time in a foreign one.

1799. A woman with a commanding air once spoke to President Lincoln as follows:

"Mr. President, you must give me a colonel's commission for my son. I demand it of you, sir, not as a favor but as a right. My grandfathers fought at Lexington; my uncle was the only man who did not run at Bladensburg; my father fought at New Orleans and my husband was killed at Monterey."

PATRIOTISM

"I guess, madam," said Lincoln, "your family has done enough for our country. It's time to give somebody else a chance."

1800. Patriotism is not necessarily included in rebellion. A man may hate his king, yet not love his country.

— DR. SAMUEL JOHNSON

1801. We should behave toward our country as women behave toward the men they love. A loving wife will do anything for her husband except stop criticizing and trying to improve him. We should cast the same affectionate but sharp glance at our country. We should love it, but also insist upon telling it all its faults. The noisy, empty "patriot," not the critic, is the dangerous citizen.

— J. B. PRIESTLEY, *Rain Upon Godshill*
(Harper and Brothers)

Patron

1802. Patron: a wretch who supports with insolence and is paid with flattery.

— DR. SAMUEL JOHNSON

Peace see also *War*

1803. If there is righteousness in the heart there will be beauty in the character. If there be beauty in the character, there will be harmony in the home. If there is harmony in the home, there will be order in the nation. When there is order in the nation, there will be peace in the world.

— Chinese proverb

1804. It also takes two to make up after a quarrel.

1805. The world will never have lasting peace so long as men reserve for war the finest human qualities. Peace, no less than war, requires idealism and self-sacrifice and a righteous and dynamic faith.

— JOHN FOSTER DULLES

Penalty

1806. In Washington, a man returning from Moscow told friends that the front door of the American Embassy was never locked. "Aren't there any thieves in Moscow?" asked a surprised listener.

"Oh, yes," he replied, "there are thieves all right. But the penalty for being seen entering the American Embassy is stiffer than the penalty for larceny."

Pension

1807. Pension: in England, understood to mean pay given to a state hireling for treason to his country.

— DR. SAMUEL JOHNSON

People

1808. Igloo: an icicle built for two.

1809. Name five internationally famous people who were all born on the same day.
Answer: The Dionne Quintuplets.

1810. The voice of the people is the voice of God. (Vox populi, vox Dei.)

— ALCUIN, *Epistle to Charlemagne*

1811. Governments are nation-minded; religions are church-minded; labor unions are union-minded; businessmen are business-minded. But, altho all of these exist for the benefit of humanity, none seems to be truly people-minded.

— HARRY E. BARNES, introduction to book by
Manmatha Nath Chatterjee, *Out of Confusion* (Antioch Press)

Perfection

1812. If you expect perfection from people, your whole life is a series of disappointments, grumblings and complaints. If, on the contrary, you pitch your expectations low, taking folks as the efficient creatures which they are, you are frequently surprised by having them perform better than you had hoped.

— BRUCE BARTON

1813. We all know it isn't human to be perfect and too many of us take advantage of it.

— *Corbin* (Kentucky) *Daily Tribune*

PERFECTION

1814. It is only imperfection that complains of what is imperfect. The more perfect we are, the more gentle and quiet we become towards the defects of others.

— François Fénelon

1815. The finer the nature, the more flaws it will show through the clearness of it; and it is a law of this universe, that the best things shall seldomest be seen in their best form.

— John Ruskin

1816. Years ago, when the Dow Chemical Company was just getting started, H. H. Dow, the founder, stood talking to the head of the electrical shops when a stranger walked up to them, stating that he was an electrician and had heard there might be an opening. He went on at great length about his qualifications, repeatedly emphasizing that he never, never made a mistake.

Before the head of the electrical shops could say a word, Dow spoke up. "Sorry, mister. But I've got 3,000 men working at the plant, and they make at least 3,000 mistakes a day. It wouldn't do at all to hire a man who never makes a mistake!"

— Pete Derrio

1817. A man can do his best only by confidently seeking (and perpetually missing) an unattainable perfection.

— Ralph Barton Perry

Performance

1818. Pressure is on us by the nature of the job. Performance releases pressure.

Permission

1819. The chief vice of many people consists not in doing evil but in permitting it.

— Roy M. Pearson, *This Do—And Live*
(Abingdon Press) Reprinted by permission

Persecution see also *Intolerance*

1820. Persecution is not wrong because it is cruel; but it is cruel because it is wrong.

— Richard Whately

Perseverance

1821. Perseverance is more prevailing than violence; and many things which cannot be overcome when they are together yield themselves up when taken little by little.

— PLUTARCH

1822. Fight one more round. When your feet are so tired that you have to shuffle back to the center of the ring, fight one more round. When your arms are so tired that you can hardly lift your hands to come on guard, fight one more round. When your nose is bleeding and your eyes are black and you are so tired that you wish your opponent would crack you one on the jaw and put you to sleep, fight one more round—remembering that the man who always fights one more round is never whipped.

— JAMES J. CORBETT

1823.
For he who fights and runs away
May live to fight another day;
But he who is in battle slain
Can never rise and fight again.

— OLIVER GOLDSMITH, *The Art of Poetry
on a New Plan*

1824. The great composer does not set to work because he is inspired, but becomes inspired because he is working. Beethoven, Wagner, Bach and Mozart settled down day after day to the job in hand with as much regularity as an accountant settles down each day to his figures. They didn't waste time waiting for an inspiration.

— ERNEST NEWMAN

1825. If you get up one time more than you fall you will make it through.

1826. Perseverance: a lowly virtue whereby mediocrity achieves an inglorious success.

— AMBROSE BIERCE

1827. The Man Who Quits

The man who quits has a brain and hand
As good as the next, but lacks the sand

That would make him stick, with a courage stout,
To whatever he tackles, and fight it out.

He starts with a rush, and a solemn vow
That he'll soon be showing the other how;
Then something new strikes his roving eye,
And his task is left for the bye-and-bye.

It's up to each man what becomes of him;
He must find in himself the grit and vim
That bring success; he can get the skill,
If he brings to the task a steadfast will.

No man is beaten till he gives in;
Hard luck can't stand for a cheerful grin;
The man who fails needs a better excuse,
Than the quitter's whining, "What's the use?"

For the man who quits lets his chances slip,
Just because he's too lazy to keep his grip.
The man who sticks goes ahead with a shout,
While the man who quits joins the "Down and out."

— Author unknown

1828. You can do what you want to do, accomplish what you want to accomplish, attain any reasonable objective you may have in mind . . . Not all of a sudden, perhaps not in one swift and sweeping act of achievement . . . But you can do it gradually—day by day and play by play—if you *want* to do it, if you *will* to do it, if you *work* to do it, over a sufficiently long period of time.

— WILLIAM E. HOLLER

1829. To get through the hardest journey we need take only one step at a time, but we must keep on stepping.

1830. Little and often make much.

1831. The difference between perseverance and obstinacy is, that one often comes from a strong will, and the other from a strong won't.

— HENRY WARD BEECHER

1832. Never despair; but if you do, work on in despair.

— EDMUND BURKE

1833. Keep trying. It's only from the valley that the mountain seems high.

Persistence see also *Determination*

1834. Vacillating people seldom succeed. They seldom win the solid respect of their fellows. Successful men and women are very careful in reaching decisions and very persistent and determined in action thereafter.

— L. G. ELLIOTT

1835. Big shots are only little shots who keep shooting.

— CHRISTOPHER MORLEY

Personality

1836. Benjamin Franklin went through life an altered man because he once paid too dearly for a penny whistle. My concern springs usually from a deeper source, to wit, from having bought a whistle when I did not want one.

— ROBERT LOUIS STEVENSON

Persuasion

1837. A guest towel is what often persuades people their hands don't need washing after all.

Pessimism see also *Optimism*

1838. The pessimist is worried because he's afraid the optimist will be right.

1839. Pessimism is only the name that men of weak nerves give to wisdom.

— MARK TWAIN

1840. A pessimist is one who makes difficulties of his opportunities; an optimist is one who makes opportunities of his difficulties.

— REGINALD B. MANSELL

Pharmacy see *Drug Store*

Philosophy

1841. A philosopher and a theologian were engaged in a disputation. The theologian used the old quip about a philosopher resembling a blind man, in a dark room, looking for a black cat—which wasn't there.

"That may be," said the philosopher, "but a theologian would have found it."

1842. The mood of the moment must never be permitted to congeal into a permanent philosophy of life.

—Dr. A. L. Sachar, speech, April, 1955

Plagiarism

1843. All work and no plagiarism makes a dull speech.

Planning

1844. An intelligent plan is the first step to success. Planning is the open road to one's destination. If one doesn't know where he is going, how can he expect to get there?

1845. Make no little plans; they have no magic to stir men's blood and probably themselves will not be realized. Make big plans: aim high in hope and work, remembering that a noble, logical diagram once recorded will never die, but long after we are gone will be a living thing, asserting itself with ever-growing insistency. Remember that our sons and grandsons are going to do things that would stagger us. Let your watchword be order and your beacon duty.

—Daniel H. Burnham in *Daniel H. Burnham* by Charles Moore

1846. It takes as much energy to wish as it does to plan.

Pleasing

1847. It is vain to hope to please all alike. Let a man stand with his face in what direction he will, he must necessarily turn his back on one-half of the world.

Pleasure

1848. Business is always interfering with pleasure—but it makes other pleasures possible.

— WILLIAM FEATHER

1849. The greatest pleasure I know is to do a good act by stealth, and to have it found out by accident.

— CHARLES LAMB

1850. The greatest and noblest pleasure which men can have in this world is to discover new truths; and the next is to shake off old prejudices.

— FREDERICK THE GREAT

1851. Everybody is able to give pleasure in some way. One person may do it by coming into a room, another by going out.

— LADY MAUDE WARRENDER

Poet — poetry

1852. Poets are born—that's the trouble.

— WALTER WINCHELL

1853. Du Bose Heyward was once lecturing in Detroit. After his talk, a group of local women insisted upon questioning him as to his opinion of their local laureate, Edgar A. Guest. After vainly seeking to sidestep the issue, Heyward was at last driven to acknowledge that he did not consider Mr. Guest's work poetry. Great indignation resulted.

"Mr. Heyward," snapped one fearsome lady, "what kind of car do you drive?"

The poet and novelist was compelled to admit that he drove none.

"Eddie Guest," said the lady cuttingly, "drives a Packard."

Point of view

1854. There is no such thing as bad weather; there are only good clothes.

— ELIZABETH WOODBRIDGE, *Jonathan Papers*

POINT OF VIEW

1855. A certain woman with a reputation as a "manhater" announced suddenly she was going to be married. "Goodness gracious!" exclaimed a friend, "I thought you despised all men."

"Oh, I do," replied the bride-to-be, "but this man asked me to marry him."

1856. The Joneses were Europe-bound aboard a large trans-Atlantic liner with their infant child. One afternoon, in great excitement, Mrs. Jones entered their cabin and aroused her sleeping husband. "I've just been stopped by half a dozen passengers who paid me the compliment of saying that Junior looks just like me and here you've been wanting me to believe that he was the very image of you—a dead ringer for you."

"That can't be; I just don't believe it," replied the angered Mr. Jones. "Let me have that child, I'll find out for myself." And so saying, he took the child, threw him over his shoulder and bounded for the deck.

He was back in a short while with a sneer on his face.

"Looks like you? Why a dozen people stopped to tell me that the kid was the spittin' image of his dad. And here you're trying to tell me that the child looks like you. Quit kidding me, will you?"

"Well, I can understand it all right!" said Mrs. Jones. "If you'll only look, you'll see you're carrying him upside down."

1857. An Irishman, speaking of a relative who was hanged, commented that he had "died during a *tightrope* performance."

1858. A man who had invested rather steeply in some mail order uranium securities decided to have a Wall Street friend look them over.

"Don't you think I stand a good chance of making a fortune out of that mine?" he asked.

"Out of it, yes," said the broker. "In it, no."

1859. The private was whistling happily as he cleaned out the carrier pigeon cages.

"Well," said a passing officer, "that's the first time we've ever had anyone happy on that job."

"Oh," said the private, "it's not so bad. Before I was transferred here I was in the cavalry."

1860. I can complain because rose bushes have thorns or rejoice because thorn bushes have roses. It's all how you look at it.

—J. KENFIELD MORLEY

1861. Two men, a guide and a disgruntled sportsman, were standing in a thick woods half-way up the side of a mountain.

"Humph!" snorted the greenhorn, glowering at the underbrush. "Where's the beautiful scenery you were bragging about?"

"You're standing on it," the guide grinned, "as you'll see when we reach the top."

Viewpoint depends on where you stand. The basis of a man's judgment is the by-product of his experience; perspective changes constantly with the passing of time and the growth of wisdom.

1862. A parishioner called at the clergyman's home. Presently the minister's little son went up to the visiting lady and blurted, "My, how ugly you are."

Horrified, his mother remonstrated, "Johnny! Whatever can you mean by saying such a thing?"

"I only meant—meant it for a joke, mother," Johnny stammered.

"Well," his mother purred unwittingly, "how much better the joke would have been if you had said to Mrs. Smith, 'How pretty you are!' "

1863. Alfred Gwynne Vanderbilt, owner of "The Grey Horse," discovered one summer the difference between English and French women. He left London for Paris on June 23, and the English woman who drove him to the London airport remarked: "Alfred, did you know yesterday was the longest day of the year?"

That evening he attended a dinner party in Paris, and the French woman seated beside him observed: "Mr. Vanderbilt, did you know yesterday was the shortest night in the year?"

—ART BUCHWALD in the *New York Herald-Tribune*

1864. "It can't be done!" said the tear. "That's what my salt tells me!"

"Indeed it can be done," said the bead of sweat. "That's what my salt tells me!"

1865. A New York lawyer who wanted to buy a summer home

found just the right one on a small island off the Maine coast. Approaching an old man painting on a boat nearby, he inquired about the owner.

"Place belongs to the Hallet boys," the man said, and pointed to a dot in the distance. "That is Ben Hallet over there. Out haulin' his lobster traps—he'll be in in a couple of hours. Ben's the smartest feller around here. Seen him dig eight, ten bushel clams in one tide. Gits good money for 'em too."

"And the brother?" inquired the would-be buyer.

"Waal, he ain't near so smart as Ben. Didn't amount to much—lawyer or sumpin', down in Boston."

—E. M. DUNNING in *The Reader's Digest*

1866. Oscar Wilde arrived at his club one evening, after witnessing a first production of a play that was a complete failure.

"Oscar, how did your play go tonight?" said a friend.

"Oh," was the lofty response, "the play was a great success, but the audience was a failure."

Poise

1867. Poise is an acquired characteristic which enables father to buy a new pair of shoes at the same time he is ignoring a hole in his sock.

1868. *A father's advice to his son:* "Lose as if you like it; win as if you were used to it."

Policy

1869. I have never had a policy. I have simply tried to do what seemed best each day, as each day came.

—ABRAHAM LINCOLN

Politeness see also Courtesy

1870. Politeness is the art of choosing among your thoughts.

—MADAME DE STAËL

1871. On a bus a man gave a woman his seat. She fainted. On recovering she thanked him. Then he fainted.

268

1872. If we treat people too long with that pretended liking called politeness, we shall find it hard not to like them in the end.

— LOGAN PEARSALL SMITH, *All Trivia*
(Harcourt, Brace and Company)

Politics

1873. On one occasion when Lord Macaulay was running for re-election to his seat in Parliament, he was standing side by side with his opponent when he was suddenly struck by a dead cat. The member of the audience who had thrown the animal at once apologized saying that he had intended it for his opponent.

"Well," said Macaulay, "I wish you had meant it for me and struck him."

1874. In a discussion on the Senate floor of taxes on night clubs, Senator Eugene D. Millikin, ranking Republican member of the Finance Committee, frequently mentioned the "23" Club in New York. Later, reporters caught up with Millikin and told him that the celebrated spot wasn't the "23" Club but "21."

"I know," whispered the Senator, "but in politics you've got to appear to be ignorant of things like that."

— Washington Bureau, *The Cleveland*
(Ohio) *Plain Dealer*

1875. When Oliver Cromwell first coined his money, an old cavalier looking on one of the new pieces read this inscription on one side: "God is with us." On the other, "The Commonwealth of England." "I see," said he, "that God and the Commonwealth are on different sides."

1876. You cannot help being a politician. You cannot live for an hour without being a politician. But what a man generally means when he says that he is not a politician is this—that he has been all his life enjoying his political privileges and grossly neglecting his political duties; and in that sense the observation is scarcely to his credit. As a matter of fact, politics, properly understood, is simply Science of Life—the doctrine of the way in which I am to do my duty to my neighbor, which is an essential part of true religion. It is nothing in the world except religion applied to human society; in fact, it is the practical recognition of the Second Table of the Law of God.

— THE REVEREND HUGH PRICE HUGHES

1877. Bribery is a sin. It is condemned in the law of Moses: "And thou shalt take no gift; for a gift bindeth the wise, and perverteth the words of the righteous." These words are as true today as when they were written.

— THE REVEREND BERNARD PAINE

1878. A faithful setting forth of Christian duty at the polls, not to vote for this or that man, but to vote conscientiously as before God, and to make the use of the franchise a solemn duty to be prayerfully performed, is a part of the minister's function, when he is teaching his people how to live on earth as representatives of God's truth.

— HOWARD CROSBY, D.D.

1879. The trouble is not in our institutions, imperfect as they doubtless are. The crying necessity for reform springs from the fact that while our institutions are representative theoretically, our public officials are not so, actually.

— FULTON MCMAHON

1880. A Democratic political leader in Illinois always showed up at Republican rallies. He seemed to take grim pleasure in attending these gatherings, somewhat to the discomfort of assembled Republicans. His presence seemed to make their parties seem less homey.

At last one day, a Republican leader asked the old gentleman why he came to their meetings. "Is it in your mind that you might get converted or something?"

"Oh, no!" said the Democrat. "Nothing like that. I'll tell you; I just come around to your meetings just so as to keep my disgust fresh."

1881. Public office is a public trust.

— WILLIAM C. HUDSON

1882. Being allergic to unpopular viewpoints is the best mental equipment for success in politics.

— DAN KIDNEY, Scripps-Howard Newspapers

POLITICS should be...

1883. Politics is the art by which politicians obtain campaign contributions from the rich and votes from the poor on the pretext of protecting each from the other.

1884. When a man assumes a public trust, he should consider himself as a public property.

— THOMAS JEFFERSON

1885. Politicians take no interest in eugenics because the unborn have no vote.

— WILLIAM RALPH INGE

1886. Politics I conceive to be nothing more than the science of the ordered progress of society along the lines of greatest usefulness and convenience to itself.

— WOODROW WILSON

1887. Those who would treat politics and morality apart will never understand the one or the other.

— JOHN MORLEY, *Rousseau*

1888. There is a homely old adage which runs: "Speak softly and carry a big stick; you will go far." If the American nation will speak softly and yet build and keep at a pitch of the highest training a thoroughly efficient navy, the Monroe Doctrine will go far.

— THEODORE ROOSEVELT, address at
Minnesota State Fair, 1901

1889. A mugwump is a person educated beyond his intellect.

— HORACE PORTER in Cleveland,
Blaine Campaign

1890. Every time I fill a vacant office I make ten malcontents and one ingrate.

— MOLIÈRE, quoting LOUIS XIV in *Siècle
de Louis Quatorz*

1891. "My friends!" cried the energetic Congressional candidate, "as a boy I fought with our forces in World War I. As an officer I fought in the second World War. I saw service in the Korean incident. I have often had no bed but the battlefield; no canopy but the sky. I have marched over frozen ground until every step was marked with blood. I—."

"Just a minute," interrupted a listener. "Did you say you'd slept on the ground with no covers?"

"That's right!"

"And that you saw service in both World Wars?"

"That's right!"

"And that your feet have bled from walking on frozen ground?"

"That's quite right!"

"Then," concluded the listener, "you've done enough for your country. Go home and rest. I'll vote for the other fellow."

1892. Representative Jones from Illinois was awakened one night by his wife, who whispered, "John, John, get up! There's a burglar in the house."

"Burglar, nothing," he said, "there may be burglars in the Senate, but in the House, never."

1893. "It's terrible—the two great leaders of our party have split."

"How—fifty-fifty?"

1894. A politician running for office was incensed at remarks which had been made about him by the paper of the town. He burst into the editorial room and exclaimed,—"You are telling lies about me in your paper, and you know it!"

"You have no cause for complaint," said the editor. "What would you do if we told the truth about you?"

1895. A western Congressman, defeated in his fight for re-election, inserted this ad in his local newspaper: "I wish to thank all those who voted for me, and my wife wishes to thank all those who didn't."

> — From *Laughing Stock*, edited by BENNETT
> CERF. Copyright 1945 by BENNETT CERF.
> Published by Grosset & Dunlap

1896. No politician, of either party, is quite as bad and mistaken as his opponents say he is, and none is quite as good as his friends claim he is.

> — R. L. DUFFUS in *Nation's Business*

1897. The mistake a lot of politicians make is in forgetting they've been appointed and thinking they've been anointed.

> — MRS. CLAUDE PEPPER

1898. At the beginning of a political campaign, Chauncey

Depew chanced to meet one of the leading men on the other side. This man said to Mr. Depew, "Can we not carry on this campaign without any mud-slinging?" Mr. Depew replied: "That's a good idea. I'll tell you what I'll do. If you refrain from telling any lies about the Republican party, I will promise not to tell the truth about the Democratic party. Will you agree?"

1899. The county road commissioner had been re-elected for so many terms that he was said to have worn down his swivel chair to the point where it would fit no one else, but he did a good job. Suddenly a self-styled reform candidate of doubtful sincerity threatened to unseat the old commissioner.

"You all know that Commissioner Williams has charge of the road system," the "reform" candidate thundered in one speech. "Let me remind you taxpayers that the widest, best-paved road runs right past Commissioner Williams' farm!"

As he paused to let this sink in, a voice from the crowd rang out, "That's why we should re-elect Williams—he's already got *his* road."

> — Helen M. Heppell in *Saturday Evening Post*

1900. If you think politics easy, try standing on a fence while keeping one ear to the ground.

1901. The donkey first appeared as a Democratic party symbol in 1870 in a Thomas Nast cartoon in *Harper's Weekly*. Nast also drew the GOP elephant, the Tammany Tiger, and the standard depiction of Uncle Sam.

> — *Quote*

1902. An election campaign should not be an orgy of mud-slinging. An election campaign should be the opportunity for calm, unselfish, mature—if you will, scientific—study of the issues. Therein lies America's great need, that politics should cease to be childish, that politics should follow not the way of the guttersnipe but the way of the mature, responsible, conscientious adult.

> — Rabbi Abraham Cronbach, *The Jew Requites America, New Outlook*

1903. Party honesty is party expedience.

> — Grover Cleveland, interview in *New York Commercial Advertiser,* 1889

POLITICS

1904. All political parties die at last of swallowing their own lies.

> — Attributed to JOHN ARBUTHNOT,
> *Life of Emerson*

1905. All political power is a trust.

> — CHARLES JAMES FOX

1906. These are exciting days in Washington. Some are getting posts while others are getting the gate.

1907. A politician has to be able to see both sides of an issue so he can get around it.

1908. Politics makes strange bedfellows, but they soon get accustomed to the same bunk.

1909. John Cameron Swayze used to tell of the history professor who asked his class for a clear, concise definition of a politician.

"I'll give you one," replied the son of a Congressman, "if you'll just tell me to which party you refer."

1910. Asked what he thought of the two candidates for the election, an enlightened voter replied:

"Well, when I look at them I'm thankful only one of them can be elected."

1911. Back in 1885, John Allen, of Tupelo, Miss., sought election to the House of Representatives. His principal opponent was a General Tucker, of the Army of the Confederacy, in which John Allen had served as a private. In one memorable debate, the general contrasted his own high rank with Allen's lowly military status.

"Yes sir," was Allen's rebuttal, "I admit I was only a private. In fact, I was just a picket who stood guard over the general when he slept. And now, all you fellows who were generals and had privates standing guard over you, you vote for General Tucker. All you boys who were privates and stood guard over the generals, you vote for Private John Allen."

They did, and John Allen served in the House of Representatives for the next 16 years.

> — HODDING CARTER in *Saturday
> Evening Post*

1912. There are two political parties in this country, not because there are two sides to every question, but because there are two sides to every office—outside and inside.

1913. In politics the paths of glory lead but to the gravy.

1914. He that accuses all mankind of corruption ought to remember that he is sure to convict only one.

— EDMUND BURKE

1915. A political platform is just like the one on the back of a street car—not meant to stand on, just to get in on.

1916. The Alabama Democrat who ran for sheriff managed to get only 55 votes out of a total of 3500. The next day he walked down Main Street with two guns hanging from his belt.

"You were not elected and you have no right to carry guns," fellow-citizens told him.

"Listen, folks," he replied, "a man with no more friends than I've got in this county needs to carry guns."

1917. The political community needs to be taught how and what to laugh at; how and what to scorn and pity; needs to be taught continuously that honor is not the same as fame or notoriety; that physical bravery is not the only form of courage. It needs to be taught the proper objects of anger or of love. It needs to be taught the nature of justice. And above all, the political community needs to be taught that the capacity of the human mind has yet to be explored, that there can be new possibilities for men themselves.

— SENATOR J. WILLIAM FULBRIGHT,
speech, January, 1955

1918. Politics: the art of looking for trouble, finding it everywhere, diagnosing it incorrectly, and applying the wrong remedies.

— GROUCHO MARX

1919. The political machine triumphs because it is a united minority acting against a divided majority.

— WILL DURANT

1920. A lot of voters always cast their ballot for the candidate who seems to them to be one of the people. That means he must have the same superstitions, the same unbalanced prejudices, and the same lack of understanding of public finances that are characteristic of the majority. A better choice would be a candidate who has a closer understanding and a better education than the majority. Too much voting is based on affability rather than on ability.

— WILLIAM FEATHER

1921. A newcomer to politics got elected to Congress and someone asked him how he did it.

"I didn't like what the incumbent Congressman was doing, so I ran against him," he said.

"But the party machine was against you," persisted the questioner. "How did you manage to win?"

"Well," answered the new Congressman, "I guess everyone who knew me voted for him, and everybody who knew him voted for me —and he knew more people."

— GEORGE DIXON, King Features Syndicate, Inc.

1922. Old politicians never die; they just run once too often.

1923. People vote their resentment, not their appreciation. The average man does not vote for anything, but *against* something.

— WILLIAM BENNETT MUNRO

1924. One sometimes wonders whether the members of Congress would have to mend their fences so often if they had not sat on them so much.

— Christian Science Monitor

1925. *Political leader at a party caucus to pick a candidate:* "He'd be all right if we could shut his mouth retroactively."

1926. The first wisdom of politics is strength.

— DAVID BEN-GURION

1927. *Haughty dowager to public-opinion poll investigator:* "I never vote! It's quite a relief not to feel responsible for what goes on in Washington."

1928. A law sired by the Democrats and damned by the Republicans.

— JOSEPH P. KENNEDY

1929. *Mrs. Deleigh (meeting a politician at a party):* "I've heard a great deal about you."
Politician (absent-mindedly): "Possibly, but you can't prove it."

1930. One of the virtues of a small town politician is that he knows he has got to stick pretty close to the truth.

— O. A. BATTISTA

Popularity

1931. Popularity: to be gifted with the virtue of knowing a whole lot of uninteresting people.

Position

1932. Pigmies placed on the shoulders of giants see more than the giants themselves.

— DIDACTUS STELLA—*Lucan*, quoted by
BURTON in *Anatomy of Melancholy*

Positiveness

1933. Positiveness is a most absurd foible. If you are in the right it lessens your triumph; if you are in the wrong it adds shame to your defeat.

— LAURENCE STERNE

Poverty see also *Wealth*

1934. Poverty is the mother of crime.

— CASSIODORUS, *Variae*

1935. Poverty is not dishonorable in itself, but only when it comes from idleness, intemperance, extravagance, and folly.

— PLUTARCH

1936. A rich Hassid came to Rabbi Dov Baer for his blessing. "What is the conduct of your household, and what table do you set from day to day?" asked the Maggid.

"My household is conducted with great simplicity," said the rich man. "My own meal consists of dry bread with salt."

Full of indignation, the Maggid looked at him and asked: "Why do you not favor yourself with meat and wine, as becomes a man of wealth."

For a long time he berated the rich Hassid until the latter finally promised that henceforth he would serve meals of more becoming

POVERTY

viands. When the Hassid had departed, the Hassidim asked the Maggid: "What matters it to you whether he eats bread with salt or meat with wine at his meal?"

The Maggid answered: "It matters a great deal. If he enjoys a good fare and his meal consists of fine viands, then he will understand that the poor man must have at least dry bread with salt. But if, being wealthy, he renounces all enjoyments of life and lives so stingily, he will believe it is sufficient for the poor to eat stones."

1937. The thing that keeps man broke is not the wolf at the door. It's the mink in the window.

Power

1938. Power intoxicates men. When a man is intoxicated by alcohol he can recover, but when intoxicated by power he seldom recovers.

— JAMES F. BYRNES

1939. Love of money often makes a man a coward, but love of power always makes a man a brute. It is the most degrading love of all. Love of material well-being seldom hurts others, but love of power and glory always does. The former makes slaves of the common people; the latter makes slaves of the great.

— Reprinted with permission of publishers, from *Looking Beyond* by LIN YUTANG. Copyright 1955 by LIN YUTANG (Prentice-Hall, Inc.)

1940. Anyone entrusted with power will abuse it if not also animated with the love of truth and virtue, no matter whether he be a prince, or one of the people.

— JEAN DE LA FONTAINE

Practice

1941. Paderewski, the great pianist, once explained that he practiced faithfully every day.

"If I miss one day's practice," said he, "I notice it. If I miss two days, the critics notice it. If I miss three days, the audience notices it."

Praise

1942. Fool's praise is censure.

1943. Praise a fool and you may make him useful.

— Old proverb

1944. The Praise you take, although it be your Due,
Will be suspected if it come from you.

— BENJAMIN FRANKLIN, *Poor Richard's
Almanac*

1945. He who praises everybody praises nobody.

— DR. SAMUEL JOHNSON in BOSWELL's
Life of Johnson

1946. There is nothing like undeserved praise for putting human beings in a good temper. Praise not only pretends that we are better than we are; it may help to make us better than we are.

— *The New Statesman*

1947. Cal Johnson, the former Republican congressman from Illinois, used to tell the story about the minister who knew he was preaching the worst sermon of his life. When he had finished, a normally testy member of the congregation praised the sermon to the skies.

"But why?" asked the minister.

"Because," answered his new admirer, "I don't like no preachin' at all, and that's as near no preachin' at all as I ever heard."

— *Chicago Tribune*

1948. Never praise a woman too highly. If you stop she'll think you don't love her any more. If you keep it up she'll soon think she's too good for you.

1949. It's only eighteen inches between a pat on the back and a kick in the pants.

1950. Praise is like a shadow. It follows him who flees from it, but flees from him who follows it.

1951. A refusal of praise is a desire to be praised twice.

— FRANÇOIS DE LA ROCHEFOUCAULD

PRAISE

1952. Parents and teachers who give affection and praise only when it is deserved are withholding the most important food of life ... It is time we recognized that love and praise are just as important as discipline—just as basic to sound development—and that there are no strings attached. A child who has to *earn* love or recognition from the most important people in his life—mom and dad—cannot be blamed for lying, cheating, or stealing to get it.

> — From *Understanding Teen-Agers* by PAUL H. LANDIS. Copyright 1955 (Appleton-Century-Crofts, Inc.)

1953. Praise, like gold and diamonds, owes its value to its scarcity.

> — DR. SAMUEL JOHNSON

1954. Those who are greedy of praise prove that they are poor in merit.

> — PLUTARCH

1955. Praise: what you receive when you are no longer alive.

1956. A unanimous chorus of praise is not an assurance of survival; authors who please everyone at once are quickly exhausted.

> — ANDRÉ GIDE

1957. I know of no manner of speaking so offensive as that of giving praise, and closing with an exception.

> — SIR RICHARD STEELE

Prayer

1958. Prayer is the peace of our spirit, the stillness of our thoughts, the evenness of our recollection, the sea of our meditation, the rest of our cares, and the calm of our tempest.

> — JEREMY TAYLOR

1959. A burly officer of the law was standing outside one of our temples during Yom Kippur, carefully scrutinizing the tickets. A little Jew approached, but was stopped by the "cop."

The Jew said, "I want to go in for just one minute to visit my brother."

"Nothing doing," replied the officer in a marked brogue. "If you have no ticket, you can't get in."

"Please," the Jew continued, "I just want to tell him something important, I'll be right out."

The officer thoughtfully scratched his head. "Well," he relented, "if you're sure you're just going to speak to your brother, it will be all right. But mind, DON'T LET ME CATCH YOU PRAYING!"

1960. After Sunday morning services in a Boston church, a woman stayed to chat with a friend, leaving her purse on the seat. When she returned for her purse, it was gone, but she quickly found it in the possession of the clergyman himself.

"I thought I had better hold it," he said. "You must remember that there are some in the congregation so simple that they might consider it an answer to prayer."

— ELLEN LUCINDA BURNAP

1961. A quick thinking employe came up with a new one when his foreman demanded, "How come you're sleeping on the job?"

"Goodness," replied the employe, "can't a man close his eyes for a minute of prayer?"

1962. The head of a monastic order heard that one of the monks was expressing doubt of the order's motto, "Pray and work." So he invited the young man to go rowing with him, and took the oars himself. After a while the monk shook his head and commented, "But if you just use one oar you'll continue to go around in circles and you won't get anywhere."

"That is right, son," replied the elder man. "One oar is called prayer, and the other is called work. Unless you use both at the same time, you just go in circles and don't get anywhere."

1963. The influence of prayer on the human mind and body is as demonstrable as that of secreting glands. Its results can be measured in terms of increased physical buoyancy, greater intellectual vigor, moral stamina, and a deeper understanding of the realities underlying human relationship.

— DR. ALEXIS CARREL

1964. Prayer is the soul's sincere desire unuttered or expressed.

— JAMES MONTGOMERY

1965. Prayer covers the whole of a man's life. There is no thought, feeling, yearning, or desire, however low, trifling, or vulgar we may deem it, which, if it affects our real interest or happiness, we may not lay before God and be sure of sympathy. His nature is such that our often coming does not tire him. The whole burden of the whole life of every man may be rolled on to God and not weary him, though it has wearied the man.

—HENRY WARD BEECHER

1966. Who rises from prayer a better man, his prayer is answered.

—GEORGE MEREDITH

Preaching

1967. He first practices what he preaches, and then preaches according to his practice.

—CONFUCIUS, *Analects*

1968. At the close of a rather long Sunday service, a little old lady approached the minister, extended her hand and said, "Reverend, I really must apologize for dozing just a little during your fine sermon. But," she concluded stoutly, "I want you to know I didn't miss a thing!"

1969. *Woman, shaking hands with the preacher after the service:* "Wonderful sermon! Everything you said applies to somebody or other I know."

1970. A minister illustrated a point in his sermon by saying that a beneficent wisdom knows which of us grows best in sunlight and which of us must have shade. "You know you plant roses in the sunlight," he said, "but if you want your fuchsias to grow, they must be kept in a shady nook."

Afterward a woman came up to him, her face radiant. "Dr. Smith," she said, clasping his hand, "I'm so grateful for your splendid sermon." His heart glowed for a moment. But then she went on fervently, "Yes, I never knew before just what was the matter with my fuchsias!"

—DAN BENNETT, quoted in *The Reader's Digest*

1971. A visiting minister, preaching a sermon in a little church away from home while on his vacation, received the greatest compliment of his ministry from one of the natives who gripped his hand at the conclusion of the service, beamed all over, and said: "Didn't get my nap today."

1972. A little girl went to church for the first time. Afterward, the minister asked her how she liked the service.

"Well," she said, "I thought the music was very nice, but your commercial was too long."

Precedent

1973. At the foot of a stairway in the House of Commons there was an attendant, who, it was said, had been standing there for eighteen years. Nobody seemed to know why. At last it was learned that the job had been held by his family for three generations. It had originated forty years earlier, when the stairs had been newly painted, and his grandfather had been detailed to stand at the foot and tell people not to step on the wet paint.

Prediction

1974. On location for *Red Stallion* the entire company was amazed at the unfailing weather predictions made by an old Indian. He was consulted daily and his forecasts proved reliable. Then one day he refused to predict the weather. "Is anything wrong?" inquired Robert Paige.

"Yes," said the Indian, "radio broke."

— ANDREW B. HECHT

Prejudice see also *Bigotry—Intolerance*

1975. Prejudice is a great time saver. It enables us to form opinions without bothering with facts.

1976. Prejudice can be defined as a judgment which does not change, and is impervious to facts and reason. Said an Oxford student: "I despise all Americans but I have never met one I didn't like." Experience had no effect on the young man's prejudice.

— STUART CHASE, "How to Smash a Prejudice," review of *Nature of Prejudice* by GORDON ALLPORT (The Beacon Press)

1977. Prejudice is always accompanied by a rigidity of attitude,

PREJUDICE

an unwillingness to see all sides of a question or to face facts that
are not to one's liking. The prejudiced child sooner or later develops
a mental rigidity that does not limit itself to his beliefs about the
people against whom he is prejudiced. It spreads to all areas of his
thinking and proves to be a barrier in everything he does.

— From "Roots of Prejudice" by ELIZABETH
B. HURLOCK, *Today's Health*

1978. Prejudice is the child of ignorance.

— WILLIAM HAZLITT, *Essays on Prejudice*

1979. Beware prejudices. They are like rats, and men's minds
are like traps; prejudices get in easily, but it is doubtful if they ever
get out.

— LORD JEFFREY

1980. Men are blind in their own cause.

— American proverb

1981. When we destroy an old prejudice we have need of
a new one.

1982. The difference between a conviction and a prejudice is
that you can explain a conviction without getting angry.

Preparedness

1983. Our new cook seemed to be a find. We had agreed on
hours, wages and days off. "My husband is very punctual," I said.
"But sometimes," I added apologetically, "he brings home unex-
pected guests for dinner. I would suggest you always be prepared for
such an emergency."

"Yes, ma'am," Elinor nodded, "I'll keep my bags packed."

— CHRISTINE NASON

1984. A man who qualifies himself well for his calling, never
fails of employment.

— THOMAS JEFFERSON

Present, The

1985. Those who compare the age in which their lot has fallen
with a golden age which exists only in imagination may talk of de-

generacy and decay, but no man who is correctly informed as to the past will be disposed to take a morose or desponding view of the present.

— THOMAS B. MACAULAY

1986. It is children only who enjoy the present; their elders live on the memory of the past or the hope of the future.

— SEBASTIEN CHAMFORT

1987. The past, the present and the future are really one—they are *today*.

— STOWE

1988. We live in the present, we dream of the future and we learn eternal truths from the past.

— MADAME CHIANG KAI-SHEK

Pretense

1989. Pretension almost always overdoes the original, and hence exposes itself.

— HOSEA BALLOU

1990. It is no disgrace not to be able to do everything; but to undertake or pretend to do what you are not made for, is not only shameful, but extremely troublesome and vexatious.

— PLUTARCH

Pride see also *Humility*

1991. Pride is sometimes a better bill collector than dunning letters. A local physician discovered one Christmas that some of his patients hadn't paid their bills for as long as 14 months.

In the holiday spirit, he wrote to each, cancelling the bill and expressing his regret that they had had such a poor year. All but one paid, virtually by return mail.

— PHILIP BARRON

1992. You'll never get indigestion from swallowing your pride occasionally.

Principles

1993. If we work marble, it will perish; if we work upon brass, time will efface it; if we rear temples, they will crumble into dust; but if we work upon immortal minds and instill in them just principles, we are then engraving upon them tablets which no time will efface, but will brighten and brighten to all eternity.

— DANIEL WEBSTER

1994. The man that is governed by self, and not by a principle, changes his front when his selfish comforts are threatened. Deeply intent upon defending and guarding his own interests, he regards all means as lawful that will subserve that end. He is continually scheming as to how he may protect himself against his enemies, being too self-centered to perceive that he is his own enemy. Such a man's work crumbles away, for it is divorced from truth and power. All effort that is grounded upon self perishes; only that work endures that is built upon an indestructible principle.

— JAMES ALLEN, *Poverty to Power*

Procrastination see also *Delay*

1995. The way to get ahead is to start now. If you start now, you will know a lot next year that you don't know now and that you would not have known next year if you had waited.

— WILLIAM FEATHER

1996. Never do today what you can do tomorrow. Something may occur to make you regret your premature action.

— AARON BURR

1997. Don't put things off—put them over!

1998. It is well to put off until tomorrow what you ought not to do at all.

1999. Tomorrow is the day when idlers work, and fools reform, and mortal men lay hold on heaven.

Profit

2000. Prefer a loss to a dishonest gain; the one brings pain at the moment; the other for all time.

— CHILON

Profundity

2001. Where the river is deepest it makes least noise.

— Old proverb

Progress

2002. You can't hold a man down without staying down with him.

— BOOKER T. WASHINGTON

2003. Whether in or out of the government the orthodox mind because of its strength and singleness of purpose maintains and preserves progress, but the dreamer and non-conformist makes progress.

— HARRY CAIN

2004. Emergencies have always been necessary to progress. It was darkness which produced the lamp. It was fog that produced the compass. It was hunger that drove us to exploration. And it took a depression to teach us the real value of a job.

2005. If God had intended that man should go backward, he would have given him eyes in the back of his head.

— VICTOR HUGO

2006. We frequently must look backwards in order to look forward.

2007. Progress is not made by taking pride in our present standards but by critically examining these standards, hypothetically setting higher standards and attempting to achieve them.

— DR. J. L. ROSENSTEIN, Marquette University

2008. True progress consists not so much in increasing our needs as in diminishing our wants.

— IVAN NIKOLAYEVICH PANIN

2009. The reasonable man adapts himself to the world; the unreasonable man persists in trying to adapt the world to himself. Progress therefore depends on the unreasonable.

— GEORGE BERNARD SHAW

PROGRESS

2010. Restlessness and discontent are the first necessities of progress.

— THOMAS A. EDISON

2011. About the time we think we can make the ends meet, somebody moves the ends.

— HERBERT HOOVER

2012. The toughest form of mountain climbing is getting out of a rut.

Promise

2013. A promise is a debt.

2014. He who is most slow in making a promise is the most faithful in its performance.

— JEAN JACQUES ROUSSEAU

2015. I had rather do and not promise, than promise and not do.

— ARTHUR WARWICK

Propaganda

2016. Propaganda is baloney disguised as food for thought.

Prophecy

2017. A prophet is not without honor, save in his own country, and in his own house.

— New Testament: Matthew xiii, 57

Prosperity

2018. The prosperous man is never sure that he is loved for himself.

— LUCAN, *Bellum Civile*

2019. In prosperity we need moderation; in adversity, patience.

— Old proverb

2020. Prosperity is only an instrument to be used; not a deity to be worshipped.

— CALVIN COOLIDGE

Prudery

2021. It is a misfortune that many people think it is a mark of saintliness to be easily shocked; whereas the greatest saints are the people who are never shocked. They may be distressed; they may wish things different; but to be shocked is often nothing but a mark of vanity, a desire that others should know how high one's standard, how sensitive one's conscience is.

—A. C. Benson

Psychiatry

2022. The other day a man paid a psychiatrist $50 to be cured of an inferiority complex and later on that same week he was fined $25 and costs for talking back to a traffic cop.

2023. The difference between a neurotic, a psychotic and a psychiatrist: The neurotic builds castles in the air, the psychotic lives in them, the psychiatrist collects rent on them.

2024. Needing a new secretary, the firm's president decided to have applicants judged by a psychologist. Three girls were interviewed together.

"What do two and two make?" the psychologist asked the first.

"Four," was the prompt answer. To the same question the second girl replied: "It might be 22." The third girl answered: "It might be 22 and it might be four."

When the girls had left the room, the psychologist turned triumphantly to the president. "There," he said, "that's what psychology does. The first girl said the obvious thing. The second smelled a rat. The third was going to have it both ways. Now, which girl will you have?"

The president did not hesitate. "I'll have the blonde with the blue eyes," he said.

2025. A psychiatrist is a guy who, when a gorgeous hunk of woman enters a room, watches everybody else.

2026. Dr. Alfred Adler, the psychiatrist, was lecturing on the theory that people with handicaps often specialize on their handicapped functions. Thus, short-winded boys tend to train themselves into being distance runners, people with weak eyes tend to become painters, and so forth. Adler finished his exposition and asked for questions.

Immediately this one was pitched at him from the back of the auditorium: "Dr. Adler, wouldn't your theory mean that weak-minded people tend to become psychiatrists?"

—J. C. FURNAS in *Saturday Evening Post*

2027. The Army psychiatrist wanted to be sure the enlisting rookie was perfectly normal. Suspiciously he said: "What do you do for your social life?"

"Oh," the man blushed, "I just sit around, mostly."

"Hmmmm—never go out with girls?"

"Nope."

"Don't you ever want to?"

The man was uneasy. ". . . Well, yes, sort of."

"Then why don't you?"

"My wife won't let me."

2028. The lady was on vacation and spent a little time each day sending postcards to her friends back home. To her psychiatrist she wrote:

"Having a wonderful time. Wish you were here to tell me what's wrong."

2029. A psychiatrist advised his timid little patient to assert himself. "Don't let your wife bully you. Go home and show her who's boss!"

The patient went home, slammed the door loudly and roughly seized his wife. "From now on," he snarled in his best Little Caesar manner, "you're taking orders from me, see? You're gonna make my supper this minute and when it's on the table you're goin' up to lay out my clothes, see? Tonight I'm goin' out on the town—alone—and do you know who's goin' to dress me in my tuxedo and black tie?"

"You bet I do," was her answer. "The undertaker."

—E. E. KENYON. Reprinted by permission
"The Wit Parade" in *The American Weekly*

2030. A middle-aged man stepped into the doctor's office and asked to see the psychiatrist. He was granted an immediate reception.

"What seems to be the difficulty?" asked the doctor.

"Plenty, doctor," said the worried man. "I have developed the habit of making long distance calls to myself and it's costing me a lot of money."

"Hmmm," mused the psychiatrist, "why not try reversing the charges?"

2031. Kindliness antedates psychiatry by hundreds of years; its antiquity should not lessen your opinion of its usefulness.

— ROSEWELL GALLAGHER, M.D., Adolescent
Unit, Children's Hospital, Boston

2032. A friend of mine, threatened with a nervous breakdown, was persuaded to consult a psychiatrist. After their first session, he gave her a list of things to do and made a weekly appointment for her. Two weeks later he telephoned her and asked why she had failed to keep her appointments.

"But, Doctor," she explained, "you said for me to stay away from people who irritate me, and I don't know anyone who irritates me more than you do."

2033. The army assigned a group of eminent psychiatrists to determine the best way to select soldiers for duty on the various fighting fronts. After many tests the learned professors made their report. The best way to find out whether a soldier would be more effective in the desert or in the north was to ask him: "What kind of weather do you like—hot or cold?"

— *Journal of the American Medical Association*

Psychology

2034. Leaving a potential customer's apartment, the not-too-well-to-do insurance salesman was ushered by the doorman towards a sleek convertible parked near the entrance.

"That's not mine," said the flattered salesman. He walked over to an ancient coupe and, as the doorman opened the door, tipped him a quarter.

"Confidentially, that car belongs to me," confided the doorman. "I paid for it out of tips—psychology, you know."

— B. W. SMITH in *The Reader's Digest*

PUBLIC OPINION

Public opinion

2035. Private opinion creates public opinion. Public opinion overflows eventually into national behavior and, as things are arranged at present, can make or mar the world. That is why private opinion and private behavior, and private conversation are so terrifyingly important.

— JAN STRUTHER

2036. The pressure of public opinion is like the pressure of the atmosphere; you can't see it—but, all the same it is sixteen pounds to the square inch.

— JAMES RUSSELL LOWELL

Public speaking

2037. Continued eloquence is wearisome.

— BLAISE PASCAL

2038. When Dr Walter Williams once spoke in a Chinese university, an interpreter translated into Chinese symbols on a blackboard. Dr. Williams noted that the interpreter stopped writing during most of the speech and at the conclusion he asked why. "We only write when the speaker says something," was the blithe reply.

2039. Oratory: the art of making deep noises from the chest sound like important messages from the brain.

2040. Having to speak at a public dinner in Chicago, I found my place at that pillory of torment, the speakers' table; and there, seeing a magnificent man in evening dress, I gave him my name and grasped his hand with what cordiality I could command.

"I'm the headwaiter, sir," he replied.

"Shake hands again, old man," I cried. "You don't know how I envy you."

— WILLIAM LYON PHELPS, *Autobiography*
(Oxford University Press)

2041. A young peer once asked Disraeli what course of study he had best take to qualify himself for speaking so as to gain the ear of the House of Lords. "Have you a graveyard near your house?" asked Disraeli. "Yes," was the reply. "Then," said Disraeli, "I should recommend you to visit it early of a morning and practice upon the tombstones."

— *The Personal Papers of Lord Rendel*
(Ernest Benn)

2042. The quality of oratory might not be raised, but the quantity would certainly be cut if every speaker delivered his remarks first to his family, and asked them for their comment.

— SENATOR SOAPER, *Chicago Daily News*

2043. Mayor McNair of Pittsburgh, speaking in the city of Greensburg, once made a mistake and got out of it very neatly.
"I am glad to be in your fine city of Johnstown—"
"GREENSBURG!" called someone in the audience.
"I know, I know," said the mayor, recovering quickly, "I just wanted to see if you were awake. Now, I hope you'll stay awake until I finish."

2044. Many speakers need no introduction; what they need are conclusions.

2045. A prayer: From our traducers and introducers, may we be delivered.

2046. That speaker speaks the best who gives his audience the most knowledge and takes from it the least time.

2047. Speaking without thinking is shooting without taking aim.

— Old proverb

2048. An itinerant preacher, who rambled in his sermons, when requested to stick to his text, replied that a scattering shot would hit most birds.

2049. "You, sir, speak for the present generation, but I speak for posterity," a dull and long-winded member of Congress once said to Henry Clay.
To which Clay responded, "And it seems that you are resolved to keep on speaking until your audience arrives."

2050. James Whitcomb Riley, the poet, and a fellow writer were once discussing their platform experiences.
The other fellow confessed that his engagements had not been too

successful. He asked Riley if he could point out the trouble. "Why are you such a success," he asked, "while my talks fall so flat?"

"Well," said the Hoosier poet, "I'll tell you. It's like this: I talk until I get tired and then I quit—whereas you talk until the audience gets tired before you realize it's time to quit!"

2051. "Has he finished yet?" one suffering auditor inquired of another as he was leaving the auditorium by a side door.

"Yes," replied the other who had preceded him. "He finished long ago; but he just won't stop."

2052. The minister of a local congregation approached the desk of the city editor. "I just dropped by," he said, "to thank you for the very generous report on my sermon in your morning edition, and also to register a mild protest. In your article you referred to me as 'the reverend' but you spelled it 'neverend'."

2053. Chauncey Depew once played a trick upon Mark Twain on an occasion when they were both to speak at a banquet. Twain spoke first for some 20 minutes and was received with great enthusiasm. When Depew's turn came, immediately afterwards, he said, "Mr. Toastmaster, Ladies and Gentlemen. Before this dinner Mr. Twain and I made an agreement to trade speeches. He has just delivered mine and I'm grateful for the reception you have accorded it. I regret that I have lost his speech and cannot remember a thing he had to say." And with that he sat down to much applause.

2054. No speech can be entirely bad if it is short enough.

—IRVIN S. COBB

2055. A small town minister during the course of one of his discourses said: "In each blade of grass there is a sermon."

Later that afternoon one of his parishioners discovered the good man pushing a lawn mower about his garden and paused to remark:

"Well, parson, I am glad to observe you engaged in cutting your sermons short."

2056. "Doctor," a wife asked a renowned medical man, "can you tell me why it is that some people are born dumb?"

"Why—" replied the medical man, "it is due either to some congenital inhibition of the faculty of articulation, or to some anatomical deficiency in the organs of vocalization."

"There, now," she remarked triumphantly, glancing at her husband, "see what it is to have an education? I've asked Henry more than a hundred times why it was, and all he could say was, 'because they're naturally born that way.' "

— *The Anthology of Anecdotes* (Droke House)

2057.   The Speaker bores you, gentlemen?
He's also boring me.
But praise him gently when he's thru—
He comes to us for free!

— VIRGINIA MOORE

2058.   A fraternal organization once asked George Jessel to play a benefit, and since it was in Brooklyn, his home territory, he agreed.

A few days later someone phoned him and suggested that he might also be able to line up Eddie Cantor. George said he would try and soon thereafter was able to report Cantor's acceptance.

"Ah, that's fine," beamed the chairman of the program committee. "Now, just one thing more. If you can also get Bing Crosby, you won't have to come."

2059.   The president of a leading Chicago bank was addressing a large group of bankers in Louisville when the microphone ceased to function. Raising his voice, he asked a man in the back row if he could hear.

"No," said the man. Whereupon a man in the front row stood up. "I can hear," he shouted to the gent in back. "And I'll change places with you."

— *Chicago Tribune*

2060.   One Sunday morning, after attending church services in Hartford, Conn., Mark Twain said to Dr. Doane the minister: "I enjoyed your service this morning, doctor. I welcomed it like an old friend. I have, you know, a book at home containing every word of it."

"You have not," said the indignant Dr. Doane.
"I have so," countered Twain.
"Then send it to me. I'd like very much to see it."
"I'll send it," promised Mark and the following day he sent the Reverend Dr. Doane an unabridged dictionary.

2061. A toastmaster is a man who eats a meal he doesn't want so he can get up and tell a lot of stories he doesn't remember to people who have already heard them.

— GEORGE JESSEL

2062. During the course of a lecture he was once delivering, Charles Lamb heard a loud hiss which came from somewhere in the audience. There was an embarrassed moment of silence. Lamb, not turning a hair, said, "There are only three things that hiss—a goose, a snake, and a fool. Come forth and be identified."

2063. At a dinner concluding a long and boring convention, a parade of reluctant speakers had been pried from their chairs to "say a few words." As the 16th orator took his seat, a sigh of expectation filled the room. Deliverance was in sight. But no! The chairman was on his feet again. "I'm sure this meeting does not want to break up without our hearing from our good friend, Ken Roe."

Mr. Roe stood up. "Gentlemen," he said, "I am reminded of the story of the two skeletons. For days they had been imprisoned in the mustiest closet imaginable. Finally, one skeleton said to the other, 'What are we doing here anyhow?' whereupon the other skeleton replied, 'I'll be darned if I know. But if we had any guts, we'd get the hell out of here.'"

— MATT ROBERTS, *Saturday Evening Post*

2064. It is not sufficient to know what one ought to say, but one must also know how to say it.

— ARISTOTLE, *Rhetoric*

2065. A boring lecturer while speaking one time during a torrential rainstorm said to his audience, "I'm afraid I've kept you too long."

"Keep right on going," replied a voice from the rear, "it's still raining outside."

2066. Will Rogers, acting as toastmaster at a dinner one evening, was annoyed by the lengthy talk of the man he introduced. The long-winded bore finally ended his oratory. Will Rogers arose and said, "Friends, you have just listened to that famous Chinese statesman, On Too Long."

2067. When Agriculture Secretary Benson found himself facing an unfriendly audience he tried to soften them up with a story of an elderly spinster and her first train ride. As he told it, the lady was puzzled by the antics of the conductor in getting the train moving.

"This is my first train ride," she told the conductor when he collected her ticket. "I understood what you meant when you said 'all aboard,' but why were you waving your hand over your head?"

"That's my way of telling the engineer to get the hell out of here," came the gruff reply.

Later the conductor realized he had been discourteous and went back to apologize, only to have the spinster look him in the eye and wave her hand vigorously above her head.

"And every time I face an audience," said Benson, "I sort of expect to see some waving hands."

— WALTER TROHAN in *Chicago Tribune*

2068. The story is told of Orson Welles, that he once lectured in a small Midwestern town before a very sparse audience. He opened his remarks with a brief sketch of his career. Said he: "I'm a director of plays and also a producer of plays. I am an actor of the stage and motion pictures. I write and produce motion pictures and I write, direct, and act on the radio. I'm a magician and painter. I've published books. I play the violin and the piano." At this point he paused and surveying his audience, remarked, "Isn't it a pity there's so many of me and so few of you!"

2069. Introducing Thomas Alva Edison at a dinner, the toastmaster mentioned his many inventions, dwelling at length on the talking machine. The aged inventor then rose to his feet, smiled and said gently: "I thank the gentleman for his kind remarks but I must insist upon a correction. God invented the talking machine. I only invented the first one that can be shut off."

— LOUIS SOBOL

2070. A visiting bishop delivered a speech at a banquet on the night of his arrival in a large city. Because he wanted to repeat some of his stories at meetings the next day, he requested reporters to omit them from their accounts of his speech. A rookie reporter, commenting on the speech, finished with the line: "And he told a number of stories that cannot be published."

2071. There was a Senator who was to introduce another Senator as the principal speaker at a big luncheon in Washington.

"What can I say about you?" asked the first Senator. "Oh, be as generous as you like," replied the second, "you won't be under oath."

2072. One way to save face is to keep the lower part of it shut.

2073. *Chairman at a Liverpool meeting:* "In most associations half the committee does all the work, whilst the other half does nothing. I am pleased to put on record that in this society it is just the reverse."

— *Liverpool Echo*

2074. The chairman was introducing a speaker who had complained to him in advance that he would have difficulty because he had left his dental plate at home. The chairman was prepared to be helpful. He reached into his pocket and brought forth a set of false teeth which he asked the speaker to try. They were a bit loose and he handed them back to the chairman who reached into another pocket and brought out a second set. These were too tight. The chairman was prepared. He reached into yet another pocket and came up with a third set. They fit perfectly. The speaker was elated and lost no time in expressing his gratitude.

"You must be a dentist," he remarked, "and a good one at that."

"No, I'm sorry, I'm not," replied the chairman, "I'm only an undertaker."

2075. On a lecture tour, Louis Untermeyer, the poet, told a Texas audience all his best stories. After the lecture he was presented with his check, which he realized had been rather a burden on the committee. With a wave of his hand, he offered it back to be put to some good use. The committee faltered. They retired to a back room to decide what to do. The problem settled, they returned, accepted the check and then said that it would be the beginning of a special fund. "And the purpose of this fund?" asked Mr. Untermeyer. Their eyes fluttered unhappily. "It's a fund to get better lecturers next year," they said.

— "The Stage," *Fun Fare*

2076. Rabbi Stephen S. Wise was once scheduled to address an anti-Nazi meeting in Brooklyn. He received several letters warning that unless he stayed away he would most certainly be shot. But he was not one to be intimidated and the threat did not daunt him. Soon after the meeting was brought to order he was called upon to speak. Taking a characteristic position, he spread his outstretched arms and opened by saying, "I have been warned to stay away from this meeting under pain of being killed. If anyone is going to shoot me let him do it now. I hate to be interrupted."

2077. At a banquet given by a native king in Samoa for Dr. Victor C. Heiser, time came for the tribute to the guest of honor, but His Majesty still squatted at the feast, while a professional orator laid on the palaver for Dr. Heiser. When he ended, the doctor moved to rise but the King restrained him: "Don't get up; I have provided an orator for you. In Polynesia we don't believe public speaking should be engaged in by amateurs."

— *The Commentator*

2078. When the noted French author André Maurois vistied the United States some years ago, he gave a series of lectures in French before a woman's club. Maurois was delighted with the response to his talks, for the women attended regularly, hung on his every word and took reams of notes.

One morning, with their usual promptness and notebooks, the women arrived in the lecture hall, only to find Maurois was not present. After waiting an hour, they got in touch with the writer's secretary.

"Monsieur Maurois will not be there today," the surprised secretary said. "He announced that very clearly at last week's talk!"

— E. E. Edgar

2079. Once, when asked to make a speech in England, John G. Winant stood in agonized silence for four minutes, finally said, softly:

"The worst mistake I ever made was in getting up in the first place."

— *Time*

2080. I never resort to a prepared script—anyone who does not have it in his head to do thirty minutes' extemporaneous talking is not entitled to be heard.

— Bishop Fulton J. Sheen, quoted by
James L. Kilgallen

2081. Eamon de Valera was once arrested on a street corner while making a speech. He was tried and sentenced to a year and a day in jail. He served his sentence and when he got out he went back to the same street corner and resumed his harangue with these opening words: "As I was saying when I was so rudely interrupted . . ."

2082. A thoughtful hostess, when she introduces two people, gives them a lead, so they won't stare blankly at each other with nothing to talk about. The introducer tries to indicate a mutual interest, a possible bond between two strangers . . .

When you introduce a speaker, you are doing practically the same thing. You draw the audience and the speaker together so they can "communicate."

— MOLLY GATES DAUGHERTY, "I Am Happy
to Present," *Farm Journal*

2083. A prominent politician was due to arrive for a speech in a little western town. Members of the Arrangements Committee formed a motorcade to meet the distinguished man at the edge of town and escort him to the Public Hall with proper fanfare.

But there was a mix-up—the speaker arrived by train. The cavalcade came dejectedly back to town.

After completing his address that evening, the visitor was approached by the chairman of the Welcoming Committee.

"Sir," said the chairman, "we're powerful sorry that we didn't have the opportunity to escort you into our city, but we'll take great pleasure in escorting you out of it."

— JACK KYTLE, *Quote*

2084. Banquet: an affair where you eat a lot of food you don't want before talking about something you don't understand to a crowd of people who don't want to hear you.

2085. She's the kind of woman who talks on and on about the things that leave her speechless.

2086. Public relations is the ability to translate, with good taste and good sense, the activities and aims of an organization or individual into terms found understandable and sympathetic to other groups—or to the public at large.

— MILBURN McCARTY

2087. Clarence Budington Kelland was acting as master of ceremonies at a huge dinner party. The speakers' table was distressingly populous. Mr. Kelland got up, a slip of paper in his hand.

"Gentlemen," he began, "the obvious duty of a toastmaster is to be so infernally dull that the succeeding speakers will appear brilliant by contrast." The succeeding speakers began to chuckle heartily.

"I've looked over this list, however," added Kelland, "and I don't believe I can do it."

Those at the speakers' table stopped chuckling and the diners bellowed.

— JOHN GOLDSTROM quoted in
The Reader's Digest

2088. Banquet: a plate of cold chicken and anaemic green peas completely surrounded by dreary speakers and appeals for donations.

2089. My method is to take the utmost trouble to find the right thing to say, and then to say it with the utmost levity.

— GEORGE BERNARD SHAW

2090. Talking and eloquence are not the same: to speak, and to speak well are two things. A fool may talk, but a wise man speaks.

— BEN JONSON

2091. A gentleman having an appointment with another who was habitually unpunctual, to his great surprise found him waiting. He thus addressed him: "Why, I see you are here first at last. You were always behind before, but I am glad to see you have become early of late."

2092. It is better to leave your audience before your audience leaves you.

2093. Many after-dinner speakers remind us that to er-r is human.

— FRANCES RODMAN

2094. "You can be the mastoid of ceremonies."
"You mean 'master of ceremonies.'"
"No, I mean 'mastoid.' That's a pain in the ear, isn't it?"

2095. "I'm glad I attended your lecture on insomnia, Doctor."
"Good, and did you find it interesting?"
"Not especially, but it did cure me of my insomnia."

2096. What many orators lack in depth they give you in length.

2097. After-dinner speaker: a person who only has a few words to say, but seldom stops when he has said them.

2098. A friend of mine who goes about the country delivering speeches before business organizations, used to wonder why people did not laugh more heartily at his stories. One day he wished to quote briefly from the Bible, and couldn't remember the exact scriptural phrase without reaching into his pocket for notes. The crowd laughed uproariously.

Thus he discovered an important secret—that it is easier to make a crowd laugh at you than to laugh with you. Since then he regularly appears to forget his Bible quotation and frantically consults his notes; to the great delight of his audiences. It seems everybody likes a man who makes mistakes or who has petty human weaknesses better than if he were too smart.

— FRED C. KELLY, quoted in
The Reader's Digest

2099. The late Senator William Alden Smith of Michigan used to tell about the introduction he was accorded at a farmers' picnic in his home state. "Senator Smith will now talk for an hour," the chairman said, "after which the band will call you together again."

— C. LYNN SUMNER, *We Have With Us
Tonight* (Harper and Brothers)

2100. Soon after becoming a minister, I was invited to preach in my Texas college town. Being young and more ambitious than wise, I used every illustration I knew that could possibly apply to my theme, and it was after 12 before I finished.

After the service, the college president grasped my hand and said, "Your voice was clear and your thoughts were good, but I like to see a man have his hay baled before he tries to deliver it."

— ALBERT C. GRIFFIN, quoted in
The Reader's Digest

2101. The mind is a wonderful thing. It starts working the minute you're born and never stops until you get up to speak in public.

2102. What this country needs is less public speaking and more private thinking.

— ROSCOE DRUMMOND

2103. Some people speak from experience. Others—from experience—don't speak.

2104. When Bill O'Dwyer was running for District Attorney in Brooklyn, he would appear on the platform with a piece of paper in his hand, ostensibly covered with notes. Looking around the audience, he would say, "Hello, Joe," "Hello, Harry," and remark that he hadn't known there'd be so many friends there tonight. "I don't need a prepared speech to talk to *you* people," he would say. "To you I can speak from my heart." And with that he would throw away his piece of paper.

A reporter who had seen O'Dwyer do this in every Brooklyn neighborhood mounted the platform one night and picked up the discarded paper. It was an old laundry bill.

2105. Lord Halifax used to attribute his success in speaking to a bit of advice he was given by his friend Winston Churchill. "It's quite simple," Churchill once told him. "Say what you have to say and when you come to a sentence with a grammatical ending, sit down."

2106. Upon entering a room in a Washington hotel, a woman recognized a well-known government official pacing up and down and asked what he was doing there. "I am going to deliver a speech shortly," he said.

"Do you usually get very nervous before addressing a large audience?"

"Nervous?" he replied. "No, I never get nervous."

"In that case," demanded the lady, "what are you doing in the Ladies' Room?"

2107. To make a speech immortal you don't have to make it everlasting.

— LORD LESLIE HORE-BELISHA

2108. The speaker who hops to the platform, skips his introduction and jumps to his conclusion is roundly applauded.

— *Wall Street Journal*

2109. I am frequently reminded of the Vermont woman who admitted she never knew what she thought about the matter under discussion until she heard what she had to say about it.

2110. ... I am glad to be here among my new-made as well as my old-made (old maid) friends.

2111. The problem with speeches isn't so much not knowing when to stop, as knowing when not to begin.
— FRANCES RODMAN

2112. Public speakers fall into three categories:
Those who put down on the table in front of them each page of their speech as they read it. These honest ones enable the audience to keep track of how much more is to come.
Those who cheat by putting each sheet under others in their hand.
And, worst of all, those who put down each sheet as read and then horrify the audience by picking up the whole batch and reading off the other side.

2113. A good speaker is one who rises to the occasion and promptly sits down.
— O. A. BATTISTA in *Saturday Evening Post*

2114. Woodrow Wilson was once asked how long he took to prepare a ten-minute speech. He said, "Two weeks."
"How long for an hour speech?"
"One week."
"How long for a two-hour speech?"
"I am ready now."

2115. During the course of most speeches the audience as a rule can figure out what the subject is, but not the object.

Publishing

2116. The trouble with the publishing business is that too many people who have half a mind to write a book do so.

Pullman

2117. A man boarded the train in New York late one evening and said to the Pullman porter, as he prepared to retire, "I have an important engagement in Syracuse in the morning and must get off there. I am a very hard man to awaken but I am going to give you this $5.00 bill. You see that I get off the train in Syracuse."

Some time later the man awakened and discovered that the sun was shining. He called the porter and asked, "Where are we now?"

The porter replied, "We'll be getting into Buffalo in a short time."

The traveler burst out in an angry protest to the porter, using words that do not ordinarily appear in print.

The Pullman conductor overheard the conversation and called the porter. He said, "You are expected to be courteous to people on the train but you don't have to stand for conversation of that kind."

The porter replied, "If you think that is bad, you should have heard the man I put off in Syracuse."

Punctuality

2118. We overheard a question from a young man who must have had experience with women. The girl with him was boarding a bus and called over her shoulder, "Meet me at the Library at 7!" "Okay," he answered cheerily. "What time will you be there?"

— FRANCES RODMAN

2119. The movie colony is notorious for being late for all dates. So this is how you get an invitation for dinner: "Please come on time for our 7:30 dinner. That doesn't mean 7:29 or 7:31— but 8 o'clock sharp!"

— Kup's Column, *The Chicago Sun-Times*

2120. Nothing inspires confidence in a businessman sooner than punctuality, nor is there any habit which sooner saps his reputation than that of being always behind time.

— W. MATHEWS

2121. Appointments once made, become debts. If I have made an appointment with you, I owe you punctuality; I have no right to throw away your time, if I do my own.

— RICHARD CECIL

Punishment

2122. Punishment is justice for the unjust.

— ST. AUGUSTINE

QUALITY

2123. A child may be quiet and industrious by beating, but it seldom happens, I believe, that kindheartedness, morality, and intelligence are induced by whipping.

> — B. K. PIERCE in *A Half-Century with Juvenile Delinquents*

Quality

2124. Quality is never an accident; it is always the result of high intention, sincere effort, intelligent direction and skillful execution; it represents the wise choice of many alternatives, the cumulative experience of many masters of craftsmanship. Quality also marks the search for an ideal after necessity has been satisfied and mere usefulness achieved.

> — WILLA A. FOSTER

2125. The animals were arguing about who had the biggest litters. Some talked big about their twins or triplets, some bragged of a dozen.

Finally, they asked the lioness, who rather quietly replied, "Only one—but that one is a lion."

> — Adapted from AESOP'S fables

Quest

2126. What we see depends mainly on what we look for.

> — JOHN LUBBOCK

Question

2127. No man really becomes a fool until he stops asking questions.

2128. A father and his young son were walking one day when the boy asked how the electricity went through the lighting wires.

"Don't know," said the father. "Never knew much about electricity."

A little later the boy asked what caused lightning and thunder.

"To tell the truth," said the father. "I never exactly understood that myself."

"Say, Pop," began the lad after a while. "Oh, well, never mind."

"Go ahead," said the father. "Ask questions. How else are you going to learn?"

— Mrs. Steven M. Siesel as quoted in
The Reader's Digest

Quick answer

2129. Cardinal Vaughan and Dr. Adler, the late Chief Rabbi of England, were next to one another at luncheon. "Now, Dr. Adler," said the Cardinal, "when may I have the pleasure of helping you to some ham?"

The rabbi replied without a pause: "At your Eminence's wedding."

Quotation

2130. *Convention speaker:* "Those are not my own figures I am quoting. They are the figures of someone who knows what he is talking about."

2131. I quote others only in order the better to express myself.

— Michel de Montaigne

Radical

2132. If a man is right, he can't be too radical; if he is wrong, he can't be too conservative.

Radio

2133. The longest word in the English language is the one following the phrase: "And now a word from our sponsor."

2134. A dramatist employed to write stories from the Bible in radio form was astonished, at the end of a broadcast, to hear the announcer say:

"Will Cain kill Abel? Tune in at the same time tomorrow morning and find out."

— From an article by Albert R. Perkins
in *Vogue*

Reading see also *Books*

2135. When they clean up all the comic books and literature that might be harmful to children, many adults will not have anything to read.

2136. A classic is a book everyone wants to have read, but no one wants to read.

2137. In science, read by preference the newest works; in literature the oldest. The classics are always modern.

— LORD LYTTON

Reason

2138. A man always has two reasons for doing anything—a good reason and the real reason.

— JOHN PIERPONT MORGAN

Recognition

2139. Along one of the main corridors of the City Hall in Stockholm are several niches occupied by bronze busts of men who had to do with building the Hall—not members of the building commission or the Chamber of Commerce but men who actually *did* the building. One is of the man who laid the first brick; another of the man who worked the greatest number of days; another man distinguished himself in metal work. All these men had been voted by their trade associates as most worthy to be memorialized.

— FRED C. KELLY in *The Reader's Digest*

Regret

2140. Make the most of your regrets . . .
To regret deeply is to live afresh.

— HENRY DAVID THOREAU

2141. If I've said anything for which I'm sorry, I'm glad of it.

Rejection

2142. Many Masons feel that rejection for membership in a Masonic lodge is a serious blot on a man's character, from which it will take him a long time to recover. In the first place, it should never become a matter of public property. It is nobody's business outside of Masonry who has applied and been rejected, and if we are true to our obligations and the laws of the order no outsider will ever know it. In the next place, we take ourselves too seriously. Not all good men are Masons—not all of them care to be. In fact, not all Masons are good men, and when this is the case it is not much of a reflection on a man to be rejected by those who have proved themselves really unfit. No—in itself, a rejection for membership in a Masonic lodge need not worry any man.

— *Seattle Masonic Tribune*

Relationships

2143. The relation between superiors and inferiors is like that between the wind and the grass. The grass must bend when the wind blows over it.

— CONFUCIUS, *Analects*

Relative

2144. Years ago when Ernie Pyle, the famous war correspondent, was on the Washington *News* as a $30-a-week copyreader, he tagged a story with the headline: "Man Inherits Huge Fortune of $15,000."

"Where do you get the idea that $15,000 is a huge fortune?" his executive editor asked.

"If you were earning the same dough I am," Ernie replied, "you'd think so, too."

— LARRY BOARDMAN

2145. Motoring west one hot August, too weary to drive farther, we stopped for the night in a small country town. Neither of the two hotels looked particularly attractive, so we asked the garage attendant which one he would recommend. He hesitated. "Can't say I recommend the National House," he said slowly. "But I do say the folks who come for their cars after staying at the National aren't quite so mad as those from the Commerical."

— R. D. JONES

Relatives

2146. Kindred: fear that relatives are coming to stay.

— WES LAWRENCE in *The Cleveland* (Ohio) *Plain Dealer*

Religion

2147. Thou Mayest Choose

If God knows all that shall befall,
How can my soul be free?
What power have I to dare defy
Or change His high decree?
I may but climb the arch of time,
And scan the endless sea.

Yet man is more than vertebrate,
For he can dream and plan;
By love created to create
As fate's custodian.
His faithfulness shall consummate
What Providence began.

The world is wide; with God for guide
I need not hide nor flee.
My destined course will be the source
Of immortality.
One choice alone must be my own—
That God and I agree.

— ROBERT LEE STRAUS

2148. Every American military plane that flies over water carries a collapsible boat which contains food rations and a copy of the Bible in a waterproof package. Army officers say, "We know that spiritual equipment can be as important as food and drink in saving lives."

2149. The extent of some people's religion is that they know the name of the church they stay away from.

2150. I have treated many hundreds of patients. Among those over 35, there has not been one whose problem in the last resort was not that of finding a religious outlook on life.

— DR. CARL JUNG

2151. A western rancher had asked the district superintendent that a pastor be assigned to his community.

"How big a man do you want?" asked the superintendent.

"Well," the wiry rancher replied, "we're not overly particular, but when he's on his knees we'd like to have him reach heaven."

2152. You cannot cash checks on heaven's bank without first making deposits.

2153. Religious feeling is as much a verity as any other part of human consciousness; and against it, on the subjective side, the waves of science beat in vain.

— John Tyndall

2154. Religion is either applied or denied.

2155. A blacksmith, known for his strong faith, had a great deal of illness. He was challenged by an unbeliever to explain why his God would let him suffer. He explained, "I take a piece of iron, put it into the fire, bring it to white heat, then I strike it once or twice on the anvil to see if it will take temper. I plunge it into water to change the temperature, put it into the fire again. Then I put it on the anvil and make a useful article. If, when I first strike it on the anvil, it will not take temper, I throw it into the scrap heap and sell it at half-penny a pound.

"I believe God has been testing me to see if I will take temper. I have tried to bear it as patiently as I could, and daily my prayer has been, 'Lord, put me into the fire if You will; put me into the water if You think I need it; do anything you please, O Lord, only don't throw me into the scrap heap.'"

These may be trying and difficult days and our tribulations may be many. God may test us to see if we are worthy of His laws and decrees. Therefore, let us endure our difficulties and pray that God will not cast us aside.

— Rabbi Adam Neuberger

2156. Going to church doesn't make you a Christian any more than going to a garage makes you an automobile.

— W. A. "Billy" Sunday

2157. Every child is born into the religion of nature; its parents make it a Jew, a Christian, or a Magian.

— The *Koran*

RELIGION

2158. We have just enough religion to make us hate, but not enough to make us love one another.

> — JONATHAN SWIFT, *Thoughts on Various Subjects*

2159. While just government protects all in their religious rites, true religion affords government its surest support.

> — GEORGE WASHINGTON

2160. Men who make a business of religion are not likely to make a religion of business.

2161. Some people's religion is just like a wooden leg. There is neither warmth nor life in it; and although it helps them to hobble along, it never becomes a part of them, but has to be strapped on every morning.

2162. Clergyman: a man who undertakes the management of our spiritual affairs as a method of bettering his temporal ones.

> — AMBROSE BIERCE, *The Devil's Dictionary*

2163. When Phillips Brooks was recovering from an illness, and was denying himself to all visitors, Robert G. Ingersoll, the agnostic, called.

"I appreciate this very much," said Ingersoll, "but why do you see me when you deny yourself to your friends?"

"It is this way," said the bishop, "I feel confident of seeing my friends in the next world, but this may be my last chance of seeing you."

2164. Abraham Lincoln once remarked to a friend that his religion was like that of an old man whom he had known in Indiana. He heard this man speak at a church meeting once and this is what he said: "When I do good I feel good; when I do bad I feel bad; and that's my religion."

2165. The distinguishing mark of religion is not so much liberty as obedience, and its value is measured by the sacrifices which it can extract from the indivdiual.

> — HENRI FREDERIC AMIEL

2166. An atheist is a man who doesn't care who wins the Notre Dame—S.M.U. football game.

2167. The Golden Rule did not originate in Christianity. It was a component part of seven other religions—Hinduism, Buddhism, Confucianism, Taoism, Zoroastrianism, Judaism and Greek philosophy—centuries before the time of Christ.

2168. Religion is what the individual does with his own solitude. If you are never solitary you are never religious.

— DEAN WILLIAM RALPH INGE

2169. Our great-grandfathers called it the holy Sabbath; our grandfathers, the Sabbath; our fathers, Sunday, but today we call it the week end. We have substituted a holiday for the holy day.

— *Wesleyan Methodist*

2170. A good Moslem believes in Mohammed far more passionately than anyone believes in the multiplication table. That is just because in the case of the multiplication table he knows and is done with it; in the case of Mohammed he does not know, and makes up for his lack of knowledge by passionate feeling.

— GILBERT MURRAY, *Tradition and Progress*
Reprinted by permission of George Allen &
Unwin Ltd. (London)

2171. Mother was ill and couldn't go to church, but small Janice went as usual, being cautioned to remember the text of the sermon. When she returned, Janice remembered proudly that it was: "Don't be scared, you'll get your quilts."

Mother couldn't figure it out until she learned from the minister that his text had been: "Fear not, thy Comforter will come."

2172. Church: an institution supported by the husbands of the members.

2173. I am an agnostic; I do not pretend to know what many ignorant men are sure of.

— CLARENCE DARROW

2174. They that deny a God destroy man's nobility; for certainly man is of kin to the beasts by his body; and, if he be not kin to God by his spirit, he is a base and ignoble creature.

— FRANCIS BACON

2175. *True* religion is the life we *live,* not the creed we profess, and some day will be recognized by quality and quantity, and not by brand.

—J. F. WRIGHT

2176. Religious truth is not fixed. No religion has a sole priority on truth. All liberal religions have great and abiding principles which are their cornerstones: the brotherhood of man, the fatherhood of God, the perfectability of man, the superiority of reason to superstition, the presence in the universe of certain undergirding laws of justice, goodness, mercy and love which cannot be broken without paying a penalty.

—Dr. RICHARD C. HERTZ

2177. No university can take away the religion a child gets at its mother's knees.

—A. LAWRENCE LOWELL

2178. It is only when men begin to worship that they begin to grow.

—CALVIN COOLIDGE

2179. In their essence there can be no conflict between science and religion. Science is a reliable method of finding truth. Religion is the search for a satisfying basis for life. . . . Yet a world that has science needs, as never before, the inspiration that religion has to offer . . . Beyond the nature taught by science is the spirit that gives meaning to life.

—Dr. ARTHUR H. COMPTON

2180. When an agnostic informed Woodrow Wilson that the continuing troubles that afflict the world prove that religion has failed, he replied: "Think this over. If men are wicked with religion —what would they be without it."

2181. I have lived long enough to know what I did not at one time believe—that no society can be upheld in happiness and honor without the sentiment of religion.

—PIERRE SIMON DE LA PLACE

2182. A modern scientist, A. Cressy Morrison, gives the following seven reasons for his belief in God.

1. By unwavering mathematical law we can prove that our universe was designed and executed by a great engineering intelligence.

2. The resourcefulness of life to accomplish its purpose is a manifestation of all-pervading intelligence.

3. Animal wisdom speaks irresistibly of a good Creator who infused instincts into otherwise helpless little creatures.

4. Man has something more than animal instinct—the power of reason.

5. Provision for all living is revealed in phenomena which we know today but which Darwin did not know—such as the wonder of the genes.

6. By the economy of nature we are forced to realize that only infinite wisdom could have seen and prepared with such astute husbandry.

7. The fact that man can conceive the idea of God is itself a unique proof.

2183. What we need in religion is not new light, but new sight; not new paths, but new strength to walk in the old ones; not new duties, but new strength from on high to fulfill those that are plain before us.

— TRYON EDWARDS

2184. Religion: betting your life there is a God.

2185. My Son

My son, when you were just a child,
You asked me, "What is Heaven?"
I answered, "Our blessed home,
Where love and understanding roam,
And peace makes our roof a dome,
Of these things, God makes Heaven."

My son, when you were just a boy,
You asked me, "Where is God?"
I told you, "Mother's selfless ways
That guided you through childhood days,
Her sacred love, her words of praise,
These, are akin to God."

And now that you're a man, my son,
You make my life—a Heaven.

> The love I give, which you return
> Through righteousness, you chose to learn,
> The "good name" which you strive to earn,
> Bring me a glimpse of Heaven.
>
> Each day, as you mature, my son,
> You bring me close to God.
> The humble things you do and say,
> The "unseen" voice that you obey,
> The "love of neighbor" you display,
> Through these, my soul sees God.
>
> — LUD ISAAC

Reluctance

2186. There is nothing so easy but that it becomes difficult when you do it with reluctance.

— TERENCE, *Heauton Timorumenos*

Remorse

2187. There are some people who are very
resourceful
At being remorseful,
And who apparently feel that the best
way to make friends
Is to do something terrible and then
make amends.

— OGDEN NASH, *Hearts of Gold*

2188. It does not do any good just to remember sins which we cannot undo. To sit and brood over them, to keep saying to oneself, "What a fool I've been"—all that is futile remorse. Like a rocking chair, remorse keeps us moving, but it doesn't get us anywhere. Worse than that, it tortures the mind without cleansing the conscience.

— DR. RALPH W. SOCKMAN

Reputation

2189. It is a maxim with me that no man was ever written out of reputation but by himself.

— RICHARD BENTLEY, *Monk's Life of Bentley*

2190. To disregard what the world thinks of us is not only arrogant but shameless.

— CICERO, *De Oficiis*

2191. There are two very difficult things in the world. One is to make a name for oneself and the other is to keep it.

— ROBERT SCHUMANN

2192. It is really not honor based on virtue which men seek today, but rather reputation, which is measured more by its width than by its depth. Reputation is often only popularity, and, like a breeze, it cannot be kept. You must enjoy it while it blows. It is like a ball—men generally start kicking it when it stops rolling.

— BISHOP FULTON J. SHEEN

2193. But he that filches from me my good name,
Robs me of that which not enriches him,
And makes me poor indeed.

— WILLIAM SHAKESPEARE, *Othello*

2194. The great difficulty is first to win a reputation; the next to keep it while you live; and the next to preserve it after you die, when affection and interest are over, and nothing but sterling excellence can preserve your name.

— BENJAMIN ROBERT HAYDON, *Table Talk*

2195. Whatever you lend let it be your money, and not your name. Money you may get again, and, if not, you may contrive to do without it; name once lost you cannot get again, and, if you cannot contrive to do without it, you had better never been born.

2196. A good name is seldom regained. When character is gone, all is gone, and one of the richest jewels of life is lost forever.

— J. HAWES

2197. An honest reputation is within the reach of all men; they obtain it by social virtues, and by doing their duty. This kind of reputation, it is true, is neither brilliant nor startling, but it is often the most useful for happiness.

— CHARLES PINOT DUCLOS

2198. Reputation is to notoriety what real turtle is to mock.

REPUTATION

2199. The reputation of a man is like his shadow: it sometimes follows and sometimes precedes him, it is sometimes longer and sometimes shorter than his natural size.

— French proverb

2200. Garments that have once one rent in them are subject to be torn on every nail, and glasses that are once cracked are soon broken; such is man's good name once tainted with just reproach.

— BISHOP JOSEPH HALL

2201. My name and memory I leave to men's charitable speeches, to foreign nations, and to the next age.

— FRANCIS BACON

2202. Associate with men of good quality, if you esteem your own reputation; for it is better to be alone than in bad company.

— GEORGE WASHINGTON

2203. Gain at the expense of reputation is manifest loss.

— PUBLILIUS SYRUS

2204. The way to gain a good reputation is to endeavor to be what you desire to appear.

— SOCRATES

2205. I would rather make my name than inherit it.

— WILLIAM MAKEPEACE THACKERAY

2206. A good name is better than precious ointment.

— Old Testament

2207. We sometimes speak of winning reputations as though that were the final goal. The truth is contrary to this. Reputation is a reward, to be sure, but it is really the beginning, not the end of endeavor. It should not be the signal for a letdown, but rather, a reminder that the standards which won recognition can never be lowered again. From him who gives much—much is forever after expected.

— ALVAN MACAULEY

2208. You can't build a reputation on what you are going to do.

— HENRY FORD

318

Research

2209. What we need is not the will to believe, but the wish to find out, which is the exact opposite.

— BERTRAND RUSSELL, *Scientific Monthly*

2210. Tomorrow's "help-wanted" advertisements are being written by the research of today. Industry's progress and the employment opportunities it will bring are being determined now in the quiet confines of the laboratory.

— From *The Story of Employment Possibilities*

2211. Research teaches a man to admit he is wrong and to be proud of the fact that he does so, rather than try with all his energy to defend an unsound plan because he is afraid that admission of error is a confession of weakness when rather it is a sign of strength.

— H. E. STOCHER

Resourcefulness see also *Ingenuity*

2212. She stood at the counter, an obviously new bride, while a clerk explained various household gadgets to her. He waxed enthusiastic about an electrically timed egg cooker, explaining that her husband's boiled eggs would be just right when timed by it.

"But I wouldn't need that," she said. "John likes his eggs the way I do them. I just look out the window at the traffic light, give them one red and two greens, and they're done."

— JOHN POWELL

2213. One night William Howard Taft, then a young law reporter, finished studying a case in Somerville, Ohio, and discovered that he could not get back to his office that night unless he could stop a through express. He wired division headquarters: "Will you stop through express at Somerville to take on large party?" Promptly came back the reply: "Yes."

When the train arrived, the conductor said to Mr. Taft, "Where's the large party we were to take on?"

Mr. Taft regarded his own comfortable bulk ruefully and laughed. "I'm it," he said, stepping aboard the train.

— *Christian Science Monitor*

RESOURCEFULNESS

2214. A lawyer had been made custodian of twenty thousand dollars by two partners, who arranged that he would make no outlays without the signatures of both. But when one of the partners went off on a trip, the other told the lawyer that a note was falling due, and that fifteen thousand dollars must be paid on it to keep the partners from bankruptcy. The lawyer asked for the two signatures, but the partner at home explained that his associate could not be reached and that in business it was necessary to use discretion. With much misgiving the lawyer paid him the fifteen thousand dollars for the note. The partner took the money and disappeared completely.

When the second partner returned home, he instituted a suit against the lawyer in court. The lawyer explained the circumstances, and finding that the partner was insistent said: "I paid out the money for the note, not from the partners' fund, but from my own."

"Then give me the fifteen thousand dollars," said the partner.

"All right," said the lawyer, "but you must produce the two signatures!"

2215. It is told that Disraeli got rid of an unfortunate applicant for a baronetcy upon whom, for many reasons, it was impossible to confer the honor, by telling him, "You know I cannot give you a baronetcy but you can tell your friends I offered you one and you refused it. That is far better."

2216. A few months after my husband and I moved to a small Massachusetts town I grumbled to a resident about the poor service at the library, hoping she would repeat my complaints to the librarian. The next time I went to the library, the librarian had set aside two best-sellers for me and a new biography for my husband. What's more, she appeared to be genuinely glad to see me.

Later I reported the miraculous change to my friend. "I suppose you told her how poor we thought the service was?" I asked.

"No," she confessed. "In fact—I hope you don't mind—I told her your husband was amazed at the way she had built up this small-town library, and that you thought she showed unusually good taste in the new books she ordered."

— LILLIAN MOORE in *The Reader's Digest*

2217. At a large dinner party a financier was placed next to a lady whose name he didn't catch. During the first course he noticed

320

at the left of the host a man who had bested him in a business transaction. "Do you see that man?" he muttered ferociously to his dinner partner. "If there's one man on earth I hate he's it."

"Why," exclaimed the lady, "that's my husband!"

"Yes, I know," said the financier glibly. "That's why I hate him."

— Thomas L. Mason, Listen to These,
(Doubleday & Co., Inc.)

2218. At a busy intersection in Oklahoma City, as a traffic signal turned red, a four-door sedan rolled to a stop, completely blocking the pedestrian crosswalk. Instead of following a flow of pedestrians around the front and rear of the car, a middle-aged man walked straight ahead, opened the rear door, climbed through the car and stepped out the other door, leaving both doors wide open, while amid the honking of horns the driver stared bewildered after his retreating form.

— Oscar E. Gram

2219. For several years, a minister and a professor had regularly played golf together. They were very evenly matched, and there was a keen rivalry. Then one spring the professor's game suddenly improved so much that the minister was regularly beaten. The preacher's efforts to improve his own game were unsuccessful, but finally he came up with an idea. At a bookstore, he picked out three how-to-play golf texts, and had them sent to the professor for a birthday present. It wasn't long before they were evenly matched again.

— Havilah Babcock

2220. A young mother was having great difficulty with her three-year-old son who had locked himself in the bathroom and either could or would not unlock the door. Finally, in desperation, she called the fire department.

After a brief wait, a burly fire captain ran up the front steps with an axe in one hand, a fire extinguisher in the other. She explained her predicament, but instead of going back for a ladder, he asked her the sex of the child. When she had told him, he climbed the stairs and said in his most authoritative voice, "You come out, little girl!" Aroused at being called a little girl, the boy unlocked the door and marched out to confront the fireman. "It works just about every time," explained the grinning captain.

— Bernard G. Silberstein

RESOURCEFULNESS

2221.   A man failed to remove his hat when he entered a church, and was presently sighted by a horrified deacon who quietly drew the man's attention to his apparent forgetfulness.

The man explained that he had been worshipping in that church for three years without anyone speaking to him, and he thought the hat might do the trick.

— *The Methodist Recorder*

2222.   Francis X. Bushman was a small-time, $250 a week actor in Chicago when he met Harry Reichenbach, the "father of bally-hoo." Reichenbach tells this story:

"I wanted to raise his salary to a commanding figure. When we arrived (in New York) I had 2,000 pennies in my pocket. As we walked along 42nd Street toward the Metro office, I dropped handfuls of pennies in our line of march. At first children followed to pick up the coins, then everybody followed.

"By the time we reached Metro the streets were black with milling crowds . . . When the officers of Metro looked out of the window they judged Bushman's popularity by the vast throngs that had followed us and he received $1,000 a week without any argument.

"The fact was, not a living soul in the mob knew Bushman."

— From *Grand Deception: World's Most Spectacular Hoaxes*, edited by ALEXANDER KLEIN. (J. B. Lippincott Co.) copyright 1955 by ALEXANDER KLEIN

2223.   Alexander Dumas, the French novelist, was once stopped in Paris by a beggar who asked for a handout. "Why do you not take off your hat to me when you ask for money?" asked the famous author.

"If I took off my hat to you," said the bum, "that policeman on the corner would know I was begging and arrest me. As it is, he thinks we are old acquaintances having a chat."

Dumas was so impressed by the man's logic that he quickly handed him 100 francs.

— *Wall Street Journal*

2224.   Henry Clay, finding himself in need of money, went to the Riggs Bank and asked for the loan of $250 on his personal note. He was told that while his credit was perfectly good, it was the inflexible rule of the bank to require an endorser. The great statesman hunted up Daniel Webster and asked him to endorse the note.

"With pleasure," said Webster. "But I need some money myself. Why not make your note for five hundred, and you and I will split?"

This they did. And rumor has it that today the note is still with the Riggs Bank—unpaid.

2225. Henry Ford was always dropping into the offices of the executives of his automobile plant. One day he was asked why he didn't have them come to him.

"Well, I'll tell you," Ford answered. "I've found that I can leave the other fellow's office a lot quicker than I can get him to leave mine."

— HAROLD HELFER

2226. A wise clergyman kept on his desk a special notebook labeled "Complaints of Members." Whenever one of his people began to criticize another's doings, he would say, "I'll just write it out so I can take it up with the board."

The sight of the complaint book and the ready pen had its effect. The clergyman kept the book for 40 years, opened it hundreds of times, and never had occasion to write a line in it.

— LEEWIN B. WILLIAMS, *The Master Book of Humorous Illustrations* (Cokesbury)

2227. A large trailer truck, attempting to go through a railroad underpass almost made it—but not quite. With a grinding crash, the truck was wedged tightly between the pavement and the steel girders overhead. Soon traffic was stalled for blocks on both sides of the underpass.

Experts from the State Highway Department tugged and hauled to no avail. When an acetylene torch was suggested to burn a little steel off the girders, railroad officials objected. Talk of dismantling the truck drew a sharp veto from the driver.

About this time, a little boy who had been watching with interest, tugged at the sleeve of the wrecking crew foreman. "Say, mister, I know how to get that truck out," he said.

The foreman looked at him irritably. "All right, how would you do it?"

RESOURCEFULNESS

"Well," said the youngster, "I'd let some of the air out of the tires."

In a few minutes the truck was on its way.

2228. Horace Dutton Taft, late headmaster of the Taft School, was noted for his strictness as a disciplinarian—and also for his sense of humor. There was one school rule which could never be broken: unscheduled private vacations, no matter what the excuse, were simply not countenanced. Yet a special problem arose when the son of the headmaster's brother, William Howard Taft, asked permission to attend his father's inauguration as President of the United States. After deliberation, the request was granted—not, however, as an exception to the strict rule, but by authority of a new rule duly passed and to this day a part of the school's legal code. The new rule: "Any boy whose father is elected to the Presidency of the United States shall be permitted to attend the inauguration ceremony."

2229. A hillbilly heard that the job of watchman at a railroad crossing was open.

"You'll have to undergo a strict examination," the man in charge said.

"Ask me anything!" bragged the hillbilly.

"All right," spoke up the examiner. "Supposing you are at the crossing and two trains are coming along 60 miles an hour—head on. What would you do?"

"Waall, I'd blow m' whistle."

"Yes, but supposing your whistle was out of order."

"I'd always wear a red shirt and I'd take it off and flag the train."

"Let's say this happened at night."

"Then I'd swing m' lantern."

"But suppose you had no oil in your lantern?"

"In that case," said the hillbilly, "I'd call m' sister."

"Your sister? What for?"

"I'd just say to her, 'Come on down, sis, and see the guldarndest wreck you ever saw in your life.' "

— EDDIE CANTOR quoted in *The Reader's Digest*

2230. Every business day, promptly at noon, a timid little man would check in at the safe deposit department of a large Chicago bank and obtain his safe deposit box which he would open, peer into, and carry away to one of the small coupon rooms where he would remain for exactly 30 minutes. After several months, one young clerk managed to pluck up enough courage to ask the visitor a few questions which he answered in a thin, colorless voice. The deposit box was empty, and always had been. He had simply rented it so as to have a quiet spot in the little coupon room to eat his lunch, carried in his coat pocket.

—BILL KAY

Respect

2231. Young people were more respectful of their elders in the old days. Perhaps because they had more to respect.

2232. Respect is what we owe; love, what we give.

—PHILIP JAMES BAILEY, *Featus*

Respectability

2233. The more things a man is ashamed of, the more respectable he is.

—GEORGE BERNARD SHAW, *Man and Superman*

Responsibility

2234. That which is everybody's business is nobody's business.

2235. You cannot escape the responsibility of tomorrow by evading it today.

—ABRAHAM LINCOLN

2236. I've never known of an instance in the history of our company where an executive unloaded responsibilities and duties on one lower in the ranks, that he did not find himself immediately loaded from above with greater responsibilities.

—ARTHUR F. HALL

Retirement

2237. Composer Johannes Brahms once startled friends with the announcement that he was going to stop composing music.

"Why shouldn't I enjoy my old age?" he asked. "I'll not write another note."

Several months passed and Brahms kept his promise. Then one evening a new masterpiece of his was played in public. A friend heard it and hurried to see the elderly composer.

"I thought you weren't going to write any more music," he said.

"I wasn't," replied Brahms, "but after a few days' leisure I was so happy at the thought of not writing, the music just came to me without effort!"

— Dan Bennett in *Quote*

Revenge

2238. Time spent in getting even would be better spent in getting ahead.

2239. The noblest vengeance is to forgive.

— Henry George Bohn, *Handbook of Proverbs*

2240. To forget a wrong is the best revenge.

— Old proverb

2241. Revenge is always the weak pleasure of a little and narrow mind.

— Decimus Juvenal

2242. You'll notice a Fire Department never fights fire with fire.

— Elizabethtown (Kentucky) *News*

2243. Revenge is an act of passion; vengeance of justice: injuries are revenged; crimes are avenged.

— Dr. Samuel Johnson

2244. An act by which we make one friend and one enemy is a losing game; because revenge is a much stronger principle than gratitude.

— Charles C. Colton

2245. Some people do odd things to get even.

2246. The cruelest revenge of a woman is to remain faithful to a man.

— Jacques Bossuet

2247. The best manner of avenging ourselves is by not resembling him who has injured us.

— JANE PORTER

2248. It is a work of prudence to prevent injury, and of a great mind, when done, not to revenge it. He that hath revenge in his power, and does not use it, is the great man; it is for low and vulgar spirits to transport themselves with vengeance. To endure injuries with a brave mind is one half the conquest.

Reverse English

2249. The little boy wanted to go to a night baseball game, so he told his grandmother that his boss had died.

Revolution

2250. Every revolution was first a thought in one man's mind.

— RALPH WALDO EMERSON, *Essays*

2251. A South American was describing his country to an American woman.

"Our most popular sport is bullfighting," he told her.

"Isn't it revolting?" she asked.

"No," smiled the man. "That's the second most popular sport."

— *Wall Street Journal*

Reward

2252. The reward of a thing well done, is to have done it.

— RALPH WALDO EMERSON, *New England Reformers*

2253. Service without reward is punishment.

Ridicule

2254. Whenever men wax out of proportion, overblown, affected, pretentious, bombastical, hypocritical, pedantic, fantastically delicate; whenever the comic spirit sees them self-deceived or hoodwinked, given to run riot in idolatries, drifting into vanities, congregating in absurdities, planning shortsightedly, plotting dementedly;

whenever they are at variance with their professions, and violate the unwritten but perceptible laws binding them in consideration one to another; whenever they offend sound reason, fair justice; are false in humility or mined with conceit, individually or in bulk—the Spirit overhead will look humanely malign and cast an oblique light on them, followed by volleys of silvery laughter.

— GEORGE MEREDITH

Right

2255. Every man at the bottom of his heart wants to do right. But only he can do right who knows right; only he knows right who thinks right; only he thinks right who believes right.

— TIORIO

2256. One may go wrong in many different directions, but right only in one.

— ARISTOTLE

Righteous

2257. A Jew and an Englishman were having an argument about the ways of their respective races.

"You people," said the Jew, "have been taking things from us for thousands of years. The Ten Commandments, for instance."

"Well, yes," said the other. "We took them from you all right, but you can't say we've kept them."

2258. It is not what people eat but what they digest that makes them grow. It is not what they read, but what they remember that makes them learned. It is not what they profess, but what they practice that makes them righteous.

— Lake Mills (Iowa) *Graphic*

Romance

2259. Playboy: a man who summers in the Alps, winters in Miami, and springs at blondes.

Rules

2260. Absolute rules are a device of cowardice to escape the difficulty of decision when an exceptional case occurs. A consistent refusal is always easier than an occasional compliance.

— JOHN STUART BLACKIE

Sacrifice

2261. If you begin by sacrificing yourself to those you love, you will end by hating those to whom you have sacrificed yourself. Self-sacrifice is suicide.

— GEORGE BERNARD SHAW

Safety

2262. A ship in harbor is safe, but that is not what ships are built for.

— JOHN A. SHEDD, *Salt from My Attic*

2263. In case of an air raid go to the nearest slot machine. It hasn't been hit in years.

Saintliness

2264. A man can be as truly a saint in a factory as in a monastery, and there is as much need of him in the one as in the other.

— ROBERT J. McCRACKEN, D.D.

Salary see also *Wages*

2265. It isn't so hard to live on a small salary if you don't spend too much money in trying to keep it a secret.

2266. Most people nowadays are interested in the higher things of life—wages.

Salesmanship

2267. There are some organizations that could stimulate more sales by sticking pins into the salesmen instead of into maps.

2268. Salesmen: people with both feet on the ground who take orders from people with both feet on the desk.

SALESMANSHIP

2269. When 20th Century-Fox advertised in the New York papers to fill a vacancy in its sales force, one applicant replied: "I am at present selling furniture at the address below. You may judge my ability as a salesman if you will stop in to see me at any time, pretending that you are interested in buying furniture.

When you come in, you can identify me by my red hair. And I will have no way of identifying you. Such salesmanship as I exhibit during your visit, therefore, will be no more than my usual workaday approach and not a special effort to impress a prospective employer."

From among more than 1,500 applicants, the redhead got the job.

— Irving Hoffman in *The Reader's Digest*

2270. A salesman, like the storage battery in your car, is constantly discharging energy. Unless he is recharged at frequent intervals he soon runs dry. This is one of the greatest responsibilities of sales leadership.

— R. H. Grant

2271. Anyone can kiss a girl once. The art is in being invited again! It's the same in salesmanship. It's the first impression that your prospect gets of you, your product and your company that counts up to long run profits.

2272. The big businessman had died and gone to—well, not to Heaven. But he had hardly settled down for a nice long smoke when a hearty hand slapped him on the back, and into his ear boomed the voice of a persistent salesman who had pestered him on earth.

"Well, Mr. Smith," chortled the salesman, "I'm here for the appointment."

"What appointment?"

"Why, don't you remember?" the salesman went on. "Every time I entered your office on earth you told me you'd see me here!"

2273. The object of a salesman is not to make sales, but to make customers.

2274. "I had a marvelous day," said the first salesman, "made lots of friends of our company."

"Me, too," said the second salesman quite understandingly. "I didn't sell anything either."

2275. Salesmen who keep passing the buck never seem to make many of them.

2276. A salesman went into a grocery store to buy a bottle of catsup. The shelves of the entire store were solidly lined with bags of salt—hundreds and hundreds of them. To get the catsup the proprietor had to go down to the cellar. The customer went with him, and there to his surprise saw more salt stacked on all sides. "Say," commented the customer, "you certainly must sell a lot of salt!" "Nah," answered the grocer, "I can't sell no salt at all. But the fellow who sells me salt! Can *he* sell salt!"

2277. An advertising salesman arrived at a large hotel and took a room. He carried with him only a small grip and the hotel porter asked him for the tags to his trunks.

"I have none," said the salesman.

"Why, I thought I understood you to say that you were a salesman," said the porter.

"That's right, I am. But I don't need any trunks. You see, I sell brains."

The porter scratched his head for a moment and said, "Well, sir, you're the first traveling salesman who's ever come here without any samples."

2278. You have a message which seems old to you because you have known it so long, but a new generation has arrived which does not know it.

You are selling a standing army, you are selling a parade; part of your market every year is passing out and another part is coming in. The part that is coming in is a generation more susceptible to advertising than any generation we have ever had.

— CHARLES COOLIDGE PARLIN

2279. Salesmen should bear in mind that more mature men who have reached a certain point in business buy rather than are sold. A real salesman does not attempt to sell his prospect but instead directs his efforts towards putting his prospect in a frame of mind so that he will be moved to action by a given set of facts.

— ROY HOWARD

2280. Try this at your next sales meeting: Hold this card up and ask a group of salesmen what it means:

SALESMANSHIP

Y C S I U Y T I

Then hold up another card which reads:

You can't sell it
unless you tell it!

They'll soon get the idea.

2281. The super-salesman neither permits his subconscious mind to "broadcast" negative thoughts nor give expression to them through words, for the reason that he understands that "like attracts like" and negative suggestions attract negative action and decisions from prospective buyers.

— NAPOLEON HILL

2282. Salesmanship consists of transferring a conviction by a buyer to a seller.

— PAUL G. HOFFMAN

2283. *Sailor, walking into recruiting office:* "Gimme that ol' sales talk again. I'm gettin' kinda discouraged."

Salvage

2284. How many a thing which we cast to the ground
When others pick it up becomes a gem!

— GEORGE MEREDITH, *Modern Love*

Sarcasm

2285. At a luncheon party an actress, noted for her sarcasm, looked significantly at Rosalind Russell and said: "I dread to think of life at 45."

"Why?" asked quick-witted Miss Russell. "What happened then?"

2286. *Tourist (sneeringly):* "What does this pig-sty cost?"
Motel proprietor: "For one pig, five dollars; for two pigs, seven dollars."

2287. During World War II, the harassed attaché of the American Consulate at Lisbon once told this story: A shy little man leaned across his desk and said, "Please, could you tell me if there is any possibility that I could get entrance to your wonderful country?"

The attaché pressed by thousands of such requests and haggard from sleepless nights, roughly replied, "Impossible now. Come back in another ten years!"

The little refugee moved torward the door, stopped, turned and with a wan smile asked, "Would morning or afternoon be better?"

2288. The man at the bar finished his second glass of beer and turned to ask the manager of the place, "How many kegs of beer do you sell here in a week?"

"Thirty-five," the manager answered with pride.

"Well, I've just thought of a way you can sell 70."

The manager was startled. "How?"

"It's simple. Fill up the glasses."

2289. At a party, one woman called across the room to another: "I have been wondering, my dear, why you weren't invited to the Asterbilt's party last week." The other woman smiled. "Isn't that a coincidence?" she said. "I was just wondering why you were."

2290. Asked if a Broadway producer had called him a pinhead, as reported, George Jean Nathan loftily replied: "That's impossible. Pinhead is a word of two syllables."

> —EARL WILSON, quoted in
> *The Reader's Digest*

Satire

2291. Arrows of satire, feathered with wit, and wielded with sense, fly home to their mark.

> — C. SIMMONS

Savoir-faire

2292. An American professor met three staid members of the Académie Française in Paris and asked for their definition of *savoir-faire* to include in his modern dictionary. "Eet is not deefeecult," one said. "Eef I go home and find my wife kissing another man and I teep my hat to heem and say, 'Excuse me,' that is savoir-faire."

"Not quite," said the second. "Eef I go home and find my wife kissing another man and I teep my hat and say, 'Excuse me. Continue,' that is savoir-faire."

"No—not quite," rumbled the third, fingering his beard. "Eef I go home and find my wife kissing another man and teep my hat and say, 'Excuse me. Continue,' and he can continue—he has savoir-faire."

— IRVING HOFFMAN in *The Hollywood Reporter*

Scandal

2293. A lot of molehills become mountains when someone adds a little dirt.

Science

2294. The wife of the great physicist, Robert A. Millikan, happened to pass through the hall of her home in time to hear her maid answer the telephone. "Yes," Mrs. Millikan overheard, "this is where Dr. Millikan lives, but he's not the kind of doctor that does anybody any good."

2295. In science the credit goes to the man who convinces the world, not to the man to whom the idea first occurs.

— SIR WILLIAM OSLER

2296. Science is the great instrument of social change, all the greater because its object is not change but knowledge, and its silent appropriation of this dominant function, amid the din of political and religious strife, is the most vital of all revolutions which have marked the development of modern civilization.

— A. J. BALFOUR in *Scientific Monthly*

2297. The great Thomas A. Edison had a very beautiful summer home in which he took great pride. One day while showing some guests about, he pointed out all the labor-saving devices he had around the place. Turning back to the house, it was necessary to pass through a turnstile which led onto the main path; to get through the device took some considerable force.

"Mr. Edison," asked one of his guests, "how is it that with all these wonderful things around here, you still retain such a heavy turnstile?"

"Well, you see," replied the great inventor, his eyes lighting up, "everyone who pushes the turnstile around, pumps eight gallons of water into the tank on my roof."

2298. Greater even than the greatest discovery is it to keep open the way to future discovery.

— JOHN JACOB ABEL in *Science*

2299. This modern electro-mechanical age is getting to the point where it's just too complicated. Take the man in Eldorado, Ill., who had a new air conditioner installed in his home, turned it on and blissfully retired for a comfortable night's sleep.

But, when the conditioner brought the temperature down to a delightful 68 degrees, his furnace automatically switched on.

— *St. Louis Globe-Democrat*

2300. If we are to become the masters of science, not its slaves, we must learn to use its immense powers to good purpose. The machine itself has neither mind nor soul nor moral sense. Only man has been endowed with these godlike attributes. Every age has its destined duty—ours is to nurture an awareness of those divine attributes and a sense of responsibility in giving them expression.

— GENERAL DAVID SARNOFF

2301. Science has sometimes been said to be opposed to faith, and inconsistent with it. But all science, in fact, rests on a basis of faith, for it assumes the permanence and uniformity of natural laws —a thing which can never be demonstrated.

— TRYON EDWARDS

2302. Science—in other words, knowledge—is not the enemy of religion; for, if so, then religion would mean ignorance; but it is often the antagonist of school-divinity.

— OLIVER WENDELL HOLMES

Search

2303. Dr. Samuel Johnson used no filthy words, but when two ladies praised him for omitting them, he answered in mock surprise: "What, my dears? Then you have been looking for them!"

SECLUSION

2304. Things are always in the last place you look, because after you find them you don't look any more.

Seclusion

2305. When we have shut all the world out, we find that we have shut ourselves in.

— WILLIAM GRAHAM SUMNER, *The Forgotten Men and Other Essays*

Secret

2306. *He:* "Can you keep a secret?"
She: "I'll tell the world."

2307. When Colonel Frank Knox was Secretary of the Navy he was once asked by an old friend some casual question about the movement of certain ships in Atlantic waters. The question was thoughtless and Knox leaned over with an air of confidence and said, "Look here, can you keep a secret?"

"Of course, I can," replied the friend eagerly.

"Well," said the Secretary, "so can I."

2308. A woman looks on a secret in two ways: either it is worth keeping, or it is too good to be kept.

2309.   THE SECRETS OF MASONRY

Freemasons keep secret only certain signs of identifications and rituals by means of which the unity of the members of association scattered over all parts of the earth is made possible. In this way they guard against the possibility of people, who do not belong to the Masonic community, forcing themselves into the confidence and into the ceremonies which build up their inner life, and thus interfering with the efficiency of the brotherhood. Masonic lodges do not pursue any secret hidden purpose. The direction is prescribed by certain fundamental ideas which are openly confessed in Masonic writings everywhere. There is a common belief that the Masonic craft is a secret society, and this notion is based on the secret signs and grips by which its members recognize one another. Thus it has come to pass that the main aims of Freemasonry are assumed to be a secret policy, but, in fact, there is no secrecy about them. The secrecy of Masonic grips is a mere externality and is as unessential to Freemasonry as are the secrets of students fraternities, whose members are not allowed to betray the hidden meaning of the Greek letters by which they are called.

— *South African Masonic Journal*

2310. To keep your secret is wisdom; but to expect others to keep it is folly.

— OLIVER WENDELL HOLMES

2311. One often wonders why they are called the secrets of success when everybody is always telling them to everybody else.

2312. When a secret is revealed, it is the fault of the man who has intrusted it.

— JEAN DE LA BRUYÈRE

Security

2313. With all its alluring promise that someone else will guarantee for the rainy day, social security can never replace the program that man's future welfare is, after all, a matter of individual responsibility.

— HAROLD STONIER

2314. Uncertainty and expectation are the joys of life. Security is an insipid thing, though the overtaking and possessing of a wish discovers the folly of the chase.

— WILLIAM CONGREVE

2315. By a divine paradox, where there is one slave there are two. So in the wonderful reciprocities of being, we can never reach the higher level until all our fellows ascend with us. There is no true liberty for the individual except as he finds it in the liberty of all. There is no true security for the individual except as he finds it in the security of all

— EDWIN MARKHAM

2316. The trouble with worrying so much about your "security" in the future is that you feel so insecure in the present.

— HARLAN MILLER

Self

2317. A man has to live with himself, and he should see to it that he always has good company.

— CHARLES EVANS HUGHES

2318. Why is it we judge ourselves by our ideals and others by their acts?

2319. Your greatest problem is yourself. You are also your greatest treasure. If you can get yourself determined upon—find out what you are and what you are for—and if you can discover and develop the elements of value in your nature, your life will take on the beauty of orderliness and your need of the savings bank will be less and less, for you will be your own riches. I say, if you can, for this procedure takes wisdom and wisdom is a fruit which ripens slowly. Perhaps you are not yet wise; perhaps you are still incapable of self-analysis; perhaps you are confused amid the surfaces and appearances of life; perhaps your code of conduct is based upon the customs of the times and the sayings of the alleged sages; perhaps you are disheartened and discouraged—even in frenzy of retreat before the things in your life which seem to oppose you and beat you back. But even so, this is but a condition or mood which is not final. The condition will right itself, the mood will pass.

— RICHARD WIGHTMAN

2320. Here I am talking about myself when it's you I want to talk about me.

2321. A woman complained to a friend that the walls of her new apartment were so thin that the neighbors on either side could hear everything she said.

"Oh, I think you could eliminate that trouble," the other replied. "Just hang some tapestries over your walls."

The woman considered the suggestion briefly, then shook her head. "No, that wouldn't do," she replied. "Then we couldn't hear what they say."

2322. Yes, this is an age of materialism. And when we transform it into an age of reborn morality, in which the courage of a God-given spirit shall guide us as it did our forefathers, then we will discover anew that the hope of the world is really to be found dormant within our own bosoms—within ourselves.

— DAVID LAWRENCE

2323. We see things not as they are, but as we are.

— H. M. TOMLINSON in *Capper's Weekly*

2324. When you are good to others you are best to yourself.

— DR. LOUIS L. MANN, *In Quest of the Bluebird*

Self-analysis

2325. Judging others is a dangerous thing; not so much because you may make mistakes about them but because you may be revealing the truth about yourself.

Self-appraisal

2326. Do not judge a man by his opinion of himself.

— J. L. SCHNADIG

2327. When a man turns the light on others he must not expect to stay in the shade himself.

2328. Say nothing good of yourself, you will be distrusted; say nothing bad of yourself, you will be taken at your word.

— JOSEPH ROUX

2329. A prominent scientist has just published an article stating that a man of 50 is doing the best work of his life. Want to bet that he's the same scientist who wrote, 10 years ago, that a man of 40 was at the height of his ability?

— *Weltwoche*, Zurich

2330. It was a hot sultry night. A young man entered a drug store, asked the proprietor to change a quarter, entered a phone booth and dialed a number. For better ventilation he left the door of the booth ajar. The druggist couldn't help overhearing the conversation.

"Hello," said the young man, "is this Superior 3344?" "It is?" "Then may I talk to the boss." "You say this is the boss?" "Well, then can you tell me, do you need a good office boy?" "You say you have a good one?" "Well wouldn't you like to make a change; it might be for the better." "What's that?" "You say you don't care to make a change?" "O.K., that's all right, thank you." The young man hung up and proceeded to leave the store but before he got out, the proprietor stopped him.

"You'll have to forgive me but I couldn't help overhearing that conversation," he said. "I'm sorry you didn't land that job—better luck next time."

"Thanks very much for your interest," replied the lad, "don't worry, everything is all right. That was my boss I was talking to. I was only checking up on myself."

Self-appreciation

2331. H. T. Webster, the newspaper cartoonist, amused himself one summer day by sending telegrams to twenty acquaintances selected at random; each message containing the one word, "Congratulations." So far as he knew, not one of them had done anything in particular to be congratulated on. But each took the message as a matter of course and wrote him a letter of thanks. Everyone of them had done something that he himself regarded as clever and worthy of a congratulatory telegram.

— FRED C. KELLY

Self-assurance

2332. Do not attempt to do a thing unless you are sure of yourself; but do not relinquish it simply because someone else is not sure of you.

— STEWART E. WHITE

Self-blame

2333. No mud can soil us but the mud we throw.

— JAMES RUSSELL LOWELL

2334. When you shake your fist at someone, remember that all your fingers are pointing at yourself.

Self-confidence

2335. Doubt whom you will, but never doubt yourself.

— CHRISTIAN BOVEE

2336. The world has a way of giving what is demanded of it. If you are frightened and look for failure and poverty, you will get them, no matter how hard you may try to succeed. Lack of faith in yourself, in what life will do for you, cuts you off from the good things of the world. Expect victory and you make victory. Nowhere is this truer than in business life, where bravery and faith bring both material and spiritual rewards.

— DR. PRESTON BRADLEY

Self-control

2337. There is many a man whose tongue could govern multitudes, if he could only govern his tongue.

2338. Those who can command themselves, command others.

— WILLIAM HAZLITT

Self-destruction

2339. A man who trims himself to suit everybody will soon whittle himself away.

— CHARLES M. SCHWAB

Self-education

2340. The young man of native ability, the will to work and good personality, will, in the long run, get the equivalent of a college education in the tasks he will set for himself. If he has ability and determination, he will find ways to learn and to get ahead.

— EDWARD G. SEUBERT

Self-esteem

2341. He who does not think too much of himself is much more esteemed than he imagines.

— JOHANN WOLFGANG VON GOETHE

Self-hatred

2342. It is not love of self but hatred of self which is at the root of the troubles that afflict our world.

> — Eric Hoffer, *The Passionate State of Mind* (Harper and Brothers)

Self-importance

2343. A man who is pulling his own weight never has any left over to throw around.

> — O. A. Battista, quoted by Gurney Williams in *Look*

2344. Gregory Peck made his first visit to the Stork Club after he had appeared in a few movies. He wanted to sit in the Cub Room, but the tables were occupied and he was told that he'd have to wait. "Tell him who you are, Greg," Peck's companion whispered.

"If I have to tell 'em who I am," replied Peck, "then I ain't."

2345. Blessed are those who go around in circles, for they shall be called "Big Wheels."

2346. Man must realize his own unimportance before he can appreciate his importance.

> — R. M. Baumgardy

Self-improvement

2347. People seldom improve when they have no other model but themselves to copy after.

> — Oliver Goldsmith

2348. When an archer misses the mark he turns and looks for the fault within himself. Failure to hit the bull's-eye is never the fault of the target. To improve your aim improve yourself.

> — Gilbert Arland

Self-independence

2349. Every young man should aim at independence and should prepare himself for a vocation; above all, he should so manage his life that the steps of his progress are taken without improper aids;

that he calls no one master, that he does not win or deserve the reputation of being a tool of others, and that if called to public service he may assume its duties with the satisfaction of knowing that he is free to rise to the height of his opportunity.

— CHARLES EVANS HUGHES

Selfishness

2350. What you keep to yourself you lose; what you give away you keep forever. What is the good of hoarding your money? Death has another key to your safe.

— AXEL MUNTHE, *The Story of San Michele*

2351. One day a rich but miserly Hassid came to a Rabbi. The Rabbi led him to the window. "Look out there," he said, "and tell me what you see."

"People," answered the rich man.

Then the Rabbi led him to a mirror. "What do you see now?" he asked.

"I see myself," answered the Hassid.

Then the Rabbi said, "Behold—in the window there is glass and in the mirror there is glass. But the glass of the mirror is covered with a little silver, and no sooner is a little silver added than you cease to see others and see only yourself."

— From *The Dybbuk* by ANSKY, published by Liveright Publishers, New York. Copyright 1953 by HENRY G. ALSBERG and WINIFRED KATZIN

2352. Selfishness is the only real atheism; aspiration, unselfishness, the only real religion.

— ISRAEL ZANGWILL, *Children of the Ghetto*

2353. The man who lives for himself is a failure. Even if he gains much wealth, position or power he is still a failure. The man who lives for others has achieved true success. A rich man who consecrates his wealth and his position to the good of humanity is a success. A poor man who gives of his service and his sympathy to others has achieved true success even though material prosperity or outward honors never come to him.

— DR. NORMAN VINCENT PEALE

SELFISHNESS

2354. People who live to themselves are generally left to themselves.

— GEORGE KELLY, *Craig's Wife*

2355. Whenever you are too selfishly looking out for your own interest, you have only *one* person working for you—yourself. When you help a dozen other people with their problems, you have a *dozen* people working with you.

— WILLIAM B. GIVEN, JR.

2356. If you wish to travel far and fast, travel light. Take off all your envies, jealousies, unforgiveness, selfishness and fears.

— GLENN CLARK

2357. Be unselfish. That is the first and final commandment for those who would be useful, and happy in their usefulness. If you think of yourself only, you cannot develop because you are choking the source of development, which is spiritual expansion through thought for others.

— CHARLES W. ELIOT

Self-limitation

2358. When a man has put a limit on what he will do, he has put a limit on what he can do.

— CHARLES M. SCHWAB

Self-mastery

2359. I count him braver who overcomes his desires than him who conquers his enemies; for the hardest victory is victory over self.

— ARISTOTLE

2360. No man is fit to command another that cannot command himself.

— WILLIAM PENN, *No Cross, No Crown*

Self-praise

2361. Self-praise is half slander.

344

Self-reformation

2362. A man who has reformed himself has contributed his full share towards the reformation of his neighbor.

— NORMAN DOUGLAS

Self-reliance

2363. Humility is the better part of wisdom, and is most becoming in men. But let no one discourage self-reliance; it is, of all the rest, the greatest quality of true manliness.

— FERENC KOSSUTH

2364. Whoever serves his country well has no need of ancestors.

— VOLTAIRE

Self-respect

2365. He that respects himself is safe from others; he wears a coat of mail that none can pierce.

— HENRY WADSWORTH LONGFELLOW

2366. Never esteem anything as of advantage to thee that shall make thee break thy word or lose thy self-respect.

— MARCUS AURELIUS

2367. These three are the marks of a Jew—a tender heart, self-respect, and charity.

— Hebrew proverb

Self-sacrifice

2368. Self-preservation is the first law of nature, but self-sacrifice is the highest rule of grace.

Self-understanding

2369. When a man begins to understand himself he begins to live. When he begins to live he begins to understand his fellow men.

— NORVIN G. McGRANAHAN

Sensibility

2370. A man must not think he can save himself the trouble of being a sensible man and a gentleman by going to his lawyer, any more than he can get himself a sound constitution by going to his doctor.

— EDGAR W. HOWE

Servant

2371. A young physician and his wife had considerable difficulty teaching a new maid to answer the telephone properly. In spite of repeated instructions she persisted in answering: "Hello," instead of "Dr. Jones' residence." After many practice sessions, everything seemed to be all right. Then one morning the extension in the bedroom rang, and the maid, busy making the bed, grabbed the phone and blurted: "Dr. Jones' bedroom."

— J. M. ROSBROW

Service

2372. What we have done for ourselves alone dies with us. What we have done for others and the world remains and is immortal.

— ALBERT PINE

Sex

2373. The battle of the sexes will never be won by either side; there is too much fraternizing with the enemy.

Sham

2374. The time men spend in trying to impress others they could spend in doing the things by which others would be impressed.

— FRANK ROMER

Sharing

2375. "Darling," scolded the mother, "you shouldn't always keep everything for yourself. I told you before that you should let your little brother play with the toys half the time."

"I've been doing it, too!" Darling defended himself. "I take the sled going down hill and he takes it going up hill."

Silence

2376. There are times when silence is the best way to yell at the top of your voice.

— O. A. BATTISTA

2377. Wise men say nothing in dangerous times.

— JOHN SELDEN, *Table Talk*

2378. Vessels never give so great a sound as when they are empty.

— BISHOP JOHN JEWELL

2379. Moral cowardice that keeps one from speaking his mind is as dangerous as irresponsible talk.

2380. Winston Churchill once blandly remarked of a parliamentary opponent that he had "missed a very fine opportunity for keeping quiet."

2381. When Calvin Coolidge was Vice-President, Channing N. Cox, who had succeeded him as Governor of Massachusetts, came to Washington and called on his predecessor. Cox noted that Coolidge was able to see long lists of callers daily and finish his work at five o'clock, while Cox found himself held at his desk as late as nine P.M. "How come the difference?" he asked.

"You talk back," Coolidge explained.

— WALTER TROHAN, *The Chicago Tribune Press Service*

2382. *Sign in an office at a Southern air base:* CAUTION—Be Sure Brain Is Engaged Before Putting Mouth in Gear.

2383. You have not converted a man because you have silenced him.

— JOHN MORLEY

2384. We can refute assertions, but who can refute silence?

— CHARLES DICKENS

2385. A distinguished clergyman and one of his parishioners were playing golf. It was a very close match, and at the last hole the clergyman teed up, addressed the ball, and swung his driver with great force. The ball, instead of rolling down the fairway, merely rolled off the tee and settled slowly some twelve feet away.

The clergyman frowned, glared and bit his lip, but said nothing. His opponent regarded him for a moment, and then remarked:

"Doctor, that is the most profane silence I have ever witnessed."

2386. It is better to remain silent than to speak the truth ill-humoredly, and so spoil an excellent dish by covering it over with bad sauce.

— ST. FRANCIS DE SALES

2387. Silence brings friendship.

2388. Well-timed silence hath more eloquence than speech.

— M. T. TUPPER

2389. To say the right thing at the right time, keep still most of the time.

— JOHN W. RAPER, *What This World Needs*
(The World Publishing Co.)

2390. The best time for you to hold your tongue is the time you feel you must say something or bust.

— JOSH BILLINGS

2391. Speech may sometimes do harm; but so may silence, and a worse harm at that. No offered insult ever caused so deep a wound as a tenderness expected and withheld; and no spoken indiscretion was ever so bitterly regretted as the words one did not speak.

— A *Pocketful of Pebbles* by JAN STRUTHER.
Used by permission of Harcourt, Brace and Company

2392. Silence is often guilt instead of golden.

2393. The most difficult thing in the world is to know how to do a thing and to watch somebody else doing it wrong, without comment.

— T. H. WHITE in *The Atlantic Monthly*

2394. A man who lives right, and is right, has more power in his silence than another has by his words.

— PHILLIPS BROOKS

2395. Joseph Welch, the Boston lawyer, who achieved a measure of fame as chief counsel for the Army in the McCarthy hearings (1954) in reminiscing before a convention of Iowa farmers once quipped about "those hearings where I gained stature as a public figure by keeping still."

— The Des Moines Register

Simplicity

2396. Nothing is more simple than greatness; indeed, to be simple is to be great.

— RALPH WALDO EMERSON, Literary Ethics

Sin

2397. Seven deadly sins: politics without principle, wealth without work, pleasure without conscience, knowledge without character, business without morality, science without humanity, and worship without sacrifice.

— E. STANLEY JONES

2398. Saints and Sinners

When some fellow yields to temptation,
   And breaks a conventional law,
We look for no good in his make-up
   But God! how we look for a flaw!
No one will ask, "How tempted?"
   Nor allow for the battles he's fought;
His name becomes food for the jackals;
   For us who have never been caught.

"He has sinned!" we shout from the house-tops,
   We forget the good he has done,
We center on one lost battle,
   And forget the times he has won.
"Come, gaze on the sinner!" we thunder,
   "And by his example be taught,
That his footsteps lead to destruction,"
   Cry we who have never been caught.

> I'm a sinner, O Lord, and I know it,
>   I'm weak, I blunder, I fail.
> I'm tossed on life's stormy ocean,
>   Like ships embroiled in a gale.
> I'm willing to trust in Thy mercy;
>   To keep the commandments Thou'st taught,
> But deliver me, Lord, from the judgment
>   Of saints who have never been caught!

— Author unknown

Singing

2399. Samuel Foote once asked a man why he forever sang one tune.

"Because it haunts me," replied the other.

"No wonder," said Foote, "you continually murder it."

Smallness

2400. Little pots soon boil over.

2401. Little words are the sweetest to hear; little charities fly furthest and stay longest on the wing; little lakes are the stillest; little hearts are the fullest, and little farms are the best tilled. Little books are read the most and little songs the dearest loved. And when Nature would make anything especially rare and beautiful, she makes it little; little pearls, little diamonds, little dews. Agar's is a model prayer but then it is a little one; and the burden of the petition is for but the little. The Sermon on the Mount is little, but the last dedication discourse was an hour long. Life is made up of little things that count and death is what remains of them all. Day is made up of little beams, and night is glorious with little stars.

— Anonymous

Smile

2402. There is a very simple test by which we can tell good people from bad. If a smile improves a man's face, he is a good man; if a smile disfigures his face, he is a bad man.

— William Lyon Phelps

Smoking

2403. Two men met on the street, and one asked the other for a cigarette. His friend gave him the cigarette, commenting, "I thought you had quit smoking."

"I'm just to the first stage," replied the other. "I've quit buying."

2404. Fat man: one who knows where his cigar ashes are going to land.

2405. A friend of mine who commutes to New York always avoids the smoking car—can't stand smoking himself and doesn't like other people to smoke. One day he took a seat as usual in a nonsmoking car, but to his dismay a man came in, sat down facing him, and lighted up a cigar. Not wanting to make a scene, my friend waited till the conductor came around to punch his 26-trip ticket. As he handed it to the conductor, he nudged him and nodded at the brazen smoker. The conductor nodded back, punched the ticket again and went on.

— IRVING HOFFMAN

2406. Much smoking kills live men and cures dead swine.

2407. Sign in a hotel room: "Don't smoke in bed. The ashes that fall on the floor may be your own."

Society

2408. Upper crust: a bunch of crumbs stuck together with their own dough.

2409. Life in a populated world cannot be lived by human beings in isolation but only in societies, and the moment organized society impinges on the individual the ugly facts of force and constraint make their appearance and the age-long struggle between power and liberty begins.

— ARTHUR BRYANT, *Illustrated London News*

Solitude

2410. They are never alone that are accompanied with noble thoughts.

— SIR PHILIP SYDNEY

SOLITUDE

2411. We walk faster when we walk alone.

— NAPOLEON BONAPARTE

2412. The worst solitude is to have no real friendships.

— FRANCIS BACON

Sorrow

2413. You cannot prevent the birds of sorrow from flying over your head, but you can prevent them from building nests in your hair.

— Chinese proverb

2414. Sorrows are like thunder clouds: in the distance they look black, but overhead they are hardly gray.

— JEAN PAUL RICHTER

2415.

I walked a mile with pleasure,
She chattered all the way;
But left me none the wiser,
For all she had to say.

I walked a mile with sorrow,
Not a word, said she;
But oh the things I learned
When sorrow walked with me.

— ROBERT BROWNING HAMILTON

Souvenir

2416. Former Vice-President Garner had lost a $10 bet on a Washington baseball game, and the winner asked him to autograph the bill. "I'm giving it to my grandson for a souvenir," he explained. "He wants to frame it and hang it in his room."

"You mean the money's not going to be spent?" asked the Texan. "That's right."

"Well," said Garner, "in that case, then I'll just write you a check."

Speculation

2417. Warning to Wall Street speculators: "A new boom sweeps clean."

2418. The bulls win sometimes, the bears win sometimes, but the hogs always lose.

Speech see also *Talk*

2419. The trouble with a silver tongue seems to be that when it gets too sharp, it tends to cut the owner's throat.

— *The Chicago Daily News* on the chastisement of British Laborite ANEURIN BEVIN

2420. Too many people confuse free speech with loose talk.

— FRANKLIN P. JONES

2421. Think all you speak, but speak not all you think.— Thoughts are your own; your words are so no more.

— PATRICK DELANY

Speech, Freedom of see *Freedom of Speech*

Spelling

2422. Roger V. Devlin of The Tulsa (Okla.) *Tribune* at one time drove his readers crazy with this: What is the five-letter word whose pronunciation isn't changed by removal of four of the letters? Answer: Queue.

— MATT WEINSTOCK, *The Los Angeles Mirror-News*

Spending

2423. I would rather be a beggar and spend my money like a king, than be a king and spend money like a beggar.

— ROBERT G. INGERSOLL

Sports

2424. Win or lose (and when he was manager for the Chicago Cubs, it was mostly lose), Charlie Grimm always kept his sense of humor. One time, when the Cubs were digging deep in the barrel for new talent, one of Grimm's scouts excitedly phoned him from somewhere in the sticks.

SPORTS

"Charlie," he shouted, "I've landed the greatest young pitcher in the land. He struck out every man who came to bat—27 in a row. Nobody even got a foul until two were out in the 9th. The pitcher is right here with me. What shall I do?"

Back came Grimm's voice, "Sign up the guy who got the foul. We're looking for hitters."

— JOE MILLER

2425. Jeff Cravath once explained why he prefers running a ranch to his old job, coaching the Southern California football team: "Cattle don't have any alumni."

— S. PERRIN in *Coronet*

2426. Football season; The only time of the year when a man can walk down the street with a blonde on one arm and a blanket on the other without encountering raised eyebrows.

— BENNETT CERF in *Saturday Review*

2427. I think it was F.P.A., Commander of the Conning Tower on the New York *World* who first told the story of the gawky, naive, and wide-eyed freshman who approached his coach at the first football practice of the year. He was none too sure of himself and had his alibi prepared in advance.

"I'm a little stiff from bowling, sir," he said.

"I don't care where you're from," the coach replied. "Get your clothes on and get out there and show me what you've got."

2428. One afternoon while baseball's colorful Frankie Frisch was piloting the Pittsburgh Pirates, he was the victim of a loud-voiced heckler who kept shouting instructions as to how the game should be played. When it was over, Frankie went up to the man and politely asked his name and business address.

Flattered, the heckler told him, then asked why he wanted the information.

"Because," Frankie replied pleasantly, "I'm gonna be at your office bright and early tomorrow morning to tell you how to run your business."

— JAMES KELLER, *Just for Today*
(The Christophers, Inc.)

2429. Lefty Gomez, the baseball player, was nearing the end of his illustrious career and the time came for him to sign a new contract. Colonel Jacob Ruppert, owner of the Yankee club, called

354

him in and offered him a cut in salary from $22,000 to $8,000.

"I'll tell you what," cracked Gomez. "You keep the salary and I'll take the cut."

2430. A track meet is where a lot of young men, suddenly discovering themselves caught outdoors in their underwear, start running like hell.

2431. The game between Notre Dame and Southern Methodist had scarcely begun when the Fighting Irish scored a touchdown. A spectator sprang to his feet, let out a screech of delight and pounded his neighbor on the back.

A few minutes later, SMU scored and the same spectator went through the same routine. The neighbor's curiosity was aroused. "Who you rootin' for, friend?" he asked.

"I don't care who wins," replied the spectator. "I just came out to enjoy the game."

"Aha," sneered the neighbor, "an atheist."

2432. The small-time football coach with a reputation for optimism came into the locker room to give the boys a pre-game pep talk. "All right, boys," he cried cheerily, "here we are, unbeaten, untied, and unscored upon—and ready for the first game of the season."

2433. The devil was always challenging St. Peter to a game of baseball, but St. Peter never took him up. Finally, the Dodgers, the Giants and the Yanks all went to heaven. So naturally St. Peter called up the devil.

"Now I'll play you that game of baseball," he said.

"You'll lose," said the devil. "You'll lose."

"Oh, yeah?" replied St. Peter. "Right now I've got the greatest collection of baseball players you ever saw."

"You'll lose," said the devil. "You'll lose!"

"What makes you so sure we'll lose?"

"Because," laughed the devil, "we got all the umpires down here."

Sportsmanship

2434. The cheerful loser is a winner.

—ELBERT HUBBARD, *One Thousand and One Epigrams*

SPORTSMANSHIP

2435. The only bad part of being a good sport is that you have to lose to prove it.

— WALTER WINCHELL in *Coronet*

2436. He conquers twice who conquers himself in victory.

— PUBLILIUS SYRUS

2437.
To brag little, to lose well,
To crow gently if in luck,
To pay up, to own up,
To shut up if beaten,
Are the virtues of a sportingman.

— OLIVER WENDELL HOLMES

Statistics

2438. There are three kinds of lies: lies, damned lies, and statistics.

— BENJAMIN DISRAELI

2439. Statistics are no substitute for judgment.

— HENRY CLAY

2440. He uses statistics as a drunken man uses lampposts—for support rather than for illumination.

— ANDREW LANG

2441. Statistics can be used to support anything—especially statisticians.

2442. Statistics are like a Bikini bathing suit. What they reveal is suggestive, but what they conceal is vital.

— AARON LEVENSTEIN
— also credited to DR. CHARLES HILL

Story-telling

2443. They say I tell a great many stories; I reckon I do, but I have found in the course of a long experience that common people, take them as they run, are more easily informed through the medium of a broad illustration than in any other way, and as to what the hypercritical few may think, I don't care.

— ABRAHAM LINCOLN

2444. Anecdotes are stories with points. They are tools—nail-sinkers to drive home arguments firmly. They are the origin of all teaching.

—EDMUND FULLER, *Thesaurus of Anecdotes*
(Crown Publishers, 1942)

Strength

2445. Better to be a strong man with a weak point, than to be a weak man without a strong point. A diamond with a flaw is more valuable than a brick without a flaw.

—WM. J. H. BOETCKER

2446. If any man is rich and powerful he comes under the law of God by which the higher branches must take the burnings of the sun, and shade those that are lower; by which the tall trees must protect the weak plants beneath them.

—HENRY WARD BEECHER

2447. A man's strength cannot always be judged by his strongest actions; in many instances he is judged by his weakness.

—J. W. A. HENDERSON

Stubbornness

2448. Those who never retract their opinions love themselves more than they love the truth.

—SIR WALTER KING VENNING

2449. John H. Holliday, peppery founder and editor of *The Indianapolis* (Indiana) *News,* stormed into the composing room one day, determined to find the culprit who had spelled height—"hight." A check of the original copy showed that it was spelled "hight" and that, furthermore, the copy had been written by Mr. Holliday.

"If that's the way I spelled it, that's correct," he said—and the word was spelled "hight" in *The Indianapolis News* for the next thirty years.

—STEVE GOMORI in *Coronet*

2450. Firmness: the admirable quality in ourselves that is detestable stubbornness in others.

Subtlety

2451. *Pastor:* "Good morning, Betty. I hear God has seen fit to send you two little twin brothers."

Little Betty: "Yes sir, and He knows where the money's coming from, too. I heard daddy say so."

2452. Eugene Field used probably the gentlest method known of dealing with a plagiarist. When Field, a Chicago columnist, found that a small-town editor was lifting his column word for word and signing his own name, the poet didn't hit the ceiling. Instead he made sure to include in his column a glowing tribute to that editor, lauding him as a writer of unusual talent.

—*St. Louis Post-Dispatch*

2453. An irate landowner posted the following sign on his property: "No hunting or fishing. Survivors will be prosecuted."

2454. A beautiful blonde was seated in a hotel lobby. A well-known wolf was trying his best to strike up an acquaintance. After several unsuccessful attempts, she finally suggested that he quit bothering her.

Quick as a flash the man-about-town replied, "Pardon me, Miss, I thought you were my mother."

With that she smiled prettily and replied, "I couldn't be. I'm married."

2455. Little Georgie received a new drum for Christmas, and shortly thereafter, when father came home from work one evening, mother said: "I don't think that man upstairs likes to hear Georgie play his drum, but he's certainly subtle about it."

"Just what do you mean?" asked the father.

"Well," said Georgie's mother, "this afternoon he gave Georgie a knife, and asked him if he knew what was inside the drum."

2456. George Bernard Shaw once autographed one of his works to a friend with the following inscription:

To ——————
with esteem
George Bernard Shaw

Several years later he found the volume on the shelves of a used-book store. He purchased it and sent it back to his friend with the following inscription added:

With renewed esteem
George Bernard Shaw

Success see also *Failure*

2457. When James Burrill Angell, for 38 years president of the University of Michigan, was asked for the secret of his success, he answered, "Grow antennae, not horns."

2458. You cannot climb the ladder of success with your hands in your pockets.

2459. "I don't want to be a success. I want to be like you."

2460. Nothing is particularly hard if you divide it into small jobs.

— HENRY FORD

2461. The measure of success is not whether you have a tough problem to deal with, but whether it's the same problem you had last year.

— JOHN FOSTER DULLES, quoted by C. B. PALMER in *The New York Times Magazine*

2462. Success is in the way you walk the paths of life each day;
It's in the little things you do, and in the things you say.
Success is not in getting rich, or rising high to fame.
It's not alone in winning goals, which all men hope to claim.
Success is being big of heart, and clean and broad in mind;
It's being faithful to your friends, and to the stranger, kind.
It's in the children whom you love, and all they learn from you;
Success depends on character, and everything you do.

— *Pepper Box*, St. Louis Rotary Club

2463. When your superior receives you as an equal, you are already his superior.

2464. Our business in life is not to get ahead of others, but to get ahead of ourselves.

— STEWART B. JOHNSON

2465. Do you know how to fail? If you do, then you will know also the secret of succeeding, for the two are forever locked together. On a thousand gridirons, coaches each fall prepare their charges to take the field of battle in the grand sport of football. Do you know the first lessons those candidates for the team will be taught? Not how to make a touchdown—that is easy. The first thing they must learn is to fall down and for days the coaches will be teaching their teams how to be tackled, how to fall limp so as not to be hurt, how to expect to fall and then rise again and press onward toward the goal.

— The Reverend William E. Phifer, Jr.,
Christian Observer

2466. It's a shame that when success turns a person's head it does not also wring his neck just a little.

— *Grayson County* (Kentucky) *News*

2467. In the race towards success, don't look back because someone might be gaining on you.

2468. If you want to succeed you should strike out on new paths rather than travel the worn paths of accepted success.

— John D. Rockefeller, Sr.

2469. The rung of a ladder was never meant to rest upon, but only to hold a man's foot long enough to enable him to put the other somewhat higher.

— Thomas Henry Huxley

2470. The men who succeed best in public life are those who take the risk of standing by their own convictions.

— James A. Garfield

2471. If I wanted to become a tramp, I would seek information and advice from the most successful tramp I could find. If I wanted to become a failure I would seek advice from men who have never succeeded. If I wanted to succeed in all things, I would look around me for those who are succeeding, and do as they have done.

— Joseph Marshall Wade

2472. No age or time of life, no position or circumstance, has a monopoly on success. Any age is the right age to *start doing!*

2473. Experience shows that success is due less to ability than to zeal. The winner is he who gives himself to his work, body and soul.

— CHARLES BUXTON

2474. I have observed that to succeed in the world one should appear like a fool but be wise.

— BARON DE LA MONTESQUIEU

2475. Success covers a multitude of blunders.

2476. A wise old trainer, asked for advice on winning races, said: "Well, sir, the thing to do is get out in front at the start and *improve your position from there on.*"

2477. Success is getting what you want; happiness is wanting what you get.

2478. The secret of success is to be able to make more money to meet obligations you wouldn't have had if you hadn't made so much money.

2479. Nothing *recedes* like success.

2480. There never has been any 30-hour week for men who had anything to do.

— CHARLES F. KETTERING

2481. Success has ruined many a man.

— BENJAMIN FRANKLIN, *Poor Richard's Almanac*

2482. Nothing succeeds like success.

— ALEXANDRE DUMAS, SR., *Ange Pitou*

2483. The man who fails while trying to do good has more honor than he who succeeds by accident.

2484. He who will not listen to the teaching of failure shall never hear the voice of success.

2485. Success slips away from you like sand through the fingers, like water through a leaky pail, unless success is held tight by hard work, day by day, night by night, year in and year out. Everyone who is not looking forward to going to seed looks forward to working harder and harder and more fruitfully as long as he lasts.

— STUART SHERMAN, *Shaping Men and Women*, edited by JACOB ZEITLIN (Doubleday & Co., Inc.)

2486. Far better it is to dare mighty things, to win glorious triumphs, even though checkered by failure, than to take rank with those poor spirits who neither enjoy much nor suffer much, because they live in the gray twilight that knows not victory nor defeat.

— THEODORE ROOSEVELT

2487. In Hollywood success is relative. The closer the relative, the greater the success

— ARTHUR TREACHER

2488. At age 25 a man has about 100,000 hours of work ahead of him before his retirement at 65. How much he broadens his scope of knowledge and abilities through the years reflects his degree of success.

2489. Albert Einstein once gave what he considered the best formula for success in life. "If a is success in life, I should say the formula is a equals x plus y plus z, x being work and y being play."

"And what is z?" inquired the interviewer.

"That," he answered, "is keeping your mouth shut."

2490. If at first you don't succeed, try try again. Then quit. No use being a damn fool about it.

— W. C. FIELDS

Suffering

2491. Those who have suffered much have lived long. Never suppose that lonely spirits know nothing of the world; they see and judge it.

— HONORÉ DE BALZAC

2492. Present suffering is not enjoyable, but life would be worth little without it. The difference between iron and steel is fire, but steel is worth all it costs.

— MALTBIE BABCOCK

Sufficiency

2493. In an orchard there should be enough to eat, enough to lay up, enough to be stolen, and enough to rot upon the ground.

— SAMUEL MADDEN

Superiority

2494. A person who talks about his inferiors hasn't any.

2495. The superior man is the providence of the inferior. He is eyes for the blind, strength for the weak, and a shield for the defenseless. He stands erect by bending above the fallen. He rises by lifting others.

— ROBERT G. INGERSOLL

2496. We gain nothing by being with such as ourselves; we encourage each other in mediocrity. I am always longing to be with men more excellent than myself.

— CHARLES LAMB

Superstition

2497. Superstition is the religion of feeble minds.

— EDMUND BURKE, *Reflections on the Revolution in France*

Surprise

2498. Surprise: opening your laundry to see what you got.

2499. When a woman called Police Constable Crawford in Owen Sound, Ont., to report a skunk in her cellar, he advised: "Make a trail of bread crumbs from the basement to the yard and wait for the skunk to follow it outside."

A little later the woman called back: "I did what you told me. Now I've got two skunks in my cellar."

Suspicion

2500. Suspicion is far more apt to be wrong than right; oftener unjust than just. It is no friend to virtue, and always an enemy to happiness.

— HOSEA BALLOU

2501. Suspicion is no less an enemy to virtue than to happiness. He that is already corrupt is naturally suspicious, and he that becomes suspicious will quickly be corrupt.

— DR. SAMUEL JOHNSON

2502. It is hardly possible to suspect another without having in one's self the seeds of the baseness the other is accused of.

— SAINT STANISLAUS

2503. Suspicion always haunts the guilty mind.

— WILLIAM SHAKESPEARE, *Henry VI*

Sympathy

2504. Sympathy without judgment is like wine without water, apt to degenerate into intoxication; judgment without sympathy is like water without heat, destined to end in ice.

— JOHN STUART BLACKIE

Tact

2505. Tact is the unsaid part of what you think; its opposite, the unthought part of what you say.

— HENRY VAN DYKE

2506. Silence is not always tact, and it is tact that is golden—not silence.

— SAMUEL BUTLER

2507. The perfect hostess needs quick wit and tact—like the Chungking matron who invited a few Americans to Thanksgiving dinner, promising them the incredible treat of turkey.

As the first guest entered the dining room, the servant, carrying the tray, slipped and the priceless bird skidded to the floor. "Never mind, Boy," said the hostess quietly and kindly. "Take it back to the kitchen and bring in the other one."

— *The Reader's Digest*

2508. Tact is the ability to describe others as they see themselves.

2509. "One of the most tactful men I ever knew," says a California manufacturer, "was the man who fired me from my first job. He called me in and said, 'Son, I don't know how we're ever going to get along without you, but starting Monday we're going to try.'"

2510. A woman well on in years entered a drugstore and asked a clerk, "Have you any cream for restoring the complexion?"

"Restoring, Miss?" inquired the clerk in a surprised tone. "You mean preserving." So he sold the woman eighteen dollars' worth of cosmetics.

Talent see also *Hidden talent*

2511. Mozart was once asked by a lad how to write a symphony. "You're a very young man," Mozart told him. "Why not begin with ballads?"

"But you composed symphonies when you were ten years old," the youth urged.

"Yes," replied Mozart, "but I didn't ask 'how'."

2512. A young lady called one day on Rubinstein, the great pianist, who had consented to listen to her playing.

"What do you think I should do now?" she asked when she had finished.

"Get married," was Rubinstein's answer.

2513. Edward Fitzgerald had to pay for the printing of his "Rubaiyat of Omar Khayyam" before he could get it before the public. No editor could see anything to it. Burns and Kipling had to pay for the printing of their poetry at first. Carrie Jacobs Bond, turned down by innumerable song publishers, borrowed $1,500 and published her own works.

— E. V. DURLING in *The Chicago American*

2514. Talent is built in solitude; character in the stream of the world.

— JOHANN WOLFGANG VON GOETHE

Talk see also *Speech*

2515. Some people make a practice of talking to strangers; others make a practice of talking to themselves, and still others make a practice of talking too much.

2516. The danger lies not in the big ears of little pitchers, but in the large mouths.

Target

2517. A gangster rushed into a saloon shooting right and left, yelling, "All you dirty skunks get outta here."

The customers fled in a hail of bullets—all except an Englishman, who stood at the bar calmly finishing his drink.

"Well?" snapped the gangster, waving his smoking gun.

"Well," remarked the Englishman, "there certainly were a lot of them, weren't there?"

Taxation — taxes

2518. Taxation without representation was tyranny, but taxation with it is pretty expensive.

2519. The average taxpayer no longer feels that Congress will let him down. He just hopes that Congress will let him up.

2520. We've never had it so good nor taken away from us so fast.

— From "In This Corner" by CEDRIC ADAMS
in *The Minneapolis Sunday Tribune*

2521. Taxpayer: a government worker with no vacation, no sick leave, and no holidays.

2522. People who squawk about their income taxes may be divided into two classes. They are: men and women.

2523. "What is the difference between a taxidermist and a tax collector?"

"The taxidermist takes only your hide."

2524. Each citizen contributes to the revenues of the State a portion of his property in order that his tenure of the rest may be secure.

— BARON DE LA MONTESQUIEU

2525. A man owes it to himself to become successful—after that he owes it to the Bureau of Internal Revenue.

2526. The voters of a North Carolina county were considering an increase in the schoolteachers' salaries, which would entail a rise in taxes. I asked a farmer who was much interested in the schools what the general sentiment seemed to be.

"Well," he said slowly, "as best I can see it, almost everybody is in sympathy with it, but hardly anybody is in favor of it."

— J. CALVIN REID

Teaching see also *Education*

2527.   There were two unemployed schoolteachers; one had no *class;* the other had no *principal.*

2528.   The devotion of teachers to the subjects they teach as a thing of prime importance often means the inevitable neglect of the object of instruction, the boys and girls to be taught.

— DR. WILLIAM H. BURHAM

2529.   To teach is to learn twice.

— JOSEPH JOUBERT

2530.   The well-educated teacher is not the one who has mastered the jargon of pedagogy, but the one who is himself so constantly in quest of knowledge and intellectual power that learning in him begets learning in his students.

— Reprinted from *The Restoration of Learning* by ARTHUR BESTOR, by permission of the publisher, Alfred A. Knopf, Inc. Copyright 1955 by ARTHUR BESTOR.

2531.   Who teaches, learns.

Tears

2532.   I do believe there is many a tear in the heart that never reaches the eye.

— NORMAN MACEWAN

Telephone

2533.   An angry subscriber, having trouble with the telephone, bellowed at the operator, "Am I crazy, or are you?"

"I'm sorry, sir," she replied in her sweetest professional voice, "but we do not have that information."

TELEVISION

2534. "Miss Jones," said the science professor, "would you care to tell the class what happens when a body is immersed in water?"

"Sure," said Miss Jones. "The telephone rings."

— BENNETT CERF, *Anything for a Laugh*
(Grosset & Dunlap)

Television

2535. Television certainly helps you get acquainted with a lot of new people. Mostly repairmen.

2536. It seems to me that movies on television are just like furniture—they're either early American or old English.

2537. Television isn't replacing radio half as fast as it is homework.

2538. My objection to television is not merely that the quality of programs is depressingly low; it is also that the screen exercises a hypnotic effect on the majority of watchers . . . It is a terrible slavery of the mind—and, as Aristotle warned us a long time ago, "the worst thing about slavery is that eventually the slaves get to like it."

— SYDNEY J. HARRIS, *The Chicago Daily News*

Temper

2539. Don't be a fault-finding grouch; when you feel like finding fault with somebody or something, stop for a moment and think; there is very apt to be something wrong within yourself. Don't permit yourself to show temper, and always remember that when you are in the right you can afford to keep your temper, and when you are in the wrong you cannot afford to lose it.

2540. Keep your temper. Do not quarrel with an angry person, but give him a soft answer. It is commanded by the Holy Writ and, furthermore, it makes him madder than anything else you could say.

Temperance

2541. Temperance is the control of self by self; control of the lower self by the higher self.

2542. Temperance is moderation in the things that are good and total abstinence from the things that are foul.

— Frances E. Willard

Temptation

2543. Every moment of resistance to temptation is a victory.

2544. A woman flees from temptation, but a man just crawls away from it in the cheerful hope it may overtake him.

2545. The easiest way to resist temptation is publicly.

— Franklin P. Jones

2546. Opportunity knocks only once but temptation bangs on the door for years.

Testimonial

2547. It seems to me we are giving too many testimonial dinners these days to people who have simply done a job they were paid to do. Anyone who works for pay—and that includes presidents of corporations as well as janitors—is paid to do a *good* job, not a bad one. If he does what he is paid to do, then why give him a medal? Don't do it on the basis that he may have done something beyond the call of duty. It's a man's duty, when he takes money, to do a job to the limit of his ability. And by that word "limit" I mean the *extreme* limit.

— Cy Fox

Theory

2548. One of the tragedies of life is the murder of a beautiful theory by a brutal gang of facts.

Thievery

2549. A thief passes for a gentleman, when stealing has made him rich.

—Ancient proverb

Thought — thoughts — thinking

2550. There's nothing either good or bad, but thinking makes it so.

—WILLIAM SHAKESPEARE

2551. If men would think more, they would act less.

—EARL OF HALIFAX

2552. Those who deny freedom to others deserve it not for themselves, and, under a just God, they cannot long retain it.

—CHARLES SUMNER

2553. The pleasantest things in the world are pleasant thoughts; and the great art of life is to have as many of them as possible.

—MICHEL DE MONTAIGNE

2554. He thinks by infection, catching an opinion like a cold.

—JOHN RUSKIN

2555. The greatest thoughts seem degraded in their passage through little minds. Even the winds of heaven make but mean music when whistling through a keyhole.

2556. When you stop to think, don't forget to start again.

2557. The only reason some people become lost in thought is because it's unfamiliar territory to them.

2558. If you make people think they're thinking, they'll love you; but if you really make them think, they'll hate you.

—DON MARQUIS

2559. The best and clearest thinking in the world is done and the finest art is produced, not by men who are hungry, ragged and harassed, but by men who are well-fed, warm and easy in mind.

—H. L. MENCKEN

2560. Be careful of your thoughts. They may break into words at any time.

Thrift see also *Economy*

2561. Mere parsimony is not economy . . . Expense, and great expense, may be an essential part of true economy.

— EDMUND BURKE, *Letter to a Noble Lord*

2562. Save a part of your income and begin now, for the man with a surplus controls circumstances and the man without a surplus is controlled by circumstance.

— HENRY H. BUCKLEY

2563. Work hard and save your money. Then, when you're old, you can have the things that only young people can enjoy.

2564. Resolve not to be poor; whatever you have, spend less.

— DR. SAMUEL JOHNSON as quoted in
Boswell's Life of Johnson

2565. Thrift is that habit of character that prompts one to work for what he gets, to earn what is paid him; to invest a part of his earnings; to spend wisely and well; to save, but not hoard.

— ARTHUR CHAMBERLAIN

2566. It took thrift and savings, together with tremendous character and vision, to make our nation what it is today. And it will take thrift and savings, together with constant ingenuity and stamina, to conserve our remaining resources to enable us to continue to be a great nation.

— JOHN W. SNYDER

2567. All the money in the world is no use to a man or his country if he spends it as fast as he makes it. All he has left are his bills and the reputation of being a fool.

— RUDYARD KIPLING

2568. We are not to judge thrift solely by the test of saving or spending. If one spends what he should prudently save, that certainly is to be deplored. But if one saves what he should prudently spend, that is not necessarily to be commended. A wise balance between the two is the desired end.

— OWEN D. YOUNG

THRIFT

2569. So often we rob tomorrow's memories by today's economies.

— John Mason Brown, *Morning Faces*
(Whittlesey)

2570. A woman's idea of thrift is saving enough on one purchase to buy something else.

2571. The secret of financial success is to spend what you have left after saving, instead of saving what is left after spending.

2572. Little Sandy arrived home from school completely out of breath. His father asked him what was the matter.

"I ran all the way home behind a streetcar and saved a nickel," Sandy replied proudly.

"Not bad, my boy—not bad!" said his father. "But why didn't you run home behind a taxi and save a quarter?"

Time

2573. Paul Barnes, radio actor, tells of the receptionist at NBC in New York who was helping an aspiring actress fill out an audition blank. When the actress was asked her age she hesitated. The receptionist waited patiently while seconds ticked by, then she quipped, "Better hurry up. Every minute makes it worse!"

2574. The good old days: when you got the landlord to fix anything by just threatening to move.

2575. The real secret of how to use time is to pack it as you would a portmanteau, filling up the small spaces with small things.

— Sir Henry Haddow

2576. Sorting a collection of books left to me by my grandfather, I came across a dictionary printed in 1901. I leafed through it, and my eye fell upon "uranium." The definition read: "A worthless white metal, not found in the United States."

— Owen W. Stout in *The Reader's Digest*

2577.   TIME

Time *was* is past—thou canst it not recall.
Time *is* thou hast—employ thy portion small.

> Time *future* is not, and may never be.
> Time *present* is the only time for thee!
>
> —Inscription on an ancient sun dial

2578. Time is the one thing that can never be retrieved. One may lose and regain a friend; one may lose and regain money; opportunity once spurned may come again; but the hours that are lost in idleness can never be brought back to be used in gainful pursuits. Most careers are made or marred in the hours after supper.

—C. R. LAWTON

2579. An engineer engaged on railroad construction in Central America explained to one of the natives living alongside the right-of-way the advantages the new road would bring him. Wanting to illustrate his point, he asked the native, "How long does it take to carry your produce to market by muleback?"

"Three days, señor."

"Then," said the engineer, "you can understand the benefit that road will be to you. You will be able to take your produce to market and return home on the same day."

"Very good, señor," the native agreed courteously, "but, señor, what shall we do with the other two days?"

—*The Anthology of Ancedotes* (Droke House)

2580. Those who make the worst use of their time are the first to complain of its shortness.

—JEAN DE LA BRUYÈRE

2581. Blotter: something you spend time looking for while the ink is drying.

2582. The past is present in the future.

—DR. LOUIS L. MANN

Timidity

2583. He will never get a good thing cheap, that is afraid to ask the price.

Timing

2584. Junk: something you keep ten years and then throw away two weeks before you need it.

TIP — TIPPING

2585. The easiest way to get into trouble is to be right at the wrong time.

Tip — tipping

2586. A taxi driver whose fixed fee was 20 cents from the Mayflower Hotel in Washington to the Navy building received just that amount from a prosperous-looking customer.

"That's correct, isn't it?" the man asked as the cabby stared at the two dimes.

"It's correct," answered the cabby cryptically, "but it ain't right."

2587. Tips: wages we pay other people's help.

2588. A Stanford University professor took his young son with him on a trip across the country. One day after their return, a package was delivered with postage due. Neither the professor nor his wife had the necessary $3, but their son produced it. Surprised, his mother asked how he came to have that much money. "Well," he said, "Dad was always careless with his money on our trip and nearly always left some on the table when we ate. So I just picked it up."

Tit for tat

2589. A contractor out in the Northwest had been trying for months to collect an overdue bill. As a last resort, he sent a tear-jerking letter accompanied by a snapshot of his little daughter. Under the picture he wrote, "The reason I must have the money."

The prompt reply was a photo of a voluptuous blonde in a bathing suit labeled: "The reason I can't pay!"

2590. A bumptious playwright who had a new show opening sent a couple of tickets for the first night to the mayor of the city with a note suggesting that the chief executive could bring a friend "if you have one."

The mayor returned the tickets with a courteous letter stating that previous engagements made it impossible for him to see the show the opening night, but he would purchase two tickets for the second performance—if there was one.

— JOHNNIE MACINTYRE, quoted by JOE HARRINGTON in *The Boston Sunday Post*

2591. Cambridge University recently received an inquiry from a sugar refining firm: "We would like to purchase some of your books for use in our library. Would it be possible to do so at wholesale prices?" The Press made a counter proposal: "We would like to purchase some sugar for our coffee break. Would it be possible to do so at wholesale prices?"

2592. When Cornelia Otis Skinner opened in a revival of Shaw's *Candida,* he called, "Excellent. Greatest." Miss Skinner, overwhelmed, cabled back, "Undeserving such praise." Shaw answered, "I meant the play." Miss Skinner bristled and replied, "So did I."

— BENNETT CERF in *Saturday Review*

2593. "I am a daughter of the American Revolution," a woman told the rabbi's daughter, "and we go back 160 years."

"That's nothing," she replied. "I'm a daughter of the Egyptian revolution, and we go back 3300 years."

Toasts

2594.
I drink to one, and only one,—
And may that one be he
Who loves but one, and only one,—
And may that one be me!

2595. May misfortune follow you all the days of your life and never overtake you.

2596. May we have more and more friends and need them less and less.

2597.
Here's to the ships of our navy and the
ladies of our land.
May the former be well rigged and the
latter well manned.

2598.
Here's to the land which gave me birth,
Here's to the flag she flies,
Here's to her sons—the best on earth,
Here's to her smiling skies,
Here's to a heart which beats for me,
True as the stars above,

Here's to the day when mine she'll be,
Here's to the girl I love.

2599. Here's that you may live a hundred happy years,
And I may live a hundred less one day,
For I don't care to live any longer,
When you good fellows have all passed away.

— RICHARD CARLE

2600. Here's to the girl I love,
And here's to the girl that loves me,
And here's to all those that love her that I love,
And to those that love her that loves me.

2601. Another candle in your cake?
Well, that's no cause to spout,
Be glad that you have strength enough
To blow the darn thing out.

2602. I come from good old Boston,
The home of the bean and the cod,
Where the Cabots speak only to Lowells,
And the Lowells speak only to God.

— SAMUEL C. BUSHNELL, toast at Harvard
alumni dinner at Waterbury

Here's to the town of New Haven,
The home of the truth and the light,
Where God speaks to Jones,
In the very same tones,
That he uses with Hadley and Dwight.

— DEAN JONES, reply to DR.
BUSHNELL's toast

2603. At a dinner of the foreign ministers, following the American Revolutionary war, the British ambassador gave this toast. "England—the sun, whose bright beams enlighten and fructify the remotest corners of the earth."

The French ambassador followed with: "France—the moon, whose mild, steady and cheering rays are the delight of all nations, controlling them in the darkness, and making their dreariness beautiful."

Benjamin Franklin then rose and, with his usual dignity and simplicity, said: "George Washington—the Joshua, who commanded the sun and moon to stand still, and they obeyed him."

2604. Here's to those who love us,
   And here's to those who don't,
   A smile for those who are willing to,
   And a tear for those who won't.

2605. Here's to the man who drinks when he's dry,
   And drinks till his humor is mellow;
   And here's to the man who perhaps isn't dry,
   But drinks just to be a good fellow.

2606. God made man frail as a bubble;
   God made Love, Love made Trouble.
   God made the Vine; was it a sin
   That Man made Wine to drown Trouble in?

2607.   One drink is plenty;
   Two drinks too many,
   And three not half enough.

2608. Here's to our creditors—may they be endowed with the three virtues—faith, hope, and charity.

2609. Here's to freedom—may the shackles of prejudice never fetter the mind.

2610. Here's to the happiest days of my life
   That I spent in the arms of another man's wife,—
   My mother, God bless her!

Tolerance see also *Intolerance—Prejudice—Bigotry*

2611. A man who took great pride in his lawn had a heavy crop of dandelions. After trying every known device to get rid of them, he wrote the Department of Agriculture, enumerating all the things he had tried, and ending, "What shall I do now?"
   In due course came a reply, "We suggest you learn to love them."

2612. The test of tolerance comes when we are in a majority; the test of courage comes when we are in a minority.

— DR. RALPH W. SOCKMAN

TOLERANCE

2613. I believe with all my heart that civilization has produced nothing finer than a man or woman who thinks and practices true tolerance. Someone has said that most of us don't think, we just occasionally rearrange our prejudices. And I suspect that even to-day, with all the progress we have made in liberal thought, the quality of true tolerance is as rare as the quality of mercy. That men of all creeds have fundamental common objectives is a fact one must learn by the process of education. How to work jointly toward these objectives must be learned by experience.

— COLONEL FRANK KNOX

2614. Tolerance is the positive and cordial effort to understand another's beliefs, practices and habits without necessarily sharing or accepting them.

— DR. JOSHUA LOTH LIEBMAN

Tomorrow
2615. One of the greatest labor-saving devices of today is to-morrow.

Tradition
2616. Tradition does not mean that the living are dead but that the dead are alive.

— G. K. CHESTERTON

Traffic
2617 "What's your name?" demanded the traffic cop.
"Abraham O'Brien Goldberg," replied the motorist.
"What's the O'Brien for?" asked the officer.
"Protection, sir," replied Goldberg.

2618. Edgar Bergen was driving calmly along a peaceful stretch of road one day when a woman driver came weaving down the road behind him. She tooted her horn once and rammed him with a crushing impact. While they were trying to untangle bumpers, the lady said breezily, "Well, I'm afraid this was all my fault."

"Don't be silly," Bergen said gallantly. "The blame is entirely mine. I saw you fully three blocks away, and had plenty of time to duck down a side street."

2619. The way blood flows in them these days, it's easy to see why they're called traffic arteries.

2620. A schoolteacher, brought before a traffic judge for having driven through a red light, requested an immediate disposal of her case that she might hasten away to her classes. A wild gleam came into the judge's eye. "You're a schoolteacher eh?" said he. "Madam, I shall now realize my life-long ambition. Sit down at that table and write 'I went through a red light' five hundred times."

2621. Traffic light: a trick to get pedestrians halfway across the street safely.

— WALTER WINCHELL, quoted in *Coronet*

2622. Pedestrian: man who thought there was still a couple gallons of gas left in the tank.

2623. Pedestrian: a fellow whose wife beats him to the garage.

2624. You can tell Americans trust in God by the way they drive.

2625. *Wifey, explaining the smashed fender to hubby:* "And the policeman was really very nice about it. He even asked me if I'd like for the city to remove all the telephone poles."

2626. A motorist is a person who, after seeing a wreck, drives carefully for several blocks.

2627. The police of Zagreb (Yugoslavia) at one time required violators of traffic ordinances to pull over to the side of the road and deflate all tires. As a consequence, the number of accidents on the streets of that city fell off considerably.

2628. A tourist speeding along a highway at 100 miles an hour was stopped by a patrolman. "Was I driving too fast?" asked the tourist apologetically.

"Heck, no," replied the officer. "You were flying too low."

2629. Pedestrian: a man who falls by the wayside.

2630. A lot of auto wrecks result from the driver hugging the wrong curve.

— OLIN MILLER

2631. Detour: the roughest distance between two points.

TRAVEL

2632.
Here lies the body of William Jay,
   Who died maintaining his right of way—
He was right, dead right, as he sped along,
   But he's just as dead as if he were wrong.

2633. Don't drive as if you own the road; drive as if you own the car.

2634. Detour: something that lengthens your mileage, diminishes your gas, and strengthens your vocabulary.

      — OLIVER HERFORD

2635. The automobile approached the coroner at 60 miles an hour.

2636.
    If a grave I'll soon be needing
    It's because I drive while reading.

2637. There wouldn't be nearly as many pedestrian patients if there were more patient pedestrians.

2638. To insist on drinking before driving is to put the quart before the hearse.

2639. A woman driver is a person who drives the same way a man does—only she gets blamed for it.

      — DAN VALENTINE in *Saturday Evening Post*

2640. The most annoying kind of Sunday driver is the one who is out trying to drive a hard bargain.

      — O. A. BATTISTA

Travel

2641. *Trans Continental Airlines passenger:* "I hate riding locals. We've stopped at Denver, Chicago and now Pittsburgh."

      — TOM BLAKLEY, reprinted by permission of *Collier's*

2642. Only that traveling is good which reveals to me the value of home and enables me to enjoy it better.

      — HENRY DAVID THOREAU

2643. It isn't the travel that broadens one—it's all that rich foreign food.

2644. A little figuring on the fatality rate for United States railroads and scheduled air lines for 1955 (.78 per billion passenger miles on railroads, .92 on air lines) proves interesting.

It shows that if you spent every minute of your life on commercial planes, hurtling about the country at 300 m.p.h.—and did not die of some other cause—you would live an average of 400 years.

On the railroads it means you could ride continuously at 75 m.p.h. with the chance of a fatality only once in about 2,000 years.

No doubt the companies will strive for even safer records; but even so, you can't do better lying in bed.

— John T. McCutcheon Jr., *Chicago Tribune*

2645. A large car skidded to the curb in front of the Capitol in Washington, and a well-dressed tourist couple hurriedly got out. After quickly surveying the surrounding scene, the man said: "All right, dear, you do the outside and I'll take the inside. We should be through in a half hour."

— Harold Helfer

2646. Usually speaking, the worst bred person in company is a young traveler just returned from abroad.

— Jonathan Swift

2647. He who never leaves his own country is full of prejudices.

— Carlo Goldoni

Trifles

2648. The journey of a thousand miles begins with one pace.

— Lao-Tze

Trouble – troubles

2649. Troubles, like babies, grow larger by nursing.

— Lady Holland

2650. Never bear more than one kind of trouble at a time. Some people bear three kinds—all they have had, all they have now, and all they expect to have.

— Edward Everett Hale

2651. The man who starts out to borrow trouble soon finds his credit is always good.

2652. Trouble, it seems, defies the law of gravity. It's easier to pick up than to drop.

2653. The eternal stars shine out as soon as it is dark enough.

— THOMAS CARLYLE

2654. When you help out a man in trouble, you can be sure of one thing. He won't forget you—the next time he's in trouble.

2655. Remember, when you are telling people your troubles, half of them aren't interested and the other half are glad to see you're finally getting what's coming to you.

2656. "Don't tell your troubles to others," a Nantucket sea captain once advised me. "Most of 'em don't care a hang; and the rest are damn glad of it."

— ROBERT HAVEN SCHAUFFLER, *Enjoy Living*, Reprinted by permission of Dodd, Mead Company, Inc.

2657. A trouble shared becomes a trouble halved.

— DOROTHY SAYERS, *Suspicious Characters*

2658. You can't keep trouble from coming, but you needn't give it a chair to sit on.

2659. When we can't make light of our troubles, we can keep them dark.

2660. Trouble is only opportunity in work clothes.

— HENRY J. KAISER

2661. Troubles are often the tools by which God fashions us for better things.

— HENRY WARD BEECHER

Trust

2662. You may be deceived if you trust too much, but you will live in torment if you do not trust enough.

— DR. FRANK CRANE

2663. The chief lesson I have learned in a long life is that the only way to make a man trustworthy is to trust him; and the surest way to make him untrustworthy is to distrust him and show your mistrust.

— HENRY L. STIMSON

Truth

2664. A man that seeks truth and loves it must be reckoned precious to any human society.

— FREDERICK THE GREAT

2665. This is the punishment of a liar: he is not believed, even when he speaks the truth.

— Babylonian Talmud, *Sanhedrin*

2666. The truth is always the strongest argument.

— SOPHOCLES

2667. Things are never quite the same somehow after you have to lie to a person.

— From *Kitty Foyle* by CHRISTOPHER MORLEY, reprinted by permission of The J. B. Lippincott Co., Copyright 1939

2668. Falsehoods not only disagree with truths, but usually quarrel among themselves.

— DANIEL WEBSTER

2669. The bare assertion of a fact is not always the naked truth.

2670. Truth is a thing immortal and perpetual, and it gives to us a beauty that fades not away in time.

— EPICTETUS

2671. Truth uttered before its time is dangerous.

— MENCIUS

2672. An army rookie from the South ran afoul of the loyalty investigation system that requires everyone in the defense department to fill out a loyalty questionnaire. When he came to the question about whether anyone in his family had ever advocated the overthrow of the government he replied, "yes" in bold block letters. He was called up for an interview.

"Yes, suh," he told the interrogator, "it was my grandpappy. He fought for the Confederacy."

2673. When in doubt, tell the truth.

2674. It is twice as hard to crush a half-truth as a whole lie.

— Austin O'Malley

2675. Those are weaklings who know the truth and uphold it as long as it suits their purpose, and then abandon it.

— Blaise Pascal

2676. The liar's punishment is not in the least that he is not believed, but that he cannot believe anyone else.

— George Bernard Shaw

2677. The pursuit of truth shall set you free—even if you never catch up with it.

— Clarence Darrow

2678. It is not hard to find the truth; what is hard is not to run away from it once you have found it.

— Etienne Gilson, *Ladies' Home Journal*

2679. A liar begins with making falsehood appear like truth, and ends with making truth itself appear like falsehood.

— William Shenstone

2680. A lie has always a certain amount of weight with those who wish to believe it.

— Elliott W. Rice

2681. It is error only, and not truth, that shrinks from inquiry.

— Thomas Paine

Turn-about

2682. Mark Twain met a friend at the races one day in England who complained he was broke and asked Mark to buy him a ticket back to London.

"Well," Mark Twain said, "I'm nearly broke myself, but I'll tell you what I'll do. You can hide under my seat and I'll hide you with my legs." To this the friend agreed.

Then Mark went down to the ticket office and bought two tickets. When the train pulled out, his friend was safely under the seat. The conductor came around for the tickets and Mark gave him two. "But where is the other one?" the conductor asked.

Tapping his head, the humorist said in a loud voice, "That is my friend's ticket! He is a bit eccentric and enjoys riding under the seat."

Understanding

2683. A big-league umpire once remarked that he could never understand how crowds in the grandstand, hundreds of feet from the plate, could see better and judge more accurately than he, when he was only 7 feet away.

Another man commented that in life, too, we call strikes on a chap when we are too far away to understand. Perhaps, if we had a closer view of the man and his problems, we would reverse our decisions.

2684. It is better to understand little than to misunderstand a lot.

— ANATOLE FRANCE, *Revolt of the Angels*

2685. The best way to be understood is to be understanding.

2686. Meteorologist: a man who can look into a girl's eyes and tell whether.

— BENNETT CERF, *Saturday Review*

2687. If a man is worth knowing at all, he is worth knowing well.

— ALEXANDER SMITH

Unexpected, The

2688. Anyone who doesn't realize that anything can happen to anybody at anytime doesn't know what kind of a world we are living in.

— DR. LOUIS L. MANN, *In Quest of the Bluebird*

Unity

2689. A husbandman who had a quarrelsome family, after having tried in vain to reconcile them by words, thought he might more readily prevail by an example. So he called his sons and bade them lay a bundle of sticks before him. Then having tied them up into a fagot, he told the lads, one after another, to take it up and break it. They all tried, but tried in vain. Then, untying the fagot, he gave them the sticks to break one by one. This they did with the greatest ease. Then said the father: "Thus, my sons, as long as you remain united, you are a match for all your enemies; but differ and separate, and you are undone."

— AESOP

Vacation

2690. How long should a vacation be? Just long enough for the boss to miss you, but not long enough for him to discover that he can get along without you.

Value

2691. Coarse stones, if fractured, may be cemented again; precious stones, never.

— WALTER SAVAGE LANDOR

2692. Nothing is cheap which is superfluous, for what one does not need, is dear at a penny.

— PLUTARCH

2693. La Gabrielli, a celebrated singer, having asked 5,000 ducats from the Empress of Russia as her fee for singing at St. Petersburg for two months, the latter replied: "I pay none of my field marshals on that scale." "In that case," said La Gabrielli, "Your Majesty has only to make your field marshals sing." The Empress paid the 5,000 ducats without further demur.

— SEBASTIAN CHAMFORT

Vanity

2694. Oscar Levant is said to have once asked George Gershwin, "Tell me, George, if you had it to do all over, would you fall in love with yourself again?"

2695. An English newspaper once carried this gossip item:

VIRTUE

"James McNeill Whistler and Oscar Wilde were seen yesterday at Brighton, talking as usual about themselves." Whistler clipped the item and sent it to Wilde with a note saying: "I wish these reporters would be accurate. If you remember, Oscar, we were talking about me." To which Oscar sent the following telegram in reply:

"It is true, Jimmie, we were talking about you, but I was thinking of myself!"

2696. Never undertake what you can delegate. It is personal vanity, business folly and timewasting to do everything yourself.

— J. WILSON NEWMAN, president of
Dun & Bradstreet, Inc.

Verbatim

2697. A Chinese student at the University of Michigan who memorized phrases from an etiquette book, had his first opportunity to try them out at a reception that was given by the president of the University. When a cup of tea was handed to him, he solemnly responded: "Thank you, sir or madam, as the case may be."

Vice

2698. Thomas R. Marshall, Vice-President under Wilson, was a great admirer of the President. One of the books Marshall wrote was dedicated: "To President Wilson from his only Vice."

Vigor

2699. The unforgivable crime is soft hitting. Do not hit at all if it can be avoided; but *never* hit softly.

— THEODORE ROOSEVELT

Virtue

2700. He who is virtuous is wise; and he who is wise is good; and he who is good is happy.

2701. Virtue is woman's honor; honor, man's virtue.

Vision

2702. You must have long-range goals to keep you from being frustrated by short-range failures.

— CHARLES C. NOBLE

Vocabulary

2703. The average woman's vocabulary is said to be about 500 words. That's a small inventory, but think of the turnover.

Wages see also Salary

2704. Unless the job means more than the pay it will never pay more.

— H. BERTRAM LEWIS

War see also Peace

2705. The peoples of the world wouldn't have to resort to arms if they'd use their heads.

2706. The only war I ever approved was the Trojan war; it was fought over a woman, and the men knew what they were fighting for.

— WILLIAM LYON PHELPS

2707. In time of war, the first casualty is truth.

— BOAKE CARTER

2708. Social problems can no longer be solved by class warfare any more than international problems can be solved by wars between nations. Warfare is negative and will sooner or later lead to destruction, while good will and cooperation are positive and supply the only safe basis for building a better future.

— WILLIAM LYON PHELPS

2709. Even the lion has to defend himself against flies.

— German proverb

2710. War is the surgery of crime. Bad as it is in itself, it always implies that something worse has gone before.

— OLIVER WENDELL HOLMES

2711. Peace is the common language of the day, which governments everywhere, irrespective of any concealed motivations and designs, must speak to their people . . . Though the will of the peoples of the world is for peace, the means of welding that will into irresistible strength across barriers of nationalism and through impenetrable curtains is not readily discernible. Men, however peaceloving, may be called upon to engage in battle. In authoritarian societies, they may readily be led into war by their governments. In free societies, they may find themselves under the compulsion of waging war, even though reluctantly, in order to protect and preserve their liberties. Nor can it be ignored that nations and peoples, free or otherwise, could merely blunder into war through fear and hysteria or failure to understand and employ the available instruments of peace.

— Dr. Ralph J. Bunche

2712. There is no such thing as fighting on the winning side: one fights to find out which is the winning side.

— G. K. Chesterton

2713. One murder makes a villain, millions a hero.

Warning

2714. How is it possible to expect mankind to take advice when they will not so much as take warning?

— Jonathan Swift

Waste

2715. Don't be fooled by the calendar. There are only as many days in the year as you make use of. One man gets only a week's value out of a year while another man gets a full year's value out of a week.

— Charles Richards

2716. Most people spend more time and energy in going around problems than in trying to solve them.

— Henry Ford

2717. The man who wastes today lamenting yesterday will waste tomorrow lamenting today.

— Philip M. Raskin

WEALTH

2718. If you have half an hour to spare, don't spend it with someone who hasn't.

Wealth see also *Poverty*

2719. When most Americans read about the corruption and ruthlessness of the rich, they are inclined to grin. These malefactors are their dreamselves. The American does not aspire to overthrow the thieves and oppressors half as much as he does to become one of them.

— BEN HECHT, *A Child of the Century*, Simon & Schuster, Inc. Copyright 1954, reprinted by permission

2720. Some may have more material goods than others but no man is poor who has eyes to see, ears to hear, and, above and beyond all, a heart to understand.

— ALMA WEIZELBAUM, *Wealth*

2721. Wealth is not his who hath it, but his who enjoys it.

2722. If you want to know how rich you really are, find out what would be left of you tomorrow if you should lose every dollar you own tonight.

— WM. J. H. BOETCKER

2723. It ain't so much trouble to get rich as it is to tell when we have got rich.

— JOSH BILLINGS

2724. That man is the richest whose pleasures are the cheapest.

— HENRY DAVID THOREAU

2725. Wealth is not only what you *have* but it is also what you *are*.

— STERLING W. SILL

2726. There is a burden of care in getting riches; fear in keeping them; temptation in using them; guilt in abusing them; and a burden of account at last to be given concerning them.

— M. HENRY

2727. If a rich man is proud of his wealth, he should not be praised until it is known how he employs it.

— SOCRATES

2728. The man who dies rich dies disgraced.

— ANDREW CARNEGIE

2729. The true way to gain much is never to desire to gain too much. He is not rich that possess much, but he that covets no more; and he is not poor that enjoys little, but he that wants too much.

— FRANCIS BEAUMONT

2730. Beach: a place where people lie upon the sand about how rich they are in town.

2731. No good man ever grew rich quickly.

— PUBLILIUS SYRUS

2732. Some people may have their first dollar, but the man who is really rich is the one who still has his first friend.

2733. Not what we have, but what we enjoy, constitutes our abundance.

— JEAN PETIT-SENN

2734. A man is rich in proportion to the number of things which he can afford to let alone.

— HENRY DAVID THOREAU

2735. Rich man: one who isn't afraid to ask the clerk to show him something cheaper.

2736. There are two things needed in these days; first, for rich men to find out how rich men live; and, second, for poor men to know how rich men work.

— EDWARD ATKINSON

Weather

2737. Sunshine is delicious, rain is refreshing, wind braces up, snow is exhilarating; there is no such thing as bad weather, only different kinds of weather.

— JOHN RUSKIN

2738. Bad weather always looks much worse through a window.

— JOHN KIERAN, *Footnotes on Nature,*
(Doubleday & Co., Inc.)

WIFE

Wife see also *Husband and wife*

2739. Everybody all over the world takes a wife's estimate into account in forming an opinion of a man.

— HONORÉ DE BALZAC

2740. It was that gallant soldier and brilliant poet, Sir Philip Sidney, who was the first man to refer to his wife as "my better half." Abraham Lincoln was the first to refer to a matrimonial mate as "the little woman."

Will see *Determination*

Willingness

2741. The world is full of willing people; some willing to work, the rest willing to let them.

— ROBERT LEE FROST

Will-power

2742. An old Negro preacher once cautioned his flock, "When you're looking at your neighbor's melon patch, brethren, you can't keep your mouth from watering, but you can run."

Wills

2743. Lawyer, reading client's last will and testament to circle of expectant relatives: "And so, being of sound mind, I spent every damn cent I had before I died."

2744. "Where did you get that beautiful diamond stick pin?" Smith asked of his friend who was sporting a two carat brilliant.

"This?" asked Jones, pointing to the "searchlight" which shone from his necktie. "This is a testamentary stone."

"A testamentary stone! What is that?" asked Smith.

"Well, I'll tell you, it's like this," replied Jones. "A friend of mine died leaving a will. In the will he named me his executor and further provided that his executor should take three thousand dollars out of his estate and buy a stone to his memory. This is it!"

2745. There is a strange charm in the thoughts of a good legacy, or the hopes of an estate, which wondrously alleviates the sorrow that men would otherwise feel for the death of their friends.

— MIGUEL DE CERVANTES, *Don Quixote*

2746. Just heard a terribly pathetic story: For years a young actor vied for his rich aunt's affections by being nice to her dogs. And when she died, sure enough, she remembered him in her will. Left him the dogs.

— MIKE CONNOLLY, *The Hollywood Reporter*

Wind

2747. The wind that fills my sails
      Propels; but I am helmsman.

— GEORGE MEREDITH, *Modern Love*

Wisdom see also *Knowledge*

2748. Wisdom is divided into two parts: (a) having a great deal to say, and (b) not saying it.

2749. A man should never be ashamed to own he has been in the wrong, which is but saying in other words, that he is wiser today than he was yesterday.

— ALEXANDER POPE

2750. Wisdom is the right use of knowledge. To know is not to be wise. Many men know a great deal, and are all the greater fools for it. There is no fool so great a fool as a knowing fool. But to know how to use knowledge is to have wisdom.

— CHARLES H. SPURGEON

2751. Wisdom: knowing when to speak your mind and when to mind your speech.

2752. After his 60th year a man is more surprised to find himself right about something than he was at 20 to find himself wrong about anything.

2753. A wise man changes his mind, a fool never.

2754. It isn't so much that a man becomes wiser and better as he grows older as it's that he just doesn't feel like acting the fool.

2755. In our present society, there seems to be no lack of efficient people, but there is an almost complete absence of wisdom. It is not as if wisdom has become extinct. Rather, it has been abandoned as a social value (the highest there is) and therefore many of us live in desperation and fear, looking in vain for the purpose of our existence.

> —DR. ANTON J. CARLSON from paper presented at the International Gerontological Congress, London, 1954

2756. There is one person that is wiser than anybody, and that is everybody.

> —ALEXANDER A. TALLEYRAND-PERIGORD

2757. No man is wise enough by himself.

> —PLAUTUS

Wit

2758. Jokes are a segment of generally anonymous information which often reflects the qualities of the nation, or the status of the people or the character of the people from whom they spring.

> —NAT SCHMULOWITZ, *The Nazi Joke Courts*

2759. The good die young was never said of a joke.

2760. If Adam came on earth again the only thing he would recognize would be the old jokes.

> —T. R. DEWAR

Woman — women

2761. The only way to fight a woman is with your hat. Grab it and run.

> —JOHN BARRYMORE

2762. We would give her more consideration, when we judge a woman, if we knew how difficult it is to be a woman.

> —P. GERALDY

2763. Girls are like newspapers: they all have forms, they always have the last word, back numbers are not in demand, they have great influence, you can't believe everything they say, they're thinner than they used to be, they get along by advertising, and every man should have his own and not try to borrow his neighbor's.

2764. No friendship is so cordial or so delicious as that of a girl for girl; no hatred so intense or immovable as that of woman for woman.

— WALTER SAVAGE LANDOR

2765. Female friends: women mad at the same person.

2766. Bridge: a game which gives women something to try to think about while they are talking.

✳ **2767.** God made woman beautiful so man would love her, and He made her foolish so that she would love him.

2768. A woman's mind is cleaner than a man's—she changes it oftener.

— OLIVER HERFORD, *Epigrams*

2769. Career girl: one who is more interested in plots and plans than in pots and pans.

2770. According to the Scriptures, woman was borrowed from man. That was a long time ago, but the principal has never ceased to draw interest.

2771. Some women spend money like it was going out of style.

2772. Maybe it's a good thing men don't understand women. Women understand women and don't like them.

2773. The fickleness of the women I love is only equaled by the infernal constancy of the women who love me.

— GEORGE BERNARD SHAW

2774. Fashions exist for women with no taste, etiquette for people with no breeding.

— QUEEN MARIE OF RUMANIA

2775. If a woman has been loved, hated and envied, her life was worth living.

— AKIHO YANAGIWARA

2776. To women, beauty is what money is to man—power.

— DOROTHY MAY

2777. Give a woman an inch and she thinks she's a ruler.

2778. The best ten years of a woman's life are between 28 and 30.

2779. A woman in love never wants to rule: she wants to obey. When a woman seeks authority she never finds love.

2780. A woman's fondest wish is to be weighed and found wanting.

— WALTER WINCHELL

2781. Women like audacity; when one astounds them he interests them; and when one interests them he is sure to please them.

— THEOPHILE GAUTIER

2782. For a man to pretend to understand women is bad manners; for him really to understand them is bad morals.

— HENRY JAMES

2783. Women are wiser than men because they know less and understand more.

— JAMES STEPHENS

2784. The liveliest desire of a woman's heart is not so much to please but to please more than other women.

— ECKHARTHAUSEN

2785. One thing you can be sure of about a silent partner—it's not a woman.

2786. She has an hour glass figure and makes every minute count.

— ERNIE FORD

2787. This is certainly a woman's world. When a man is born, the first question is, "How's the mother?" When he marries, everyone says, "What a lovely bride." And when he dies, the question is, "How much did he leave her?"

2788. The trouble with women is that they have become too much like men. They work, smoke, drink and swear like men. Some even tell stories like men. In becoming the equals of men, they have sacrificed their superiority as women.

— HENRY C. LINK

2789. A career woman is one who goes out and earns a man's salary instead of sitting at home and taking it away from him.

2790. Women are like money. If you don't keep them busy they'll lose interest.

Woman's club

2791. Woman's Club: a place where they knock after they enter.

2792. "Do you believe in clubs for women?" a friend asked W. C. Fields.
"Yes," replied Fields, "if every other form of persuasion fails."

2793. My advice to the Women's Clubs of America is to raise more hell and fewer dahlias.
— WILLIAM ALLEN WHITE

Wonderment

2794. A Navy physician in the Pacific received from his fiancée a snapshot taken on a beach and showing two couples smiling contentedly while his girl sat alone at one side, forlorn and lonely. The accompanying letter explained that this was how she was fretting away the time until he returned. At first the physician was delighted, displaying it proudly to several fellow officers. That night, however, after studying it a long time in silence, he turned to his roommate. "John," he said, "I wonder who took that picture?"
— ROBERT J. DOYLE

2795. A friend once said to Cato the Elder, "It's a scandal that no statue has been erected to you in Rome! I am going to form a committee to see that this is done."
"No," said Cato, "I would rather have people ask 'Why isn't there a statue to Cato?' than 'Why is there one?' "
— THOMAS L. MASSON, *The Best Stories in the World* (Doubleday & Co., Inc.)

Words

2796. Some of mankind's most terrible misdeeds have been committed under the spell of certain magic words or phrases.
— JAMES BRYANT CONANT

WORDS

2797. Words, like glasses, obscure everything which they do not make clear.

— Joseph Joubert

2798. *Shh! "Sub Rosa" Comes from a Greek Legend*

A romantic tale lies behind the phrase "sub rosa."

According to ancient legend, the Greek god of silence, Harpocrates, stumbled upon Venus, the goddess of love, in the course of one of her amorous adventures.

Cupid, Venus' son, happened along at an opportune moment and, by making a gift of a rose to Harpocrates, bought his pledge of secrecy.

Since that time, the rose has been the symbol of silence.

During the Renaissance and later during the reigns of the pre-Revolutionary kings of France, the rose was a favorite architectural motif and often was sculpted on ceilings of dining and drawing rooms where diplomats gathered.

The obvious implication was that matters discussed "under the rose" were considered to be held in confidence.

— William Morris, *The Chicago Daily News*

2799. Some of the phrases we use every day don't mean what we think. "Beer and skittles" is an oftquoted example, on the theory that most of us think skittles are some sort of cookies you eat with beer. Almost everybody knows by now that skittles is a sport like bowling.

"Kith and kin" is a phrase used over and over, often indicating that the two are synonymous. This is not the case. Kin, like kindred, applies to relatives, and always has. But kith started out as cuth, an adjective meaning known or familiar. It is the long lost opposite of uncouth, which correctly means strange or alien. Kith gradually became a noun and refers properly to the home land, the "auld sod," or the home folks.

"Flotsam and jetsam," although they don't sound it, are highly legalistic terms. Laws defining them, however, have varied through the years. Flotsam, a cousin of the word float, once meant the wreckage of a ship and its cargo when found floating on the sea. Jetsam, related to jettison, was material deliberately thrown overboard to save a ship in rough weather. If jetsam sank, it rested on the bottom and became lagan, lagon, or ligan. More recently ligan has applied only when the material was marked by buoy for purposes of salvage.

These distinctions have always been important in settling cases where material is found at sea.

Then there is "nip and tuck." A correspondent has asked us, "Who were they?" We've seen no satisfactory explanation, but can offer a reasonable one of our own. Nip, in sailors' talk, is the pull of a rope on, for example, a ship's winch. If there's too much nip, the rope tends to slip and they have to take another tuck, or loop the rope around again. Too much tuck is equally bad because then they can't let the rope slip when they want to. The delicate balance between these, according to our theory, led to the phrase "nip and tuck."

— "A Line O'Type or Two," *Chicago Tribune*

Work

2800. I've met a few people in my time who were enthusiastic about hard work. And it was just my luck that all of them happened to be men I was working for at the time.

— BILL GOLD, Washington (D.C.)
Post and Times Herald

2801. There is no pleasure in having nothing to do; the fun is in having lots to do and *doing* it.

2802. There is no pleasure in having nothing to do; the fun is in having lots to do and *not* doing it.

2803. Queer thing, but we always think every other man's job is easier than our own. And the better he does it, the easier it looks.

— EDEN PHILLPOTTS

2804. Even in the meanest sorts of labor, the whole soul of a man is composed into a kind of real harmony the instant he sets himself to work.

— THOMAS CARLYLE

2805. I want to be thoroughly used up when I die, for the harder I work, the more I live. Life is no brief candle for me. It is a sort of splendid torch which I have got hold of for the moment, and I want to make it burn as brightly as possible before handing it on to future generations.

— GEORGE BERNARD SHAW

WORK

2806. Slow down. The job you save may be your own.

2807. Some people think they are overworked because it takes them all day to do a three hour job.

2808. Work does more than get us our living; it gets us our life.

— HENRY FORD

World

2809. Sometimes we think the world is growing worse, but it may just be that the news and radio coverage is better.

2810. "I want a new suit made," the customer said, "and I want it in a hurry."

The tailor shrugged. "I can make it for you," he said, "but it'll take me thirty days."

"Thirty days! Why, the Lord created Heaven and Earth in only six!"

"Sure," said the tailor quietly. "And have you taken a look at it lately?"

2811.
If we noticed little pleasures,
    As we notice little pains—
If we quite forgot our losses
    And remembered all our gains.

If we looked for people's virtues
    And their faults refused to see.
What a comfortable, happy, cheerful place
    This world would be!

— Reprinted from *Forbes Magazine of Business*

Worry

2812. People with vertical furrows on their foreheads are intellectual fighters and enjoy arguing. Horizontal furrows indicate the worrier.

— From "The Story in Your Face" by NANCY VAN COURT, *The American Magazine*, January, 1939

2813. The reason worry kills more people than work is that more people worry than work.

— Robert Lee Frost

2814. Worry, whatever its source, weakens, takes away courage, and shortens life.

— John Lancaster Spalding

2815. Worry is a thin stream of fear trickling through the mind. If encouraged, it cuts a channel into which all other thoughts are drained.

— Arthur Somers Roche

2816. When we have nothing to worry about we are not doing much, and not doing much may supply us with plenty of future worries.

— Chinese proverb

2817. Anxiety and worry are the parents of temper and disease.

2818. Don't tell me that worry doesn't do any good. I know better. The things I worry about don't happen!

2819. A woman worries about the future until she gets a husband, while a man never worries about the future until he gets a wife.

Writing

2820. The ABC of good writing:
    A—Accuracy
    B—Brevity
    C—Clarity

Youth

2821. A lot of young people these days seem to think that the three R's stand for Rah! Rah! Rah!

2822. By the time we appreciate how important youth is, youth isn't.

— Dr. Louis L. Mann

2823. Young men have a passion for regarding their elders as senile.

— Henry Adams

2824. The only way any woman may remain forever young is to grow old gracefully.

— DR. W. BERAN WOLFE

2825. The time to start worrying about a boy is when he leaves the house *without* slamming the door.

2826. The Youth of a Nation are the trustees of Posterity.

— BENJAMIN DISRAELI, *Sybil*

2827. Boy: a pain in the neck when he is around; a pain in the heart when he isn't.

2828. The most difficult job teenagers have today is learning good conduct without seeing any.

— H. G. HUTCHESON in *Augusta* (Kansas) *Gazette*

2829. "Going with girls keeps you young."
"How do you figure that?"
"I started going with them when I was a freshman. And I'm still a freshman."

2830. Youth is a wonderful thing. What a crime to waste it on children.

— GEORGE BERNARD SHAW

2831. Probably the most powerful head of steam ever created is that of young people trying to set on fire a world that is all wet.

2832. In the old days when a youth started sowing wild oats, father started the thrashing machine.

2833. Many a small boy is the kind of kid his mother tells him not to play with.

2834. Oh, the eagerness and freshness of youth! How the boy enjoys his food, his sleep, his sports, his companions, his truant days! His life is an adventure; he is widening his outlook; he is extending his dominion; he is conquering his kingdom. How cheap are his pleasures; how ready his enthusiasms! In boyhood I have had more delight on a haymow with two companions and a big dog—delight that came nearer intoxication—than I have ever had in all the subsequent holidays of my life. When youth goes, much goes with it. When manhood comes, much comes with it. We exchange a world of delightful sensations and impressions for a world of duties and studies and meditations. The youth enjoys what the man tries to understand. Lucky is he who can get his grapes to market and keep the bloom upon them; who can carry some of the freshness and eagerness and simplicity of youth into his later years; who can have a boy's heart below a man's head.

— JOHN BURROUGHS

2835. *Small boy at piano to mother:* "Gosh darn it, mommy; I wish you hadn't been deprived of so many things as a child!"

— PERRY BARLOW in *Ladies' Home Journal.* Peproduced courtesy of Curtis Publishing Co.

2836. Give the neighbors' kids an inch and they'll take a yard.

2837. A boy becomes a man when he walks around a puddle of water instead of through it.

2838. Of all the animals, the boy is the most unmanageable, inasmuch as he has the fountain of reason in him not yet regulated.

— PLATO, *Laws*

2839. A nation is strong or weak, it thrives or perishes upon what it believes to be true. If our youth is rightly instructed in the faith of our fathers; in the traditions of our country; in the dignity of each individual man, then our power will be stronger than any weapon of destruction that man can devise.

— HERBERT HOOVER at reception given him by the State of Iowa on his 80th birthday.

2840. As I approve of a youth that has something of the old man in him, so I am no less pleased with an old man that has something of the youth. He that follows this rule may be old in body, but can never be so in mind.

— CICERO

2841. Tell me what are the prevailing sentiments that occupy the minds of your young men, and I will tell you what is to be the character of the next generation.

— EDMUND BURKE

YOUTH

2842.   It is most important for our young men, as it is for our nation, that they be taught in their homes from their early youth that a man has work to do; that one who merely seeks his own pleasure proves himself unworthy of a place in the world. Our rapidly increasing wealth and unwise parental love are as ever leading to our indulgence and many weak, worthless lives.

— SAMUEL FESSENDEN CLARKE

SUBJECT INDEX

(Numbers in the index refer to selections in the text, not to page numbers.)

A

Ability, *1-4*, 1390, 1399, 1920, 2340, 2473, 2488, 2547
Absence, *5*, 425
Absent-minded, *6*
Abstinence, 2542
Absurd—absurdity, 325, 873, 1933, 2254
Abundance, 2733
Abuse, 1140, 2726
Académie Francaise, 2292
Acceptance, 1112, 1475, 2614
Accident, *7*, 1040, 1491, 2124, 2229
Accident, airplane, 2644
Accident, automobile, 2618, 2626, 2627, 2637
Accident insurance, 1264
Accident, railroad, 2644
Accomplishment, *8-16*, 106, 425, 613, 633, 1129, 1579, 1755, 1828, 1997, 2252, 2801
Accord, *17*, 278
Accordion, 901
Accountability, 2726
Accumulation, 14, *18*
Accuracy, *19-21*, 164, 1063, 2695, 2820
Accuse—accusation, 1914
Accustomed, 1868
Acetylene torch, 2227
Achievement, 15, *22-24*, 106, 461, 482, 1828, 2007, 2252
Acid, 139
Acorn, 308
Acquaintance, 265, 1672, 1773, 2223, 2535
Acquiescence, 25, 237
Acquittal, 568, 1350, 1613
Act, 1026
Action, 12, *26-28*, 172, 767, 1186, 1645, 2318, 2551

Actor—actors—acting, *29-33*, 889, 1698, 2068, 2573
Actress, 1316, 2285, 2573
Adam, 1224, 2760
Adaptation, 2009
Address, 1239
Adjective, 1013
Adjustment, *34*, 759
Admiral, 1254
Admiration, 925, 1004, 1470, 1834
Admit—admission, 805, 2749
Admonition. See also Warning, 824, 2742
Adolescence, *35*
Adulation, 1095
Adult, 225, 2135
Adulthood, 1902
Advantage, 932, 1220, 1487, 1490, 2366, 2579
Adventure, 2834
Adversity, *36, 37*, 509, 2019
Advertisement, 1895, 2210, 2269
Advertising, *38-56*, 75, 1249, 2277, 2763
Advice, *57-70*, 382, 616, 683, 824, 918, 1061, 1332, 1360, 1535, 1727, 1733, 1858, 1868, 2105, 2471, 2476, 2499, 2714, 2793
Advice, professional, 1410
Affability, 1920
Affectation, *71*, 927, 1167, 2254
Affection—affectionate. See also Love, 378, 561, 1070, 1801, 1952, 2194
Affiliation, 2719
Affirmative, 489
Affront, 904
Africa, 1243
Age. See also Middle age—Old age, 9, 72-92 1269, 2573, 2778
Age, middle, 72-75, 2030
Agent, 233

SUBJECT INDEX

Age, old, 694
Aging, 1131, 1739, 2573, 2824, 2840
Agitate—agitator, 954
Agnosticism, 2163, 2173, 2180
Agony, 1455
Agreement, 93, 452, 1752, 2147
Agriculture. See also Farming, 885, 1774
Agriculture, Department of, 2611
Aid, 1226
Aim, 883, 1566, 1619, 1845, 2047, 2348
Air, 1208, 2023, 2227
Air conditioning, 1218, 2299
Air force, 1246, 1616
Air, hot, 644
Airplane, 1524, 2148, 2644
Air raid, 2263
Air transportation, 2641
Alamo, the, 819
Alarm, 682, 796
Alarm clock, 1236
Alcohol, 4, 94-103, 1247, 1938, 2638
Alcoholism, 94, 95, 99, 101, 669
Alertness, 6
Alibi, 104, 1640
Alien, 2799
Alimony, 1551
Alive, 137, 440, 934, 1094, 1147, 1413, 1955, 2616
Allergy—allergic, 1882
All-inclusive, 2048
All-pervasive, 2048
All-pleasing, 1847
Almond, 748
Alone, 1340
Aloofness, 1598
Alphabet, 247, 1793
Alps, 2259
Altar, 1428
Alternative, 2124
Alumni, 2425, 2602
Amass—amassing, 18
Amateur, 2077
Ambassador, 1608
Ambition, 105-115, 749, 834, 910, 1153, 1674, 2100
Ambulance, 311
Amend—amendment, 1108, 2228
Amends, 891, 2187
America—American, 56, 116-132, 436, 470, 562, 810, 859, 977, 1079,

America—American (cont.)
1165, 1226, 1669, 1888, 1902, 1976, 2148, 2251, 2566, 2624, 2719, 2839, 2842
America, Central, 2579
America, South, 56, 2251
American, early, 2536
American Revolution, 2593
Amherst College, 64
Analysis, 133, 1322
Anarchy, 2672
Anatomy, 1313, 1716
Ancestor—ancestry, 116, 134-138, 157, 339, 1002, 1028, 1154, 2364
Ancient, 2593
Anecdote, 2444
Anesthetic, 770
Anger, 17, 139-147, 805, 1917, 1982, 2145, 2540
Animal—animals, 148, 458, 1070, 1443, 2145, 2174, 2182, 2838
Animalculae, 1443
Anointed, 1897
Annoyance, 427, 764, 1010, 1219
Announcer, 2134
Annuity, 1495
Anonymity, 31
Answer, 12, 400, 1960, 1966, 2540
Antagonism, 149, 2302
Antennae, 2457
Anthropology, 981
Anticipation, 844, 1651
Anti-Nazi, 2076
Antique, 150
Antiquity, 2031
Anvil, 1792, 2155
Anxiety, 897, 973, 2817
Apartment house, 1247, 1375
Apartment walls, 2321
Apology, 151, 152, 1174, 1873, 1968, 2067
Appeal (charity), 2088
Appearance—appearances, 90, 153, 154, 207, 1874, 2204
Appeasement, 155
Appendicitis, 669
Appetite, 895, 1144, 1672, 1685
Applause, 156, 443, 504, 2108
Apple, 308, 558, 657, 1099
Application blank, 1240, 2266, 2573
Appointment, 1489, 2091, 2121
Appointment, political, 1890, 1897

SUBJECT INDEX

Back fire, 995
Back number, 2763
Backward, 977, 1745
Backward-looking, 2467
Backwards, 1740, 2005, 2006
Bacon, 643
Bait, 658, 1230
Balance, 2568
Balance of power, 759
Bald—baldness, 30, 205-210, 418, 981
Bale—baled, 2100
Balkan states, 828
Ballad, 2511
Balloon, 659
Ballot, 1920
Ballyhoo, 2222
Baloney, 644, 903, 2016
Banana, 503
Bandit, 638
Bank—banks—banking, 211-214, 215, 467, 545, 887, 1536, 2059, 2152, 2224, 2230
Bank account, 1438
Bank deposit, 2152
Bankruptcy, 57, 215, 216, 280, 795, 1370, 1641, 1687, 1937, 2214
Banner, 1028
Banquet, 2053, 2070, 2077, 2084, 2088
Baptism, 774
Barber shop, 208, 1642
Bargain—bargaining, 217, 218, 1245, 2583, 2640
Bark—barking, 556
Barn, 887
Baronetcy, 2215
Baseball, 395, 577, 1301, 1776, 2249, 2416, 2424, 2428, 2429, 2433, 2683
Basket, 1099
Basketball, 743
Bathing beach, 2730, 2794
Bathing suit, 2442
Bathroom, 2220
Battery, storage, 2270
Battle, 948, 1028, 1823, 2373, 2398
Battle field, 1891
Battleship, 1700
Beach, bathing, 2730, 2794
Beans, 643
Bear—bears, 993, 2418
Beatitude, 456

Beauty, 172, 219, 220, 241, 441, 786, 981, 1126, 1178, 1568, 1586, 1735, 1803, 1862, 2401, 2603, 2670, 2767, 2776
Bed, 466, 651, 873, 1891, 2407, 2644
Bed fellows, 1908
Bedroom, 2371
Bee—Bees, 250, 1204
Beer, 2288
Beer and skittles, 2799
Beg—begging—beggar, 266, 2223, 2423
Beginner, 1861
Beginning, 383, 502, 1756, 2207, 2648
Behavior. See also Conduct, 221-231, 369, 393, 736, 935, 1089, 1304, 1372, 1562, 1797, 1869, 2828
Beholden, 1877, 1998, 2035, 2164
Belief. See also Credo, 232, 526, 868, 1061, 1321, 1644, 2182, 2209
Believing, 687, 2676
Belittling, 894
Benefactor—benefaction, 339
Beneficence, 1077
Benefit, 1024, 1321
Benefit performance, 2058
Benevolence, 361
Bequest, 233, 354, 1425, 1681, 2746, 2787
Best, the, 1447
Best-seller, 2215
Bet—betting. See also Gambling, 234, 235, 2184, 2416
Betray—betrayal, 236, 958, 2312
"Better-half", 2740
Betterment. See also Improvement, 448
Bible, the, 237, 238, 1299, 1666, 2017, 2098, 2148, 2206, 2540, 2770
Biblical, 2134
Bicycle, 1250
Big—bigness, 239, 276, 1277
Bigamy—bigamist, 1555, 1568
Bigotry. See also Prejudice, 240
Big shot, 456, 1835, 2345
Big stick, 1888
Bikini suit, 2442
Billboard, 48
Billiards, 981
"Big wheel", 2345

408

SUBJECT INDEX

Brooding, 2188
Brooklyn, N.Y., 2058, 2104
Broom, 1285
Broom-sandal, 1775
Broomstick, 1762
Brother, 657, 2375
Brotherhood, 273, 338, 382, 2176
Brute—brutal—brutish, 1939
Bubble, 2606
Buddhism, 2167
Budget, 274
Buffalo, N.Y., 2117
Bug, lightning, 1117
Build, 824
Building, 559, 1031
Bull—bulls, 993, 2418
Bull-dozer, 731
Bullet, 1344
Bullfighting, 2251
Bull's-eye, 2348
Bullying, 2029
Buncombe, 1908, 2016
Bunk, 1908
Buoyancy, physical, 1963
Burden, 1391, 1703
Bureau of Internal Revenue, 2525
Burglar, 1892
Burial, 844, 1413
Burlesque show, 889
Burma, 278
Bus, 1871, 2118
Bushel, 1518
Business. See also Industry, 41, 44,
      47, 54, 55, 57, 93, 239, 275-
      295, 586, 760, 859, 880, 1006,
      1059, 1229, 1236, 1239, 1245,
      1249, 1265, 1401, 1641, 1744,
      1848, 1858, 2098, 2160, 2217,
      2234, 2236, 2267, 2397, 2428,
      2696
Business executive, 2236
Businessman, 131, 215, 814, 1293,
      1360, 1416, 1449, 1524, 1811,
      2120
Business-minded, 1811
Busy, 385, 1742
Butcher, 218, 1410
Butler, 784
Buttons, 353, 1516
Buyer, 2282
Buying, 2279
By-product, 1861

C

Cabbage, 748
Cabinet, 1658
Cable, 1109
Cabots, the, 2602
Cackling, 51
Caddie, 1046
Cadillac, 844
Cage, 1858
Cake, 242, 1216, 2601
Calamity, 241, 476
Calcutta, India, 744
Calendar, 2715
California, University of, 417
Callousness, 818
Calmness, 698, 853, 1395, 1902, 1958
Cambridge University, 2591
Campaign, political, 1883, 1898, 1902,
      1922
Canal Zone, Panama, 1242
Canasta, 1685
Cancellation, 295, 1991
Candidate, political, 1891, 1910, 1916,
      1920, 1925
Candle, 5, 113, 242, 1402, 1450, 1525,
      2601, 2805
Candor, *296*
Candy, 1237, 1597
Cane, 1290
Cannibal, 1061, 1443, 1717
Canonization, 1095
Canopy, 1891
Capacity, 297, 724
Capital—capitalism, 57, 276, *298-302*,
      1284, 1334, 1335, 1674
Capital punishment, 1857
Capitulation, 1827
Captain, 1615, 1620
Card game—card playing, 4, *303*,
      1746, 2766
Care—careful—carefulness, 401, 2560,
      2626, 2726
Career, *304*, 587, 855, 2068, 2578,
      2769, 2789
Carelessness, 160, 1181, 2588
Cargo, 2799
Carrier, 1700
Car sickness, 1259
Cartoonist, 2331
Carve, 304
Cashier, 1197

410

Curiosity, 45, 558, 710, 754, 1028, 1236, 1249, 1716, 2456
Currency, 1054, 1664, 1671
Curse, 362
Curve, 2630
Custodian, 2214
Custom, 1412, 1744
Customer, 294, 295, 1237, 2273
Customs (Duty), 278, 325, 398, 559-562, 1634, 2319
Customs inspector, 1250
Customs official, 744, 1250
Cyclone, 1279
Cynic—cynicism, 527, 563-565, 600

D

Dahlias, 2793
Daily, 1869
Dairy, 1774
Damage, 1066
Dancing, 1651
Dandelion, 2611
Danger—dangerous, 562, 566, 777, 1077, 1145, 1391, 1426, 2377, 2671
D. A. R., 2593
Dare, 436
Darkness, 113, 475, 1179, 1525, 2004, 2603, 2659
Dating, 567
Daughter, 1685
Daughters of the American Revolution, 2593
Day, 2401
Deacon, 2221
Dead, 1748, 2616
Deaf—deafness, 263, 1111
Death, 10, 26, 168, 221, 354, 361, 568-571, 668, 756, 813, 844, 1022, 1094, 1203, 1343, 1413, 1431, 1433, 1436, 1437, 1446, 1757, 1922, 2350, 2401, 2632, 2636, 2728
Debase—debasement, 1095
Debate, 572, 628, 1911
Debt—debtor, 282, 523, 531, 573, 574, 911, 983, 1991, 2013, 2121, 2232, 2525
Debt, public, 1080
Debutante, 1572
Decalogue, the, 2257

Decay, 1198, 1729, 1985
Deceit, 1476
Decency, 315
Deception, 52, 575, 576, 701, 1267, 1513, 2222, 2662
Decisions, 577, 578, 621, 671, 829, 1108, 1298, 1390, 1834, 2260, 2683
Declaration of Independence, 1265
Decoration, 1316
Decoy, 2104, 2221
Dedication, 2698
Deep-freeze, 733
Defeat, 107, 563, 859, 948, 1868, 1895, 1916, 1933, 2437, 2486
Defeatism, 580, 581, 860, 1006
Defense, 707, 1409, 2709
Defenseless, 2495
Deference. See also Respect, 935
Defiance, 2147
Definition, 359, 1909, 2292
Deflation, 582
Deformity, moral, 1677
Deformity, physical, 1677
Degeneracy, 1985
Degree, college, 414, 419
Degree, third, 466
Deity. See also God, 2020, 2254
Dejection, 183, 1100
Delay. See also Procrastination, 140, 348, 583-585
Delegation of authority, 586, 2236, 2696
Deliberate—deliberateness, 39, 167, 1796
Delinquency. See also Crime—Juvenile delinquency, 225, 587-591
Deliverance, 2398
Demagogue—demagogy, 1406
Democracy, 127, 592-602, 1428
Democrat, 1632, 1880, 1898, 1928
Democratic party, 1777, 1901
Demon, 1762
Denmark, 128
Dénouement, 1539
Dentist—dental—dentistry, 307, 603-605, 652, 1146, 2074
Denture, 2074
Denunciation, 1332
Denver, Colo., 2641
Department store, 1044, 1282, 1761, 2212, 2735

415

SUBJECT INDEX

SUBJECT INDEX

Fasting, 356
Fatality, 2644
Fate, *888*, 1040, 1096, 2147
Father, 686, 705, 822, 839, 879, 889,
    935, 1107, 1685, 1687, 1781,
    1797, 1867, 1868, 1952
Fatherhood, 2176
Father-in-law, 209
Father's day, 890
Fatigue, 635
Fault—faults, 315, 437, 465, *891-893*,
    958, 1103, 1432, 1801, 2348,
    2618, 2811
Fault-finding, *894*, 2539
Faux pas, 895
Favor, 1363, 1799
Fear, 318, 361, 367, 381, 509, 514,
    566, 597, 647, *896, 897*, 1646,
    1727, 1762, 1838, 2146, 2171,
    2336, 2356, 2711, 2735, 2755,
    2815
Fearlessness, 600
Feast, 1175
Feeble-mindedness, 2497
Feeling, 1135, 1643, 1965, 2170
Fees, professional, 233, 667, 678, 679,
    684, 1410, 2075
Fellow man, 1306
Felon—felony, 1366
Feminine, 1701
Fence, 311, 1704, 1900, 1907, 1924
Fiancée, 2794
Fiasco, 1778
Fickleness, 2773
Fiction, 1348
Fidelity, 507
Fifty-fifty, 2073, 2375
Fight—fighting, 1822, 1823, 2249
Figure, 90, 407
Filch, 2193
Finality, 1647
Finance—financial, 730, *898*, 1858,
    1920
Finances, public, 1920
Financier, 2217
Find—finder—finding, 1244, 2304
Fine—fines, 396
Fingers, 963, 2334, 2485
Finish—finished, 323, 2051
Fire, 5, 284, 540, 775, 791, 1331,
    1371, 1642, 2155, 2242, 2491,
    2831

Fire arms, 261
Fire department, 775, 2220, 2242
Firmness, 1888, 2450
First (foremost), 111, 421
First-rate, 3
Fish—fishing, *899, 900*, 1230, 1502,
    2453
Fist, 963, 2334
Fitness, 351
Flag—flags, 118, 121, 124, 128, 1028,
    2598
Flame, 648
Flask, 1778
Flattery, 493, *903-912*, 1802
Flaw, 1815, 2398, 2445
Flea, 514, 1288
Fleet, 1254
Flirtation, *913*, 1172, 2454
Float, 1110
Flock, 1138
Florist, 45, 104, 775
Flotsam, 2799
Flour, 133
Flowers, 250, 309, 585, *914, 915*,
    1291, 1585, 1685, 1970, 2739,
    2792
Fly—flying, 1524, 2628
Fog, 1254, 2004
Foible, 1933
Follow—follower, 1396, 1397, 1404,
    1405, 1407
Folly. See also Fool, 831, 1724, 1935,
    2310, 2314, 2696, 2767
Food, 769, *916, 917*, 1672, 2016,
    2088, 2148, 2643, 2834
Fool—foolish. See also Folly, 63, 143,
    317, 633, 770, 833, *918-929*,
    946, 1207, 1323, 1486, 1628,
    1674, 1748, 1942, 1943, 1999,
    2062, 2090, 2127, 2188, 2474,
    2490, 2567, 2750, 2754
Foot—feet, 510, 797, 1208
Football, 413, 743, 771, 859, *930*,
    1505, 2166, 2192, 2425, 2426,
    2431, 2432, 2465
Football coach, 2425, 2427, 2432,
    2465
Footsteps, 2398
Forbearance, 1797
Forbidden, 2129
Force, 382, 949, 1334

420

Forecast, 1124, 1974
Forecaster, weather, 1721
Forehead, 2812
Foreign, 1798, 2643
Foreign minister, 2603
Foreman, 1961
Forerunner, 1034
Foresightedness, 1493
Forest, 490
Forewarning, 931
Forge, 2155
Forget—forgetting—forgotten—forget-
  fulness, 6, 15, 932, 933, 937,
  1029, 1344, 1606, 1773, 1897,
  2221, 2240, 2398, 2654, 2811
Forgiveness, 1183, 1314, 1541, 1789,
  2238, 2356
Form, 811, 1036, 1650, 2763
Formal attire, 2040
Formula, 716, 1237, 2489
Fortitude, 2063
Fortune, 326, 1217, 1227, 1483, 1856,
  2144
Forward, 275, 977, 2006
Foul, 2542
Foundation, 293
Fountain, 709, 1784
Fountain pen. See pen
Fox, 356
Fracture, 2691
Frailty, 2606
Frame, 2416
France. See also French, 247, 644,
  777, 2798
Franchise, 1878
Frankness. See also Candor, 436,
  1399, 1801, 1862, 2673
Fraternal organizations, 338, 394,
  2058, 2142, 2309
Fraternity, student, 2309
Fraternization, 2373
Fraud, 943
Free, 491, 1320, 2057
Freedom, 469, 571, 597, 600, 620,
  944-949, 1086, 1226, 1428,
  2147, 2552, 2608, 2677
Freedom of conscience, 950
Freedom of speech, 469, 622, 950-954,
  1086, 2420
Free enterprise, 434
Freemasonry, 2309
French. See also France, 247, 489,

French (cont.)
  1671, 1863, 2078, 2223, 2292,
  2603
Freshman, 421, 1404, 2427, 2829
Friars club, 1603
Friction, 540, 1309
Friend—friendship, 28, 57, 236, 405,
  552, 935, 955-972, 1057, 1306,
  1366, 1418, 1672, 1916, 2104,
  2110, 2187, 2244, 2274, 2387,
  2412, 2578, 2590, 2595, 2691,
  2732, 2745, 2764, 2765
Friendliness, 517, 590, 601, 789
Fright—frighten, 381, 682, 2336
Frigidity, 517
Frontier, 1760
Fruit, 13, 696, 1245
Fruitless, 1199
Frustration, 565, 685, 2702
Fuchsia, 1970
Fuel, 56, 733
Full measure, 2288
Fun, 1042, 1553
Fund, special, 2075
Funeral, 812, 1409, 2638
Fur coat, 1937
Furniture, 1251, 1779, 2269, 2536
Futility, 1462, 2188, 2831
Future, the, 138, 296, 313, 592,
  973-986, 1124, 1244, 1463,
  1626, 1986, 1987, 2316, 2322,
  2577, 2582, 2708, 2805, 2817,
  2841
Future intention, 2208

G

Gadget, household, 2212
Gain. See also Profit, 997, 2000, 2203,
  2811
Gambling. See also Bet—betting, 21,
  234, 235, 356, 987-998, 1719,
  2184
Game—games, 638
Gangster, 2517
Gangsterism, 588
Garage, 1225, 2156, 2623
Garden—gardener, 999, 1000, 1012,
  1042, 1282, 1470, 2055
Garment. See also Clothes, 1454,
  2200
Garrulity, 98, 1001

SUBJECT INDEX

Gasoline, 2622, 2634
Gastric ulcer, 1148
Gear, 2382
Gem—gems, 278, 2284, 2401, 2691
Gender, 1312
Gene—genes, 2182
Genealogy, *1002*
General, 1614, 1615
Generality, 445
Generation, 490, 948
Generosity, 354, 361, *1003*, 1012, 1508, 2071
Genius, 1, 318, 330, 461, 718, 875, *1004-1010*, 1239
Gentility, 1814
Gentleman, 282, *1011-1014*, 2370, 2549
Genuine—genuineness, 153, 433, 944
Geology, 1625
German, 777
Ghost, 474, *1015*
Giant, 1932
Gift, 45, 339, 346, 449, 571, 792, 820, 911, 972, *1016-1019*, 1021, 1028, 1029, 1032, 1252, 1877, 2219
Gin, 127, 1247
Girdle, 406, 407
Girl—girls, 313, *1020*, 1319, 2686, 2763, 2764
Give-away program, 753
Giving. See also Charity, 336, 337, 339, 346, 359, *1021-1034*, 1118, 1332, 2350, 2728
Glacial theory, 1625
Gladness, 789
Gland—glands, 1963
Glare, 893
Glass, 1483, 2351
Glassblowing, 1778
Glasses, eye, 2200, 2797
Glassware, 1778
Glory, 2, 24, 382, 1723, 1913, 1939
Glow—glowing, 1117
Goal, 789, 1464, 1844, 2207, 2211, 2465, 2702
God, 34, 68, 122, 127, 237, 257, 331, 345, 390, 432, 449, 526, 578, 600, 769, 801, 843, 950, 1000, *1035, 1036*, 1053, 1054, 1423, 1504, 1683, 1706, 1810, 1875, 1965, 2005, 2069, 2147, 2155,

God (*cont.*)
2174, 2176, 2182, 2184, 2446, 2552, 2602, 2624, 2767, 2810
Godlike, 2185
Godliness, 401
Gods, 349, 716
Gold—golden, 1155, 1953, 2392, 2506
Gold-digger, *1037-1039*
Golden rule, 229, 1371, 2167
Golf, 235, 603, *1040-1051*, 1602, 2219, 2385
Golf professional, 1044, 1051
Good—goodness, 67, 221, 223, 348, 349, 505, 716, 863, *1052-1057*, 1092, 1253, 1299, 1352, 1744, 1849, 2164, 2176, 2324, 2398, 2550, 2700, 2731
Good-bye, 933
Good fellow, 2599, 2605
Good humor, 782
Good taste, 1014
Good will, 385, *1058, 1059*, 2708
Goose, 2062
G. O. P., 1901
Gossip, 226, 331, 959, *1060-1073*, 2308, 2695
Govern, 871, 1406, 2777, 2779
Government, 434, 594, 712, 945, *1074-1087*, 1284, 1385, 1575, 1714, 1811, 2003, 2159, 2518, 2521, 2672, 2711
Grace, 640, 2368
Graciousness, *1088*
Graduate—graduates, 412, 420
Graft, 1914
Grain, 133, 571, 790
Grammar, 163, 1312, 2105
Grandchild, 1089
Grandee, 1028
Grandeur, 1028
Grandfather, 1799, 1973, 2169, 2576, 2672
Grandmother, 1215, 1690, 2249
Grandparents, 608
Grandson, 1845, 2416
Granite, 1681
Grapes, 356
Grass, 1287, 2055, 2143
Gratefulness. See also Gratitude, 1092
Gratification, 635
Gratitude, *1090-1092*, 1970, 2243
Grave, 568, 1681, 2636

422

SUBJECT INDEX

Heartstrings, 1029
Heat, 660, 2504
Heaven, 98, 112, 571, 1054, 1179, 1184, 1540, 1999, 2151, 2152, 2163, 2185, 2272, 2555, 2810
Heaviness, 1473
Hebrew. See also Jewish, 640
Hebrew Union College, 1278
Heckler, 2428
Heir, 138, 672, 1731
Hell, 59, 98, 184, 775, 1144, 1708, 1735, 2272, 2793
Helmsman, 2747
Help, 357
Helpfulness, 1151-1153, 1159, 1610
Helping hand, 1152, 1153
"Help-wanted", 2210
Heredity, 209, 1154
Heritage, 948, 1425
Hero—heroism, 26, 614, 819, 1095, 1698, 2713
Hesitation, 491, 918, 2573
Hidden talent, 1155
Highball, 102
High school, 72, 420
Hillbilly, 1388, 2229
Hinduism, 2167
Hiss—hissing, 2062
History—historical, 399, 592, 629, 1156-1161, 1224, 1909
History, American, 125, 470, 1275
Hoarding, 2350, 2565
Hobby, 1162
Hobgoblin, 1762
Hobo, 1602
Hog. See also Pig, 993, 2418
Hole, 574
Hole-in-one, 1040
Holiday, 124, 618, 2169, 2521
Hollywood, Calif., 30, 233, 384, 808, 874, 1163, 1192, 1238, 1538, 2487
Holy—holiness, 401, 724
Holy day, 2169
Holy water, 1634
Holy Writ. See also Bible, 2540
Homage, 1363
Home, 538, 725, 731, 822, 1116, 1164, 1165, 1168, 1506, 1803, 2642
Homemaker, 615
Home study, 751

Home, summer, 1865
"Home Sweet Home", 162
Homework, 2537
Hone, 330
Honesty. See also Integrity, 20, 339, 822, 1014, 1104, 1167, 1351, 1903, 1989, 2275
Honey, 2216
Honeymoon, 6, 1518
Honor, 160, 525, 910, 1096, 1168, 1169, 1195, 1449, 1744, 1917, 2017, 2181, 2192, 2483, 2701
Honorarium, 2057, 2075
Honor, guest of, 2077
Honors, 636, 1796, 2353
Honor system, 417
Hope, 701, 924, 1035, 1170, 1276, 1456, 1845, 1847, 2322, 2544, 2608
Hopefulness, 1236, 1471
Hopelessness, 1006
Horizon, 382, 585, 729, 1196
Horns, 2457
Horse, 779, 790, 1332, 1349, 1405, 1775
Horseback, 1770, 2046
Horse racing, 991, 1719, 2476, 2682
Horse sense, 1171
Horse shoe, 1775
Horse trainer, 2476
Hospital, 669, 680, 1172
Hospitality, 120, 1744
Hospital, mental, 783
Host, 532, 800, 1249
Hostage, 1433
Hostess, 808, 895, 1112, 1216, 1711, 2082, 2507
Hot air, 644
Hotel, 1173, 1506, 1519, 1613, 1627, 2106, 2145, 2277, 2407, 2454
Hot water, 765, 2653
Hour glass, 2786
House, 559, 1430, 1779
Household, 1936
Household gadget, 2212
House of Commons, 1973
House of Lords, 2041
House of Representatives, U. S. See also Congress, 1892, 1911
Housewife, 1236, 1568
Housework, 1552
Hovel, 1166

Human, 347, 369, 516, 1813, 2093
Humane, 392
Humanity, 348, 382, 1302, 1345, 1811, 2353, 2397
Human nature, 585, *1174, 1175*
Human race—humanity, 1391
Human relations, 517, 1963
Human society, 1876, 2664
Human weakness, 2098
Humble, 1177
Humility, 32, 172, 401, 1100, 1102, *1176-1179,* 1508, 1639, 2363
Humor. See also Wit, 782, 1240, 2605
Humor, good, 782
Humor, sense of, 2228
Hunger, 2004, 2558
Hunting, 1468, 2453
Hurdle, 458
Hurry. See also Haste, 1137, 1138
Hurt, 650
Husband, 50, *1180, 1181,* 1544, 2218
Husband and Wife. See also Marriage, 212, 411, 439. 561, 575, 776, 902, 1045, 1150, 1217, 1248, 1286, 1414, 1533, 1557, 1561, 1609, 1983, 2029, 2056, 2172, 2292, 2623, 2625, 2739, 2819
Husbandry, 2182
Husk, 1672
Hut, 1166
Hypercritical, 2443
Hypnotic, 2538
Hypochondria, 1149, *1182*
Hypocrisy, 1003, *1183-1188,* 2254
Hysteria, 2711

I

Iberian, 111
Ice 517, 2504
Ice cream, 344, 1530
Icicle, 1808
Idea—ideas, 325, 717, 759, 818, 826, 827, 1026, *1189-1193,* 1695, 1771, 2219
Ideal—ideals, 116, 949, *1194-1196,* 1226, 1727, 2318
Idealism, 565, 1805
Identification, 929, *1197,* 2062, 2269, 2309

Idiosyncrasy, 1005
Idleness, 107, *1198, 1199,* 1935, 1999, 2578
Idolatry, 2254
Igloo, 1808
Ignobility, 2174
Ignorance, 7, 68, 416, 500, 818, 1270, 1359, 1874, 1978, 2173, 2302
Ignore—ignored, 1071
Ill—illness, 61, 76, 247, 676, 1470, 2155, 2163, 2171
Illegality, 624
Illegibility, 673, 1112
Illinois, State of, 1947
Illinois Central Railroad, 811
Illumination, 2440
Illusion, 745, 1135, 1932
Illustration, 2100, 2443
Image, 1856
Imagination, 587. 588, 711, 867, *1200, 1201,* 1507, 1783, 1985
Imitate—imitation, 587, 1685, 2247
Immaturity, *1202*
Immigration, 905, 2287
Immodesty, 561, 1658, 1950
Immorality, 624, 1353
Immortality, 382, 401, *1203,* 2107, 2147, 2372, 2670
Immunity, 55
Impatience, *1204*
Imperfect—imperfection, 1814, 1815, 1879, 2445
Impersonal, 1079
Impertinence, 196
Implant—implanted, 1208
Importance—important, 3, 126, 596, 616, *1205,* 1835, 2346
Impossible, 68, 928, *1206, 1207,* 1614
Impostor, 1342
Impoverished, 2682
Impractical, *1208*
Impress—impression, 1445, 2271, 2374
Imprisonment, 1370
Imprisonment, life, 541
Improve—improvement, 105, 116, 369, 632, 1046, *1209,* 1379
Impulsive, *1210*
Inaccuracy, 20, *1211*
Inaction, 1230
Inattention, *1212*
Inauguration, 2228
Incentive, *1217*

Patriot—patriotism, 124, *1798-1801*, 1891, 2364
Patrol, 392
Patron, *1802*
Pattern, 620, 1036, 1159
Pawn—pawning, 1247
Pay—payment, 307, 424, 753, 1991, 2547
Peace, 560, 571, 642, 716, 1004, 1672, 1765, *1803-1805*, 2185, 2711
Peace conference, 644
Peace, Justice of the, 1565
Peacemaker, 1373
Peach, 748
Pearl, 2401
Peck, 1518
Peculiar—peculiarity, 702
Pedagogy. See also Teaching, 2530
Pedantry, 2254
Peddler, 1495
Pedestrian, 2218, 2621-2623, 2629, 2637
Peer, 2041
Pen—fountain pen, 673, 714, 850
Penalty, 530, 534, *1806*, 2176
Pendulum, 692
Penitentiary. See also Prison, 531
Penmanship, 1112
Penny, 2222
People, common, 599, 2443
Pension, *1807*
Pentagon, 1246, 1616
People, 15, 34, 288, 790, 881, 1060, 1061, 1079, 1159, 1268, 1403, 1443, 1549, *1808-1811*, 1920, 1931, 2351, 2758
People-minded, 1811
Pep talk, 2432
Percentage, 233, 990, 1007
Perception, 2182
Perfection, 1521, 1544, *1812-1817*, 1879, 2176
Performance, 297, 461, 544, 694, 1812, *1818*, 2014, 2015, 2258
Performance, benefit, 2058
Perfume, 1530
Permanence, 256, 362, 948, 1842
Permission, 810, 1238, 1361, *1819*
Perpetual, 2670
Persecution, *1820*
Perseverance, 247, 525, 1006, 1797, *1821-1833*, 1941

Persia, 278
Persistence, 618, 866, 1006, *1834, 1835*, 1872
Personal, 281
Personality, 328, 586, 1203, 1484, *1836*, 2340
Personnel, 1197, 2033, 2266
Perspective, 1861, 2414, 2683, 2738
Perspicuity, 1209
Perspiration, 1007, 1126
Persuasion, 448, 466, 473, 910, 954, *1837*, 2792
Perversity, 1787
Pessimism—pessimist, 1556, *1838-1840*
Petition, 2401
Pettiness, 597
Pew, 353
Pharmacy. See Drug store
Philadelphia, Pa., 800, 1670
Philanderer, 1258
Philanthropy. See also Charity, 358
Philosophy, 423, 818, 1226, *1841, 1842*
Phoenicians, 159
Photograph — photographer, 1238, 1515, 2794
Physical deformity, 1677
Physician. See also Doctor—Medicine, 76, 371, 670, 1112, 1150, 1991, 2371, 2794
Physicist, 2294
Pianist, 1941, 2511, 2512
Piano, 1251, 1432, 1686, 2835
Picket, 1911
Pickpocket, 989
Picnic, 2099
Pictures, motion, 536, 1192, 1346, 1974, 2119, 2536
Piecemeal, 984, 1821
Pierian spring, 739
Pig, 1367, 2406
Pigeon, 1858
Pigmy, 1932
Pigsty, 2286
Pill—pills, 1597
Pilot, 24, 1246, 1401
Pin—pins, 2267
Pinhead, 2290
Pioneer—pioneering, 977, 1655, 2468
Pipe, 811
Pitcher, 2516

437

SUBJECT INDEX

Promotion, 244, 1615, 1906
Promptness. See also Punctuality, 579, 1025, 1260
Pronunciation, 2422
Proof, 152, 232, 436, 2435
Proof positive, 1107
Propaganda, 2016, 2707
Pro patria, 1623
Proper—propriety, 1312
Property, 804, 1081, 1884, 2524
Prophecy—prophet, 2017
Prosecution, 2453
Prospect, 2271, 2279
Prosperity, 884, 886, 1152, 2018-2020, 2353
Protection, 1081, 1356, 1883, 2159, 2617
Protest, 1107, 2052
Protocol, 1409
Proverb, American, 836, 1056, 1980
Proverb, ancient, 2549
Proverb, Arabian, 504, 556, 1323
Proverb, Chinese, 113, 114, 1803, 2413, 2816
Proverb, Danish, 1707
Proverb, Dutch, 1794
Proverb, English, 143
Proverb, French, 310, 528, 2199
Proverb, Gaelic, 979
Proverb, German, 960, 2709
Proverb, Hebrew, 2367
Proverb, Hindu, 343
Proverb, Hungarian, 1181
Proverb, Jewish, 1683
Proverb, Norwegian, 1341
Proverbs, old, 12, 13, 257, 309, 607, 654, 923, 1033, 1792, 1943, 2001, 2019, 2046, 2047, 2240
Proverb, Sanskrit, 1022
Proverb, Scotch, 1590
Proximity, 1132
Prudence, 794, 950, 2248, 2568
Prudential Life Insurance Co., 1124
Prudery, 2021
Psychiatry—psychiatrist, 530, 616, 2022-2033, 2150
Psychology, 1694, 2024, 2034
Psychotic, 2023
Public—publicly, 2545
Publication, 1719, 2070
Public debt, 1080
Public figure, 2395

Public finances, 1920
Public mind, 777
Public office, 1881, 1884
Public official, 1879
Public opinion, 196, 724, 1104, 1714, 1927, 2035, 2036
Public property, 1884
Public relations, 2086
Public service, 2349, 2470
Public speaking, 443, 1843, 1853, 2036-2115
Publisher, 185
Publishing, 2116, 2513, 2591
Puddle, 2837
Pugilism, 1822
Pullman porter, 2117
Pulse, 1694
Pump—pumping, 2297
Punctuality, 1417, 1983, 2091, 2118-2121
Punishment, 97, 530, 534, 536, 541, 650, 1257, 1262, 1806, 2122, 2123, 2253, 2665, 2676
Punishment, capital, 1857
Pupils, 2528
Purchase, 1018
Puritans, 1275
Purity, 401, 1815
Purpose, 525, 2115, 2706, 2755
Purpose, singleness of, 2003
Purse, 679, 1244, 1960
Pursuit, 1403, 1950, 2314, 2677
Push and pull, 1754
Puzzle, crossword, 1685

Q

Quaker, 90
Qualifications, 1816
Quality, 1032, 1659, 1744, 2042, 2124, 2125, 2175
Quantity, 251, 1032, 2042, 2175
Quarrel—quarrelsome, 444, 1469, 1472, 1804, 2540, 2668, 2689
Quart, 2638
Quest, 1101, 1116, 2126
Question, 159, 227, 400, 572, 1853, 1912, 2127, 2128
Questionnaire, 1404, 2033, 2672
Queue, 2422
Quick-answer, 2129
Quick-thinking, 1961, 2507

438

SUBJECT INDEX

SUBJECT INDEX

SUBJECT INDEX

SUBJECT INDEX

SUBJECT INDEX

Symbol—symbolism, 1028, 1291, 1775, 1901
Sympathy, 557, 1123, 1965, 2353, *2504*, 2526
Symphony, 2511
Symptom, 2031
Synagogue, 694, 1959
Synonyms, 2799
Synthesis, 1322
Syracuse, N. Y., 2117

T

Table, 1746
Table, speaker's, 2087
Tact, 2292, *2505-2510*
Taffy, 440
Tailor, 455, 2810
Taint—tainted, 1663, 2200
Talent, 515, 718, 804, 1399, 1660, 2340, 2424, 2452, *2511-2514*
Talent, hidden, *1155*
Talent, native, *1699*
Talk—talking. See also Speech, 28, 494, 543, 1001, 1070, 1214, 1358, 1645, 2337, *2515, 2516*, 2766
Talking machine, 2069
Talk, loose, 2420
Talmud, the, 157, 356, 401, 429, 568, 1243
Talmud, Babylonian, 2665
Tammany Hall, 1901
Taoism, 2167
Tapestry, 2321
Tardiness, 841, 2091
Target, 2291, 2348, *2517*
Target practice, 1619
Taste, 818, 1507, 2774
Taste, good, 2086
Taxation, 1078, 1085, *2518-2526*
Tax collector, 2523
Taxes, 1041, 1874
Taxi cab, 32, 982, 1605, 2572, 2586
Taxidermy—taxidermist, 733, 2523
Taxpayer, 1899
Tea, 1216
Teacher—teaching, 375, 536, 591, 650, 657, 713, 731, 741, 742, 753, 777, 822, 995, 1638, 1665, 1685, 1781, 1793, 1878, 1952, 2620

Tea kettle, 37
Tear—tears, 46, 1864, *2532*, 2604
Technical education, 432
Technicality, 1355, 1613
Tediousness, 1160
Teen-age—teen-agers, 715, 2828
Teeth, 981, 1146, 2074
Teetotal, 96, 103
Telegram, 295, 690, 2331
Telephone, 74, 389, 390, 2030, 2330, 2371, *2533, 2534*
Telephone information, 2533
Telephone pole, 2625
Telescope, 176
Television, 43, 374, 536, 725, *2535-2538*
Temper—tempering—tempered, 224, 1150, 2155, *2539, 2540*, 2817
Temperament, 364
Temperance, 94, *2541, 2542*
Temperature, 517, 2155, 2299
Tempest, 24, 1958
Temple, 1993
Temporal, 387, 2162
Temporary, 447, 1422
Temptation, 990, 1122, 1299, 1550, 1559, 2398, *2543-2546*, 2726
Ten Commandments, 1371, 2257
Tenderness, 1477, 2367
Tennis, 936
Tension, 34
Terror, 180
Test, 2155, 2732
Testamentary, 2744
Testament, Old, 2206
Test, aptitude, 2033
Testimonial, 440, *2547*
Texas, state of, 267, 694, 819
Text, 2048, 2171
Textbook, 2219
Thanks, 2331
Thanksgiving Day, 2507
Theatre. See also Stage, 31, 543, 555, 743, 889, 1241, 1866, 2590
Theatrical producer, 2290
Theft, 617, 1301, 1349, 1410, 1952, 2257
Theologian, 1841
Theory, 534, 599, 729, *2548*
Theory, glacial, 1625
Thief—theft, 99, 333, 1806
Thievery. See also Theft, *2549*, 2569

447

SUBJECT INDEX

U.S.S.R., 455
Utensils, kitchen, 2769
Utility, 2715

v

Vacancy, 1890, 2269
Vacation, 731, 2028, 2228, 2521, 2690
Vacillating—vacillation. See also Indecision, 1406, 1834, 1924
Vacuum, 459
Vagueness. See also Uncertainty, 445
Vainglory, 597
Valet, 1098
Valley, 311, 1833
Valor. See also Courage, 819, 1431
Valuable, 1440
Value, 278, 424, 491, 1320, 1418, 1791, 1953, 2004, 2165, 2691-2693, 2715
Valueless, 1134
Vandalism, 466
Vanity, 1001, 1238, 1493, 2021, 2254, 2694-2696
Vassar College, 1404
Vegetables, 1443
Vengeance. See also Revenge, 1677, 2239, 2243
Venturesome, 2262
Verbatim, 2697
Verbosity, 1001, 1563, 2042, 2056
Verification, 1711
Vermont, state of, 128, 1880
Vermouth, 1247
Versailles, France, 644
Vessel—vessels, 2378
Vest, 455
Veterinarian, 151
Vexations, 1990
Vibration, 692
Vice, 1183, 1819, 2698
Vice-president—vice-presidency, 211, 2698
Vice versa, 1921
Victory, 571, 581, 948, 1614, 1868, 2336, 2359, 2398, 2436, 2486, 2543, 2712
Viewpoint. See also Point of view, 1861, 1882
Vigilance, 1423
Vigor, 2699

Vigor, intellectual, 1963
Villain, 2713
Vim, 1827
Violence, 1821
Violin, 162, 544, 550, 1474, 1581
V.I.P., 1608
Virtue, 2, 363, 1826, 1930, 1940, 2192, 2500, 2501, 2700, 2701, 2811
Virtue, social, 2197
Virtuous, 882
Vision, 26, 796, 977, 2566, 2702
Visit—visiting—visitor, 826, 1862, 2163
Vocabulary, 916, 2634, 2703
Vocation, 652, 1113, 2349
Voice, 90, 367, 474, 1810
Voluntary, 466
Vote—voter—voting, 1087, 1226, 1878, 1883, 1885, 1895, 1910, 1916, 1920, 1921, 1923, 1927
Vow, 1827
Vow, marriage, 1470
Vox populi, 1810
Vulgar — vulgarize — vulgarity, 196, 1095, 1338

w

Wager. See also Betting—gambling, 234
Wages. See also Salary, 571, 837, 1255, 1665, 1730, 2586, 2704
Wagon, 110
Waiter, 163, 783, 801, 810, 987
Waiter, head, 2040
Walk—walking, 611, 653, 981, 1048, 1169, 1535, 1770, 2046, 2411, 2415
Wall—walls, 1467
Wallet, 1564
Walls, apartment, 2321
Wall Street. See also Stock Exchange, 1858, 2417
Wants, 1242
War, 283, 392, 560, 716, 1243, 1616, 1805, 2705-2713
War, Civil (U.S.), 303, 1332, 2672
Warden, 1050
Warfare, class, 2708
Warmth, 2504
Warning, 736, 2714

SUBJECT INDEX

AUTHOR AND SOURCE INDEX

AUTHOR AND SOURCE INDEX

AUTHOR AND SOURCE INDEX

Casson, Herbert N., 1391
Castle, Dave, 214
Cato, 297
Catton, Bruce, 1159
Cecil, Richard, 237, 2121
Cecil, Robert, 551
Cerf, Bennett, 29, 543, 545, 782, 1173, 1409, 1895, 2426, 2534, 2592, 2686
Cervantes, Miguel de, 1018, 1496, 2745
Chamberlain, Arthur, 2565
Chamfort, Sebastien, 1368, 1986, 2693
Channing, William Ellery, 1083
Chapin, E. H., 873
Chapman, Rev. J. B., 241
Chase, Stuart, 1976
Chatfield, John, 1491
Cherbuliez, Victor, 1493
Chesterfield, Lord, 1338, 1629
Chesterton, G. K., 175, 489, 630, 803, 805, 1479, 2616, 2712
Chiang Kai-Shek, Madam, 1988
Chilon, 2000
Churchill, Sir Winston, 81, 155, 516
Cicero, 2, 349, 885, 1430, 1439, 1728, 1770, 2190, 2840
Clark, Caroline, 78
Clark, Glenn, 2356
Clark, Justice Tom C., 1301
Clarke, Adam, 7, 284
Clarke, Samuel Fessenden, 162, 915, 1462, 2842
Clay, Henry, 2439
Clayton, J. J., 1225
Cleveland, Grover, 1335, 1903
Cobb, Irvin S., 2054
Cochran, Hal, 1020
Cocteau, Jean, 171
Coleridge, Samuel T., 431
Collins, John C., 1643
Colton, Charles C., 190, 250, 1209, 1267, 1508, 2244
Commager, Henry Steele, 743
Compton, Dr. Arthur H., 2179
Conant, James Bryant, 2796
Confucius, 511, 676, 940, 1697, 2143
Congreve, William, 2314
Connolly, Mike, 2023, 2746
Cook, Ted, 1696, 1790
Coolidge, Calvin, 2020, 2178

Cooper, Judge Irving Ben, 535
Corbett, James J., 1822
Corneille, Pierre, 1262
Cortelyou, George B., 1425
Cousins, Norman, 746
Cowley, Prof. W. H., 416
Cox, Coleman, 1371, 1494
Cox, Marcelene, 373
Craig, John, 586
Crane, Dr. Frank, 2662
Cromwell, Oliver, 863
Cronbach, Rabbi Abraham, 1902
Crosby, Dr. Howard, 1878
Crosby, John, 1603
Crum, Bartley C., 526, 1086
Cudahy, John, 745
Cuilhe, Mrs. Paul A., 48
Curran, John Philpot, 1423
Cushing, Dr. Harvey, 1721
Cyrus The Elder, 1082

D

Daly, Arnold, 1043
Dandemis, 1294
Daniels, Jonathan, 21
Dante, 1708
Darrow, Clarence, 184, 1161, 1677, 2173, 2677
Daugherty, Molly Gates, 2082
Davenport, Russell, 620
Davy, Sir Humphrey, 1457
Dawes, Charles G., 71, 1598
Deeping, Warwick, 259
Delany, Patrick, 2421
Demosthenes, 1756
Derrio, Pete, 1816
De Sales, St. Francis, 2386
Dewar, T. R., 2760
Dewey, Mrs. Carroll M., 774
Diane, Comtesse, 1306
Dickens, Charles, 1364, 2384
Didactus Stella, 1932
Digiovanni, Joseph, 1669
Disraeli, Benj., 182, 460, 761, 2438, 2826
Dixon, George, 1107, 1921,
Doane, W. C., 571
Dodd, Bella V., 735
Dodd, Harold W., 1511
Doherty, Henry L., 1353
Donaghy, Rev. Wm. A., 733

455

AUTHOR AND SOURCE INDEX

Dorsey, Dr. George A., 367
Douglas, Norman, 2362
Doyle, Robert J., 2794
Dreier, Thomas, 1143, 1272
Dressler, Marie, 86
Drummond, Roscoe, 2102
Dryden, John, 189, 658, 1499
Duckett, Hansell B., 952
Duclos, Charles Pinot, 2197
Duffus, R. L., 1896
Dughet, Gaspard, 1055
Dulles, John Foster, 1805, 2461
Dumas, Alexander, 521, 2482
Dunn, Elizabeth, 324
Dunning, E. M., 1865
Durant, Will, 26, 700, 1137, 1919
D'Urfey, Thomas, 1693
Durling, E. V., 207, 999, 1773, 2513
Duvall, E. M., 992

E

Eddy, Sherwood, 869
Edgar, E. E., 2078
Edison, Thomas A., 1007, 2010
Edson, Gus, 573
Edwards, Tryon, 20, 2183, 2301
Eisenhower, Dwight D., 315, 1226
Eliot, Charles W., 2357
Eliot, George, 337
Elliott, L. G., 1834
Emerson, Ralph Waldo, 9, 23, 110,
    156, 316, 755, 870, 1261, 1684,
    1771, 2250, 2252, 2396
Emery, De Witt M., 276
Emmons, Nathaniel, 1228
Epictetus, 463, 500, 2670
Epicurus, 24
Erasmus, 1025
Erskine, John, 64
Essex, Lord, 1004
Euripedes, 1025
Evans, Melvin J., 601
Evremond, Charles de Saint Denis,
    1735

F

Fadiman, Clifton, 1455
Farbstein, W. E., 238
Feather, William, 1848, 1920, 1995
Fénelon, François, 698, 1814

Ferris, Dr. E. N., 747
Fielding, Henry, 223, 253
Fields, W. C., 1172, 2490
Fillmore, Lowell, 1189
Fine, Benj., 1300
Fischer, Chester O., 986
Fleishman, Jerry, 90
Fletcher, Frank Irving, 1223
Flexner, Dr. Abraham, 1788
Florio, John, 1400
Flynn, Lyle D., 659
Forbes, B. C., 1751
Ford, Ernie, 900, 1534, 2786
Ford, Henry, 277, 867, 2208, 2460,
    2716, 2808
Fosdick, Harry Emerson, 595, 1426,
    1549
Foster, Willa A., 2124
Fox, Charles James, 1905
Fox, Cy, 2547
France, Anatole, 710, 1160, 2684
Frank, Dr. Glenn, 41
Frankfurter, Justice Felix, 597
Franklin, Benj., 164, 188, 683, 1422,
    1533, 1541, 1779, 1944, 2841
Frederick the Great, 1849, 2664
Freehof, Dr. Solomon B., 818
Freeman, Robert, 334
French, Daniel Chester, 174
Friendlich, Dick, 417
Frost, Robert Lee, 1704, 2741, 2813
Froude, James A., 1352
Fulbright, Sen. J. William, 1917
Fuller, Edmund, 2444
Fuller, Thomas, 1105, 1654
Furnas, J. C., 2026

G

Gallagher, Buell G., 565
Gallagher, Dr. Roswell, 2031
Gallant, Morrie, 1303
Galsworthy, John, 1011
Gandhi, Mohandas K., 1453
Gardiner, A. G., 1142
Gardner, Hy, 532
Garfield, James A., 612, 2470
Garrett, Paul, 432
Gautier, Theophile, 2781
George, Henry, 1334
Geraldy, P., 2762
Gibson, I. B., 999

459

AUTHOR AND SOURCE INDEX

AUTHOR AND SOURCE INDEX

S

Saadi, 1305
Sachar, Dr. A. L., 1842
Salak, John Charles, 864
Sandberg, Carl, 1169
Santayana, George, 883
Sargent, M. K., 1485
Sarnoff, Gen. David, 177, 1385, 2300
Sayers, Dorothy, 2657
Schauffler, Robert Haven, 2656
Schelling, Felix E., 718, 1028
Schereschewsky, John F., 1786
Schmulowitz, Nat, 2758
Schnadig, J. L., 2326
Schumann, Robert, 2191
Schwab, Charles M., 2339, 2358
Schweitzer, Dr. Albert, 357, 1052, 1120
Scott, Thomas, 752
Scott, Sir Walter, 1435, 1469
Seitter, Maurice, 1516
Selden, John, 1359, 2377
Seneca, 141, 1024, 1253, 1292, 1295, 1413
Seubert, Edward G., 2340
Shakespeare, William, 512, 845, 1405, 2193, 2503, 2550
Shannon, R., 1395
Shaw, George Bernard, 51, 166, 229, 232, 529, 704, 941, 1115, 1222, 1448, 1450, 1550, 2009, 2089, 2233, 2261, 2676, 2773, 2805, 2830
Shedd, Charles W., 1463
Shedd, John A., 1682, 2262
Shedd, W. G. T., 1196
Sheen, Bishop Fulton J., 903, 1176, 1178, 2080, 2192
Shelley, Percy Bysshe, 1274
Shenstone, William, 2679
Sherman, Stuart, 2485
Shofield, Herbert, 770
Siesel, Mrs. Steven M., 2128
Silberstein, Bernard G., 2220
Sill, Sterling W., 2725
Simmons, C., 975
Simmons, G., 1103
Simms, Wm. G., 318
Simons, C., 2291
Sims, Lydel, 546
Smith, Adam, 299

Smith, Alexander, 1604, 2687
Smith, Alfred E., 606
Smith, Beverly, 57
Smith, B. W., 2034
Smith, Logan Pearsall, 1872
Smith, Sydney, 1699
Smythe, Geo. H., Jr., 124
Snyder, John W., 2566
Sobol, Louis, 2069
Sockman, Dr. Ralph W., 329, 525, 2188, 2612
Socrates, 591, 1636, 2204, 2727
Sophocles, 2666
Soutar, Andrew, 888
Spalding, John Lancaster, 2814
Spinning, James M., 594, 1093
Spurgeon, Charles H., 2750
Staël, de Mme. Anne, 1053, 1870
Stainback, Arthur H., 549
Stanislaus, Saint, 2502
Starr, Jimmy, 902
Steele, Richard, 1957
Steen, Marguerite, 1102
Stefannson, V., 1190
Steinberg, Milton, 1203
Steinmetz, Charles P., 2127
Stella, Didactus, 1932
Stephens, James, 351, 2783
Stern, Philip Van Doren, 948
Sterne, Laurence, 1933
Stevenson, Robert Louis, 972, 1069, 1836
Stewart, Rev. L. Gene, 389
Stimpson, George W., 1348
Stimson, Henry L., 2663
Stocher, H. E., 2211
Stone, Justice Harlan F., 1381
Stonier, Harold, 2313
Story, Judge Joseph, 399, 1363
Stout, Owen W., 2576
Stowe, C. E., 433
Straus, Robert Lee, 2147
Struther, Jan, 2035, 2391
Stuart, Edwin H., 1255
Sturgis, Alice F., 427
Sumner, Charles, 2552
Sumner, G. Lynn, 2099
Sumner, William Graham, 531, 2305
Sunday, W. A. (Billy), 2156
Suter, Henry Charles, 809
Sutherland, Edwin H., 534
Swanson, Olga, 927

Swicegood, Henry, 501
Swift, Jonathan, 830, 904, **1155**, **2158**, 2646, 2714
Switzer, Maurice, 1220
Sydney, Sir Philip, 2410
Syrus, Publilius, 932

T

Taft, William Howard, 1221
Tagore, Rabindranath, 1504
Talleyrand-Perigord, Alexander A., 2756
Taylor, Elizabeth, 380
Taylor, Sir Henry, 443
Taylor, Jeremy, 1958
Taylor, John, 644
Taylor, Una, 1215
Terence, 61, 1354, 1472, 2186
Tewson, W. Orton, 1369
Thackeray, William Makepeace, 2205
Thatcher, Rev. P. J., 76
Thompson, Dorothy, 539, 1330
Thompson, Perle, 858
Thompson, T. Harry, 226
Thoreau, Henry David, 696, 1179, 1715, 2140
Tiffany, Fred Robert, 160
Tiorio, 391, 815, 1396, 2255
Tocqueville, Alexis Charles Henry de, 871
Tomlinson, H. M., 2323
Tonsor, Chas. A., 587
Treacher, Arthur, 2487
Tremayne, Sydney, 1752
Trigg, E. T., 10
Trohan, Walter, 2067, 2381
Tupper, M. T., 2388
Twain, Mark, 397, 748, 807, 950, 1345, 1511, 1594, 1741, 1839
Tyndall, John, 2153

U

Untermeyer, Louis, 1019

V

Valentine, Dan, 2639
Van Court, Nancy, 2812
Vanderpoel, Robert P., 279

van Dyke, Henry, 364, 385, 570, 1153, 2505
van Loon, Hendrik, 425
Venn, Archbishop, 509
Venning, Sir Walter King, 2448
Vergil, 1692
Vincent, George E., 563
Vinet, A., 25
Voltaire, 231, 251, 519, 804, 951, 1116, 1392, 2364
Voris, Stephen, 610

W

Wade, Joseph Marshall, 2471
Walker, Harold Blake, 1332
Walpole, Hugh, 1458
Walworth, Dorothy, 445
Wardlow, Ralph, 1679
Warren, Samuel, 633
Warrender, Lady Maude, 1851
Warwick, Arthur, 2015
Washington, Booker T., 886, 2002
Washington, George, 2159, 2202
Watson, John T., 390
Webb, Perry F., 651
Webster, Daniel, 154, 298, 1993, 2668
Weinstock, Matt, 2422
Weisfeld, Israel H., 694
Weizelbaum, Alma, 2720
Welch, W. K., 1388
Westcott, Brooke Foss, 614
Whately, Richard, 1227, 1820
Wheeler, Elmer, 653
White, Stewart E., 2332
White, T. H., 2393
White, William Allen, 2793
Whitman, Walt, 352
Wightman, Richard, 2319
Wilcox, Ella Wheeler, 1340
Wilde, Oscar, 66, 249, 442, 1071, 1095, 1465
Willard, Frances E., 2542
Williams, Gurney, 2343
Williams, Leewin B., 2226
Willkie, Wendell L., 623
Wilson, Earl, 567, 1737, 2290
Wilson, Ernest C., 1762
Wilson, Francis, 1663
Wilson, Woodrow, 116, 660, 691, 1886

AUTHOR AND SOURCE INDEX

INDEX TO NAMES AND PERSONALITIES REFERRED TO IN THE TEXT

(Numbers in the index refer to selections in the text, not to page numbers.)

INDEX TO NAMES AND PERSONALITIES

INDEX TO NAMES AND PERSONALITIES

Lewis, Joe E., 1173
Liagre, Alfred de, 543
Liberace, Wladziu (Lee), 545
Lincoln, Abraham, 124, 470, 954, 1169, 1332, 1355, 1799, 2164, 2740
Lindbergh, Gen. Chas. A., 165
Lockhart, Bruce, 130
Longacre, Sarah, 1670

M

Macaulay, Thomas B., 1837
Maimonides, 339
Mann, Thomas, 186
Marshall, Thomas R., 2698
Marx, Groucho, 384, 808, 1603
Matthews, Lord Justice, 227
Maurois, André, 2078
Michelangelo, 1437
Michelson, Charles, 1608
Milliken, Robert A., 2294
Millikin, Sen. Eugene D., 1874
Mohammed, 2170
Moody, Dwight L., 1031
Morris, Sir Lewis, 655
Morris, William, 169
Morrison, A. Cressy, 2182
Mozart, Wolfgang, 1824, 2511
Murray, Arthur, 1651
Murry, John Middleton, 853

MC

McCarthy, Sen. Jos. R., 2395
McEvoy, J. P., 94

N

Nast, Thomas, 1901
Nathan, George Jean, 2290
Nelson, Lord, 514
Nygaard, Dorrance, 247

O

Oberon, Merle, 1316

P

Paderewski, Ignace, 550, 1941
Parker, Dorothy, 800, 927

Peck, Gregory, 2344
Plutarch, 1586
Polo, Marco, 1664
Popenoe, Dr. Paul, 1530
Putnam, Israel, 514
Pyle, Ernie, 2144

Q

Quintuplets, Dionne, 1809

R

Randall, Dave, 1265
Reichenbach, Harry, 2222
Repplier, Agnes, 933
Revere, Paul, 819
Riley, James Whitcomb, 2050
Rogers, H. H., 1663
Rogers, Will, 136, 2066
Roosevelt, Franklin Delano, 390, 470, 1121
Roosevelt, Theodore, 470, 1468
Root, Elihu, 977
Rothschild, Baron, 1495
Rubinstein, Anton, 2512
Ruppert, Col. Jacob, 2429
Russell, Rosalind, 2285

S

Sayre, Joel, 190
Schling, Max, 45
Shaw, George Bernard, 269, 550, 2456, 2592
Sidney, Sir Philip, 2740
Skinner, Cornelia Otis, 1239, 2592
Smathers, Sen. Geo. A., 1107
Smith, Sen. William Alden, 2099
Snyder, Ruth, 1605
Socrates, 1591
Sparks, Frank, 532
Stevens, Thaddeus, 481
Summerfield, Arthur, 1658
Swayze, John Cameron, 1909
Szymanski, Frankie, 771

T

Taft, Horace Dutton, 2228
Taft, Lorado, 174
Taft, William Howard, 2213, 2228

467

INDEX TO NAMES AND PERSONALITIES